Savage Mind *to* Savage Machine

Racial Science and Twentieth-Century Design

GINGER NOLAN

UNIVERSITY OF MINNESOTA PRESS
MINNEAPOLIS
LONDON

This book is supported by a grant from the Graham Foundation for Advanced Studies in the Fine Arts.

Publication of this book has been aided by a grant from the Millard Meiss Publication Fund of CAA.

MM CAA Advancing Art&Design

An earlier version of chapter 1 was previously published as "Weltgeist/Wildegeist: The Savage inside 'World History,'" *Grey Room*, no. 64 (Summer 2016): 40–63. Portions of chapter 4 were published in a different form in "Between Survival and Citizenship: Yona Friedman's 'Vulgar' Media," *Perspecta* 51 (Fall 2018) and in "'Bricolage,' or the Impossibility of Pollution," *e-flux* (July 26, 2018).

Published by the University of Minnesota Press
111 Third Avenue South, Suite 290
Minneapolis, MN 55401-2520
http://www.upress.umn.edu

ISBN 978-1-5179-0585-9 (hc)
ISBN 978-1-5179-0586-6 (pb)

Library of Congress record available at https://lccn.loc.gov/2020034686

Printed in the United States of America on acid-free paper

27 26 25 24 23 22 21 10 9 8 7 6 5 4 3 2 1

To

Sydell *and* Jerome

Savage Mind
to
Savage Machine

1
3
5
10
Dieu et le diable

Contents

INTRODUCTION

Twentieth-Century Design and the Ergonomics of the Spirit

From "Primitivism" to Structuralism

It has been said that architecture's preoccupation with the "primitive" is so ubiquitous as to make any comprehensive historical analysis of the phenomenon a fruitless endeavor.[1] While certainly it would be mistaken to suggest a unifying explanation for all instances of primitivism throughout the centuries, it is nonetheless possible to offer a theoretical framework to help explain the enduring prevalence of the trope into and through the twentieth century. This book takes its cue from the fact that two significant and recurrent aspects of primitivism—its relationship to technological developments and its role in the production of race—remain underemphasized in design theory and historiography. This book shows how a racialized "savage" served in an abiding modernist project to design objects and technological processes capable of seamlessly integrating human subjects into biopolitical and capitalist programs. Language-based modes of thought could be displaced by more unconscious and affective means of integrating humans into the programs of modernity—a process in which a racialized "primitive" served as an experimental subject and object of evidence. The "savage's" purportedly unconscious and unmediated relationship to labor, society, and nature constituted a model for designed interfaces—including architecture—that could be smoothly integrated with human brains and human cultures.

To understand this endeavor as racialized entails a particular understanding of race (one applicable to this history, not to all): race was a conceptual category that helped negotiate a distinction between what is often called "the posthuman" and "the human," such that a false boundary could be maintained between, on the one hand, a sovereign predicative *human* agent that consciously wielded science and technology and, on the other hand, a nonsovereign subject that was enmeshed in—and enthralled by—technological systems. If this definition of race appears overly abstract and neglectful of histories of racial politics and racial violence, it is the aim of this book to trace some important points of connection between abstract racial formulations and actual histories of racial discrimination and subjugation.

There are several probable reasons why race has been underemphasized in scholarship on art and architectural primitivism. There is, first of all, an issue of chronological framing, with much literature either focusing predominantly on eighteenth- and nineteenth-century instantiations of the "primitive hut" or else treating the primitive as an essentially ahistorical disciplinary trope dating back to antiquity. In the first case, such literature rightly contextualizes primitivism vis-à-vis colonialist discourse and practice but generally tends to presume a self-explanatory relationship among the racial, the primitivist, and the colonial, rather than analyzing what specifically was racial about, say, the primitive hut.[2] The fact that many twentieth-century instantiations of primitivism are not strictly colonial but are still often racialized suggests that the racial undercurrents of modernism exceed the bounds of the colonial, appearing, for example, under twentieth-century techno-industrial, neocolonial, developmental, and humanitarian paradigms, even if not always as literal instantiations of "primitive huts."

In contrast to the body of literature situating the primitive hut amid colonial ethnographies or colonial exhibition practices, some authors have adduced Vitruvius's inclusion of a primitive hut in the *Ten Books of Architecture* (commissioned by the Roman emperor Caesar Augustus) as evidence that this trope belongs to timeless disciplinary concerns, as if an essential continuity might be said to stretch across the eighteen centuries intervening between Vitruvius's and Marc-Antoine Laugier's (very different) rhetorical presentations of the primitive hut. This tacit assumption of disciplinary autonomy, downplaying historical context, makes the racial character of modern primitivism fade from focus.[3] On the other hand, to circumscribe primitivism too narrowly—identifying it with a few architectural protagonists—risks downplaying its centrality (and thus the centrality of race) to modernist architecture and design. The reason this book charts a century-long historical relationship between savage thought and savage machines is to show that this trope is not merely a quirk of a few eccentric designers but, rather, a fundamental basis of twentieth-century modernist design, similar to the relationship that Daniel Miller has posited between primitivism and modernist art: that the former is conceptually necessary to the latter.[4]

In order to analyze the racial character of modernist primitivism, it is useful to consider cases that lie beyond the strict purview of colonialism, turning instead to the relationship among Euro-American design, technology, and social scientific research in the twentieth century. This means considering cases where the explicit scientific racism and bigotry of nineteenth-century colonialism have given way to more subtly racialized representations of epistemic and cultural difference—leading to what I call a *racialized science* (in contrast to scientific racism). This move entails a concomitant shift away from the category of primitivism to that of twentieth-century structuralism, provided that we expand the boundaries of "structuralism" to include an array of figures not typically identified as "structuralists" (a move to be explained later). The shift from scientific racism to structuralism's racialized science was never total, as scientific racism repeatedly resurfaces. Nonetheless, the general arc traced by this book is one in which the forcible subjugation of nineteenth-century "savages" incrementally gave way to structuralist-based architectures and technologies designed to integrate a global subaltern into economic and governmental systems. Over the course of the past century, emphasis was increasingly placed on *design* relative to strategies of coercion, often as a way of circumventing the political processes through which subjugation might be resisted.

The second lacuna addressed by this book concerns the relationship between the "primitive" and the technological. Because art historical studies of primitivism have focused on the fine arts (and occasionally architecture) rather than on a wider field of applied arts, scholarship has not attended to the way primitivism appears in practices of, say, industrial design or the creation of digital graphic user interfaces.[5] Thus, primitivism—educed from painting and sculpture—has mostly been decoupled from technological development (at most, appearing in artistic *representations* of technologies, such as with some Dadaist and surrealist depictions of automatism).[6] This decoupling is evident, for example, in Bauhaus scholarship, where a disciplinary partition between the fine arts and the applied arts has given rise to a false corresponding partition between the primitivist, painterly Bauhaus and the technorational Bauhaus. To focus on the fine arts as the locus of modernist primitivism leads, moreover, to a general impression (with some exceptions) that primitivism fizzles out more or less contemporaneously with the erosion of Asian and African colonialism from the late 1940s through the 1960s. Thus, rather than being racial per se, primitivism appears dependent on specific colonial-era practices of art collection and exhibition, such that when colonial governance ends, the racial character of modernist aesthetic theory and practice likewise seems to disappear.[7]

By taking the relationship between twentieth-century Euro-American design and the structuralist social sciences as its historic object, this book brings the racial and technological aspects of primitivism to the fore, highlighting the ways primitivism was integral to structuralist-inflected disciplines of design starting in the late nineteenth century. The book thus follows a chronology from the late nineteenth through the late twentieth centuries, proposing that the late nineteenth-century rise of social Darwinism, Freudian psychology, ethnology, and structuralist linguistics frame the beginnings of a long twentieth century.[8] The book moves from late nineteenth-century entanglements between the industrial arts and social scientific theories of human cognition to several mid-twentieth-century disciplinary developments in architecture, urbanism, and environmental design, concluding with designers' forays into computation in the late twentieth century. Organized according to four disciplinary groupings—industrial design, architecture, environmental design, and the media arts and sciences—the chapters trace aesthetic technologies' movement from the context of Euro-American industrial production to a global field of communications, labor, and consumption.

Rather than seeing colonialism as the exclusive force behind themes that have typically been termed primitivist, this book focuses on a broader relationship between capitalism and "savage thought" under shifting historical circumstances in which race played a significant role. Structuralism, which shuttled between the social sciences and applied sciences, formed an epistemic support to evolving forms of commodity production, circulation, and consumption, following the expansion and transformation of capitalism from late nineteenth-century industrialism up through the Cold War. Hence, various historic developments of capitalism—including neocolonial economic relationships, an industrial (and ethnoracial) division of labor, mid-twentieth-century disinvestment in U.S. cities, post-Fordist investment in digital research, and the rise of structural adjustment programs—are seen to shape the racial and technological character of modernist design, while design conversely helped shape those economic movements.

The entanglements of the racial and the technological form a significant aspect of the modernist pursuit I call "the ergonomics of the spirit," referring to the design of the human cognitive apparatus in relation to new technologies of production, consumption, and governmentality. Whereas bodily ergonomics (exemplified by industrial Taylorism) tended to presuppose the basic fungibility of human bodies, the ergonomics of the spirit rested on an implicit cartography of cognitive difference, taking the so-called primitive as a primary object of evidence from which to extrapolate theories about the mechanics of human intelligence. The cognitive difference presupposed by twentieth-century structuralism was, however, different from that posited by nineteenth-century scientific racism. With structuralism the evidence extrapolated from social scientific studies of nonwhite societies (along with studies of children and sometimes animals) is typically offered as proof of the structures of human cognition, structures that were presumed common to all humans. This would seem to undercut assumptions of racial difference, begging the question, however, of why white cultures almost never figured as objects of anthropological interest prior to the end of the twentieth century.

We can see in *The Savage Mind* (*La pensée sauvage*), a classic work of structuralist anthropology, how Claude Lévi-Strauss becomes entangled in this basic methodological contradiction as he begins by refuting two long-standing anthropological postulations of racial cognitive difference. After discrediting widespread assumptions of a "primitive" inaptitude for abstract and theoretical reasoning and after disavowing the term "primitive," Lévi-Strauss offers instead a distinction between "bricolage" and "engineering" to account for fundamental differences he detects between the methods of Western technoscience (implicitly aligned with "engineering") and "the thought of people we call 'primitive.'"[9] He does not premise this distinction on racial–biological difference, and he asserts, moreover, that engineering is not intellectually superior to bricolage. Nonetheless, there are troubling implications to the bricolage–engineering distinction in the context of a book that adduces the cognitive structures of the bricoleur as evidence of the cybernetic nature of human intelligence, a theme that is central to *The Savage Mind* and to much of Lévi-Strauss's oeuvre.[10] I regard Lévi-Strauss's work and "savage thought" as especially cogent formulations of subtly racialized methods of thought that are found throughout late nineteenth- to late twentieth-century fields of research and design.

Given that cybernetic research was concerned with developing technologies of artificial intelligence and societal control in such a way as to obviate political dissensus, the engineer in Lévi-Strauss's account should be understood not as an ahistorical abstraction but as a part of a technoscientific field in which the bricoleur/primitive served as laboratory material for developing depoliticizing technologies of governmentality and economic organization. Lévi-Strauss coaxes forth from the (nonwhite) bricoleur the technoanthropological secrets of human intelligence that are to form the basis of cybernetic technologies, apparently unconcerned by the efforts of cybernetics to supplant political and micropolitical processes with self-regulating systems of control.[11] It is no coincidence that mid-twentieth-century research on urban cybernetics was often undertaken in especially brutal contexts of racial injustice, such as in apartheid-era South Africa and the United States, where technological means of remote governmentality were deemed instrumental to maintaining power across racially segregated territory and a racial division of labor.[12] Thus, while Lévi-Strauss considered bricolage a metaphor for universal structures of human cognition, the technological harnessing of those structures figured a power differential between the engineering and the engineered, a differential that often had a racialized character.

That being said, it would be misleading to draw this distinction between the engineering and the engineered too sharply, as of course the engineer is her- or himself also engineered. Hence, the engineering/engineered binary maps not onto different humans as much as onto semiotic and cognitive practices that all humans participate in, some of which are engineered or designed in such a way as to short-circuit conscious negotiation. The contradictory method of structuralist anthropology—which, in the very act of positing an epistemic distinction between, say, the "bricoleur" and the "engineer," posits the *universality* of epistemic mechanisms—is indicative of how "race" is defined in this book, insofar as the "savage" is meant to reveal certain universal tendencies while at the same time being implicitly implicated in a hierarchy of racial difference. A racialized notion of cognition does not always *strictly* correspond to ethnic categories of humans; instead, it supersedes race as such, as it describes different categories of thought and subjectivity related to questions of self-determination, capacities of contestation, and political agency.

The racialized character of this power differential is presupposed by the structuralist social sciences, appearing—both explicitly and implicitly—in the enduring distinction between two different models of cognition ascribed to different classes and races of humanity. Even as nineteenth-century scientific racism ceded ground to mid-twentieth-century conceptions of a biologically uniform cognitive apparatus, there persisted a deeply ingrained dichotomy (born of Enlightenment thought) between "primitive" forms of consciousness and apperceptive consciousness (that is, consciousness of the mind's modes of consciousness, a theme pursued by René Descartes, John Locke, Immanuel Kant, G. W. F. Hegel, and Sigmund Freud, to name just a few). The idea that "savages" were effectively unconscious of their own modes of thought came to undergird the structuralist social sciences and related practices of design and technological development. Essentially, structuralism became the apotheosis of apperception, as Euro-American sciences explained (and designed) the cognitive apparatus. The sovereign, apperceptive subject assumed the role of analyzing and designing systems, technologically optimizing the relationships between cognition, on the one hand, and production, consumption, and governmentality, on the other hand, whereas the putatively nonapperceptive (and hence nonsovereign) subject—a global subaltern—was to be woven *into* those systems while also serving as the object of evidence from which to extrapolate structuralist theories. The instatement of racialized difference increasingly rested not on supposed biological difference between brains but on a growing distinction between the designers of systems (and, by extension, those who benefited from those systems) and those who were to be interpolated within the systems, allegedly incognizant of their workings.

Whether this meant that the cognitive apparatus would be trained to be more creatively productive (as with nineteenth-century industrial arts pedagogy) or that architectures and digital interfaces would be designed to work in concert with the brain's native proclivities, the general thrust of the ergonomics of the spirit was to inculcate a deep intimacy between daily habits and new technologies of production and consumption. This book's ultimate object of critique has to do with the development of the ergonomics of the spirit as means of depoliticizing society through technologies and methods aimed at seamlessly integrating humans into the programs of capitalist modernity, often involving the simultaneous production of *and* technological mediation of (racialized) class difference. Accordingly, the book hypothesizes that savage thought serves the disciplines of design as an apparatus for circumventing the political negotiation of difference (that is, what has been called "dissensus").[13] In lieu of dissensus, design is configured as a natural (and hence inevitable) extension of the human brain and of particular cultures, such that negotiation is rendered obsolete.

This emphasis on the depoliticizing thrust of spiritual ergonomics is aligned with recent critiques of what some architectural historians have called "governing by design."[14] However, the grotesque racial constructions appearing in the histories examined here often exceed the immediate agenda of governmentality, taking on lives of their own—similar to what is often referred to as "an imaginary." Essentially, spiritual ergonomics—at once fantastical and instrumental—shuttles between the imagined and the actualized. As such, the forms of power described in this book, though sometimes hewing to a Foucauldian concept of governmentality, are often suggestive of something closer to spectacle in the sense given by Guy Debord and to ideology in the sense given by Louis Althusser.[15] According to Althusser, ideology does not appear in an arbitrary form, not as an illusory veil bearing no specific relationship to the conditions of existence; rather, ideology resembles the Freudian dreamwork, emerging as a wishful translation of the conditions of existence into a distorted version of those same conditions. To take a simple example from the history presented in this book, a racial (and racialized) division of labor might take the ideological form of a philosophy of racial cognitive difference.

Applied to a history of architecture, media, and technology, the implications of Althusserian ideology suggest an alternative to the antinomies sometimes arising between Marxian critique and Kittlerian genealogies of technology that bracket out discourse, fantasy, and ideology.[16] That circumstances of production and consumption might be translated into a distorted image suggests not an ideological veil concealing reality but, rather, a perforated, fluid boundary through which the presumed categories of "the real" and "the imagined" mutually penetrate and influence each other. While Althusser does not explicitly disavow the possibility of delimiting ideology from that which is external to it, his framing does figure ideology as something approaching a poststructuralist imbrication among practices, beliefs, and discourse, rendering them hard to delimit. Hence, what this book critiques is not ideology as much as the rendition of institutionalized social practices (such as a racialized division of labor) into racialized discursive constructions and, reciprocally, the activation of such discursive constructions *through* new social practices and technologies.

This reciprocal movement between discourse and practice can be seen in a recurring theme of spiritual ergonomics that forms a central motif of this book—the abiding search to displace the primacy of language with magical or supernatural techniques of communication. This fantasy of a post-Babelian world of nonlinguistic global telecommunications did not only constitute a utopian distortion of various grim realities (for example, the ongoing extinction of myriad world languages); it has also helped drive those realities, guiding the specific concerns and decisions taken by the designers of new aesthetic and semiotic technologies. In coining the expression "pentecostal technologies," I try to capture the magico-theological aspects of the twentieth-century search to aesthetically and technologically circumvent human language.

Pentecostal Technologies

In the secularized disciplines of twentieth-century design and social science, magic does not disappear as much as mutate. No longer the purview of priests and shamans, magical authority permeates aesthetic technologies designed to short-circuit slow processes of deliberation, interrogation, and political dissensus—that is, processes of negotiating meaning. The pentecostal fantasy is explicitly articulated by Marshall McLuhan in his 1964 book *Understanding Media: The Extensions of Man*:

> Language as the technology of human extension . . . may have been the "Tower of Babel" by which men sought to scale the highest heavens. Today computers hold out the promise of a means of instant translation of any code or language into any other code or language. The computer, in short, promises by technology *a Pentecostal condition of universal understanding*. The next logical step would seem to be, *not to translate, but to by-pass language* in favor of a general cosmic consciousness which might be very like the collective unconscious. . . . The condition of "weightlessness" . . . may be paralleled by the condition of speechlessness that could confer a perpetuity of collective harmony and peace.[17]

In other words, by technologically abolishing the incommensurable difference between signified and signifier—by minimizing the role of language—thought itself can be short-circuited. As I've shown elsewhere, McLuhan's fantasy of a pentecostal state of perpetual peace arose largely from his interest in neocolonial and geopolitical propaganda.[18] His assertions that the medium of print had instilled in "Western man" habits of skepticism and independent thought often bled indistinguishably into theories of racial cognitive difference. Yet the search for the "pentecostal condition of human understanding" suggested that, underlying alleged racial differences, there existed shared mechanisms of cognition that might soon enable humanity to be harmonized in a state of "general cosmic consciousness." In other words, there lurked beneath conscious linguistic thought a primitive and universal stratum of *quasi*-semiotic thought, capable of binding together brains with a nonlinguistic *aesthetic* semiosis.

McLuhan's preoccupation with late-colonial and neocolonial techniques of mass propaganda (and related theories of cognitive difference) did not preclude but gave impetus to his dream of "universal understanding." The whole point was that Euro-American global power demanded magical means "to by-pass language," not only because of linguistic diversity and nonliteracy, but also because of the incredible effectiveness of film, television, and radio in enchanting their audiences, instating a form of indirect authority. For McLuhan, these magical technologies were akin to the "primitive" rituals and incantations practiced by nonwhite societies. Yet for designers of aesthetic technologies, the global south did not constitute the sole intended subjects of magical communication technologies. Rather, the putatively "primitive" mind was taken as the exemplary and universalizable model for new media that were to govern across different cultures and across class strata, through an aesthetic logic of cognitive seduction, distraction, and absorption. The "savage mind" would thus give rise to savage machines, to aesthetic–semiotic technologies, such as personal computing devices, intended to displace prose with enchanting forms of communication supposedly more native to the brain's aesthetic proclivities. The "savage mind" had to be invented by Euro-American human sciences so that an actual savage mind could be technologically produced, this symbiosis between savage minds and savage machines lying at the crux of spiritual ergonomics.

McLuhan's description of the "pentecostal" is suggestive of how magic itself was, over the course of the twentieth century, submitted to social scientific, structuralist analysis so that it could be technologically reproduced in the form of various media, including architecture and digital interfaces. I define magical thought as the belief in the seamless congruity between human codes of representation and that which is represented (that is, erasing the arbitrariness of, for example, the signified–signifier relationship). Following Freud's argument that "primitive" people believed words to exert magical power over their referents, the twentieth-century social sciences often conceived of magical thought as a form of semiotic delusion.[19] However, magical thought was central to the modernist aesthetic project of producing a seemingly unmediated infrastructure between human cognition and the world. An *un*mediated medium (a pentecostal technology) capable of circumventing the arbitrariness of signifiers, would likewise circumvent the need for translation and discourse. In this respect, the disciplines of aesthetic and technological design came to assume growing importance over the course of the long twentieth century, with architecture serving as one art form that typically obviated the distinction between signified and signifier.

Twentieth-century instantiations of "primitive huts" resuscitated a logic found in Enlightenment texts, albeit bringing to bear on this logic a comparative, structuralist methodology. In mid-eighteenth-century France, the architectural essayist Marc-Antoine Laugier offered, in lieu of the blatantly signifying features of an "architecture parlante," the idea of ancient architecture as a translation of a primordial architectural *eidos*.[20] The originary architecture of a hypothetical "savage" constituted a semiotic artifact that did not rely on signifiers but instead reified the nonlinguistic cognitive processes through which humans confronted a prelapsarian state of nature. The primitive hut thus seemed to express a natural (magical) unity between nature and human thought, foreshadowing the pentecostal. The *eidos* does not belong to the realm of language, yet its ideational aspect assigns it to a realm quite proximate to language—that of *expression,* thereby enabling the *eidos* to serve as a subtle mediating device among the realms of nature, materiality, and human cognition. Its fluidity among these domains—belonging equally to them all—exempts it from the arbitrariness inherent to the linguistic signifier–signified relationship, attesting to the possibility of communicative means that were nonarbitrary. By the mid-twentieth century the Platonic *eidos* was largely supplanted by the idea of "structures" (that is, in the social scientific sense of elementary mechanisms underlying biological and anthropological phenomena), an idea that was used to develop a spiritual ergonomics.

Whereas bodily ergonomics pursued industrial efficiency, rational discipline, and uniformity, spiritual ergonomics were preoccupied with the mechanics of creative, aesthetic, and even magical thought as well as with variation between individuals and cultures. The fact that this ergonomics was beholden to anthropologists' and psychologists' structuralist analyses of magical thought has led me to reevaluate a commonplace critique of structuralism. Whereas twentieth-century structuralism is usually critiqued for its reductive, mechanistic understanding of the world, the obverse corollary to that reductiveness consisted in structuralism's inclusion of magical thought within the purview of mechanistic phenomena, enabling magical thought to be conceived as technologically producible. In this sense, structuralist discourse was concerned not only with rational analysis but also with transcendental synthesis—that is, pentecostal understanding—as magical thought consisted in a transcendental, numinous relationship between the thinking subject and the external world.

By "structuralism" I refer to a very broad approach (one that goes beyond the practices of self-identified structuralists), comprehending a diffuse and ill-defined set of epistemic practices and suppositions. These have roots in eighteenth-century European human sciences but fully coalesced in the last decades of the nineteenth century, given impetus by Darwinian evolution, Ferdinand de Saussure's linguistics, and the rise of Freudian psychology. Structuralism, as I use it in this book, entails a dissective analysis of any phenomenon within the scope of the human sciences, with the intent of revealing constituent mechanisms or natural laws to account for the phenomenon in question and often presupposing those constituent mechanisms to be integral to other phenomena as well (for example, the binary electric signal fundamental to a range of organic and inorganic phenomena).[21] This approach, which would dovetail with systems thinking in the mid-twentieth century, was useful in linking the human to the technological, as "structures" lent themselves to mechanistic understandings of human cognition and culture. To be clear, by "structuralist" I'm referring not exclusively to scholarship that self-consciously articulated a theory of structure but more broadly to the search for systematicity and pattern within human habits and practices.

The design practices and discourses examined in this book, even when not explicitly engaging with any structuralist figures, are all characterized by a preoccupation with a search for underlying mechanisms, with a kind of systems thinking, often *avant la lettre*. Intrinsic to this method of study was the use of comparative analysis, presumably applied to compensate for the general dearth of empirical evidence on the mechanics of human culture and human cognition. For example, when twentieth-century architects derived design principles from so-called vernacular architectures, they typically amassed a range of examples from different cultures, adducing any shared architectural traits as proof of some universal and natural logic of human habitation.

As such, the hegemonic potentials of structuralism did not lie only in its usefulness to rationalist regimes of technological expertise. The potentials also lay in the constant weaving between technics and culture, between the technorational and the seductively magical, in efforts to integrate the irrational tendencies of human thought into technical systems of communication and labor. Moving away from a scholarly tendency to see the occult and irrational as the repressed and paradoxical underbellies of the rationalist programs of modernity, this book charts a persistent and deliberate tendency to *rationally*, technologically harness the mechanics of what I call (following Freud) magical thought. To the extent that this book constitutes a poststructuralist critique, it is concerned with structuralism's neoliberal tendencies, and in this sense it regards structuralism not as a wholly modernist project but as one lending itself to a post-Fordist mediation between cultural particularity and technoscience. The phantasm of primitive thought was indispensable to twentieth-century technomagic because it seemed to offer a model (a technologically reproducible model) of a magical unison between brains and "natural" machines (that is, machines modeled after the primordial nature of human thought).

Over the course of the long twentieth century, the project of codifying and optimizing the basic structures of the aesthetic imagination gradually expanded in its scope, concerns, and technical applications. The arc of this book begins in the late-nineteenth-century United States, when the ergonomics of the spirit was largely a question of improving aesthetic inventiveness and adaptability in the burgeoning field of industrial design pedagogy, related to the formation of the designer as an intellectual proprietor of the technologically reproducible artwork. I examine the case of the Public Industrial Arts School of Philadelphia, where the curriculum was informed by ethnographic theories and by the racial politics of labor and education in postemancipation United States. The racial logic undergirding this approach to design differentiated the virtuosic but *unconscious* aesthetic techniques of "savages" from a privileged (white) form of apperception, according to which designers were said to consciously harness the brain's otherwise unconscious methods of creativity. Techniques and theories undertaken at the school's experimental program were promoted at various artistic institutions in central and eastern Europe, eventually turning up, as will be discussed in chapter 2, at the Bauhaus, where a "racial theory of the arts" intersected with prevalent mystical strains such as Theosophy as well as with a keen interest in new technologies of artistic production and reproduction.

The preoccupations of early nineteenth- and twentieth-century design pedagogues might seem to have little to do with the pentecostal project at hand. However, a refrain articulated by the instructors developing the spiritual ergonomics of design was that the unconscious aesthetic creativity evinced by "savages" constituted a language of sorts—or rather, a substitute for language as such: an aesthetic semiosis that, rooted deep in the primordial mechanisms of the brain, might be rendered reproducible by machines, as attested by one nineteenth-century design pedagogue's fantasy of an intelligent machine that could magically produce architecture. Chapters 1 and 2, on industrial design, along with four subsequent chapters, present a particular prehistory of the digital. In these chapters, we witness how allegedly unconscious and autochthonous attributes of human cognition were considered to be either technologically reproducible or at least capable of producing a better rapport between human brains and machines.

Moving forward in this prehistory of the digital, the third and fourth chapters examine a systems-thinking approach to the relationship between design and culture evinced within post–World War II architectural modernism in Europe, as architects developed notions of the systematicity of architectural "vernaculars," persuaded that "culture" provided requisite evidence of the mechanics of human thought. Architects' comparative, diagrammatic studies acted as a latently racialized form of translation between allegedly unconscious modes of life and allegedly apperceptive modes of structuralist analysis and design. Following the cues of anthropology, architects looked at interrelationships between cultural practices and beliefs as a quasi-semiotic fabric distinct from linguistic signification. "Primitive" habitat was believed to reveal cognitive habitus, and in turn, habitat could subtly shape human habits, thus serving as a potentially potent apparatus of the ergonomics of the spirit. Architects' anthropological adventures of observing and diagramming cultural practices had a performative element, often serving as a potential alibi (in contexts of neocolonial and welfare-related urbanism). These chapters thus focus on how a purported anthropological method was used to mediate between "needs" of subaltern classes and the programs of technomodernity, foregrounding the way claims to respect cultural particularities would later inform the design and spread of digital technologies. Habitats modeled on certain aspects of cultural habitus would also be used to subtly refashion daily habitus.

By the last decades of the twentieth century, this relationship between habitat–habitus became key to designers' understanding of the digital interface, which, like architecture, might mesh seamlessly with the mind's innate proclivities. In other words, architecture served as a precedent of a technological interface between world and brain. The computer interface was conceived as something to be tailored to the brain's primitive methods, rather than as something requiring linguistic input. Reciprocally, computer-aided design held out the promise of a globally applicable system of architectural design that might be easily tailored to accommodate the nuanced variations and complexities of culture. The architects Yona Friedman and Christopher Alexander are the most evident exemplars of this tendency, as they applied anthropological frameworks to developmentalist efforts in the postcolonial world while also contributing significantly to early experiments in computer-aided design.[22] Additionally, though, a host of architects in the 1950s and '60s could be seen as influential to subsequent computational research insofar as this generation applied to architecture anthropological ideas about the systematicity or "pattern" of culture, a systematicity then taken up in research on how computers might help tailor architectural design according to cultural specificities. This generation includes architects treated in chapter 3—Alison and Peter Smithson, the office of Candilis-Josic-Woods, Herman Haan, and Aldo van Eyck—illuminating the affinities between their work and cybernetic anthropology with important implications for late twentieth-century technohumanitarianism.

The fifth and sixth chapters of this book turn to another racialized discourse that likewise developed around notions of conscious thought and unconscious habitus. Beginning in chapter 5 with the post–World War II emergence of the new paradigm of the global environment and concomitant forms of global management, I examine how two overlapping definitions of the environment (that is, as an object of global management and as an organism's immediate perceptory milieu) informed late-colonial and especially U.S. designs and applications of technological media in the domain of global governance. Moving into chapter 6, we witness how this set of interests contributed to the eventual formation of environmental design and environmental psychology, two disciplines appearing in the United States in the late 1960s and motivated largely by redevelopment agenda in the nation's racial ghettoes. Both this chapter and the preceding one look to the Aspen Institute of Humanistic Studies and the related International Design Conferences at Aspen to examine how notions of cognitive subjectivity were submitted to racial categories vis-à-vis postwar constructs of the environment. The human brain was believed to be unconsciously governed by its immediate sensory environment. However, in contrast to this subjugated form of environmentally governed consciousness, "Western man" had developed modes of thought allowing "him" to cognitively surpass the boundaries of "his" perceptory milieu so as to attain a global environmental perspective (essentially, a twentieth-century high-tech version of what Mary Louise Pratt has called "planetary consciousness").[23] The environmentally submerged form of cognition ascribed to "non-Westerners" had implications for the development of technological media, lending itself ultimately to the development of personal computing technologies.

The final chapters of this book are directly concerned with the development of personal computing technologies. As a supplement to existing literature on the Massachusetts Institute of Technology's Media Lab and its predecessor, the Architecture Machine Group, chapter 7 considers the Media Lab's longtime orientation toward the global south, showing the racial dimensions of the lab's early work. During the Media Lab's formative years, two of its cofounders, Seymour Papert and Nicholas Negroponte, served as consultants for France's Centre mondial informatique et ressource humaine (CMI), abetting the CMI's initiative to cultivate the global south (especially France's former African colonies) as an enormous untapped market for personal computing technologies. Regarding his research in Senegal under the aegis of the CMI, Negroponte retrospectively observed that "kids from the jungle learned faster than kids from the city."[24] In pointing to this alleged cognitive kinship between computers and "kids from the jungle," Negroponte was effectively claiming that nonliterate rural African children augured well for the feasibility of graphic user interfaces and indexical devices (for example, the computer mouse) as nontextual means of interaction, suggesting a mode of increased global capitalist integration that would not require widespread literacy. As the CMI's work in Senegal occurred contemporaneously with the development of graphic user interfaces, the "kids from the jungle" served as the Media Lab's muse. Personal computing technologies would increasingly seek to minimize the need for writing as a form of human–machine interaction.

To contextualize these developments in relation to the power dynamics between technology-importer and technology-exporter states, the final chapter turns to international debates around technology transfer during the 1970s and '80s, showing how Third World demands for technological parity and for protection from data mining gradually gave way under the pressures of 1980s debt crises in the global south, the resulting structural adjustment programs, and the contemporaneous expansion of intellectual property law. Rather than technological parity, the 1990s witnessed an expansion of humanitarian aid. I argue that philanthropic and biopolitical paradigms of international assistance helped carve out a domain in which pentecostal technologies could take root and flourish and that philanthropic programs of technological diffusion became apologies for enduring inequities between technology-importing and technology-exporting states.

Although intellectual property forms an explicit focus of only two of the book's chapters, the historical relationship between savage thought and savage machines has long acted as a discourse supporting economic and technological inequality amid globalization, and intellectual property—in an expanded sense of the term—is thus an important object of this book's critique. Supplementing scholarship that looks at intellectual theft in colonial contexts, I chart a racialized understanding of the intellect that, in ascribing the artistic products of many societies to unconscious processes, disqualifies those products from the status of intellectual property, as the latter requires the conscious codification of technique. Intellectual property is thus studied here not only in its literal sense but also as a general construct of conscious versus unconscious forms of epistemic subjectivity. This split mirrored the ways capitalist labor produced intellectual alienation between the laboring human and the larger technical apparatus of production. Pentecostal mysticism was often offered as a remedy against the capitalist phenomenon of alienation that arose from a techno-industrial division of labor.

Thanks to the global connectivity enabled by pentecostal technologies, laboring bodies and brains could be more effectively incorporated into a global market, as such technologies cut across differences of language and education, thus allowing race- and class-based systems of caste differentiation to be maintained even while elided. The construct of savage thought thus lent itself to both the differentiating thrust of capitalism and the universalizing thrust of capital. It worked toward the fabrication and enforcement of racial, epistemic, and semiotic castes, while it also reached across those castes. The fact that savage thought was capable of abetting these contradictory tendencies—toward both homogenization and differentiation—is crucial to the history presented here. For this reason, the book repeatedly identifies certain spatial rhetorical devices such as *circumvention, elision, metalepsis,* and *suturing,* all of which worked toward bridging while simultaneously producing epistemic difference.

The Savage, the Magical, the Vernacular

The "savage," the "primitive," the "elementary," the "magical," the "vernacular," the "traditional," the "native," the "child," "Africa," the "indigenous," "nature": this cluster of terms pervades the discourses examined in this book, although the terms are not wholly interchangeable. First, it should be pointed out that the "savage" differs from the other terms in that it is decreasingly used during the course of the twentieth century, to the point of almost disappearing by the 1960s (Lévi-Strauss's tongue-in-cheek usage notwithstanding). Despite the term's disappearance, the notion of *savagery* in Euro-American discourse has deposited a historical residue of meaning onto associated terms in the present day (such as "vernacular"), terms often preferred for their supposed neutrality. Thus, "savage" is employed in this book as a strategic hyperbole, evocative of the violence and excessive representational distortions that formed the basis of colonial discourses and that persist more subtly in the terms used today in design discourses. This hyperbole constitutes an attempt to strip the other, related terms ("vernacular," "nature," and the like) of their seeming neutrality.

The usage of "savage" in this book, however, inverts the meaning of the term. "Savage thought" is used here to characterize *not* the presumed subject of savagery—for example, a racial subaltern—but, rather, structuralist efforts to analyze and recuperate basic mechanisms of thought with the goal of deploying these structures toward techno-aesthetic production. "Savage thought" is linked to efforts to technologically produce more magical modes of thought and communication. Per this usage, savage thought, though it has roots in Enlightenment thought, is first developed in the late nineteenth century, subsequently flourishing with the rise of the structuralist social sciences and related design practices in the mid-twentieth century and onward. Savage thought names an epistemic technique applied in racialized contexts, often to resolve contradictions between, on the one hand, hegemonic uses of technology (whether in the domains of war, conquest, or labor) and, on the other hand, humanist espousals of technoscientific progress and perpetual peace. Savage thought, in linking human and machine cognition, is used to render machines more humanlike while simultaneously re-creating humans in the images of their machines.

As for the larger constellation of terms—the "primitive," "nature," and the rest—these are mostly used here in paraphrasing or directly citing the discourses that employed them at the time. Some of these terms have become retrospectively affiliated with particular disciplines. For example, the "primitive" has long been an object of art historical analysis, as in studies of modernist primitivism. The "vernacular" is a preferred category of architects and architectural historians and is often taken to indicate architectures built without the involvement of professional architects, although the term is often used more vaguely to imply an opposition to "modernity."

Among the terms pertaining to savage thought, "magic" deserves special attention. The word is significant for its appearance in late nineteenth- and early twentieth-century psychological and anthropological texts, often used—as mentioned earlier—to describe what Freud referred to as the belief (the primitive delusion) that words exercised power over their signifieds, such that wishing or uttering something was tantamount to willing it into existence.[25] As distinct from this psycho-anthropological concept of magic, the category of *enchantment* has been adopted from Max Weber and the Frankfurt school in scholarship that explores cultural and scientific tendencies in eighteenth- through twentieth-century Europe.[26] While this book's usage of "magic" bears a kinship with that literature, the tendencies described here are not really about reënchantment per se, as magic is not exactly suppressed at a given historical moment only to covertly reappear. Magic has long been imbricated with violence, authority, and knowledge, all of which are subject to transformation in their means and ends, and so, correspondingly, magic too is subject to transformations in its means and ends. Savage thought / savage machines constitute one among many ever-shifting iterations of magical authority, not a return of the repressed.

The main contribution of this book to the literature on modernity's enchantment consists, first, in expanding a focus from magical *effects* to include magical forms of reasoning that underwrite structuralist approaches to design, and, second, in contextualizing this in relation to a racialized understanding of cognition. The existing literature tends to locate enchantment in the stupendous effects of scientific phenomena, in the religious cults surrounding scientific experimentation and technological developments, in notions of the technological uncanny, or in the spellbinding forms of entertainment (magic shows, cinema, panoramas, and so on) that proliferated in the late eighteenth through early twentieth centuries. These accounts tend to equate magic with the marvelous, spiritual, and eerie.[27] Departing somewhat from these historical interpretations (albeit retaining some overlaps), this book defines magic as an *espousal of transcendent subjectivity linked to aesthetic–semiotic efforts to overcome the chasms between nature and human systems of representation*. This idea of magic is closer to the Freudian conception—it involves a definite relationship between a human subject and that subject's semiotic positioning vis-à-vis the world—than it is to a concept of the marvelous, although the two are not mutually exclusive. In the following chapters, magical thought appears primarily through a mystical notion of design as capable of reconciling new machine technologies with a transcendent humanist subject.

One conventional truism concerning modernist primitivism is that it emerges as a reaction against technological modernity, as is often said of the tropical evocations of, say, Henri Matisse or Paul Gauguin.[28] While much literature of the past few decades has moved beyond such facile formulas, art historical analysis has thus far not explicitly ventured the opposite thesis—namely, that much of primitivist modernism could be construed as a part of an effort to embrace and cognitively integrate new technological developments. Because primitivism in the technical arts is detectable largely in designers' written discourses and pedagogies, several chapters of this book draw more from textual than material evidence, at least relative to the material–visual focus typical of art historical scholarship. That is, much of my analysis of savage thought comes in the form of close readings and deconstructions and is thus more aligned with work in cultural studies than with art historical tendencies to trace the interactions between "ethnographic" artifacts and modernist practices.[29]

Moreover, by focusing on the technological, this book moves in a slightly different direction from one historical explanation that pervades various critiques of primitivism—namely, the idea of otherness as a category that allows a colonizing society to project traits onto an imagined other. The positing of this projective impulse does not help explain the two opposing dialectical tendencies it describes: first, that of making the other represent all the negative aspects of one's own sociocultural constitution, and second, that of romanticizing, desiring, and mimicking the other.[30] This recourse to Freudian concepts of projection, unconscious repression, and fetishism as tools of postcolonial critique is a precarious move, given that Freud's concepts were often colonialist in their reasoning.[31] To fall back on Freudian psychology as an explanation of racial discourse risks extricating that discourse from its specific historical entanglements. A racial cartography of human cognition is linked to histories of capitalism, colonialism, and development in which technologies played a crucial role. While Euro-American discourses did generally deny their own tendencies toward magical thought, imputing those tendencies only to nonwhite races, those races do not simply serve as projection screens for any and all manner of Euro-American phobias and fantasies. Rather, exploited and subjugated classes were the practical models to refer to in developing technologies of exploitation and subjugation. Hence, the lineaments of the "primitive" bear a strong resemblance to the technological, and vice versa. The colonized and exploited were referred to as models for semiotic and aesthetic technologies that were to be applied toward integrating *all* societies into rubrics of techno-aesthetic governance. What we have here is not as much an other as a universalizable model of the future. That is, the otherness of the other was *to some extent* provisional and heuristic.

That conquered and exploited societies should serve as experimental models in the ergonomics of the spirit helps explain the troubling prevalence of "Africa" in the discourses encountered here, including the frequent conflation of Africa and Africa-America. As already mentioned, this book opens in the context of postemancipation United States amid quandaries of how to conceptualize the growing industrialization of aesthetic production in a society where an industrial division of labor often fell along ethnic and racial lines. Implicitly, questions of industrial design pedagogy revolved around the problem of distinguishing between, on the one hand, the forms of rote mechanical production suitable to subjugated portions of the population and, on the other hand, the creative inventiveness appropriate to middle-class industrial artisans, helping legitimate the latter's work as a form of intellectual labor. The book concludes with the cultivation of the global south as a growing market and experimental arena for the development of personal computing technologies, efforts in which Africa featured especially prominently (and, indeed, still features prominently, as in the current rise of "maker culture" there).

Between these historic bookends, we witness the repeated appearance of "Africa" in sundry iterations—in Hegel's world historical scheme, in a Bauhaus "racial science" of design, in ethnopsychiatric formulations of the "African mind" and related theories of media, and in the architect Aldo van Eyck's romanticization of Dogon semiotics, among others. "Africa" is not the only reference point for savage thought, but given its prominence in the development of twentieth-century techniques of domination, it is not surprising that it plays a significant part within the imaginary of savage machines. The conjuration of this mythical "Africa" is, as I elaborate in the first chapter, a matter of European "philosophical necessity" (per Hegel), but the necessity does not lie in a psychological requirement for otherness pure and simple. It lies, rather, in a magical epistemic project in which race enables a double concept of cognition: as constituting both the analyzing subject and the object of analysis. In turn, this racial cartography becomes an alibi to colonialisms and neocolonialisms.

What might come as a surprise is that in the discourses and practices examined here, neither "Africa" nor the "primitive" are stand-ins for *unreason,* as is so often assumed in critiques of colonialism. The tendency to home in on the colonizer's equations between the "primitive" and the irrational—though true in many cases—has neglected a major thrust of savage thought, which regards "primitive" people as archives of reason—*albeit a reason that is unconscious of its own processes and thus incapable of transcending its own finite subjectivity.*[32] In the twentieth-century social sciences, the "primitive" increasingly suggests an originary and thus apodictic form of reasoning, a form of reasoning that *includes* magical thought. Magical thought, according to much social scientific work in the late twentieth century, is no longer considered indicative of racial pathology; it is a natural aspect of human cognition.

Toward an Archive of Savage Thought

In asking how to identify and define the use of the "primitive" in architectural discourse, Adrian Forty has observed, "If we are to answer the question of 'where is the primitive?', then we can say that it is either nowhere, or perhaps more accurately, everywhere."[33] Forty's diagnosis explicitly disavows the historic specificity of primitivism's relationship to (neo)colonialisms, and thus also denies its racialized aspect. Nonetheless, his sense of the primitive being nowhere/everywhere rightly hints at the fact that savage thought often takes the form of a figment, a specter, an epistemic conjuration, posing a historiographic problem. What archive could possibly be linked to a device as ubiquitous and yet chimerical as savage thought? To identify savage thought with a single institutional or biographical history would be to miss the whole purport of the "savage mind," which was its flexibility and radical nonindigeneity. That is, far from being indigenous to a particular decade, place, or artistic movement, savage thought must be understood as an enduring and adaptable tool, one used to negotiate among aesthetic, technological, and ideological agendas throughout the shift from colonialism to neocolonialism. This is not the same as claiming a timeless, ahistorical status for the "primitive." Rather, the diffuseness of savage thought points to the usefulness of archaeological method, and accordingly this book comprehends a dispersal of episodes, showing how, amid permutations of savage thought, a certain underlying logic is maintained.[34] Savage thought is often situated at places of slippage where methods travel across different disciplines—for example, from linguistics to anthropology and from there to architecture—generating malapropisms that in fact are symptomatic of fundamental contradictions. For example, what is an *antithesis* to structuralist linguistics—the magical identity between signified and signifier—is shown to be structuralism's covert *thesis* when adapted to the disciplinary agenda of design. Structuralist aporia concerning the status of the human subject vis-à-vis technology is thus brought into relief through the movement of concepts from the social sciences into the fields of design and technology.

Mary Poovey's concept of a "messy" or "circuitous" history has been retrospectively helpful in understanding how to write a history of savage thought and savage machines.[35] While there are a number of connective threads strung between the numerous discursive episodes treated in the following chapters, the point is to present this history in both its density and its fragmentation and to show how disciplinary shifts over time adapted savage thought to different historical circumstances. The broad dispersal of savage thought sets in relief the methodological problem of attempting to circumscribe certain historiographic objects within national, regional, institutional, and biographical boundaries, suggesting instead that those objects be stalked in their various divergences and reemergences rather than treated as archival givens. In some chapters, this has meant, moreover, revisiting and revising well-known narratives—for example, concerning the Bauhaus and Team Ten. Rather than relying primarily on archival research, chapters dealing with such familiar moments of design history instead use archival research as a supplement to historiographic accounts to bring into relief the unacknowledged centrality of savage thought to those histories.

A history of savage thought attests to the persistence or reemergence of certain epistemic impasses over time, which is why this present work—though describing a phenomenon of the long twentieth century—is in frequent dialogue with the eighteenth century. Certain blockages within Enlightenment thought continue to haunt the discourses and figures appearing in this work. For example, the necessary and contradictory role played by anthropology in Kant's thought is mirrored by the role it plays for designers in the twentieth century. In his introduction to Kant's *Anthropology*, Foucault writes that through recourse to anthropology,

> philosophy did not manage to free itself from subjectivity as the fundamental thesis and starting point of its enquiry. On the contrary, it locked itself into subjectivity by conceiving of it as thickened, essentialized, enclosed in the impassable structure of "*menschliches Wesen*," [human essence] in which the extenuated truth which is the truth of truth keeps vigil and gathers itself.

> We can now see why, in a single movement, characteristic of the thinking of our time, all knowledge of man is presented as either dialectized from the start or fully dialecticizable—as always invested with a meaning which has to return to the origin, to the authentic.[36]

The founding problem Foucault detects in Kant's engagement with anthropology (its dialectical relation to his *Critiques*) is the question of how human cognition can be an object of thought while, at the same time, constituting the thinking subject who studies that cognition as an object. I argue that the contradictions of a subjectivity split between its finitude and its apperceptive transcendence eventually intersect historically with a racial division of labor and related precepts of class, giving rise to a split, racialized conception of humanity itself.[37] The epistemic contradictions of the Enlightenment reemerge through structuralism with its invention of savage thought.

The Present and Future of Savage Thought

A history of twentieth-century savage thought and savage machines points toward a number of recent and ongoing developments. Most fundamentally, there exists today in the fields of design, technology, and business an enduring racialized binary between the "engineer" and the "bricoleur," persisting despite the many ways in which the putative "bricoleur" is becoming a cyborg bricoleur.[38] Indeed, the bricoleur now overlaps with the broader category of "user," in that using digital technologies often entails tinkering with them, especially in economic conditions where computers must be cobbled together from e-waste. The bricoleur appears prevalently in various design, planning, and economic initiatives focused on the slums of the global south, including the recent investment in high-tech maker culture in Africa and South Asia and a more general emphasis on the creative resilience of a global indigent population. Related to such developments is the growing imbrication between data collection and methods of urban planning and redevelopment, all of these anticipated by design proposals examined in this book—especially those of Yona Friedman, the Architecture Machine Group, and the MIT Media Lab. Echoing those architects, contemporary designers and entrepreneurs alike claim to uncover the secret "logic" of the slums so as to technologically replicate that logic toward various ends. The presumed kinship between "primitive" bricolage and creative entrepreneurship renders inhabitants of substandard housing ripe for integration into neoliberal finance and data harvesting.[39] We see that the role of the unconscious has gradually expanded from discourses of creative labor to feedback loops in which people are unconsciously interpolated in systems of data analysis and planning. Throughout this expansion, the notion has persisted that one cannot *own* what one is unconscious of—whether it be one's methods of labor or one's trail of personal data.

While this book critiques specific capitalist instrumentalizations of creativity, this is not to suggest that creativity should, therefore, not be disciplined. Working from the assumption that discipline is not inimical but inherent to the effective potentials of creativity, this book reacts against a recent vein of poststructuralist thought inspired (somewhat questionably) by the work of Gilles Deleuze and Félix Guattari, which assumes that an embrace of the flexibly evolving structures of reality constitutes some kind of weapon against stultifying, rationalist, and reductive epistemic frameworks (such as structuralism).[40] This vein of cultural theory, unwittingly aligned with the rise of "design thinking," often reproduces in the name of poststructuralism the discourses of structuralism and capitalism (both of which understood structures as enabling flexible evolution and play, often in cybernetic fashion). The value of structuralist "play" can be detected now in business school literature extolling, inter alia, Lévi-Strauss's conception of savage bricolage.[41] The misguidedness of critiquing structuralism exclusively for its reductive rationality is redressed in this book by pointing to the ways figures like Lévi-Strauss, Jean Piaget, and Noam Chomsky (and their disciples and collaborators in various fields of design) were concerned precisely with how cognitive structures enabled flexible imaginative play and transformation.

Related to this emphasis on play, a fitting sequel to this narrative lies in several interrelated disciplinary developments in the fields of design appearing in the twenty-first century. I address these further in the book's Conclusion but will briefly allude to them here, as they might shed light on the book's narrative arc.

The first of these is the recent emergence of "design anthropology," which, as the name implies, involves a convergence between ethnographic observation and product development, as advanced by firms such as IDEO but now including private consulting groups that offer the services of trained anthropologists. One such consulting firm, User Experience, emphasizes on its website that its techniques can decode "users' conscious and unconscious actions."[42] Although (to the best of my knowledge) the term "design anthropology" is not yet leveraged by architects, a rising interest in humanitarian design and global-southern slums has led to a renewed pseudoanthropological sensibility in architecture schools, whereby designers—often without any substantial research—regard design as capable of resolving all manner of complex social problems.

The second disciplinary development prefaced by this history has to do with the rise of neuroscience in the fields of visual studies and design. Focusing on the cognitive circuitry of affective and aesthetic response, neurology's entwinement with visual studies and design leads away from politics and into a barely linguistic world patterned on cognitive reward behavior patterns.[43]

The third disciplinary development to be addressed in the Conclusion is the rising importance in the architecture profession accorded to digitally produced images, an importance that I relate to the rise of "postcritical" attitudes in European and U.S. schools of architecture.[44]

Taken together, these disciplinary developments point to the ways that "smart" design threatens not only contestatory politics but also the more subtle micropolitics through which people negotiate their positions vis-à-vis social and economic systems. Depoliticizing effects are not, of course, inevitable outcomes of digital technologies; rather, they arise from specific design and policy decisions along with economic and geopolitical relationships that govern their use. The aim of this book is to trace how design histories were influenced by racialized notions and also *produced* racial categories through assumptions, methods, and effects. My concern in the latter chapters of this book is specifically the way design has facilitated the global adaptation of technologies to different segments of the world's population in such a way that class difference can be maintained even while being technologically bridged. In lieu of an effective democratic discourse around the terms of technological transformation and in lieu of proportionate investments in public education, the 1970s and '80s witnessed the design of digital interfaces (with a global export market in mind) to accommodate nonliterate or minimally literate users.

This book addresses the problem of semiotic apartheids by examining hegemonic discourses and techniques rather than by looking at their effects at the more microscopic scale of the persons or communities they affect. That being said, critics of those discourses and techniques—often anonymous, little-known, or even nonliterate speakers—are sometimes cited here, their arguments against savage thought and savage machines appearing in several chapters. These representatives offer critiques of intellectual property law, they express skepticism about the desirability of Euro-American computing technologies, they suggest disenchanted understandings of the signified–signifier relationship, they critique formulations of "the environment" as an object of planetary design, and they question their participation in regimes of data collection, which is to say that these representatives from nonelite segments of society explicitly refuse both the premises and the agenda of savage thought. Those premises and agenda are to be found instead in the creases of a structuralist episteme that has long been posited as the antithesis of savage thought but that turns out to be its embodiment.

PART I

INDUSTRIAL ARTS

Spiritual ergonomics begins with the mechanization of production as a way of negotiating the utopian fantasies and dystopian anxieties inspired by that mechanization. On the one hand, automation was to deliver humans from drudgery. On the other hand, the specter of *alienation* (in German, *Entfremdung*) described a growing cleavage between bodily and intellectual labor or, for Marx, between production and mastery over the means and processes of production. The construct of alienation appeared in early nineteenth-century epistemology before it came to be seen as a social phenomenon wrought by mechanization and the related development of the capitalist metropolis. Originating with the idealist philosophies of Johann Gottlieb Fichte and G. W. F. Hegel, alienation was subsequently taken up by Karl Marx (by way of Max Stirner) and, from there, was translated by Frankfurt school authors into questions of urban life and culture. In any case, alienation referred to a perceived rupture—for Hegel, between primitive–materialist and spiritual–reasoning forms of cognition; for Marx, between the labor of the body and the larger schema of capitalist production (and the social power accruing to the dominant classes).

Noting the influence of figures like Hegel, Marx, and Walter Benjamin, the following chapters are also concerned with alienation in its more colloquial adaptations. A popular conception of alienation often conflated Marxian concern over the disempowering (and de-skilling) effects of mechanization with a quasi-Hegelian sense of alienation as a personal psychic phenomenon to be corrected through the harmonious training of the mind and body. That is, the alienation arising from mechanized forms of labor was believed to be correctable through personal spiritual exercises (such as those prescribed by occult movements such as Theosophy) and through spiritual ergonomics that sought to fine-tune body–mind–machine relationships rather than reforming relations and processes of production. The designers and theorists encountered in these first two chapters shaped industrial design pedagogy so as to allegedly counter the alienating effects of mechanized production without really challenging those means of production or the capitalist division they presupposed in the late nineteenth-century United States and subsequently in the Weimar Republic.

Savage thought was key to exorcising the specter of alienation from the growing discipline of design because the "savage" represented an originary unity between mind and body, pointing to a potential unity between humans and technologies of reproduction. Apart from this, there was a good deal of evidence suggesting the superiority of "primitive" forms of artistic production relative to mechanized arts production, as noted by many U.S. and European design pedagogues and theorists, whose ideas often hearkened back to the Gothic Revival of the mid-nineteenth century. Unlike proponents of the Gothic Revival, these pedagogues posited pseudoscientific rubrics through which to assimilate and master the "primitive" creativity of a racial subaltern. The new discipline of industrial design interrogated the points of connectivity between cognitive and corporeal functions, seeing design—as distinct from either the fine arts or crafts—as holding out a promise of a de-alienated form of aesthetic production. In these discourses, racial eschatologies emerged that regarded design in a protostructuralist light: essentially, as a scientific synthesis of "primitive" aesthetic impulses into a scientific discipline of aesthetic production.

1

THE ARCHITECTURE MACHINE

Industrial Design and Theories of Racial Evolution

The Architecture Machine

> Henceforth will be found . . . that Man can by a peculiar process based on his vital power and mechanical aid, actually decompose certain forms of matter or reduce them to an impalpable state as of dust or a vapour and then draw them together to a hard substance. . . . The result was that from earth or sand and air he [an inventor] made with great rapidity large masses of a kind of stone, in any shape required, and what was most remarkable he found it perfectly easy to put every block in place as formed. . . . One morning the people living near a hill by Springfield, Massachusetts, were astonished to behold on its summit a stone tower fifty feet high which had not been there the night before. . . . From this dated a new method of building which spread all over the world.
>
> By means of [this machine], it became as easy for a traveler in the wilderness to build a stone cottage as to pitch a tent, and any man who had a bit of ground could erect on it in a short time a manor. Forthwith castles, towers and magnificent walls and arches began to arise on all the mountains, cliffs and headlands of the world. As the method once acquired was inexpensive and easy, the poorest people, and even boys erected at will houses or huts as they pleased. . . . The results . . . in public buildings and cities was colossal, one being the perfect restoration of the pyramids of Egypt, and of well nigh all the old cathedrals and palaces of which plans had been preserved, including the rebuilding of Babylon. . . . Palmyra was restored in detail by a single hotelkeeper, and Baalbel by the Syrian Society for the Preservation of Ancient Edifices.[1]

The pyramids of Egypt would be rebuilt without slaves. The Tower of Babel would be finally completed despite the world's diversity of tongues. A stone tower would materialize as if by magic one morning in Massachusetts, prefiguring Babylon's restoration. With the aid of this imagined architecture machine, "the poorest people, and even boys" would, according to Charles Godfrey Leland, scatter huts across the earth. Huts would spring forth from rustic imaginations—imaginations uncorrupted, that is, by any cosmopolitan knowledge of architecture. In a subsequent speculation from his "Prophesies for the Twentieth Century," Leland foretold that in 1974 this architecture machine would be improved so that "photographs of a gigantic scale will be made in solid relief like stone, and used for mural decorations." People would thereby decorate their dwellings according to nature's own patterns. Finally, with this machine, Leland tells us, "Nature will be really reproduced by Nature."[2]

What could it mean for a machine to enable nature to reproduce itself? Does nature not already reproduce itself? Is this not one of its defining features? And why should the excretions of an architecture-making machine be thought natural? Perhaps the answer is simple. The machine could be said to reproduce nature because it would enable architecture to emerge directly from the untrained mind, uncontaminated by any professional consciousness. The machine would operate according to organic principles that conjoined the mechanisms of physical nature and human cognition. Because nature and mind were deemed to be governed by shared laws, a machine might finally merge the creativity of nature with that of the human brain.[3] Leland thus rewrites one of the nineteenth century's most familiar critiques of machine production: The machine need not alienate. It need not denature and destroy the mind–body integrity allegedly supported by preindustrial craft technique; rather, the machine might renaturalize art production by dint of the technologizable nature of human creativity. Rather than driving a wedge between human consciousness and human production, industrial forms of labor might weld human consciousness to the machine. Work would become a form of magic.

While Leland's own labors were polymathic, a certain consistency cut across his diverse endeavors—namely, a disregard for disciplinary boundaries delimiting science from magic. Born to a wealthy Philadelphia family in 1824, Leland traveled extensively, published magazine articles, wrote fiction, translated the poetry of Heinrich Heine, edited a literary magazine and later, during the Civil War, an abolitionist journal. In the middle and late nineteenth century, when the discipline of ethnography was still in its infancy, Leland was active in ethnographic societies, where he shared his knowledge of the Passamaquoddy language and culture. During his travels in Europe, he learned to speak fluent Romani and subsequently published volumes on Romani folklore, later engaging in similar work on African American legends, Vodou ("voodoo"), and Etruscan magic. Finally, inspired by craft techniques observed during his ethnological fieldwork, as well as by his brief involvement with craft reform movements in England, Leland advocated the implementation of "practical" or "industrial" arts as a component of public education. In 1880, as part of Philadelphia's public school system, he opened an extracurricular program of arts training that would become the Public Industrial Arts School of Philadelphia (PIASP), an institution whose influence appears to have extended as far as the Bauhaus.[4]

Leland's theories on technology, design pedagogy, ethnography, politics, psychology, and mysticism were not novel in and of themselves, but their confluence in his work anticipated a structuralist epistemic turn that would push the discipline of design to make use of ethnography and psychology.[5] Moreover, in the context of post-emancipation division of labor in the United States, Leland's thinking brought into relief racialized relations of labor and related anxieties over the expansion of mechanized forms of production. For example, his social Darwinist views concerning the triumphant evolution of the Anglo-American race relied heavily on the idea that humans would be liberated by future technologies. This view helped assuage Leland's anxieties, which he shared with many of his peers, concerning the degrading effects industrial technologies might have on the working classes.[6] Using the primitive as a way to decode the human brain—in a way that pointed toward notions of machine intelligence—Leland was able to maintain a peculiar position vis-à-vis the "pre-industrial past" (that is, as supposedly represented by "primitives") and the technological future in a world he envisioned as colonized by Anglo-America.[7]

Although Leland often echoed a Ruskinian nostalgia for medieval European arts and architecture, he avidly embraced new technological forms of production, imagining and inventing simple mechanical devices for abetting the decorative arts.[8] Against Ruskinian orthodoxy, he stipulated that such technologies need not replace the work of the creative mind. He did not argue—as Frank Lloyd Wright later would—that the aesthetic value of machine production lay in its ability to inspire formal innovations.[9] Instead, he argued that the encounter between human and machine-based labor demanded a new science of the creative mind. The imagination could be improved through rigorous systemization of its methods. Consequently, the creative imagination might come to operate more like a machine while, conversely, machines might learn to operate more like creative humans. Against Ruskinian as well as Marxian critiques of the alienating effects of industrial labor, Leland suggested an organic harmony between mechanical production and the human brain. This Taylorism of the creative imagination—what I call the ergonomics of the spirit—was closely tied to Leland's understanding of the respective competencies of conscious and unconscious thought in relation to labor. Invoking a time when creative labor was so natural as to be effectively unconscious, Leland forwarded a notion of aesthetic creativity as rooted in primordial unconscious mechanisms of human thought, an idea that suggested a potential kinship between mechanical automation and human creativity.[10]

Leland's ambition to meld mind and nature was shot through with the triumphalist European racial eschatology of world history. In his writings and pedagogical work, popularized Hegelian notions of both world historical development and cognitive development are adapted to fantasies of Anglo-American technological prowess and world conquest. (In this thinking, Leland was probably indebted to Thomas Carlyle's version of Hegelian world history).[11] This chapter will show how Leland construed the sciences of white "civilization" as essentially the conscious harnessing of savages' allegedly unconscious intellectual and aesthetic practices. In the late nineteenth century, the racial eschatology advanced by figures like Carlyle and Hegel (claiming that certain nations or races were the privileged bearers of the world's historical destiny) brushed up against—and in some ways was troubled by—Darwinian theories of evolution. The scientific (rather than theological) suggestion of a single human progenitor—and thus a single human race—cast doubt on the nineteenth century's strict racial–biological categories. However, social Darwinism would come not only to reassert but to lend scientific credence to Euro-America's racial hierarchies and related fantasies of racial world historical domination. Nonetheless, the ambivalent status of the aboriginal in these cases—as both the progenitor and the degenerate of humanity—can be glimpsed in Leland's work, which both replicated and denigrated the artistic and cognitive methods of nonwhite races whom he deemed primitive.

What I will argue is that a protostructuralist construct of savage thought served Leland as the deus ex machina with which to ideologically resolve the contradictory status of the "primitive" origin within a Darwinian-cum-Hegelian notion of racial evolution. What is ultimately important in this account is not the construct of world history in and of itself as much as its latent persistence within the protostructuralist human sciences. Leland stands as a symptomatic specimen of the evolution of nineteenth-century racial eschatology into twentieth-century structuralism, anticipating its contradictions. The fact that nonwhites served for Leland as evidence of the basic mechanisms or structures of human aesthetic cognition seems to suggest the basic equality of human brains, regardless of race; however, this suggestion of equality was undercut by eschatological narratives that helped ideologically support the actual power imbalances between Leland and his ethnographic subjects. In this respect, the Hegelian device of sublation (*Aufhebung*)—which subsumes but also cancels out that which comes before it—was prescient of twentieth-century structuralist anthropology. In Leland's ethnography-based system of design pedagogy, the labor and cognitive methods of "savages" could be at once harnessed and canceled out by Euro-American technoscientificity.

Leland's imagined architecture machine can be read as a technological analog to existing race- and class-based relations of labor, according to which the fruits of non-Anglo-American labor were sublated (absorbed and canceled out) by those controlling technological, financial, and cultural capital. In Leland's writings the machine acts as the perfect slave—automatically and instantly translating the wishes of its master. At the same time, the architecture machine's glorious reconstruction of the world's ancient monuments is based on an intellectually appropriative gesture, corresponding to actual colonial archaeological recuperations and appropriations of ancient monuments. According to Leland's description of Anglo-America's technological future, "all that man has ever done [in the past] will be as the mere alphabet of a language as compared to [the future's] grandly developed literature and oratory."[12] That is, the past or "primitive" merely furnishes the inchoate structures—the alphabet—from which Anglo-America would bring about a cosmopolitan world order. The past is absorbed—even reproduced—but also canceled out. In this sense, Leland's architecture machine appears as a cogent crystallization of several interrelated strains of Anglo-American bourgeois thought—for example, the idea of technological progress as both a mode and a justification for ethnoracial domination, the burgeoning ergonomics of the creative imagination, and the usefulness of the "savage" in respect to both of these. Leland's thinking is symptomatic of the way programs of technoscientific progress and ethnonationalist domination tended to adopt the dialectical logic of what I will refer to as sublation.

Abolition and the Postemancipation Politics of Public Schooling

Although Leland's writings allude to Hegel, he may have been, as already mentioned, swayed more by Carlyle's Anglo-American version of world historical development, as well as by Spencer's social Darwinism, both Carlyle and Spencer being fixtures of the social circles Leland frequented during his long sojourns in London.[13] Leland had eagerly procured an introduction to Carlyle through a mutual acquaintance, the Virginia-born expatriate Moncure Daniel Conway.[14] Leland and Conway shared an interest in arts education, Conway having written a book on the pedagogic success of London's South Kensington Museum with its extensive collection of decorative arts. Moreover, the two men had occupied similar roles as propagandists for abolition before and during the U.S. Civil War.[15] In this late nineteenth-century upper-class milieu, theories of white racial conquest were often intertwined with liberal bourgeois projects to abolish slavery and to reform public education and labor in the service of industrial capitalism.[16]

In his writings on education, Leland drew on various reform efforts in Europe and the United States that, though intended to improve the status of the lower classes, were often rooted in ideas of Anglo-American supremacy vis-à-vis the working classes. For Leland and many of his progressive peers, class subjugation was to be rendered more polite—that is, it was to be managed and civilized—through public education. While this might have the effect of launching the working classes on the path of upward mobility and political enfranchisement (Leland did sometimes espouse socialist sympathies in a Fourierist vein), education also served as a way to further entrench the grooves of class stratification through curricula tailored to prepare the lower classes for suitable occupations. At the same time, education provided a way to winnow out from the lowest rungs of the social hierarchy some kernels of middle-class gentility, outfitting the "better" immigrant working classes with the lineaments of civil society, in contradistinction to what was afforded to more marginalized minority groups.

The contradictions of progressive politics during the 1870s and '80s were anticipated by the particular view of abolitionism espoused by Leland and many of his compatriots during the 1850s and '60s. Leland censured black slavery for its effects not on slaves but on the white working classes, arguing that slavery robbed more deserving white people of employment, a thesis many abolitionists leveraged against white workers' fears of job competition from emancipated blacks.[17] Liberal reformers nonetheless feared that an influx of black labor would indeed bring about the pauperization of white working classes. Related to postemancipation questions of labor, education, and assimilation ("amalgamation," as it was then called), there ranged among white abolitionists a spectrum of views concerning the comparative cognitive dispositions of the various races. At one end were those upholding the absolute intellectual parity among all humans; at the other extreme were those arguing that the races actually constituted separate biological species marked by ineradicable differences. While the latter belief was espoused mostly by secessionists in the U.S. South, it was not wholly incompatible with strains of abolitionist politics.

In the middle and late nineteenth century, one of the most influential supporters of the racial theory of distinct human species was Louis Agassiz, a revered Swiss-born Harvard science professor who was active in Boston's public education reforms in the antebellum and postbellum years. Leland was well aware of his reforms, as they generally served as a model for reforms in other U.S. industrial cities, such as Philadelphia.[18] With his imposing credentials, Agassiz lent credibility to the science of white supremacy while also assuaging northern abolitionists' fears that black southerners and black refugees in Canada would come to populate northern U.S. cities. Believing that blacks were biologically bound as a *species* to tropical climates, Agassiz (who had opposed emancipation until it appeared politically inevitable) assured his white northern public that freed blacks would either stay in the southern United States or else migrate south of U.S.–Mexican border, while racially mixed persons would probably die out altogether due to degenerate constitutions.[19] In the context of Boston's pioneering educational reforms of the 1870s, this theory implied that the state's new system of universal education need not accommodate the needs of black Americans, a forecast that would be borne out by increasing processes of school segregation.[20] Leland, although rarely espousing such extreme views as Agassiz's, did express in at least two publications similarly violent fantasies of white world historical conquest.[21] More often, however, Leland subscribed to the more paternalistic forms of racism prevalent among members of his class, effectively believing that other races and ethnicities, though generally inferior to Anglo-Americans, could be greatly improved through education and modernization; he generally saw race more as a cultural than a biological attribute, although these two were never wholly separable in his thinking.

One (among many) threats to the credibility of white Americans' racial hierarchies appeared in the bulk of evidence attesting to the refined artistic skills of various minorities, including a southern class of black artisans (whose potential migration posed a risk, as we have said, to northern white workers) and Native Americans.[22] Leland, observing during his ethnographic fieldwork the impressive artistic skills of the Passamaquoddy, did not, however, allow this fact to unsettle his notions of Anglo-American supremacy. He simply ascribed such superior skills to an *inferior* form of intelligence, an intelligence that was almost unconscious, operating by dint of a simple replicable system of aesthetic forms, innate to human cognition. An acquaintance of William James, Leland seems to have been influenced by the James's idea of the unconscious automatism of bodily operations, an idea that not only motivated Leland's design pedagogy but also, I suspect, formed a basis for thinking about machine intelligence.[23]

The architecture machine Leland described in his "Prophesies for the Twentieth Century" had roots in a concept of human intelligence as *both* aesthetically gifted *and* dumbly rote—the latter aspect enabling the mechanical replication of human creativity. Like the putative savage, the architecture machine spit out endlessly varied combinations of a few basic ornamental forms and, with that simple repertoire, produced stupendous masterpieces. The predicament of reconciling the aesthetic virtuosity of savages with the belief that savage races were intellectually inferior effectively gave impetus to a new notion of technological production and aesthetics: the idea of an automaton that, though lacking language-based methods of reasoning, could still be aesthetically creative. If nonwhiteness was thus definable according to its alleged kinship with the yet-to-be invented technologies of mute aesthetic automatism, then whiteness was correspondingly constructed as the capacity to consciously organize and optimize underlying biological processes of unconscious creativity—whether those processes appeared in their natural human form or through the artifice of creative machines. Design education would thus be directed toward facilitating the *dumb* genius of the laboring classes and races, which is to say, the nonlinguistic aspects of human (non)intelligence appropriate to the industrial arts.

By opening this chapter with the architecture machine described in Leland's "Prophesies," I have really begun at the end of the story, as Leland penned that manuscript only three years before his death in 1903. The "Prophesies," though, are useful because they serve as a culmination of his life's thinking, with all its muddled contradictions, combining themes of Anglo-American racial conquest with Saint-Simonian ideals of pan-racial confederations and global communication. In the "Prophesies," these themes were wound together with various technological prognostications, including of developments in telepathy and hypnotism. For example, Leland imagined a machine capable of "projecting the brain's activities" onto paper, its projections—tellingly—taking the form of imagery, not language.[24] Although these fantasies might be dismissed as the banal rantings of a wealthy eccentric, the "Prophesies" are not simply indicative of the contours of progressive Euro-American thought at this time; they also eloquently demonstrate the gesture of intellectual appropriation that was so characteristic of Leland's thought and indicative of a burgeoning protostructuralist anthropology. This gesture appears in the "Prophesies," first, in its preoccupation with decoding the arts and cultures of the "primitive" past and the cognitive methods of the "primitive" races as a means of scripting the technological progress of the future, and second, in the fact that the year-by-year forecasts of political and technological developments appear to have been based on the divinatory work of Maddalena, a Tuscan witch who was one of Leland's principal informants and collaborators during his long years of research on Etruscan culture and magic, yet whom he does not in any way credit in the "Prophesies."[25]

The "Prophesies" were written during Leland's long sojourn in Tuscany, at a time when Maddalena paid him almost daily visits, divulging to him many aspects of Tuscan magic and fortune-telling. Much of what Leland gleaned from Maddalena was compiled in conventional nineteenth-century ethnographic formats, including volumes on Tuscan legends and one on the central scripture of Tuscan magic.[26] Little historical knowledge can be gleaned of Maddalena beyond her status as a witch, her literacy (she and Leland exchanged some written correspondences, now lost), and her consequent centrality to Leland's research on Tuscan culture.[27] Indeed, Maddalena's role in Leland's work often exceeded what is assumed to be the typical role of an ethnographic subject, as she personally amassed and transcribed various scriptures, rites, and incantations before passing them on to Leland to be translated into English and annotated.[28] (Thus, she might be rightly considered the author and he, the translator.) The "Prophesies" in

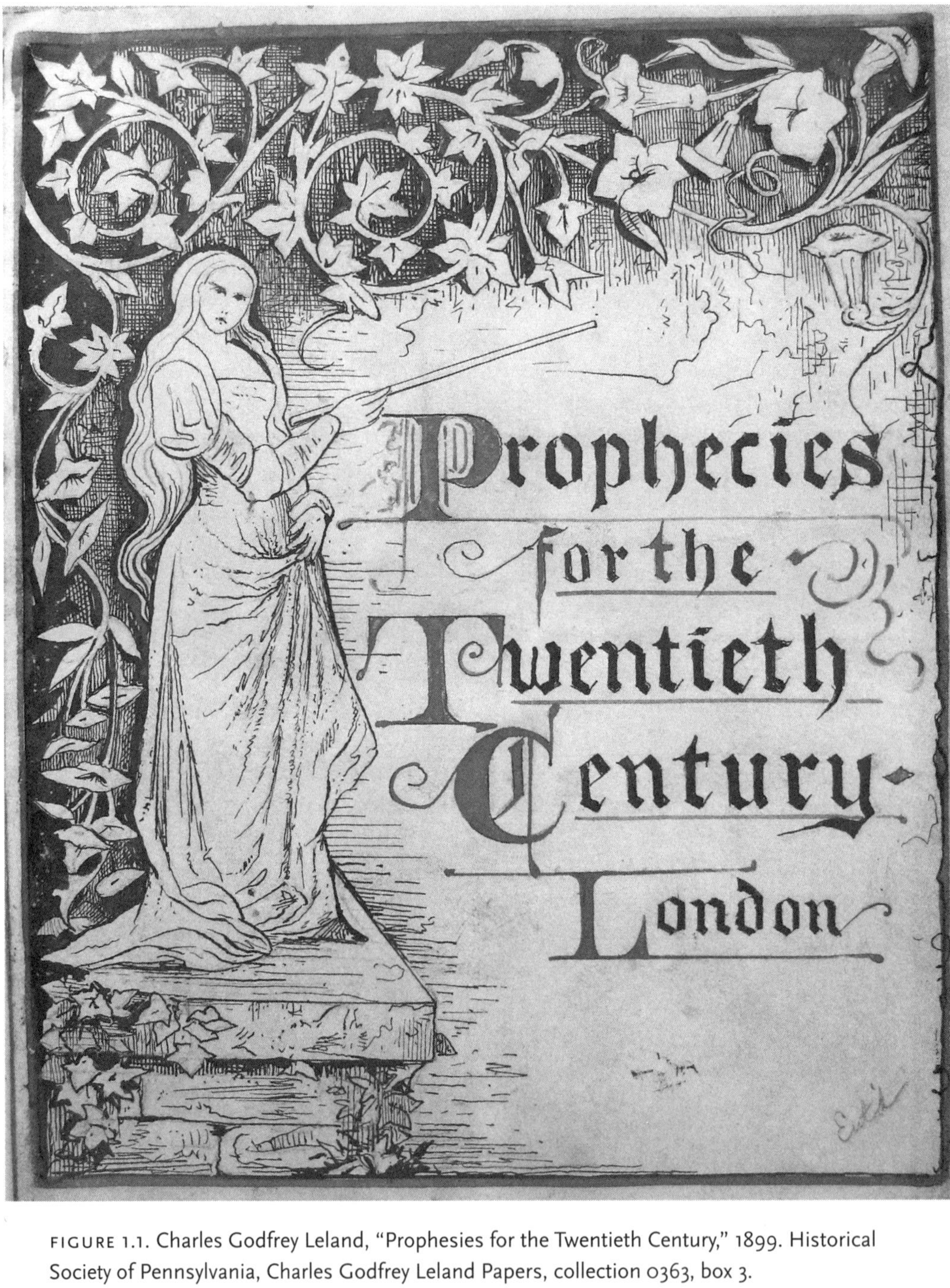

FIGURE 1.1. Charles Godfrey Leland, "Prophesies for the Twentieth Century," 1899. Historical Society of Pennsylvania, Charles Godfrey Leland Papers, collection 0363, box 3.

particular constituted a peculiar inversion of the ethnographic genre, with Maddalena's divinatory method serving as the voiceless structuring support for Leland's futurological myths. That is to say, it is the (supposed) ethnographic subject, Maddalena, who erects the narrative framework into which the (supposed) ethnographer would insert his own cultural content.

On the one hand, then, the "Prophesies" could be interpreted as the revenge of the female ethnographic subject upon the discipline of ethnography. Denied the privilege to publish, yet working as the unflagging informant, researcher, and transcriber for Leland's own publications, Maddalena may have used the "Prophesies" to stage her own ethnographic tableau, inducing Leland to be *her* informant, prompting him to jot down this torrent of fantastic obsessions, symptomatic of his class and culture. On the other hand, the "Prophesies"—though never published—repeat Leland's characteristic gesture of sublation. Assuming that their framing was indeed largely the work of Maddalena, her anonymous labor and expertise are subsumed within the scope of Leland's own authorship, thus mirroring the same movement of Anglo-American domination described in the text's forecasts. The "Prophesies" in this respect also echoed the general thrust of Leland's educational reforms and theories, which tended to simultaneously draw from and discredit the contributions of "savages."[29]

The Education of the Unconscious

> It was during a visit to the school of Miss Whatley in Cairo . . . that it suddenly occurred to me that very young children could . . . profitably and pleasantly master the decorative arts. . . . I saw very small children . . . working both sides alike of beautiful, highly elaborate designs in silk, without a pattern before them. . . .
>
> I also found . . . that . . . these children did not by any means merely follow the designs furnished by artists. In most cases they . . . had no patterns at all, *but worked like birds or bees by sympathy with the rest, modifying or varying it according to the aim of the work.*[30]

In 1879, Leland sailed home after several years in Ireland and England where he worked closely with Walter Besant and Eglantyne Jebb, who would later help develop Britain's rural crafts movement.[31] Leland's involvement in founding Britain's Cottage Arts Association (CAA) in the late 1870s gives some notion of the ways in which a concept of prehistory became instrumental to new forms of artistic production. The CAA and its later version, the Home Arts and Industries Association (HAIA), instituted programs of craft training for children in rural schools and institutionalized new practices of domicile-based industry. The programs effectively pried open the family residence to accommodate the operations of wage labor while claiming to economically empower women (anticipating so many late twentieth-century programs of development in the global south).

The CAA's plan to turn peasant homes into scattered sites of capitalist production made use of the Ruskinian image of the freely laboring medieval craftsman to represent the cottage industries as the antithesis to proletarian wage labor. For Leland, the figure of the medieval craftsman also figured within a social Darwinist account of cognitive evolution. In his 1882 pamphlet "Industrial Art in Schools," he had noted that the brain of the typical medieval European was in fact the same size as that of the average twelve-year-old boy in modern times.[32] Subsequently, in his 1883 article "An Opening for the Unemployed in Ireland," Leland described the past role of the Irish savage in art historical development, claiming that Ireland's "wild and strange" ornamental motifs derived from its prehistoric arts and subsequently formed a basis for the Gothic style that eventually spread throughout continental Europe.[33] One can thus trace the great arts and architecture of medieval Europe back to Ireland's "sculptured stones of prehistoric times" in which we "see the peculiar arts of a really savage era gradually developing into beauty."[34]

All this augured well for Ireland's unemployed. "What I would examine," Leland resumes, "is the industrial capacity of the Irish peasant." The Irish peasant's suitability for industrial employment could be deduced from his savage progenitors' artistic genius. (It was not merely incidental to the CAA's mission—or to Leland's subsequent endeavors in Philadelphia—that the Irish peasant and the Irish American immigrant were generally deemed "savages" within the nineteenth-century Anglo-American racial order.)[35] As such, cottage industries would not constitute an alienating form of exploitative wage labor but, rather, would proceed naturally from the primitive nature of Irish aesthetic cognition.

Upon returning to Philadelphia, Leland began to lecture on the advantages of industrial arts education as a means of both instilling practical skills and improving general intellectual capacities, and he began developing the program that would soon become the Public Industrial Arts School at Philadelphia (PIASP).[36] Leland followed educational developments in Boston, showing an avid interest in the founding of the Massachusetts Institute of Technology, and he knew of Walter Smith's drawing curriculum that had recently been instated as part of Boston's public school curriculum.[37] Contemporaneously with Leland's founding of PIASP, many similar vocational programs were either active or in the process of being established across the United States. Notable among these were the programs of industrial and agricultural work-study for black Americans begun during the Civil War at the Hampton Normal School in Virginia and subsequently at the Tuskegee Normal School for Colored Teachers in Alabama. There were also crafts curricula implemented at many missionary-based schools on Native American reservations preceding the establishment in 1879 of the Carlisle Indian Industrial School in Pennsylvania—the first of many compulsory off-reservation boarding schools in the United States.[38]

The discursive vectors of late nineteenth-century education reform for minorities and the working classes, spanning the Atlantic, are so numerous and entangled that it is often difficult to determine the precise trajectories of influence. For example, it seems likely—though there is no documentary evidence—that Leland's ethnographic activities among the Passamaquoddy may have brought him into contact with missionary programs emphasizing crafts education. Similarly it seems likely—though unproven—that Leland was acquainted with the pedagogical experiments in the industrial arts being contemporaneously undertaken by Booker T. Washington at Tuskegee. At the very least, PIASP and Tuskegee appear to have borrowed from common sources, as Washington's program has been linked to pedagogic exhibitions at Philadelphia's 1876 Centennial International Exposition.[39] Moreover, Leland traveled to Egypt, England, Ireland, and Prussia, where he was exposed to examples of state-sponsored and colonial missionary educational programs.

Progressive education movements in both Europe and the United States were characterized by the vexed aims of, on the one hand, a liberal notion of universal literacy and, on the other hand, assumptions that the working classes should be prepared for manual labor. While advocating that all citizens acquire knowledge exceeding the rudiments required by a given occupation, nineteenth-century proponents of public primary education strove to create curricula that were *both* universal *and* tailored to the specific (and varying) vocational requirements of the working classes, thus encouraging a conception of human brains as fundamentally identical but *also* fundamentally different.[40] The challenge was to uplift the lower classes without uplifting them beyond their assigned station. Indeed, fears of the politically emancipatory effects of public education drove the Prussian government to outlaw its popular kindergarten movement in response to the failed 1848 revolution. That kindergarten movement, led by Friedrich Fröbel, was deeply influential to Leland's own pedagogy.

In response to the conflict between progressive and conservative aims, proponents of public education often asserted the harmonious union between the cultivation of children's industrial capacities and the cultivation of their intellects. This line of reasoning lay the ground, I would argue, for a conception of the working-class intellect or (in the case of the postbellum United States) the typically non-Anglo-American intellect as harboring fundamental intellectual kinships with industrial machines, kinships that did not stunt human capacities for aesthetic creativity. Thus Leland—in the passage quoted at the beginning of this section—could interpret Egyptian child artisans as behaving like industrious automata ("working like bees"), but not in a way that impinged on their aesthetic creativity. Not merely copying patterns, these little laborers seem to have assuaged any concerns Leland may have entertained about the alienating or exploitative nature of aesthetic production, demonstrating that public education could be appropriate to the working classes (and young children) while leaving them essentially "free," creative, and self-determining.

Concerning the class politics surrounding public education programs, the German-speaking context was especially influential to U.S. movements, given that several disciples of Fröbel's kindergarten movement fled to the United States after 1848 and that influential educators like Horace Mann toured Prussia's school programs in the 1840s.[41] Fröbel had sought to render popular education appropriate to the working classes while still appearing to educate "the whole human" (not simply her or his industrial and agricultural capacities). A motivation for this program of holistic education was to be found in the late eighteenth-century German notion of *Bildung*, which described the natural unfolding of a child's various faculties. Presaging the Hegelian concept of synthesis, *Bildung* emphasized the education of the whole human and in this sense was counterposed to alienation, an estrangement between intellectual and manual faculties. (The concept of alienation appears in German idealism decades before Karl Marx ascribed alienation to the conditions of capitalist labor.)[42] Fröbel suggested that working-class childhood education offered a corrective to mind–body alienation, advancing the thesis that there was no conflict between the goals of a liberal humanist education and the development of manual dexterity.[43] Manual training and hand–eye coordination encouraged *general* intellectual competencies; hence, Fröbelian education prescribed the physical manipulation of basic forms (such as toy blocks) to impart intellectual skills while simultaneously honing the child's dexterity. According to this reckoning, alienation did not, as Marx would argue, result *inevitably* from capitalist relations of labor but, rather, could be prevented through proper education of the human organism, defeated, that is, without challenging a capitalist division of labor (a line of reasoning that would be later echoed at the Bauhaus).

Along with positing the basic harmony between the industrial laboring body and the spiritual intellect, Fröbel also suggested a basic unity between humans and nature. In this sense, educational theory was directed toward erasing the alienation not only between the laboring body and the contemplative brain but also between brain and world. This bore implications for the status of language and literacy within programs of working-class education. Leland later echoed Fröbel's conviction that in childhood education, "the representation of *things* should precede the representations of signs and words" lest words disrupt a naive and authentic relationship to the external world.[44] Language existed in a cognitive domain quite distinct from the primordial domain of the unconscious where bodily and intellectual faculties converged.[45]

There was a magico-theological dimension to Fröbel's thinking, evident especially in the didactic role he assigned to nature. Although the *-garten* (garden) component of *Kindergarten* was devised partly as an appropriate means of educating poor farmers' offspring for their future occupations, the postulation that horticulture served as a reasonable basis of general education rested on a romantic espousal of nature's divinity. Nature's theological aspect rendered agricultural training a form of spiritual education.[46] Nature, by undergirding both the material world and human intelligence, thus could form the basis for a class-appropriate education in which the fostering of agricultural and industrial competencies was cast as intellectual cultivation.

In the United States, this ideology concerning the unity of bodily and intellectual training formed a justification for racially segregated forms of education, such as at Hampton, where a curriculum designed to prepare black Americans and (for a brief time) Native Americans for a life of economic and political servility was presented as the holistic training of "the head, the heart, and the hands."[47] What Leland would contribute to this ideological construction was his belief that the unconscious mind lies at the nexus of intellectual and bodily unity and that education must be directed toward this locus of artistic productivity. He argued that the unconscious capacities of art production that had long lay dormant in the Anglo-American brain could be consciously mastered and thereby taught in public school curricula.[48]

In his 1888 treatise *Practical Education,* Leland cited Fröbel's theories in claiming the intellectual value of training in hand–eye coordination:

> The youngest child can be taught the beginning of hand-work of many kinds. It can learn to observe, its quickness of perception can be stimulated, it can be taught to draw and model in clay, and in short "begin to prepare" for serious work. No one would think of training it then to make a living, but its mind may be diverted into a channel tending in that direction.[49]

With this aim to "divert" children into vocational channels, the PIASP program opened its doors in 1880 to two hundred students selected at random from Philadelphia's public schools to receive arts instruction two afternoons a week. Leland reported anecdotally that contrary to initial fears that these students would subsequently fall behind in their regular course of studies, their teachers acknowledged that they in fact showed "an increased quickness of intellectual perception or intelligence, so that literary studies are also more easily mastered."[50] Decades later, his successor at PIASP, James Liberty Tadd, noted that the hand–eye coordination exercises were excellent training not just for the industrial arts but for the medical professions.[51] Tadd described the approach he had acquired from his mentor: "I have no sympathy with manual training methods that make the use of tools the main end. The pupils become simply machines, thoughtless mechanisms. The first tools to be used and trained are the mind, the eyes and the hands—the instrumentalities of the organism."[52]

The claim to educate students not in vocational aptitudes but, rather, in the basic organic technologies of mind and body (that is, the ergonomics of the spirit) did not simply respond to critiques of the alienating effects of industrial labor; it also tacitly responded to the ever-imminent threat of technical obsolescence. Instead of learning trade-specific skills that might become obsolete at any moment, students were trained to be high-functioning organisms, adaptable to industry's ongoing technological transformations. In 1899 Tadd published a book on Leland's methods that was later translated into German (he and Leland had both given lecture tours on their pedagogy throughout central and eastern Europe). Probably owing to the book's wide dissemination in the German-speaking world, Leland's conception of design as a mastery of unconscious cognitive mechanisms would come to undergird theories and practices at the Bauhaus. There, teachers replicated some of his exercises (as I show in chapter 2), in one case developing a program for "creative automatism" linked to a "racial theory of art."[53]

Through his ethnographic work, Leland found support for his conviction that aesthetic fecundity was rooted in primordial human aptitudes that had little to do with conscious cultivation. In an unpublished manuscript entitled "Profitable Work for Poor People," Leland noted that the Passamaquoddy were all highly skilled in a variety of crafts even though none of them specialized in craft production. He recounted the plight of

> a young sad Indian girl who believed that she was the least able to design of any of her tribe. And to prove it, in a merry mood, she scraped on birch bark with the half of an old pocket knife a series of designs. . . . They were all inspired with beautiful conventional motives.[54]

FIGURE 1.2. Exercises in ambidextrous drawing, 1900. From James Liberty Tadd, *New Methods in Education* (1900).

FIGURE 1.3. Exercises in ambidextrous drawing, 1900. From James Liberty Tadd, *New Methods in Education* (1900).

FIGURE 1.4. Drawing exercises in mind–body coordination, 1900. From James Liberty Tadd, *New Methods in Education* (1900).

Later, conceding that "red Indians do indeed have a greater aptitude than whites," Leland ascribed this artistic superiority to their familiarity from infancy onward with an aesthetic *system* consisting of "conventional motives" that could be variously configured and applied to different kinds of materials and objects. A conventional motif was not to be confused with pattern work, which Leland disparaged as a form of rote mechanical reproduction. Leland asserted the existence of an instinctive, flexible language of design, distinct from mere reproduction, that could be creatively adapted to different crafts. In *Practical Education,* he observed "that the best decoration consists of simple ornaments arranged at intervals, and that in doing this the mere

Abb. 122

Abb. 123

FIGURE 1.5. Drawing exercises in ornamental motifs, 1900. From James Liberty Tadd, *New Methods in Education* (1900).

FIGURE 1.6. Ornamentation exercises at Germantown Public School, 1900. From James Liberty Tadd, *New Methods in Education* (1900).

savage often surpasses the civilised artist. Now the average savage is not, as regards innate artistic capacity or intellect, superior to an English schoolboy."[55] Indeed, Leland tells us, "the child corresponds to primitive man." If all savages could make beautiful art, this proved that his students needed only a universal system of design. But what was this *system*? For Leland, it constituted a kind of nonlinguistic, almost supernatural form of communication: a pentecostal technology that obviated the need for language as such.

To show that the application of an aesthetic system did not entail mere mechanical copying, Leland pointed to the example, cited earlier, of Egyptian schoolchildren who "had no patterns at all, but worked like birds or bees *by sympathy* with the rest." Moreover, one could witness the architectural feats of various animal species, especially those of the marvelous mound ant:

> For the fact that ants with incredible skill and forethought anticipate and adapt a thousand circumstances, not running in mere grooves of thought or mental action, but showing a varied genius which surpasses that of man in Architecture, renders absolutely absurd the belief of Descartes . . . that animals follow in all things only "a blind instinct or mechanical impulse communicated through their external organs."[56]

Moreover, Leland noted that mound ants adapted their work not only to unforeseen circumstances but also to each other's activities. The architectural abilities of birds and bees to work "in sympathy" with their fellows—without verbal language—and to collaboratively vary their work according to circumstance indicated a cognitive stratum that, though not conscious in the sense of language-based cognition, was nevertheless not purely rote: it entailed a kind of feedback loop, or what we would now refer to as technological "smartness." In other words, birds and insects—and arguably "savages"—were intelligent or at least aesthetically creative machines, not rote machines able to perform only a single repetitive operation. The ants' *unplanned* collaboration attested to some universal grammar of design, variable enough that it could be adapted to contingent circumstances but uniform enough that its collective implementation required no plan or language for coordination. In contrast to the distinction Marx drew between bees and human architects (stressing human beings' unique ability to conceptualize an entire design in advance of its construction), Leland believed that the labor of multiple bodies could be synchronized without plans. The best design was rooted in an organic systematicity, inherent to mind and nature alike. Capitalist industrial labor could proceed organically.

Leland did not uphold the orthodox demarcation between animal instinct and human creativity because, for him, the demarcation between unconscious and conscious thought was elided by an aesthetic grammar that mediated these two spheres. In the classroom Leland's methods for improving connections between unconscious and conscious faculties included exercises in ambidexterity and in the coordination of the entire body in producing simple geometric forms in chalk (all of these exercises were later adopted by Johannes Itten at the Bauhaus). Extramurally, Leland encouraged hypnotism and directed dreaming as methods for capturing the latent productivities of the unconscious imagination.[57] Crediting Paracelsus with being the first to record systematic techniques for strengthening the cooperation between a person's two "spirits" or "minds"—(Leland preserved the original German, *Geisten*), he argued that the unconscious mind could be disciplined to work in harmony with conscious aims. Invoking a savagery of times past, he claimed that the spectacular architectures of the European Middle Ages were conceived "in a kind of slumber. . . . Instinct in its earlier or simpler form is the following of laws of Nature which are themselves formed by motive laws." That is, Nature's "motive laws" form the basis of design's "conventional motives." He continued,

> We do not sufficiently reflect on the fact that *Natura naturans,* or the action of Nature (or simply following Tradition), may . . . involve the creation of marvelously ingenious and beautiful works . . . by Instinct alone. . . . A time will come when [man] will perceive that his best work has been done unconsciously, or under influences of which he was ignorant.[58]

Unconscious creativity drew from the very structures of nature itself, whereas a conscious mind that was alienated from its slumbering counterpart could muster up only the bungled ornaments characteristic of Anglo-American industrial arts.

Leland's conceptualization of "primitive" forms of cognition was not merely condescending; there were moments when his racial precepts turned violent, hewing to the logic of social Darwinism. In a short unpublished treatise, "The Coming Race, or The New Man of Cromagnon," Leland explained that Anglo-Americans were on the verge of evolving into a new and superior race that would usurp present-day peoples just as the Cro-Magnons had usurped their contemporaries many millennia ago.[59] Proposing, in the name of science, a flurry of grave robbing ("a great exhumation of skulls and bones"), Leland's rhetoric suggests that racial cleansing is more than genocide, that it is also a means of recovering the secrets of human intelligence, fueling technological progress.[60] World history is to realize its teleology through its treatment of other races as experimental fodder for the perfection of the dominant race, appearing as a kind of eugenics *avant la lettre*. Human intelligence was to be perfected not by selective *breeding* but, rather, by a selective *fine-tuning* of the human race's intellectual faculties, scientifically translating "primitive" intelligence into a protostructuralist science of human and machine intelligence.

Holistic Education and Racial Segregation

As mentioned earlier, the class- and race-based implications of late nineteenth-century U.S. public education were, at best, ambiguous. PIASP was founded about 1880. At more or less the same time, in 1881, Philadelphia passed legislation to abolish de jure racial segregation in its public school system, though that legislation had little effect on de facto segregation, as attested by photographic evidence of black students participating in PIASP's methods in what appear to be wholly segregated schools.[61] It is worth noting that Leland had hired at PIASP a black carpentry instructor whose later dismissal by the board of directors provoked Leland to angrily sever all ties with his beloved institution.[62] Yet, his esteem for that lone carpentry instructor notwithstanding, Leland, along with many former abolitionists, believed that black Americans' and Africans' only hope of betterment lay in African colonization. That position was also adopted by some African American leaders, such as faculty at Tuskegee who participated in agricultural modernization programs intended to transform parts of West Africa, including Liberia, into a suitable plantation-based settlement colony for black Americans.[63]

Tuskegee's founding director, Booker T. Washington, had been educated at Hampton Normal School, where, according to historical accounts, he had been thoroughly indoctrinated with the school's dogma of racial submission.[64] A long-standing criticism of Washington's curriculum at Tuskegee—most famously voiced by W. E. B. Du Bois—was that it relegated African American higher education to vocational and agricultural training to the exclusion of more scholarly pursuits. Born of the Atlanta compromise, which secured for blacks the right to higher education only by outwardly divesting that education of its "higher" aims, Tuskegee's curriculum largely reflected the interests of the white ruling class.[65]

Like Leland, Washington was influenced by Fröbelian philosophies that prescribed the holistic education of mind and body.[66] At Tuskegee, however, these principles were

FIGURE 1.7. Students in workshop at Tuskegee Institute. Photograph by Frances Benjamin Johnston, 1902. Library of Congress Prints and Photographs Division.

used as a way to covertly instate aspects of liberal arts education within the framework of vocational training. Tuskegee students were asked to exhaustively analyze their manual vocational exercises through writing, drawing, and mathematics.[67] Reciprocally, courses dealing with more scholarly pursuits were to be grounded in the practical trades, thus conforming to the strictures of the Atlanta compromise. Writing classes, for example, required students to make regular diary entries describing their vocational training exercises.[68] While a generous interpretation of this strategy might deem it a compelling provocation to the ways conventional universities supported the hierarchical division between professional and manual labor, it could also be seen as an ideological maneuver, the vestige of liberal arts training serving as an apology for the demeaning mandate that the school uphold a racial division of labor. Against this program, Du Bois demanded that an intellectual elite—African America's "Talented Tenth"—receive a liberal arts education rooted in the European classics. Such an elite training—while intended to raise blacks' leadership credentials to be on par with those of the white ruling class—nonetheless left dangling the question of education for the other 90 percent.[69]

The differences between Du Bois's educational aims and those of Washington and Leland were undergirded by their divergent epistemic philosophies. Du Bois's notion

FIGURE 1.8. History class at Tuskegee Institute. Photograph by Frances Benjamin Johnston, 1902. Library of Congress Prints and Photographs Division.

of African American "double consciousness" can be directly opposed to Leland's and Washington's ideal of a holistic, nonalienated form of working-class consciousness.[70] Double consciousness, arising from the disjunctions between the dominant and minority cultures that black Americans straddled, was to enable black Americans to fulfill Du Bois's (loosely Hegelian *and* Marxian) notion of world historical liberation.[71] Alienation was not to be neatly resolved—not to be dialectically synthesized—but, rather, would serve as a guiding revolutionary force. This is significant because the nineteenth-century ideal of cognitive synthesis was so closely linked to savage thought—to the epistemic subject-positioning that regarded nonwhite intellectual and cultural products as so many clues leading toward an ultimate science of the human brain. Synthesis was, furthermore, shot through with the fantasies of merging machine and human forms of intelligence.

Africa and the Architecture Machine

The pyramids of Egypt would be rebuilt without slaves. The Tower of Babel would be finally completed despite the world's diversity of tongues. When Leland prophesied an architectural machine that would allow nature to "be . . . reproduced by Nature," he seems to have been envisioning the technological emancipation of humans from exploitative labor. The architecture machine gestured toward forms of technological production that would counter an alienating division of labor. It would integrate intellectual and physical labor—design and construction—through its magical merging of mechanical intelligence with material secretions. Yet the machine's rote labor was dependent on the apperceptive consciousness of its human inventors, and we thus might see the machine as simply a technological stand-in for existing relations of labor. The machine's inventors would distill the rich abundance of world architecture into a systematic aesthetic grammar of "conventional motives," reproducible by the machine. Leland's machine presumed natural points of connection between nature and mind that allowed the circumvention of language, enabling human beings to automatically—mutely and magically—concretize their wishes as architectural reality. Because this universal aesthetic grammar was derived from the putatively natural structures of the mind itself, it seemed plausible that all human beings could communicate with the architecture machine, transmitting their intentions to it without recourse to conventional language.

For the machine to acquire such capabilities, the architectures of the world (the pyramids of Egypt, the towers of Babylon, and the rest) would first have to be distilled into fungible components that could be somehow integrated into a single aesthetic system. So presumably all these architectural examples would be broken into their common denominators, their common lineages revealed. (Here we catch a whiff of the structuralist modes of comparison that would motivate so many mid-twentieth-century architects.) Certainly, efforts of this kind had already been undertaken in the decorative arts, Owen Jones's 1856 compendium *The Grammar of Ornament* being a case in point.[72] Efforts to compile and reveal a systematicity to the world's ornaments—to deduce a science of decorative form—pointed to the technologizable nature of ornament and, therefore, to the contiguities between human and machine intelligence.[73]

In the systematization of the world's crafts can be detected the dismal logic of world historical eschatology, according to which sublation is cast as Enlightenment liberation: the claim that what was hitherto practiced, but not *consciously* so, would now be placed in the domain of conscious knowing by integrating that unconscious practice into one's own consciousness. While the racial–nationalist biases of Hegelianism are hardly a secret, what I want to draw attention to is how Hegel's—admittedly abstract—notions of cognitive and world historical assimilation appear as an uncanny precedent for later modes of *cognitive–technological* assimilation. In this regard, Hegel's peculiar treatment of "Africa" vis-à-vis world history portends a twentieth-century structuralist project of translating cultural and cognitive habit into patterns and systems. Such translation—or sublation—requires a primordial and universalizable model of consciousness so as to reveal the systematicity of the primordial, ultimately bringing closer together human brains and aesthetic machines. Underlying this conception of the kinship between primitive (but aesthetically productive) human cognition and aesthetic machines are the various nineteenth-century racial theories of cognitive and world historical evolution.

Race was endemic to a notion that human cognition could ultimately become fully conscious of its own workings, a feat that Hegel held as the culmination of the mind's

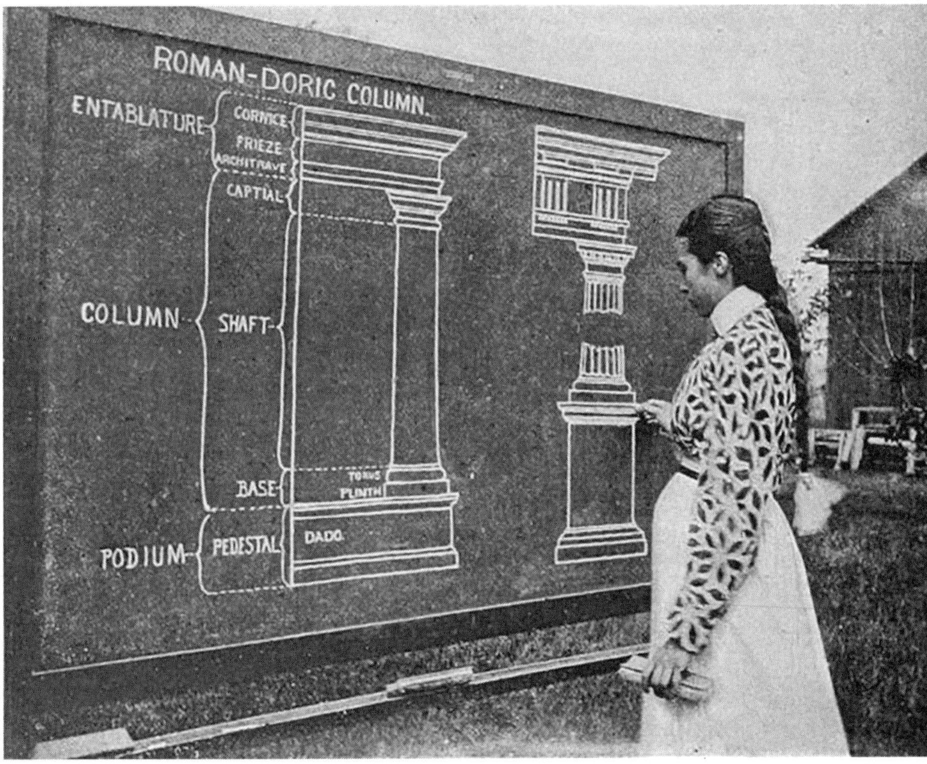

FIGURE 1.9. Drawing of Classical orders, 1900. From James Liberty Tadd, *New Methods in Education* (1900).

long historical development. In this respect, it is noteworthy that although Africa was excised from Hegel's world historical map, it nonetheless haunted his thinking in the form of a cipher, being repeatedly transposed by non-Africans (or by *alleged* non-Africans, such as ancient Egyptians) into something supposedly more advanced and universal than itself.[74] "Africa" serves as a fluid and unfixed—and thus universalizable—category for Hegel, constantly subsumed within other national "minds," offering itself as the original to be translated by other civilizations. In a much-cited passage from Hegel's lectures on history, he struggles to justify his treatment of Africa:

> At this point we leave Africa, not to mention it again. For it is no historical part of the World; it has no movement or development to exhibit. Historical movements in it—that is, in its northern part—belong to the Asiatic or European World. Carthage displayed there an important transitionary phase of civilization; but, as a Phoenician colony, it belongs to Asia. Egypt will be considered in reference to the passage of the human mind from its Eastern to its Western phase, but it does not belong to the African Spirit [or mind, that is, *Geist*]. What we properly understand by Africa, is the Unhistorical, Undeveloped Spirit, still involved in the conditions of mere nature, and which *had to be presented here only as* on the threshold of the World's History.[75]

Hegel's "had to be presented here only as" marks his awareness that Africa's liminality, its assignment to nonhistory, is a matter less of historical fact than of philosophical expediency. Africa's extrahistorical status arises, he confesses, from the exigencies of his own philosophical "presentation." But what precisely are those unnamed exigencies?

I propose that these exigencies arise from the contradictions endemic to Europe's imperialist–nationalist project, which required the geographically distant origins of human "civilization" to be somehow subsumed within the nation's own ethnonational narrative. This construction requires a transhistorical *common denominator,* a sort of invisible essence—whether a world historical spirit (*Weltgeist*) or, let's say, an always-already crossed-out "Africa." That crossed-out entity, converted into universal spirit, enables continuity across the scattered histories of diverse societies, allowing for an eschatology of racial evolution. Africa "had to be presented" as "Unhistorical" so that it could be transhistorical, an essence conserved across various historical permutations. Africa "had to be" disappeared from the map of the world spirit's historical evolution so that, effectively, it could *be* the world spirit.

The rhetorical fabrication of an always-already crossed-out "Africa" is important to the late nineteenth century because, among other things, it presages the contradictions of social Darwinism seen in this chapter, the contradictions between the idea of a single human origin and the idea of biologically distinct human races, all of them to be ultimately crossed out by the evolutionary triumph of the Anglo-American race. And this contradiction would linger on in the twentieth-century structuralist social sciences, which, though always insisting on the basic uniformity of human brains, also constantly implied that only "primitive" brains evinced the real *nature* of cognition. As for architecture's own structuralist and cybernetic adventures in the twentieth century, these are aptly presaged by Leland's imagined architecture machine. In contrast to Du Bois's notion of double consciousness, Leland's architecture machine operated according to the violent logic of the *epistemic suture*: a suture that would forcibly meld mind and nature, disavowing their mediated relationship, disavowing the importance of language as a device of that mediation, and enabling the reconstruction of the historical past as a sequence of glorious monuments (such as the pyramids of Egypt) falling under the technological regime of Anglo-American world dominance.

Leland's architecture machine was to enable the reconstruction of Egypt's ancient pyramids *without* slave labor, but this fantasy nonetheless sought recourse in the slave's imagined state of unconscious labor. This putative unconsciousness, which was believed to bear a direct, unmediated relation to nature, would be the key to technologically reproducing the mechanisms of aesthetic creativity. Through the resulting architecture machine, the white race would concretize its apperceptive transcendence over the ruptures between mind and nature. The machine would allow nature to finally be "reproduced by Nature": reproduced, that is, by a form of techno-aesthetic imperialism that masqueraded as the scientific harnessing of nature.

2

THE BAUHAUS AND THE AURA OF AUTHORSHIP

Class and Race in the Age of Technological Reproducibility

All That Is Solid Melts into Chairs

In 1926, Bauhaus instructor and former Bauhaus student Marcel Breuer produced a photomontage that would later be circulated as a fitting testament to the Bauhaus's development from its 1919 opening in the city of Weimar through its move to the small industrial city of Dessau, Germany, in 1925. Designed to resemble a film strip, the montage depicted a chronological sequence of five chairs Breuer had either designed, produced, or coproduced at the Bauhaus, ranging from his and Gunta Stölzl's so-called African or Negro chair to one of Breuer's tubular steel chairs. The five chairs were followed by a witty depiction of a woman sitting back in an invisible chair, supported only by a "resilient column of air," satirically suggesting that a modernist penchant for sleek, lightweight materials, when assisted by scientific advances, would realize its teleology by finally abolishing material altogether.[1]

Although Bauhaus historiography has reprinted this montage at various points, no scholarship has ever seriously considered the curious suggestion that a chair referred to as "African" should stand as the origin of a modernist evolution that was to lead to technologically reproducible designs and, ultimately, to the complete dematerialization of the designed object. The image tends to be used instead to illustrate familiar narratives of the Bauhaus: namely, that the Bauhaus transformed over the course of several years from a school deeply influenced by Austrian–German expressionism and magico-religious philosophies to a school dedicated to the pursuit of technological reproduction along with an aesthetic style expressive of these technological concerns. Related to this narrative are several other well-entrenched art historical narratives, such as the idea that expressionist primitivism uniformly constituted a reaction against—rather than in some cases a reconciliation with—capitalist means of technological reproduction, and the idea that Bauhaus racial evocations (such as the "African"/"Negro" chair) can be simply chalked up to an expressionist penchant for the "primitive" without requiring any serious inquiry into the racial character not only of the chair itself but also of the conceit of the chair's incremental evolution into the dematerialized essence of design.[2]

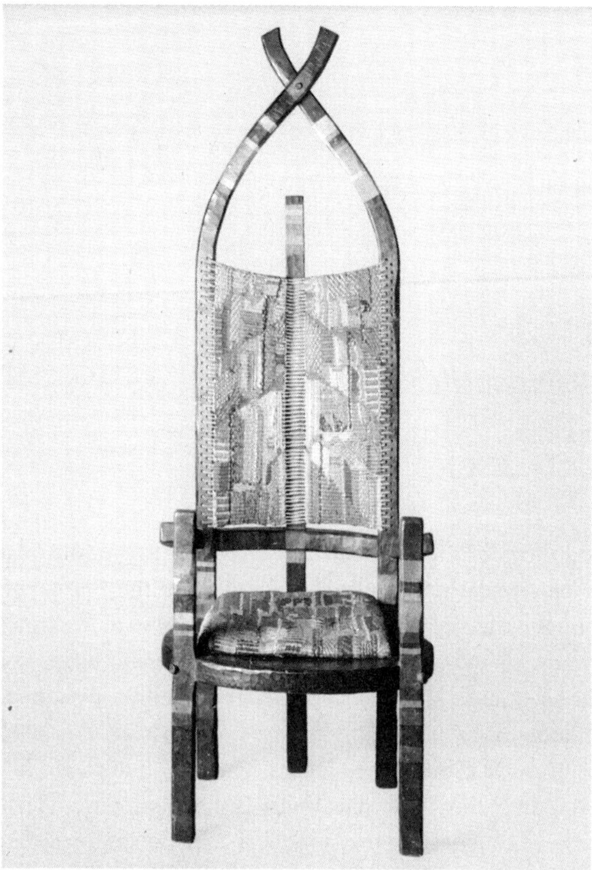

FIGURE 2.1. Marcel Breuer and Gunta Stölzl, *African Chair,* 1921. Reprinted with permission from Bauhaus-Archiv Berlin.

The aim of this chapter is to explore the imbrication between Bauhäuslers' magico-religious and technological interests during the years of Walter Gropius's directorship and dispel the lingering myth of two distinct Bauhauses—that is, the mystical, often technophobic Bauhaus that allegedly flourished during the school's first few years versus the technically oriented and no-longer-mystical Bauhaus realized in the latter half of Gropius's nine-year directorship. While recent scholarship has examined the mystical movements and psychological discourses surrounding the Bauhaus and German modernism, there has been little speculation as to how these movements and discourses may have been motivated by capitalist forms of technological reproduction and related concepts of intellectual property, class, and race.[3] The historiographic distinction between the mystical and the technorational Bauhaus arises not only from Gropius's own retrospective framing of the school but also from an enduring Euro-American schematization that segregates the magico-religious from modern technoscience, such that even when they are deeply complicit and entangled, they must be presented as a sequential succession—that is, an evolution. Although Breuer's photomontage might seem to reinforce this partitioning of the magico-religious from the technoscientific (the latter superseding the former), such an interpretation depends on the way we view the idea

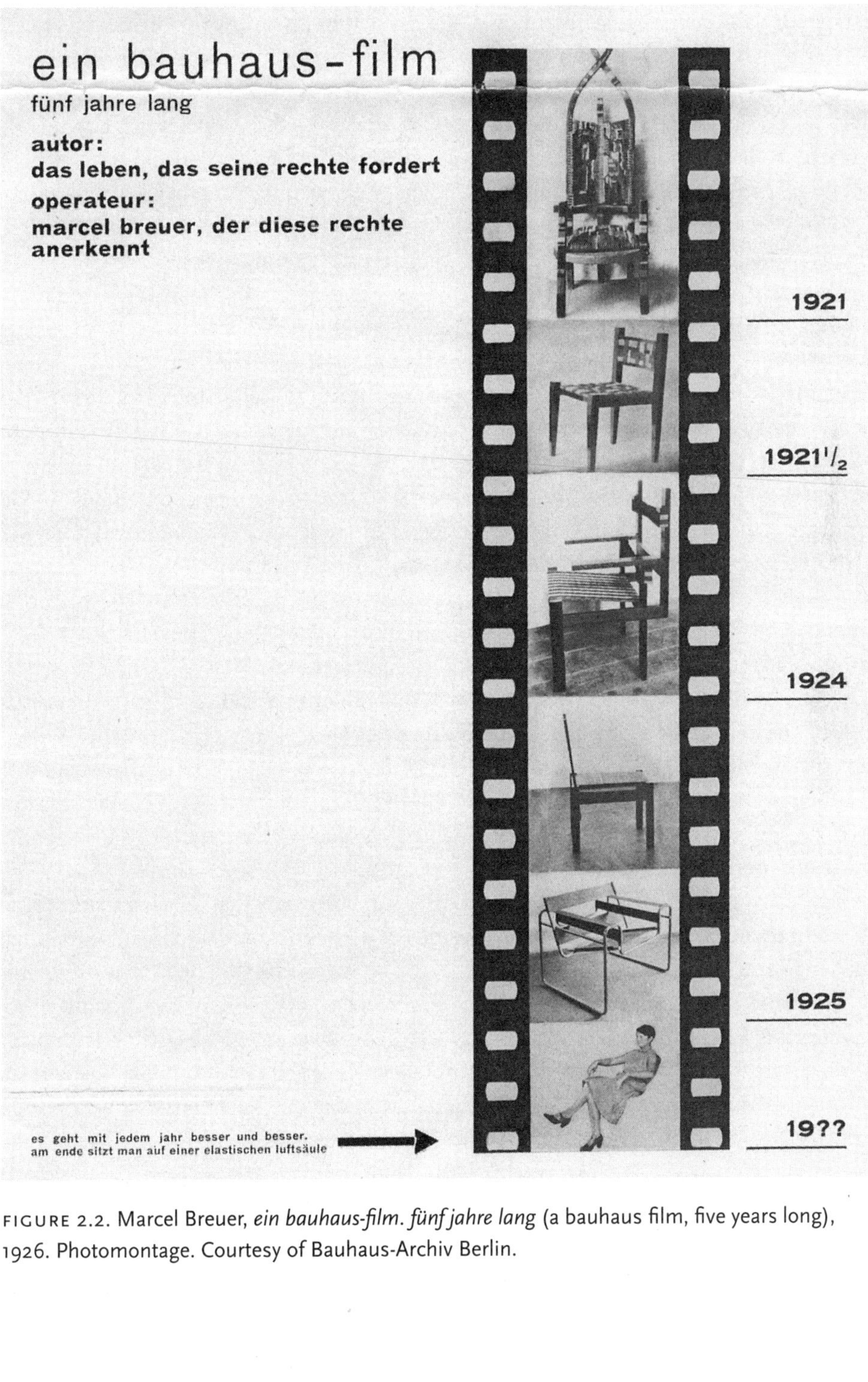

FIGURE 2.2. Marcel Breuer, *ein bauhaus-film. fünf jahre lang* (a bauhaus film, five years long), 1926. Photomontage. Courtesy of Bauhaus-Archiv Berlin.

of evolution. Given the rampant Hegelianism at the Bauhaus (evinced, for example, in Johannes Itten's "racial science"), the Hegelian notion of sublation (*Aufhebung*), introduced in chapter 1, remains relevant for Bauhaus history. Evolution, from a Hegelian perspective, emphasizes the retention of the precedent, its subsumption and inclusion (but also its cancellation) within the scope of that which succeeds it. In modernist design discourse and practice, the precedent often served as evidence of autochthonous aesthetic laws and essences that were to inform the technologically reproducible work of modernist design. These laws—grasped instinctively by primitives—were to be brought into the domain of full consciousness by twentieth-century Europeans.

Three details of Breuer's photomontage are especially relevant to the themes of this chapter: First, the tubular-steel chair it depicts was one of many such Bauhaus-designed chairs that prompted a legal battle over intellectual property in the technologically reproducible design.[4] Second, the "African chair"—far from being easily dismissed as expressionist craft—in fact constitutes an exposition of two basic modernist precepts discursively linked to aesthetic notions of technological reproducibility: the restriction of the chair's palette to the three primary colors,[5] and the chair's legible rendition of its tectonics, demonstrating a clear articulation of component parts and simple shapes, an aspect emphasized by the Van Doesburg–style chair appearing in the middle of the montage sequence. And third, the last frame of the montage, as mentioned, seems to caricaturize modernism's minimalist use of materials. The humorous exaggeration of minimalism tends to distract from other possible meanings of the chair's dematerialization. This imaginary chair, when presented (even satirically) as the telos of modernist industrial design, symptomatizes a widespread ideological response to the central dilemma of Bauhaus culture and pedagogy. This dilemma had to do with the status and nature of artistic labor in the age of the design's technological reproducibility. I mean "ideological" in the Althusserian sense of a "representation of the imaginary relationship of individuals to their real conditions of existence," a formula that captures well the Bauhaus's phantasmagoric representation of its own relationships to capitalist means of production.[6]

Much Bauhaus rhetoric and imagery expressed the fantasy that the alienating effects wrought by a capitalist division of labor might be somehow rendered inconsequential, made to vanish into thin air *despite* the school's strong support of technological reproduction (and hence of an industrial division of labor). The image of the invisible chair renders this fantasy hyperbolically, its jest belying how earnestly the fantasy was in fact pursued. In this instance, the chair's complete dematerialization renders obsolete *all* forms of labor, except the technoscientific labor of design. Karl Marx's and Friedrich Engels's formulation that "all that is solid melts into air" is turned on its head.[7] Like Leland's imagined architecture machine, the photomontage fancifully suggests that in the future, technologies of production would help displace manual labor with what was essentially magic.

In a short article concerning "racial theory," Bauhaus instructor Johannes Itten also expounded a version of the evolution of the arts, designating "the black race" as the origin to be superseded by the white race's "synthesis" of the world's arts:

> In all eras in all the realms of creation we find the creative drive. . . . It is this drive . . . that is to be finally realized with the help of electro-magnetic forces.
>
> For the black race, this drive toward realization was still an unconscious pursuit. . . .
>
> The great discovery of the white race was finding unity. . . . In all the earlier races, the foundation of creative work always formed either the material, spiritual, or intellectual system, or a combination of two such systems. Only with the white race did the purification and synthesis of the three temperaments occur . . . and henceforth everything was guided by this originary, primordial basis of individuality.[8]

Itten's racial theories will be discussed further along in the chapter; suffice it to say for now that the gist of Itten's crudely Hegelian schema of art history succinctly amends Hegelian orthodoxy in its proposition that art's teleology would "be finally realized with the help of electro-magnetic forces." What was it about *electricity* that would help fulfill art's racial eschatology? "Electro-magnetic" has two likely associations here: first, with technological reproduction, and second, with the electromagnetism of the neurologic–corporeal apparatus, linked to various mystical understandings of energy.[9] The thesis of this chapter is that the ideologies and practices surrounding technological reproduction were supported by a strong interest in the neurological body and in racial exemplars of "primitive" thought, which became sources of "natural" aesthetic laws, the latter being linked to how authorship was conceived under copyright law. These artistic developments supported a crucial and ongoing shift in the ontology of the artwork from discrete domains of material expertise (that is, crafts) toward a conception of media. In this sense, the "science" of artistic practice developed at the Bauhaus constitutes a structuralist approach to aesthetic production in which the human organism and its artistic products were submitted to (often racialized) rubrics of comparison so as to deduce underlying universal laws and elementary techniques common to all aspects of human aesthetic production.

Capitalism and Technomagic

According to Gropius, the 1919 opening of the Bauhaus heralded a new harmonious collaboration of artistic labor, in contrast to alienating modes of capitalist production:

> Architects, sculptors, painters, we must all return to the crafts! For art is not a "profession." There is no essential difference between the artist and craftsman. . . . Let us then create a new guild of craftsmen without the class distinctions. . . . Together let us desire, conceive, and create the new structure of the future, which will embrace architecture and sculpture and painting in one unity and which will one day rise toward heaven from the hands of a million workers like the crystal symbol of a new faith.[10]

Gropius's statement of educational intent was illustrated by Lyonel Feininger's woodcut print of a Gothic cathedral. The cathedral's sleek crystalline form was suggestive of the dynamism of modern technologies, while its medieval referent evoked the myth of a golden age when an architectural division of labor took the form of nonhierarchical

FIGURE 2.3. Lyonel Feininger, *Cathedral of Socialism*, circa 1919. Woodblock print. Copyright 2020 Artists Rights Society (ARS), New York / VG Bild-Kunst, Bonn.

collaboration. According to this Ruskinian notion, medieval architecture's complex coordination of labor transpired through a magico-religious synthesis of hands, rather than through a division between construction and architectural design and management.[11]

Yet in contrast to this anticapitalist vision of magical labor, Gropius in the same document stressed the Bauhaus's commitment to cutting-edge scientific research and to the formation of strong contacts with industries. That is, in order to attract financial support for its purportedly anticapitalist ideals, the school would pursue a research agenda linked to the needs of industrial capital. The school's technological enthusiasm stemmed in part from its financial straits, which deepened with the worsening economic conditions of the Weimar Republic.[12] While these financial considerations surely prompted Gropius to reflect on how moneyed patrons might judge the school's bohemian eccentricity, these concerns did not turn him into a pedagogical exorcist, as historiography has suggested. Gropius did not at any point in the 1920s decisively expel the school's mystical demons. For starters, mysticism continued to hold sway at the Bauhaus throughout Gropius's nine-year directorship and, arguably, until the school's demise in 1933. Indeed, after the school was shut down by the National Socialist Party, various mystical strains resurfaced at offspring institutions in the United States directed by ex-Bauhaus immigrants and refugees, all of them first hired by Gropius in the 1920s.[13] Over the years, the school's initial medievalist invocations were simply joined by newer organicist and technological idioms related to the Bauhaus interest in holistic spirituality, such as those expressed by László Moholy-Nagy during his leadership at the New Bauhaus in Chicago. Conversely, the expressionist strain at the Bauhaus never involved a repudiation of technological reproduction. As we will see, especially with the pedagogies of Itten and Gertrud Grunow, the mystical and technorational were deeply in complicity.

It would be more plausible to read the contradictions of Gropius's pedagogical statements not as indicating a fledgling vacillation that would be resolved within a few years as the school matured and shook off its spiritual raiment but, rather, as symptomatic of fundamental aporias arising from conflicts between, on the one hand, the artists' socialist-leaning distrust of an industrial-capitalist division of labor and, on the other hand, their deep investment and self-interest in advancing the agenda of authorship over the technologically reproducible design. Bauhaus mysticism—and the religious cults it drew from, such as Mazdaznan and Theosophy—provided designers apparent means of resolving those contradictions. Mystical exercises would help in the development of new technologically oriented practices of creative design while also helping fabricate a new form of artistic "aura." This new aura helped obfuscate the substantial difference between the labor of design and the labor of technological reproduction, such that the latter (transpiring on the factory floor) could be subsumed within the (magical) purview of the author's intellectual–spiritual labor.

In the case of the Bauhaus Manifesto, Feininger's woodcut print illustration was charged with a task of resolving the aporia implied by Gropius's coupling of industrial-capitalist with anticapitalist agendas. Woodcut printing constitutes a very particular form of technological reproduction, as it often entails no division of labor between design and technological reproduction. The woodcut block is simultaneously the machine of reproduction and the work of art crafted directly by the artist. Presumably Feininger (who had no apprentices at this time) personally printed each copy of the design, thus acting simultaneously as artist, technician, and (re)producer. Thus, the woodcut offered an ideal model according to which technological processes of reproduction could be construed as part and parcel of the artist's own labor, regardless of whether the artist was directly involved with those processes (as Feininger was) or whether technological reproduction occurred on a factory floor, far from the artist's reach, as was the intention with many Bauhaus designs.

To understand how the issue of intellectual property may have shaped Bauhaus mysticism, this chapter addresses some well-known aspects of Bauhaus pedagogy and culture along with some lesser-known aspects. Among the latter we find the influential theories and methods of Grunow, whose collaborations with the psychologist Heinz Werner shed light on some defining features of Bauhaus pedagogy, including teachers' abiding preoccupation with synesthesia (a development often incorrectly credited to Wassily Kandinsky). Itten's pedagogy, on the other hand, is well known; however, no scholarship has addressed his published theory on "racial science." Rather than dismissing Itten's religious, primitivist, and racist dogmas as yet another example of the mystical idiosyncrasies of Weimar culture, this chapter regards them as symptomatic of how that culture interacted with the rise of the technological reproduction and attendant notions of design authorship. At the Bauhaus, pedagogies shaped by the magico-religious beliefs of Mazdaznan and Theosophy formed an ergonomics of the creative spirit that helped represent design as a form of scientific mastery over nature (that is, over the natural laws of aesthetics and materiality), a mastery that was bound up with ideas of intellectual proprietorship in the age of the artwork's technological reproducibility. Although Grunow and Itten do not represent the entirety of Bauhaus culture, their teachings were quite seminal to that culture, especially as their former pupils, such as Josef Albers and Georg Muche, were promoted to teaching positions within a few years of completing Itten's and Grunow's courses. Furthermore, the centrality of these two teachers in this chapter is intended as a corrective for the general neglect of Grunow's importance and, in the case of Itten, for a general misunderstanding of his teachings as disconnected from issues of technology.

FIGURE 2.4. Gertrud Grunow's mind–body harmonization exercises, circa 1920. Photographer unknown. Courtesy of Bauhaus-Archiv.

FIGURE 2.5. Morning exercises on the roof terrace of the Itten School, Berlin, 1931. Photograph by Otto Umbehr. Copyright 2020 Phyllis Umbehr/Galerie Kicken Berlin / Artists Rights Society (ARS), New York / VG Bild-Kunst, Bonn.

FIGURE 2.6. Paul Citroen, *Mazdaznan Cures,* 1922. Copyright 2020 Artists Rights Society (ARS), New York / c/o Pictoright Amsterdam.

Related to these issues of technology—but extending beyond their ambit—was a general cultural anxiety around what was called alienation (*Entfremdung*). For Marx, alienation was the effect of an industrial division of labor—a condition arising from the fact that workers' manual labor transpired without their full knowledge or ownership (that is, "mastery" in both senses) over the means of production, leading to the estrangement between manual and intellectual work.[14] While Marx's formulation of industrial labor was surely in the minds of some Bauhäuslers, more often anxiety around alienation appeared in a form that effectively inverted Marx's critique of exploitation by being more concerned with the alienation arising from professional forms of labor such as design. According to this more abstract Hegelian notion of alienation, estrangement between the mind-spirit and the body was to be resisted through pedagogical methods addressing the whole human organism (recalling claims made not only at the PIASP but also by nineteenth-century theorists of childhood education, as described in chapter 1). For all these ideological prestidigitations, the laboring body's alienation from the larger process of production in fact formed a necessary precondition for authors' assertion of partial ownership over products produced by hands other than their own. The transindividual character of labor under the regime of technological reproduction opened up possibilities for claiming a slice of the value derived from the labor of others.

The institution of intellectual property constitutes something of a lacuna in Walter Benjamin's speculations on the way technological reproduction brings about a decay of aura and, with that decay, a weakening of the artwork's priestly authority.[15] In "The Work of Art in the Age of Its Technological Reproducibility," he suggests that technologically reproduced media such as film tended to render legible the phenomenon of working-class alienation, thereby potentially galvanizing class consciousness. In this optimistic speculation, Benjamin was primarily referring to a working-class audience's reception of film, although Samuel Weber has pointed out the subtle suggestions in Benjamin's text of the *structure* of the processes of technological reproduction.[16] But Benjamin does not address one structural aspect of capitalist technological reproduction—namely, the role of intellectual property, which effectively replaces the magical, priestly authority of the one-off artwork with a new form of priestly authority: that of aesthetic authorship in the technologically reproducible design.

In the late eighteenth through nineteenth centuries, intellectual property law was incrementally expanded in most European states in response to new technologies of reproduction. The development of intellectual property in the technologically reproduced artwork appears in tandem with burgeoning Romantic notions of authorship. It is plausible that these two developments had some connection to each other. As I will show in this chapter, artistic authorship implied a transcendental form of labor. I speculate that, by virtue of this transcendence, the author could legitimately claim property in technological reproductions manufactured by the labor of others. At the Bauhaus, it is not incidental that the construct of authorship was at times explicitly linked to a construct of racial subjectivity. Implicitly, the legal institution of intellectual property drew on—and contributed to—a hierarchical valuation of manual versus intellectual labor, a hierarchy that was linked to an imagined cartography of racial subjectivity. The *new* magical aura of the technologically reproduced artwork had a racial character, one bound up with the formulation of the "primitive." To understand this, however, requires some background on how intellectual property came to be understood during the centuries leading up to the age of the artwork's technological reproducibility.

Excursus: The Author as Nonproducer

According to what calculus—according to what formulas of value, labor, and property—could an author be said to own property in a commodity whose physical production was owed to the labor and machinery of others? This was the question around which legal debates turned in eighteenth- and nineteenth-century Europe, giving rise ultimately to a double notion of property: tangible and intangible. Beginning with the rise of the print trade in sixteenth-century Venice, new concepts of intellectual property developed through a series of legal debates around the piracy of popular literary works. Whereas monopolies, royalties, and patents had long existed throughout much of the world, these property structures were distinct from the development of intellectual property over the technologically reproducible artwork in two main respects: First, patents were usually of short duration (in Europe, from seven to fourteen years). Second, these forms of property entailed explicit relationships of patronage, including those between guilds and the state, and were often bound up with prerogatives of censorship (over texts) and efforts at secrecy (over craft technique) rather than proceeding from an idea of authorial rights.[17] However, following the rise of the printing trade in seventeenth-century England, statutes were enacted to protect what was termed an author's "intangible property" in a technologically reproducible work.[18] Gradually, European intellectual property law over artistic works incrementally expanded its scope in geography, duration of copyrights, and the kinds of art that could qualify for copyright. Eligible art started with forms of script (text and then musical scores) in the eighteenth century and then, throughout the nineteenth century, extended to textiles, the fine arts, and eventually almost all technologically reproducible designed works. According to the legal historians Lionel Bently and Brad Sherman, as intellectual property debates moved from printed texts to the decorative and industrial arts, an issue of great concern was how authors were to be distinguished from the (skilled) laborers who reproduced the works with the aid of machines.[19]

In justifying this spectral concept of "intangible property," lawyers followed the protocol established in the sciences and engineering, whereby, although a discovery of natural, universal principles did not constitute intellectual property, the *translation* of those principles into a particular use could. Bently and Sherman write that in cases of copyright it was "necessary to show that abstract principles had been reduced to practice, that Nature had been individualised or activated."[20] Bently and Sherman are making a point here about the necessity of demonstrating the author's unique *individualization* of nature's principles; that is, they are not calling attention to the fact that nature remains—rather mysteriously—a point of reference in justifying intellectual property in the technologically reproducible artwork. But in cases of art, what might constitute a discovery of nature's principles? Or even more fundamentally, why should nature's principles legitimate the slippage from value-as-labor-time to the incalculable value of the intellectual proprietor's design (incalculable because the author's remuneration depends not on the input of her labor time but on an always indeterminate number of future reproductions)?

It has been said that the formulation of artistic authorship as a form of intellectual property was facilitated by the rise of liberal economic theories of labor value, such as those advanced by John Locke and Adam Smith.[21] However, this presumed connection between liberal theories of value and intellectual property—though perhaps valid in some respects—fails to take into account some fundamental incongruities. First of all, Locke had specifically referred to a person's labor as that "of the body, the work of his hands," a stipulation that would seem to contravene the notion of an author's intangible, intellectual property in the technological reproduction.[22] Second, Smith's labor theory of value is clearly breached by the institution of intellectual property, which remunerates an author according to the number of commodities sold, not the quantity of labor time the author invests in a work, thus undermining the "natural price" of the commodity (that is, its derivation from labor time). Thus, while intellectual property rests on the principle of translating nature's principles, its structure contradicts what was considered the nature of economic principles in England at this time. Amid the rise of economic theories about the calculability of natural price qua labor time, a form of incalculability becomes secreted within the economic system. Intellectual property thus adds a metaphysical supplement to a commodity's exchange value.

The importance of "nature's principles" in early legal debates over intellectual property might be ascribed to a general reverence for natural law in the European Enlightenment. However, in light of the mystical construct of authorship that arises immediately subsequent to the development of eighteenth-century intellectual property laws, it could be said that nature serves, moreover, as an ill-defined site where metaphysical exchanges can therefore occur, authorizing transferences of ownership, much as in Locke's approach to private property. In his account, nature (in the form of land) is basically a public good (that is, the commons), but one that can be seized and privatized by anyone who has "mixed his labour with and joined to it something that is his own."[23] It seems plausible that lawyers struggling to define the scope and structure of intellectual property might have hewn to Locke's rationale, conceiving of intellectual property as an admixture of nature and labor that entitles the author to "annex" (to use Locke's word) the results of that admixture, to remove a seemingly public good (in our case, a work of design) from "the common right of other men."[24] A metaphysics of nature and labor authorizes appropriation, allowing humans, things, and processes to become bound to and unbound from each other.

It is well known that nature played a central role in the Romantic constructs of art and authorship that developed in late eighteenth- and early nineteenth-century Europe, and literary scholars have noted how tacit questions of intellectual property pervade Romantic literature.[25] Nature appears in Romantic literature as a demiurgic force stewarded by two primary agents—authorship and technology. It could be said that a Romantic representation of authorship fundamentally conforms to the lineaments of intellectual property, insofar as the author is seen as uniquely attuned to nature's divulgences and as uniquely competent to translate those divulgences into a particular form. This concept, when inherited by the twentieth-century avant-gardes, entails an auratic and mystical performance of authorship, as we see with so many Bauhaus instructors. Aura is no longer related to the singularity and presence of the one-off artwork. On the contrary, it proceeds from a magical construct of authorial transcendence, according to which the discovery of natural principles—the mixing of nature into what was once merely material craft—enables the author to enfold into the purview of his or her ownership the residue of this scientifically derived nature that is secreted within each technological reproduction.

To what extent, though, were Bauhäuslers really concerned with intellectual property? According to accounts by T'ai Smith, Frederic Schwartz, and Otakar Máčel, many were very interested in asserting the rights of intellectual property.[26] Apart from the examples furnished by these authors, Itten personally held copyrights on his textile designs, so he clearly saw himself as an author of technologically reproducible designs.[27] Regardless, though, of whether or not a particular Bauhäusler was personally concerned with copyrights, the prior invention of intellectual property profoundly changed the way artists thought of themselves and their labor. Smith, in her article "The Identity of Design as Intellectual Property," notes that Ludwig Mies van der Rohe's rhetoric develops a distinct strategy during his Bauhaus years. Mies, who sued for various patents around this time, adopted a scientific rhetoric claiming to uncover the metaphysical essence of architecture, essentially, Smith suggests, to justify his claims of intellectual property rights.[28] In this reading, one of the key characteristics of twentieth-century architectural modernism—its spurious claims to scientific, axiomatic principles—owes a good deal to the construct of intellectual property. That is, the espousal of scientificity, although surely overdetermined, appears to derive some of its impetus from the legal formulation that copyrighted work must constitute a translation of nature's principles.

Divested of religious function as such, the artwork becomes imbued with a new quasi-religious authority proceeding from the metaphysical notion that an author's claim to intellectual property lies in the priestly relation she or he occupies as mediator between nature's universal laws and human commodities. What Marx described as the displacement of social relations by material ones—and the ensuing mysticism of the commodity—has its obverse in the structure of intellectual property, according to which material labor is displaced by a mystical and hierarchical relation between two forms of social subjectivity. Simply put, the author's metaphysical "labor" on the technologically reproduced commodity displaces a portion of the worker's direct labor. As distinct from the form of appropriation Marx ascribed to "owners of the means of production" (typically understood as the literal ownership of capital and machinery), the designer's ownership consisted of neither capital per se nor physical machinery but, rather, a form of consciousness mediating between technics and aesthetics through its understanding of natural laws.[29]

From Architecture to the "Primitive" Laws of Synesthesia

In 1918, just before assuming directorship of the Bauhaus, Gropius participated in the meetings of the Arbeitsrat für Kunst (Worker's Council for the Arts) along with various artists and architects including Feininger and the architect Bruno Taut, who led the mystical Gläserne Kette group that Gropius also participated in. The Arbeitsrat heralded the end of "class distinctions," but it seemed to be suggesting not an abolishment as much as a harmonious elision of class difference through an aesthetic construct of unity.[30] The Arbeitsrat offered architecture as a material emblem of the convergence of class interests, in that it involved different specialized construction trades.[31] The trope of architecture-as-unification would endure throughout Gropius's directorship of the Bauhaus, as attested by his curricular diagram of 1922: architecture's *Gesamtkunstwerk*-like integration of disparate arts and crafts as a metalepsis for de-alienation between intellectual and manual labor. Through this metalepsis, architecture's unification of the arts became tantamount to the erasure of class difference.

Given, however, that architectural design courses were not really offered at the Bauhaus until 1927, architecture could represent de-alienation only in its rhetoric, not its

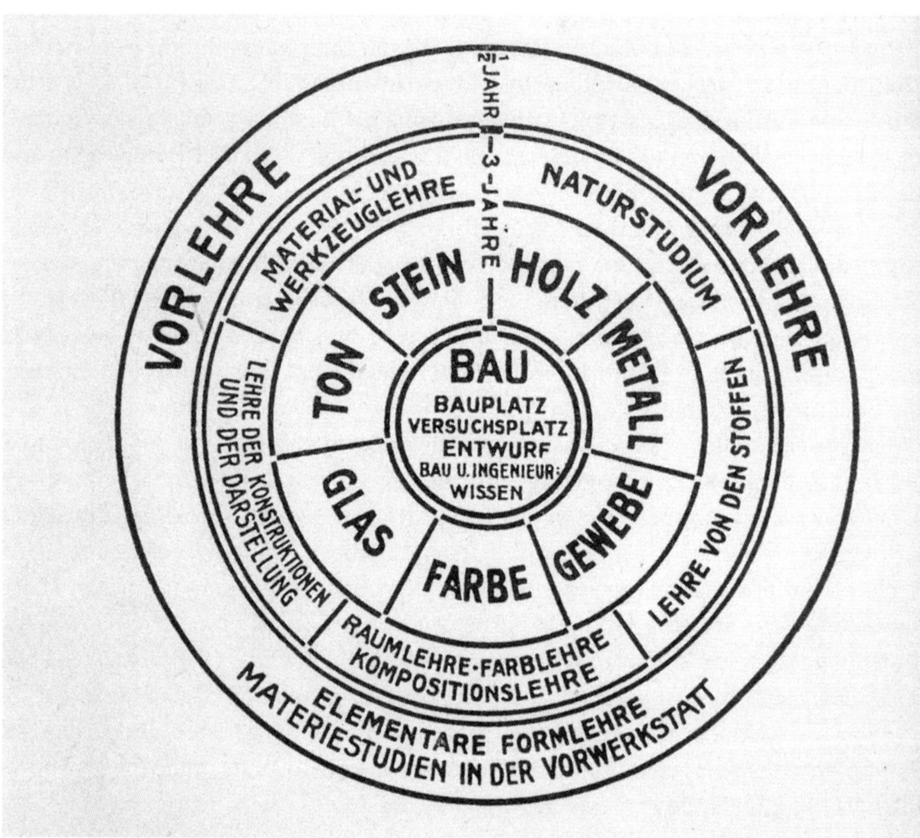

FIGURE 2.7. Walter Gropius, *Diagram of the Bauhaus Curriculum*, 1922. Copyright 2020 Artists Rights Society (ARS), New York / VG Bild-Kunst, Bonn.

practice. Apart from extracurricular projects like the Sommerfeld House or the Bauhaus exhibition structure Haus am Horn, architecture at the Bauhaus remained more of a religious specter than an object of pedagogy, perhaps because actual coursework—supporting the professionalization of architectural design, as distinct from the labor of construction—might have made it hard to maintain architecture's ideological fiction, its magical erasure of a division of labor. Itten and Grunow, among others, offered a more actionable metalepsis against the depredations of industrial forms of (re)production. Their spiritual teachings—linked respectively to Mazdaznan and Theosophy—implied that the artist's spiritual practices could heal the phenomenon of alienation arising with the labor of technological reproduction, thereby reframing the class-based problem of alienation as a private, spiritual, or psychological problem to be redressed through exercises in mind–body holism.

While Theosophy received its most explicit articulation in Grunow's courses, these teachings found their way into the theories and practices of other instructors, most notably Kandinsky. Grunow taught a mandatory first-year course consisting of musical and choreographic exercises intended to reveal each student's inborn artistic proclivities, while also expounding the natural synesthetic laws linking particular colors to particular materials, sounds, and movements. The course was taught in conjunction with Itten's required first-year *Vorkurs* (Basic Course), which had been instated with the aim of cultivating personal creativity while exposing students to a range of different media and techniques based on alleged aesthetic laws. These laws were largely derived from Mazdaznan, a religious cult whose exercises in mind–body holism were a supposed revival of ancient Zoroastrianism (perhaps influenced by Ralph Waldo Emerson's panegyrics to Zoroaster or Friedrich Nietzsche's figure of Zarathustra).[32] European disciples of Mazdaznan set up a temple in Switzerland that was soon frequented by Itten.[33]

Histories of the Bauhaus have often attributed Gropius's schism with Itten in 1923 to the director's supposed dismay over the popularity of Mazdaznan among Itten's students. According to this assumption, the schism therefore indicated Gropius's general repudiation of the school's mystical tendencies. However, Gropius did not explicitly rebuke Itten's introduction of Mazdaznan practices into the school, practices that included classroom breathing and movement exercises, the enforcement of Mazdaznan macrobiotic principles in the school cafeteria, and periodic fasts, purges, and other bodily purification rituals for his many student followers (reportedly, at least half of the *Vorkurs* students). There is no evidence to suggest that Gropius ever took Itten to task for his reported discrimination against students who declined to join Mazdaznan, to say nothing of the racist theories Itten promulgated linked to Mazdaznan.[34] (After all, Gropius, along with other Bauhaus instructors, was also known to have uttered anti-Semitic remarks.)[35] Although it's likely that Gropius harbored an unarticulated antagonism toward Mazdaznan, what he explicitly objected to was that Itten's pedagogy supposedly led students to oversubscribe to the painting workshop instead of distributing themselves more evenly across the various material workshop pursuits—work in glass, wood, stone, or pottery; weaving; wall painting; and metalworking.[36] In this sense, the *Vorkurs* was problematic in that it unwittingly rendered legible the school's ambivalent stance toward capitalist—rather than pre-Raphaelite/socialist—forms of production. Painting, however, was considered a conservative approach to the arts that eschewed *both* the anti-industrialist ideal of collaborative craftsmanship *and* the industrialist ideal of technological innovation, so it was especially objectionable that so many students wound up in the painting workshop.

Gropius in fact played an indirect role in supporting the dominance of painting at the Bauhaus, not only through his unwavering support for Kandinsky and Paul Klee but also through his emphasis on cultivating each student's unique authorial style, an agenda that probably contributed to students' pursuit of painting as a form of self-expression. The strong personal charisma exerted by so many Bauhaus painting instructors underscored the value the Bauhaus (and indeed all modernist schools of design) placed on personal authorial aura. Both Gropius and Itten were highly invested in an idea of vanguardist aesthetic authorship. For them, individual inventiveness distinguished the designer from the craftsperson who merely repeated conventional styles and techniques. In fact, the danger Gropius detected in the traditional medium of painting on canvas was that the painter risked becoming like an industrial laborer through the rote copying of the works of "old masters." Borrowing the pre-Raphaelites' coinage "Raphaels" to refer to Academy-trained painters who worked with mechanistic virtuosity, Gropius couched Itten's departure from the school in terms of the Bauhaus's mystical pedagogic mandate to instate unity among the arts:

> The Bauhaus has begun to break with the previous conventional kind of academic training which taught students how to become little Raphaels and pattern-designers. . . . The Bauhaus has quite consciously aimed to replace the principle of the division of labour by returning to collaborative work in which the creative process is perceived to be an indivisible whole.[37]

How, though—in the age of the artwork's technological reproducibility—could "the creative process" be deemed "an indivisible whole"? Gropius's injunction should not be mistaken for a Marxian repudiation of capitalist labor, or at least not in more than a very superficial way. Given Gropius's pursuit of industrial patrons, "collaborative work" might have easily referred to the transindividual labor of technological reproduction—that is, the division of labor between designer and factory worker figuring as "collaborative work." Indeed, Gropius's commission for the Sommerfeld House—typically credited as a realization of his holistic ideal of collaborative labor—reveals the disingenuousness of his vision. Although the house's design and construction did indeed entail a collaboration between Gropius and Bauhaus artists from various workshops, this collaboration extended only to the house's interior decorative flourishes. Its innovative construction technology had been pioneered by Gropius's client, the lumber magnate Adolf Sommerfeld, as a mode of efficient assembly. The bulk of the house was manufactured and assembled by an anonymous work crew. Gropius's "indivisible whole" alluded not to the actual conditions of artistic and architectural production but to a Romantic ideology of authorship.

The emphasis on authorship was what had led to the instatement of the *Vorkurs* when the school was founded. The first year, Itten and Gropius reviewed students' application portfolios and were dismayed by the applicants' lack of originality. Itten therefore proposed that the *Vorkurs,* along with Grunow's class, would act as a propaedeutic of the creative imagination, teaching first-year students basic aesthetic precepts prior to channeling them into specialized workshop trades. The creative imagination was understood as an antidote—rather than a contributor—to capitalist forms of production, creativity being the presumed antithesis of mere "pattern design"—that is, of rote reproduction.[38] In the *Vorkurs* and in Grunow's course, students were instructed in primal techniques for uniting mind, body, and nature, techniques meant to instill the capacity to translate the natural aesthetic laws into individualized artworks. These pedagogical approaches must not be understood as esoteric exceptions within a generally more rational Bauhaus culture. As the student Lothar Schreyer put it, "Itten's *Vorkurs* and Gertrud Grunow's Harmonization teachings, along with the foundations for compositional theory and color-form, were the pedagogical ammunition with which we could develop toward the Bauhaus idea."[39]

Perhaps because Grunow was not a designer (she was trained in dance and music) and perhaps because she was a woman, her contributions to Bauhaus culture and pedagogy have received only brief mentions in Bauhaus historiography, despite the seminal role she seems to have played during the school's early years, laying the groundwork for the school's preoccupation with synesthesia. Notions of synesthesia, drawn from both Theosophy and holistic psychology (*Ganzheit Psychologie*), helped ground an artist's work in supposedly universal codes, such that students could represent their work as a translation of nature's principles. Such efforts contributed to the ontological revisioning of the visual and spatial arts as constituting media, which were based on a structuralist codification of aesthetic laws and elementary techniques common to different medium-based practices.

Synesthesia describes a phenomenon whereby sensory stimuli that would appear to pertain to only one sense could also be perceived by other senses. For example, a given musical tone or a given phoneme would be experienced by a listener as emitting a particular color. This phenomenon was linked by German psychologists to "primitive" modes of thought, and its fascination for Bauhaus instructors furnishes one example of how Bauhaus culture sought recourse in "primitive" cognition as evidence of natural aesthetic principles. This is not, then, merely a romantic, expressionist conjuration of the noble savage; it is linked to serious social scientific work that regarded "primitive" people as especially legible exemplars of cognitive and perceptory mechanisms linked to aesthetics. The putative laws of synesthesia were explicitly taught by Grunow and Kandinsky, although many students and teachers also showed an interest in the phenomenon.[40] In 1923 Kandinsky circulated a questionnaire to his students asking them to assign to each of three geometric shapes—circle, square, and triangle—

one of the primary colors. Kandinsky adduced the overwhelming agreement among students' responses as scientific proof that there did indeed exist innate correspondences between particular forms and colors; these correspondences became the cornerstone of his teaching and artwork. The fact was, though, that Kandinsky's students had already been taught the "laws" of these correspondences in Grunow's course, where she imparted her theory of natural linkages between particular colors, sounds, and moods, work she would later develop further in conjunction with the renowned developmental psychologist and physiologist Heinz Werner and with the philosopher Ernst Cassirer.[41] In published articles she cited the influence of Gestalt psychologist Wolfgang Metzger, who in 1933 would join the Sturmabteilung and subsequently the National Socialist Party.[42]

Based on this synesthetic system, Grunow led the students in choreographic exercises intended to reveal, according to their personal styles of movement, their innate vocations.[43] Her concern for divining vocational leanings seems to have drawn on a long-standing concept of *Bildung*. According to German notions of education or, more literally, "formation," an individual human should develop or unfold holistically according to his or her own embryonic destiny (a notion adapted by Hegelian *Geist* and *Weltgeist*). Throughout the nineteenth century, especially in pedagogic discourses, *Bildung* was counterposed to alienation, in that it encouraged a balanced cultivation of mind and body, leading to the realization of one's full human potential. This wholeness—as a *personal attribute*—appears, then, as compensation for a capitalist division of labor within society at large. Rather than critiquing a division of labor in the world, one endeavors to heal a "division of faculties" within one's own self.

While still at the Bauhaus, Grunow began her collaboration in psychological experiments with Werner, who had contacted Bauhaus faculty out of eagerness to learn more about the phenomenon of synesthesia.[44] In his 1940 book *Comparative Psychology of Mental Development*, Werner in fact replicated Grunow's charts linking musical tones to colors.[45] Werner proposed that children and (what he called) primitive people shared a propensity to magical thought, owing to a low degree of cognitive differentiation. This lack of differentiation was the basis of both synesthesia and metaphor. "Primitive" societies, he postulated, were unaware of the idiomatic aspect of metaphors, since such an awareness would entail a high degree of differentiation between signified and signifier—that is, an understanding of the symbolic displacement distinguishing the latter from the former.[46] For "primitives," words *were* the things they named. A low level of differentiation was also, according to theories of evolutionary biology, what distinguished simple organisms from complex ones. It was thus through evolution on the scale of the species—moving from "primitive" to "civilized"—and through *Bildung* on the scale of the individual that the mind advanced from a lesser to greater capacity for perceptual and semiotic differentiation—that is, from a lesser to greater mediation between objects and representation.[47]

Since holistic unity constituted an ideal for both Werner and Grunow, it would seem likely that "primitive" people's supposed dearth of cognitive differentiation might have served as a model for "moderns" to emulate. However, "primitive" holism and synesthesia were understood as a cruder, less conscious form of the aesthetic science of perception sought by modern Europeans. Although Werner viewed "primitive cultures" as a preserve of the originary, organic bond among the senses, he also saw this very unity as preventing these people from deducing general, abstract principles from particular phenomena.[48] Here, Werner invoked a theory of magical thought indebted to Freud's understanding of "primitives." Magical incantation was not, he said, *symbolic*. Its words and rituals did not *represent* the thing that was wished for; rather, they linked together cause and (desired) effect as a unified magical event. This very propensity toward unity between words and things, between object and representation, locked things within their concrete particularity and thus precluded abstraction—precluded, that is, the detection of underlying, structural kinships among various phenomena that might point to rule-based causes.[49] "Primitive" people remained mired in an originary state in which representation and nature were still a unified whole, failing to grasp the deeper natural causes enabling that same unity. *Synthetic* unity between humans and nature (the antithesis of alienation), which entailed the scientific recuperation of a natural state, was thus ultimately the purview of what Werner called "civilization" and what Itten would more blatantly call "the white race."

Racial Science: A Cognitive Education in the Age of Technological Reproducibility

Itten supplemented Grunow's pedagogy by expanding the evidentiary objects of savage thought to include a range of sources. According to his "racial science," the "primitive" races evinced a materially oriented form of cognition, their artistic productions being motivated by merely material concerns (that is, of biological survival and reproduction).[50] As such, it lay with European modernism—or, as Itten tells us, with the white race—to uncover the scientific principles underlying materiality and thereby sublate crude materiality. Modern authorship consisted, Itten suggests, of this spiritual science of sublation. Itten was also interested in a science of the corporeal, decoding the body's material processes and fine-tuning them so as to support creative productivity. The emphasis on optimizing creative productivity—this ergonomics of the spirit—might be seen, then, as Taylorism applied to the domain of intellectual labor.

Itten's pedagogic exercises, aimed at holistically synthesizing students' corporeal and spiritual faculties, rehearsed the logic of Grunow's Theosophy, according to which alienation might be healed within the human individual rather than provoking a political response to alienating economic conditions. As Itten's course seems to have been intended largely to prepare students for creative authorship of the technologically reproducible design (as will be shown momentarily), classroom exercises for countering alienation could be interpreted as responding specifically to the alienation resulting from processes of the artwork's technological reproduction. Displacing the Marxian problem of the worker's alienation, the artist's alienation from the material processes of production becomes a problem of design theory rather than a problem of class domination. It was not the mechanization of artistic reproduction that needed to be addressed but, rather, the putative mechanization of atelier-based artistic training (that is, the making of "little Raphaels and pattern-designers," to borrow Gropius's words). Itten's methods in fact conceived of artistic production in a rather mechanized way, insofar as they prescribed bodily postures and various technologically oriented exercises. However, students were being trained to be not copy machines but creative machines, thus leading to a more perfect mechanization of body–spirit correspondence.

But what were the *mechanics* of creativity, such that creativity could be taught? The question was related to a problem that had long been contemplated in the field of childhood education: how to teach what was foundational to a child's entire cognitive development rather than simply cramming his or her head with knowledge. In fact, Itten had trained and worked as a kindergarten teacher in Switzerland prior to enrolling at Stuttgart's Academy of Fine Arts. "Artistic education," he wrote,

> will have to be substantially the same as general education, whose goal is to bring to as full a development and harmony as possible each student's natural abilities; the cognitive aptitude to develop the sense faculties and physical abilities so that the individual forces can be realized without inhibition in the creative work.[51]

It will be recalled that Leland had espoused the same approach for his industrial arts school, leading him to identify correspondences between, on the one hand, "nature" or the material world and, on the other hand, the human mind and its representational techniques. By training "the whole organism," as Leland's successor Tadd described it, in lieu of imparting skills specific to particular trades and professions, students could acquire mastery of mind–body coordination and mastery of nature's underlying grammar as a foundational basis for *all* occupations.[52]

Many of Itten's seemingly idiosyncratic exercises were identical to those advanced by Leland and Tadd at the PIASP, including exercises in ambidexterity and bodily coordination. Tadd and Leland had lectured in Germany and eastern Europe on the subject of arts pedagogy, and Tadd's book, *New Methods in Education,* was translated and published in Germany.[53] It is not clear whether Itten was personally acquainted with the book or whether he had encountered Tadd's and Leland's methods through intermediate sources. (His artistic training included stints in Geneva, Bern, Stuttgart, and Vienna, thus bringing him into contact with a wide range of pedagogic influences).[54] Whatever the case, Itten, like his forebears, maintained that the cultivation of a person's latent creativity required a *science* of design. He rejected the idea that his approach was mystical or expressionist, claiming that *Vorkurs* exercises had "nothing to do with usual expressionism"; rather, he said, they were concerned with "the *foundational principles* of the fine arts."[55] These principles were, he insisted, "scientific" (*wissenschaftliches*).[56] They were rooted in nature.

Itten's pedagogic exercises could be classed into three general categories. The first—especially indebted to his tutelage under the abstract painter Adolf Hölzel—entailed a decomposition of art making into elementary building blocks, reminiscent of Leland's fixation on a repertoire of "conventional motives" except that Itten broke things down further, into basic geometric shapes, colors, line types, hieroglyphs, and

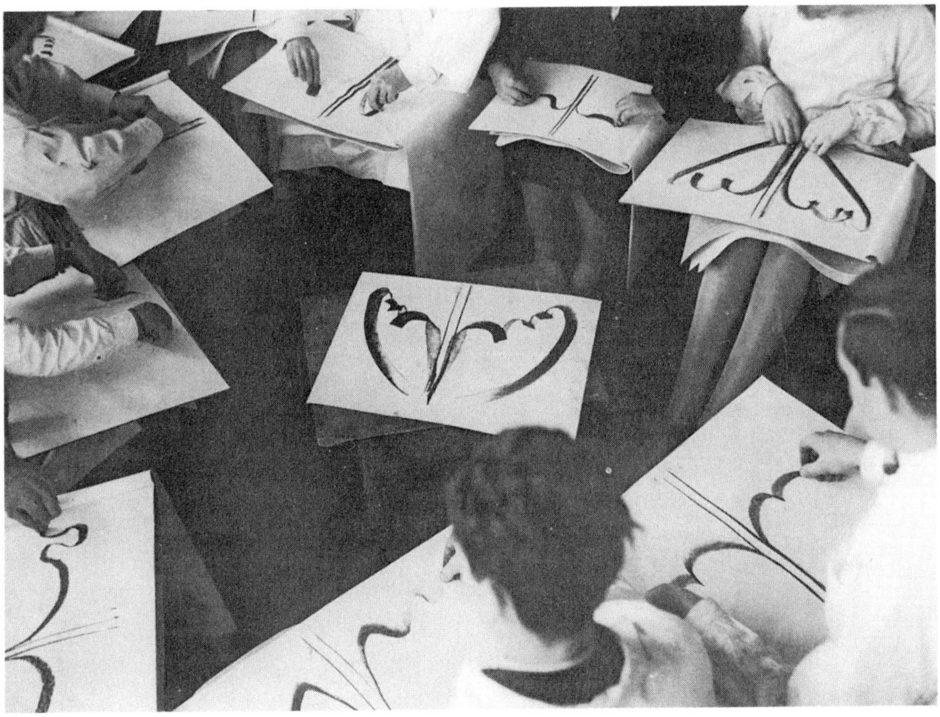

FIGURE 2.8. Drawing class of the Itten School, left- and right-handed drawing to develop the feeling for symmetry. Photograph by Otto Umbehr. Copyright 2020 Phyllis Umbehr/Galerie Kicken Berlin / Artists Rights Society (ARS), New York / VG Bild-Kunst, Bonn.

binary oppositions, many of which were based on comparative studies of more "primitive" antecedents.[57] The second entailed material experimentation, often in the form of collage and assemblage. And finally, he used a group of physical exercises aimed at mind–body–nature holism, mostly derived from Mazdaznan. Taken together, these three aspects of Itten's pedagogy constituted a reproducible code of bodily practices and formal rubrics intended to cultivate what Itten later referred to as "creative automatism" (*schöpferische Automatismus*), essentially a state of authorial production rooted in the site where nature's own principles supposedly overlapped with human inventiveness: namely, the unconscious.[58]

Well before André Breton developed the notion of "automatic writing," Itten endeavored to teach students how to short-circuit the conscious mind so as to allow nature's own laws to inscribe themselves directly upon the artwork. The unconscious, however, was not only the presumed locus of natural aesthetic principles; it also allegedly governed rote forms of industrial labor. Itten's teachings in unconscious automatism thus gave the illusion of re-creating within the design studio the supposedly unconscious modes of reproduction prevailing on the factory floor. Literary scholars have shown that amid the expansion of intellectual property in nineteenth-century England, many authors represented their work as being akin to manual labor.[59] This conflation of aesthetic authorship and the labor of technological reproduction was very much implied by Bauhaus rhetoric and pedagogical practices. However, there is a catch: at the Bauhaus designers affiliated themselves with automated labor while nonetheless distinguishing their labor from mechanistic drudgery. In the case of Itten's pedagogy, the automation of creativity produced a fanciful analog to mechanization, an imaginative distortion of the actual relations of production.

As with his methods of mind–body correlation, Itten's exercises in visual analysis also presume the existence of natural laws governing the human organism's aesthetic faculties. One *Vorkurs* exercise, falling under the larger rubric of "contrast studies," had students analyze the paintings of "old masters" by reproducing them in black ink, thus reducing original, colored works to stark black-and-white compositions.[60] The assignment implied a universal tendency to balance light against dark (a central tenet of Mazdaznan), as evidenced by its manifestation across the ages—that is, in both German medieval-style paintings and ancient Zoroastrianism.[61] The fact that in the paintings this principle was more structural and implicit than it was explicit (that is, it was only revealed through the translation of the image into black and white) underscored the idea that this tendency was in fact unconscious, suggesting a hitherto undiscovered science of aesthetic laws.

In addition to various other contrast studies, students embarked on scientific analyses of shade and color. They were asked to produce a gradation of gray-scale values from

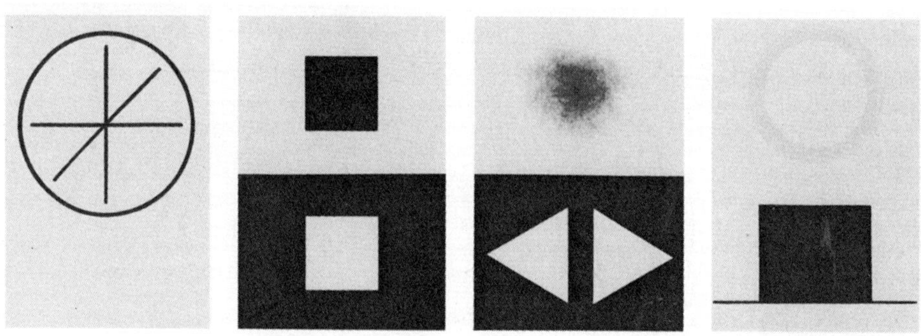

FIGURE 2.9. Johannes Itten, contrast studies. From Itten, *Gestaltungs- und Formenlehre* (1963). Copyright 2020 Artists Rights Society (ARS), New York / ProLitteris, Zurich.

FIGURE 2.10. Johannes Itten, tone-value scale. From Itten, *Gestaltungs- und Formenlehre* (1963). Copyright 2020 Artists Rights Society (ARS), New York / ProLitteris, Zurich.

FIGURE 2.11. Ascribed to Franz Singer and Friedl Dicker, dark–light studies, *Vorkurs* exercise, circa 1920–23. Photograph by Felix Jork. Courtesy of Bauhaus-Archiv Berlin.

FIGURE 2.12. Hans Mócznay, light–dark analysis of a picture by Goya (*The Duchess of Alba*), Berlin 1930. Johannes-Itten-Stiftung, Kunstmuseum Bern.

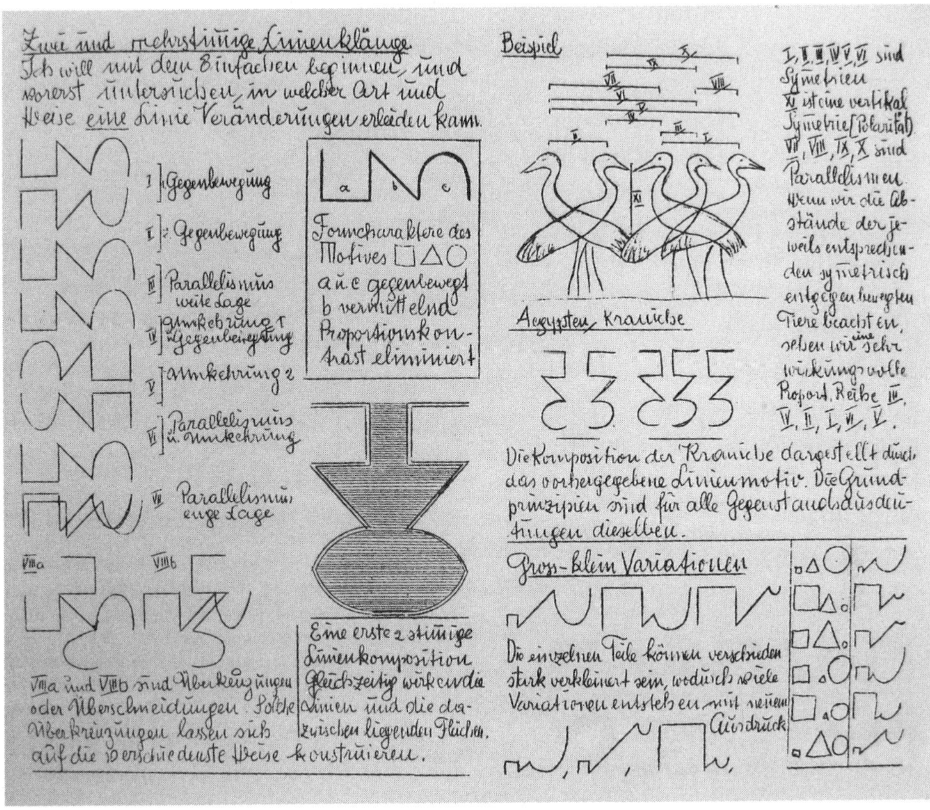

FIGURE 2.13. Johannes Itten, line-tones, shape-characters of motifs. Page from Itten, *Tagebuch* (Berlin: Verlag der Itten-schule, 1930). Copyright 2020 Artists Rights Society (ARS), New York / ProLitteris, Zurich.

light to dark, painstakingly distributed into discrete squares along a grid. With similar methodical precision, students reproduced Itten's taxonomy of line types and re-created in pencil, ink, and charcoal representations of different textures. The affinity these studies bear to present-day methods of computerized graphic manipulation is striking: the painstaking distribution of grays into a (numerically codifiable) rubric of gray scale, the palette of specific line and texture types, the disaggregation of complex imagery into simple black-and-white contrasts. This affinity does not, of course, suggest any direct lineage between Itten's methods and the late twentieth-century development of computer-graphic software. But such practices of analyzing and codifying artistic technique—widespread in the late nineteenth and early twentieth centuries—formed a precedent for the kinds of visual codification necessary to the digitization of imagery. Itten, by having his students construe representation as digital rather than analogical (that is, as reducible to a spectrum of discrete qualities rather than irreducible in its gradation of difference), partook in a more general epistemic shift that lent itself to late twentieth-century digital modes of representation and reproduction. Likewise, anticipating cybernetic discourses, Itten taught his students to translate the abundance of the perceptual world into systems of binary oppositions. "Everything we see, hear, smell, taste, touch, feel," he wrote in his pedagogical notebook, "is put in relation to a second factor which is opposed to the first."[62] Itten understood these binaries not as a human, semiotic device but as rooted in the nature of things: in the nature of both the world and the spirit as described by Mazdaznan.

Finally, there was the portion of Itten's pedagogy aimed at linking the labor of the body to that of the spirit. Itten believed that two fundamental techniques had to be mastered for all branches of design: breathing and drawing. He wrote short essays on breathing theory, explaining how mind and body merge through the respiratory process. It was necessary to *draw out* (*aufzeichnen*) the spirit with breath and pencil alike.[63] To draw—whether with one's lungs or one's pencil—was to sublimate materiality into spirit (*eidos*). When drawing anything, it was necessary, according to Itten, to first conceive the generalized essence of that thing, to dematerialize its particularity so that it was no longer a material, sensuous thing but was rarefied into the abstract idea of the thing (recalling Hegel's description of the gradual, essentializing abstraction of the material world until it conformed to the abstractness of consciousness itself). Having achieved this rarefaction, one could exhale the resulting essence, drawing it out with pencil and breath.

But how did one get to the *eidos* of a material, concrete thing? Two operations are mentioned by Itten's former students. To draw a lemon, students were required to first taste the lemon.[64] To draw a tiger, students were asked to first roar like a tiger.[65] Thus, a sensuous *experience* of the object was sublated into an intellectual *comprehension* of its inner essence, as the student translated one sensory experience into a different sensory representation. The *properties* of the object were thereby converted into *intellectual properties*. The presumed fungibility between the taste and sight of a lemon pointed to the existence of a common synesthetic root pertaining to taste and vision: a hidden, fundamental truth about the nature of the thing in question. For Itten this process of decoding material nature so as to synthesize it with the spiritual/intellectual belonged to a racial teleology of world history.

In 1923, Itten published his "Racial Theory and the Development of Art" ("Rassenlehre und Kunstentwicklung") in the journal *Masdasnan*. Itten described how the world historical trajectory of art proceeded from a primitive concern for material needs (exemplified by the arts of the "black race," or what he also called *Ur-Mensch*, "originary man") toward a concern for spirituality (exemplified by "the brown" and "grey-red" races), finally attaining the ultimate synthesis of materiality and spirituality by "the white race."[66] This Hegelian narrative was clearly also guided by Mazdaznan's racial eschatology, according to which paradise was to be attained with the purification of the "Aryan race."[67] In his manuscript notes, Itten indicated that inspiration was the goal of both art and religion and was the "true science" of the "white race." This science would consist of the "gathering," or synthesis, of all the senses as a way of attaining the "perfection of thinking."[68]

But how does one synthesize and *purify* the arts of other races? Certainly, several of the exercises mentioned above—the tasting of lemons, the breathing routines—were

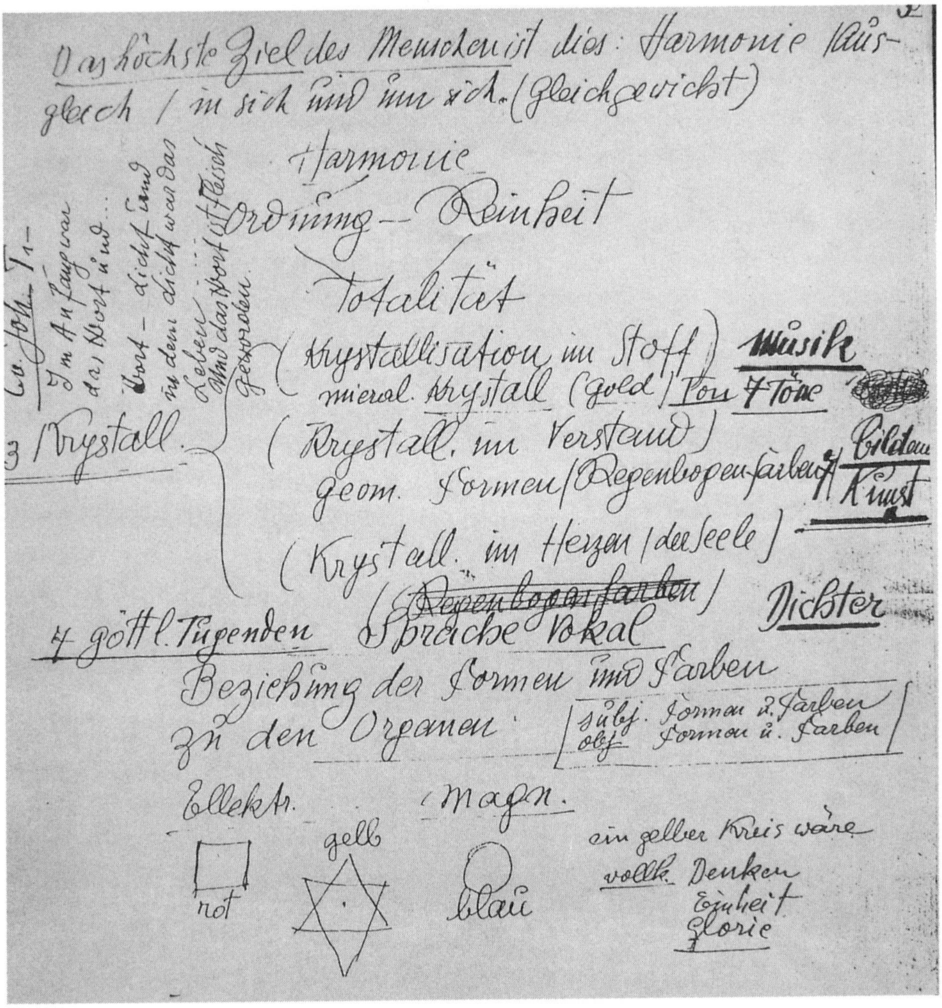

FIGURE 2.14. Johannes Itten, manuscript notes for "Racial Theory and the Development of Art," circa 1923.

meant to purify things and bodies of their merely material ontology. Moreover, Itten encouraged students in a series of extracurricular exercises intended to purify the self (and thereby, presumably, the Aryan race), exercises that included various Mazdaznan rituals of bodily cleansing. A former student belonging to Itten's inner circle described *Vorkurs* students' practice of puncturing their skins all over to allow the impurities to seep out.[69] This was in addition to fasts and what appears—from one student's sketches—to have been some kind of colonic cleansing.

Perhaps even more important to the idea of racial purification, however, was the emphasis on abstraction. Here we could point to Werner's theories: What distinguished "civilization" from savagery—or what allowed the former to *purify* itself of the latter (even while drawing heavily on the latter) was that civilization tended to abstract *general laws* from material phenomena. Whereas the savage exemplified natural cognitive *processes* and thus offered evidence of a more natural semiosis, it lay with the civilized to divine the mechanisms and rules underlying those processes. For Itten, the relation of "the white race" to "the black race" served an ideological function similar to what "architecture" performed for Gropius. Just as architecture was to synthesize the arts and thereby rescue the labor of design from capitalist forms of division and alienation, so too would "racial theory" rescue the designer (qua intellectual proprietor) from alienation vis-a-vis the immediacy of material labor. It is in this ideological and pedagogical context that Breuer's presentation of the evolution of Bauhaus chairs might be understood. The "Negro" or "African" chair is the necessary fiction enabling the larger fiction of the disappearance of manual labor, as history progresses from craft to technological reproduction to magical production.

Itten's preoccupation with codifying and thereby transcending base materiality sheds light on how the Mazdaznan fasts and purges he encouraged his students to perform may have had an indirect connection to issues of authorial production. These antimetabolic rituals are to be contrasted to Marx's references to metabolism. For Marx, metabolism constitutes the basic organic economy through which the self is converted into labor and labor into things and, reciprocally, through which things—like nutrients—are converted into self and labor.[70] In contrast to this metabolic economy, Mazdaznan rituals represented the labor of design as requiring the ritual elimination rather than intake of nourishing material. This was not simply a way to assert a racial hierarchy between the white modernist and the "primitive" artist, contrasting the latter's presumed subservience to material needs to the former's transcendence over those needs. It was, in addition, a way to obfuscate the material nature of labor. This is not, of course, to suggest that Itten specifically intended these rituals to serve as a refutation of Marxian materialism. Rather, it is to point to a culture in which the emphasis on spiritual transcendence tended to minimize the material component of production—essentially, the labor of technological reproduction.

At the Bauhaus, the mystical obfuscation of the labor of technological reproduction (its symbolic subsumption within the labor of design) has led me to propose a slight amendment to the term introduced by the Marxian philosopher C. B. Macpherson: "possessive individualism," which describes a modern European relationship between notions of selfhood and private property.[71] In reference to the rise of technological reproduction, it might be more useful to think of "possessive transindividualism," given the multiple humans involved.[72] In the age of artwork's technological reproducibility, the author's labor must be magically bound to what it does not produce concomitant with factory labor being unbound from what it does produce. If artistic labor is represented as a kind of antilabor, fueled by an incorporeal or spiritual energy (an energy literally and symbolically purged of its material basis), then this spiritual/intellectual (*geistig*) labor could perhaps "possess" commodities without having ever physically touched them. The author's property (selfhood) is seen to transcend his or her actual labor, replacing the transindividuality of labor with an imagined transindividuality: that of the author's world historical synthesis of the arts of other races.

The Useless Machine: Toward the Beginnings of "Media"

In 1922, under pressure from Gropius, Itten chose to leave the Bauhaus and spend some time at the Mazdaznan temple in Switzerland. Yet Gropius periodically invited Itten back to the Bauhaus as a guest critic at student reviews, suggesting a far more amicable relationship than some accounts have painted. In 1926 Itten opened his own design school, the Ittenschule in Berlin, which was shut down in 1934 by the Third Reich, shortly after the Bauhaus was similarly closed. Itten's subsequent career included the directorship of a textile school and a brief teaching position at the Hochschule für Gestatlung at Ulm, a design school renowned for its commitment to technological and social scientific approaches. Later he became the founding director of Switzerland's only museum of nonwhite arts.

Far from rooting out the religious associations of the *Vorkurs,* Gropius appointed Itten's favored disciple and fellow Mazdaznan devotee, Georg Muche, to instruct the course. Later, when Muche left the Bauhaus to teach at Ittenschule, Gropius assigned the *Vorkurs* to Moholy-Nagy. The changes Moholy-Nagy ushered in help illustrate the nature of the Bauhaus's transformation during Gropius's directorship. Mysticism does not disappear from the *Vorkurs,* but it becomes further nestled within scientific terminology. For example, instead of linking holism to Theosophy or Mazdaznan, Moholy-Nagy simply referred to the "organic" unity of the "biological" human.[73]

Certainly, though, as the school became more strapped for funding, Gropius increasingly sought "contacts with industry" and more explicitly emphasized technical virtuosity.[74] Amid debates over whether students were to be directed toward "individual, single pieces of work . . . or to seek contact with industry," Gropius cryptically declared his "search for unity in the *fusion*" of these alternatives.[75] He invoked the students' designs for what he called "useless machines" as proof that technological reproducibility and one-off artworks were "already converging!"[76] Hence, it was no longer the Aryan race, nor even architecture, but, rather, an unspecified aesthetic "machine" that was now invested with the magical synthetic powers to overcome the ambiguities of aesthetic authorship under a regime of technological reproduction.

There remains no evidence of what Gropius meant by "useless machines," but the term suggests that the ontology of the visual and spatial arts had passed into media. Based on archives of student work, Gropius's designation may have referred simply to the idea of the artwork as an exposition of general technical and aesthetic virtuosity, an idea cultivated under various Bauhaus instructors, including Itten. We can only surmise that the uselessness of the machine freed it from certain material constraints and from crude associations with industry, allowing it to be simultaneously a rejection of technological reproduction and an exploration of the aesthetic and mechanical principles related to the technologically reproducible prototype.

Whereas in craft work, technique is purposefully directed toward making a specific set of objects with specific sets of material, in the late twentieth-century discipline of media arts and science, the emphasis is on a codified—but expandable and rearrangeable—rubric of techniques, opening onto diverse possible applications (a tendency that came at the MIT Media Lab to be referred to as "flexible technologies," examined in chapter 7). The potentials for innovation and reinterpretation implicit to this open rubric are aligned to the systematization of design through an identification of structural linkages between different works of media. Moreover, the emphasis on technical codes, logics, and "languages," as distinct from an emphasis on *specific* applications—that is, the "uselessness" of the pursuit—gives the illusion of a certain detachment from the programs of capital. For Gropius, this meant a deferral of the distinction between the one-off artwork and technological reproduction. In the words of Samuel Weber, media "undercut the clear-cut oppositional relationship between singular and plural, general and particular, genre and work."[77] As Barry Bergdoll and Leah Dickerman have noted, one of the major outcomes of the Bauhaus was the "redefinition of the artist as a designer of systems."[78] One could thus invert the famed formula of the Bauhaus "machine aesthetic" by speaking of Bauhaus pedagogy as constituting an aesthetic machine. At the heart of this system, enabling the linkages among diverse media, styles, authors, and objects was a racial science providing a groundwork for explorations in media and persisting well after the departure of Itten and Grunow.

Years after fleeing the Holocaust and resettling in the United States, Moholy-Nagy published a circular diagram showing the evolution of the division of labor in which "primitive man" alone occupies the central axis of the circle, indicating a state prior to the division of labor, with "scientists and technicians" gradually superseding all other occupations. The striking homology between Moholy-Nagy's depiction of the division of labor and Gropius's curricular diagram for the Bauhaus can hardly be accidental. In the latter, "architecture" (*Bau*) stands as the focal point toward which all other disciplines of design converge but also as the point of origin from which they emanate, suggesting a transcendent synthesis of an architectural division of labor. Similarly, in Moholy-Nagy's diagram, "primitive man" stands at the point of both divergence and convergence within humanity's splintered vocations and classes. As with Breuer's representation of the evolution from the "African" chair (a one-off in which there is no division of labor between design and production) to the dematerialized chair (which required no manual labor at all), Moholy-Nagy's diagram suggests the complete disappearance of labor as such, the only work remaining in the future being that of science and technology. Couched within Moholy-Nagy's discussion of "organic unity," the diagram seems to be suggesting that this is a utopian rather than dystopian future. The author fulfills her or his final teleology by rendering obsolete the need for manual labor through an aesthetic and technical mastery of nature that is so complete as to require nothing outside of itself: nothing outside of *design*.

Gropius and his Arbeitsrat colleagues had dreamed of an architecture that would overcome alienation within the world, bringing about a transcendent unity—unity across a technological division of labor, and unity between nature and representation and between body and mind. This was to be achieved by dint of the designer's transposition of nature into a science of aesthetics. In chapter 3, which turns to the Cold War and decolonization movements, we see architecture appearing again as the translation of nature. In this case, however, the problem of alienation was perceived as arising not

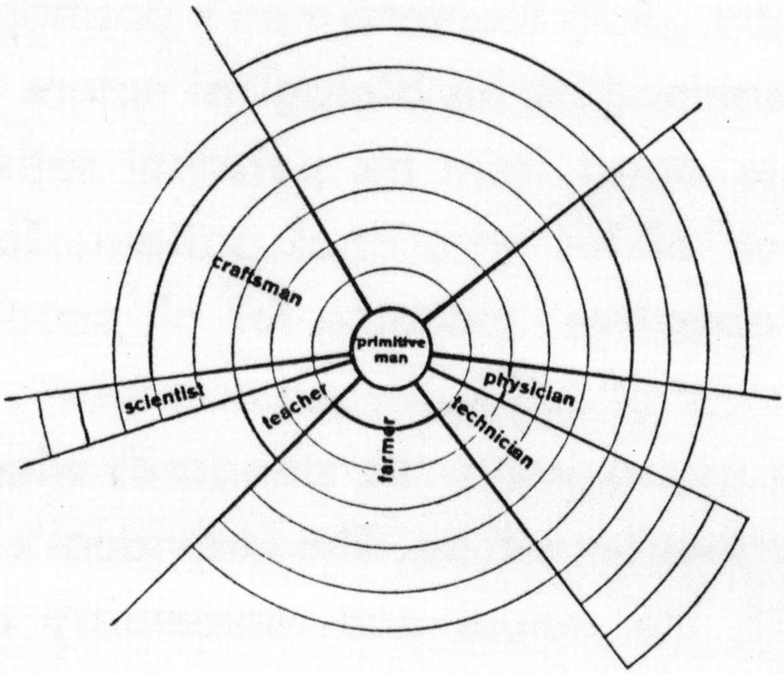

FIGURE 2.15. László Moholy-Nagy, Untitled, circa 1938. From Moholy-Nagy, *The New Vision* (1928). Copyright 2020 Estate of László Moholy-Nagy / Artists Rights Society (ARS), New York.

from a division of labor but, rather, from modernist architecture's failures to address local contexts and cultures, thus requiring new approaches to translation. Amid the rise of structuralist anthropology, postwar architectural modernism would establish new ways of analyzing and then synthesizing "vernacular" precedents. The logic of racial purification appears again, not in the context of the artwork in the age of its technological reproducibility, but in the context of urban design in the age of international expertise.

PART II

ARCHITECTURE

Chapters 3 and 4, moving into the postwar decades, turn from questions of industrial production to the formulation of international expertise in architecture and urbanism. Whereas in the preceding chapters spiritual ergonomics revolved primarily around the relationship between the psyche and technological reproduction, the chapters in Part II trace architects' efforts to understand and harness the systematicity of culture, so as to represent modernist architecture as a support for—rather than a suppression of—global cultural variation, including the cultures of Europe's own subaltern classes. In conversation with a growing body of work on postwar forms of architectural expertise (often in the context of development), these two chapters present a set of protagonists whose professional status derived to a large extent from the influence of structuralist anthropology and related social scientific theories and methods on their rhetoric and design preferences. Architects including Yona Friedman, the Smithsons, and Aldo van Eyck sought to uncover underlying structures of human culture and human architecture from which to derive a basic anatomy of design. Such anatomical architectural systems were not only deemed adaptable to diverse contexts; they also were often thought of as missionary-like devices for adapting their occupants to the programs of modernity, including those of the European welfare state and of postcolonial development. By allegedly translating cultural essentialities into modernist idioms, architecture might partly modernize "primitive" societies and classes, placing them within modern organizational schemata (such as mass housing) while still preserving many indigenous practices.

Attempts to negotiate between cultural particularities and the large-scale solutions of modernist architecture were rampant in the decades following World War II, and several dozen architects might have easily been selected as a focus for these two chapters. To provide some discursive coherence amid this diffuse genealogy, I have extracted a few exemplary figures: for chapter 3, a few designers central to the architecture group Team Ten, and for chapter 4, Yona Friedman, whose work was notable for a particular vanguardist idiom of self-help that straddled the domains of economic development, computer-aided design, structuralist anthropology, and architectural design. While Team

Ten has been exhaustively treated in architectural scholarship, a gap remains on the crucial intersection between an incipient form of systems thinking and an anthropological preoccupation with "primitive" culture, seminal to Team Ten's work. As for Friedman, with his archives made public only during the last five years, there exists to date no comprehensive, critical interpretation of his work, the existing scholarship mostly tending toward the panegyric. Chapter 4 cannot satisfactorily address the full scope and ambivalent complexity of Friedman's work, which was often utopian and critical yet suffused with the inchoate logic of a neoliberal technohumanitarian project. The chapter thus treats his work as an important precursor to architecture's more recent technohumanitarian turn.

The question of how to comprehend the myriad variations and idiosyncrasies of culture through the rubrics of modernist architectural design brushed up against the cybernetic preoccupations of the postwar decades. Both culture and cities could be thought of in cybernetic terms. As a structuralist system (derived presumably from the structures of cognition), culture held a privileged place in cybernetic discourses, as it was deemed key to understanding the systemic logics of the human organism in its social and semiotic dimensions, hence leading to the involvement of figures like Margaret Mead and Claude Lévi-Strauss in the Macy Conferences. In Team Ten discourse, cybernetics forms a weak strain, refracted through the tropes of mid-twentieth-century anthropology. Friedman was more explicitly preoccupied with cybernetic interests and related developments in global communications and computer programming. However, the sequence of these two chapters is not intended to present a continuity between Team Ten discourse and Friedman's work, as the two bodies of thought would be better seen as obverses to each other, both addressing a plurality of world cultures by identifying elemental structures deemed common throughout the global south. In the case of Team Ten, this plurality was addressed through a notion of "grammars" and what basically amounts to an architectural version of translation—translation of a so-called vernacular. Friedman, on the other hand, offers a counterpart to translation with his production of pseudovernacular architectures and media, intended for implantation within a wide range of contexts, primarily in the global south.

3

POSTWAR EUROPEAN MODERNISM, OR WHAT THE PRIMITIVE HUT REALLY SAID

The Persistence of the Primitive

> Working with the past is of course easier—the centuries have allowed meaning and language to crystallize, and the architects cannot talk back.
>
> —PETER SMITHSON, "Team X: A Proposition at Bonnieux"

In the aftermath of World War II and amid the rise of anticolonial movements throughout Asia and Africa, modernist architects found themselves in a changed geopolitical, economic, and ideological landscape. The Holocaust, in conjunction with the rising wave of independence movements, challenged European architects' assumptions about their *mission civilatrice,* prompting a subtle shift in focus from claims of *civilizing* to claims of *translating* cultural particularities into modern schemata. During this postwar period, the Marshall Plan, the World Bank, and late-colonial, postcolonial, and neocolonial architectural developments provided new professional opportunities for architects and planners both at home and abroad. Throughout much of the world, there were efforts to rapidly construct high-density housing, in many cases leading to the replacement of low-rise detached or townhouse-style architectures with medium- to high-rise apartment buildings. In efforts to conserve some vestige of existing domestic and social organization amid this conversion from lower to higher density, a certain structuralist anthropological conception of architecture emerged—as can be seen, for example, with the concerns and methods discussed throughout the 1950s and '60s at meetings of the European-based architecture group Team Ten, which will form the focus of this chapter.

The relocation of Team Ten's first meeting in 1956 from Algiers to Dubrovnik (owing to concerns over the dangers of anticolonial unrest) mirrors a shift—or really, an expansion—of European modernist interests in colonial urbanism to include new ways of understanding European urbanism in the rebuilding of postwar cities and the making of the western European welfare state. Several chapters in Mark Swenarton, Tom Avermaete, and Dirk van den Heuvel's edited volume *Architecture and the Welfare State* explore connections between colonial, postcolonial, and European urbanism during this period. Adding to a growing body of literature on these histories, this chapter suggests that a conception of the primitive was key to a burgeoning formulation of architectural expertise, an expertise capable of addressing the world's cultural diversity.[1] Alison Smithson, one of the group's founders, in her retrospective reflections on Team Ten lamented Algerian independence as a great loss to European architects.[2] Given the numerous opportunities for architectural design within postwar Europe, the perceived loss represented by Algerian independence was probably less about design opportunities in general and more about a particular kind of design opportunity, one endemic to colonialism. The colonies did not only offer a domain of architectural experimentation unconstrained by democratic institutions;[3] the circumstance of foreign occupation lent modernist architectural practice a new function: that of mediating between the biopolitical rubrics of European urbanism and extant local domestic, economic, and urbanist practices. Seminal to Team Ten's self-conceptualization was the quasi-anthropological presentation of Casablanca's North African population by the French-colonial Groupe d'architectes modernes marocaines (GAMMA) at the ninth conference of the Congrés internationaux d'architecture moderne (CIAM) in 1953.[4] Although the European welfare state was indeed a central concern for most core participants of Team Ten, I suggest that this welfare state was envisioned through a framework of spiritual ergonomics derived largely from colonial concerns and strategies.

According to colonial ergonomics of the spirit, architectures could be patterned on the basic structures underlying local cultural practices, resulting in structuralist kinships between "modern" and "traditional" architectures, thereby inculcating an intimacy between colonized populations and colonial urbanism. Such spiritual ergonomics should be distinguished from social engineering, insofar as the latter focuses on effecting a specific transformation (or transformations), whereas the former sought more generally to habituate building occupants to modernity-cum-colonization. In the context of the European welfare state (which increasingly managed immigrants from the former colonies), spiritual ergonomics appeared in efforts to transplant a small number of existing social practices into the spatial configurations of new medium-rise apartment blocks. The purpose of many of these projects, such as those designed by Alison and Peter Smithson, was not to engineer any specific societal reform but, rather, to buffer the alienating effects of such architectures and of the welfare state in general, rendering capitalist welfare urbanism as continuous with erstwhile forms of urban habitation and work.

Although the discursive vectors of postwar European architecture were both centrifugal and centripetal (design concepts moving multidirectionally between primarily Europe, its colonies, and former colonies), a fundamental device of postwar modernism—that of the primitive hut—revealed that the architectural culture of Team Ten harbored a fairly consistent racialized understanding of Europe's working classes and of late-colonial and postcolonial subjects. This enduring architectural trope, born of the Enlightenment, came to assume new powers in the age of structuralist anthropology. The primitive hut suggested methods of comparative analysis through which to derive notions of human habitus in hopes of deriving a universal anatomy of habitation, one that could be flexibly reconfigured to accommodate particular contexts.

Abstract and figurative diagrams played a significant role in these efforts and formed one of Team Ten's most recognizable contributions to modernist design.

Translation in this case assumes a very different valence than it does in literary and language studies. With language, translation presumes the arbitrariness of the signifier's relationship to the signified and, hence, of the differences between languages and the need for translation. Nowadays, in the field of translation studies, it is common, therefore, to regard translation as inherently political insofar as it entails negotiating differences and ambiguities of linguistic discourse.[5] This is notwithstanding critiques of translation in colonial contexts, such as that offered by Tejaswini Niranjana, who has noted "the powerful metaphysics of translation . . . seen even in the postcolonial context."[6] In keeping with this attentiveness to metaphysics, my examination of architectural practices and ideologies uncovers a particular version of translation. Translation becomes a mode of abstracting from different architectures humans' underlying cognitive "structures," suggesting ways to circumvent political discourse in processes of urban and architectural development. As the Smithsons wrote of the exhibition *Parallel of Life and Art,* which they designed with the Independent Group, the anthropological aspect of their work was intended as "a kind of Rosetta Stone" enabling a decoding of diverse cultural practices and artifacts.[7]

The idea of translation as the uncovering of natural structures (or principles) may sound familiar, following chapter 2's discussion of the way philosophies of intellectual property manifested themselves in modernist design pedagogy. Certainly, there are discursive connections between these histories, both of which involve colonial-era racial hierarchies and the related construct of authorship as a transcendent form of cognitive subjectivity. In the case of postwar architectural modernism, at stake was not intellectual property per se but, rather, a construction of cognitive subjectivity aligned to notions of expertise, which similarly derived its authority from claims to decode natural principles and then apply them toward aesthetic ends. Given that the "primitive"—or what architects would increasingly call the "vernacular"—was often the source from which natural principles were gleaned, and given the geopolitics undergirding western Europe's relationships with the world, there remained a racial dimension to this notion of cognitive subjectivity.

A formative example of these practices can be seen in the well-known colonial architectural scheme in Casablanca, the Nid d'abeille housing project, showcased by GAMMA at the 1953 CIAM meeting to much acclaim.[8] Intended to quell anticolonial political agitation in the city's slums, the state-sponsored project commissioned ATBAT-Afrique (the North African branch of Le Corbusier's office, run by Michel Écochard) to provide housing to relieve severe overcrowding in the narrow confines of the city's nonwhite quarters. Architecture thus became a strategy for suppressing political activity. Claiming to translate native cultural habitus—in particular, Muslim practices of purdah—into a legibly modernist idiom, the architects could claim the simultaneous aims of civilizing the colonial indigene *and* rescuing it *from* the culturally alienating effects of modernization.[9] It should be noted that the diversity of Casablanca's non-European population was collapsed into the generalizing rubric of "Islam" (and into one particular interpretation of Muslim gender relations). An architecture that translated putative indigenous practices into a modernist idiom thus reinforced a basic discrepancy between modern civil society and the colonized, given that the relevant cultural trait defining these housing occupants had to do not as much with actual (and diverse) cultural practices as with the simple fact of being non-Christian and nonwhite.

This chapter focuses on architects associated with Team Ten—especially core members Alison and Peter Smithson and Aldo van Eyck and the architectural partnership Candilis-Josic-Woods—as a way to provide narrative cohesion even though many other architectural protagonists at the time showed similar tendencies. While chapters 5 and 6 will examine more or less the same period in the United States, where military and technological resources, the rise of urban sociology, and the domestic war against the urban poor helped impel the new disciplinary configuration of environmental design, contemporaneous architectural discourses in western Europe were more aligned with colonial anthropology and with forms of economic sovereignty in the colonies and former colonies. Whereas in the United States "the environment" came to assume increasing importance in design discourses during this era for its presumed role in shaping cognitive habit, in Europe there was a greater interest in the vernacular as evidence of autochthonous forms of cognition and culture. However, these two motifs—the vernacular and the environment—were not mutually exclusive by any means, especially in light of many direct interactions between European and U.S. architects and institutions.

In seeking out innate linkages between architectural modernism and the disparate societies in which Team Ten architects conducted their design research, architects' methods and concerns dovetailed with structuralist anthropologists' interest in both the semiotic significance of village configurations and the cybernetics of communication and intelligence. Architectural primitivism thus assumed a form quite distinct from developments in the fine arts, even while it overlapped with surrealists' psychocognitive concerns. Whereas surrealists endeavored to reproduce a particular aspect of the brain's semiotic landscape—its presensical or subconscious constructions—architects sought to authorize their own sense-making prerogatives by pointing to the semiotic landscapes of "primitive cultures" and then translating them into the technocratic rubrics of modernity. The brain's semiotic mechanisms would be revealed by architectural diagrams of primitive habitus.

However, in turning toward diverse cultural precedents, architects seemed to fear a paradigm at the opposite end of CIAM urbanism, one that had been recently exemplified by fascism's *Heimatkultur,* with its replication of *völkisch* motifs. Distinct from fascism but nonetheless redolent of fascism's nostalgia for the "vernacular," some incipient strains of a postmodernism-to-come were already in the offing in the 1950s. Team Ten debates touched on the problem of attending to local particularities without slavishly mimicking historical architectural forms and motifs, to the neglect of the changes wrought by technological modernity. From the perspective of Team Ten discourse, both CIAM orthodoxy and "vernacular" copying threatened to foreclose the possibility of authentic architectural meaning: on the one hand, because of a presumed lack of signification (the pared-down, modernist International Style supposedly divesting itself of culturally *significant* features), and on the other hand, because the desultory replication of past precedents lacked any semiotic coherence and relevance to the present. Because a comprehensive history of Team Ten is certainly not the task of this chapter (and such studies already exist), I focus instead on drawing out a few exemplary strains of design strategy and theory.[10] Fundamental among these were new ways of arranging space that stressed the notion of modernism as a condensation and purification of "traditional" architectures, which were understood as untrammeled expressions of human cognitive habit.

The Primitive Hut of Tomorrow

In 1956, the same year as Team Ten took over the organization of CIAM's tenth international conference—largely under the direction of Alison and Peter Smithson—the Smithsons collaborated with two artists, Eduardo Paolozzi and Nigel Henderson, on a contribution to the group exhibition *This Is Tomorrow* at the Whitechapel Gallery in London. The four collaborators, known as the Independent Group, had already executed one gallery installation in which they borrowed to some extent from surrealist techniques of juxtaposition and amassed disparate cultural artifacts into a kind of modernist cabinet of curiosities. For the 1956 exhibition, they drew again on this technique, albeit this time arranging sundry "anthropological" artifacts and images around the focal point of a small hut. The project, *Patio and Pavilion,* was said to represent "the fundamental necessities of the human habitat."[11]

In contrast to the protopop objects produced by other artists in the exhibition, *Patio and Pavilion* was, according to architectural critic Reyner Banham, "submissive to traditional values."[12] He unfavorably contrasted the group's installation to that of John Voelcker, Richard Hamilton, and John McHale, whose futuristic technological assemblage he lauded as proper to the times. Their work, nonetheless, he said, bore a certain kinship to *Patio and Pavilion,* a kinship that

> would appear to lie in the fact that neither [installation] relied on *abstract concepts,* but on *concrete images*—images that can carry the mass of tradition and association, or the energy of novelty and technology, but resist classification by the geometrical disciplines by which most other exhibits were dominated.[13]

Ending on this note, Banham left his readers to speculate on the relative uses and values of "concrete images" versus "abstract concepts." A few years later, Lévi-Strauss would ascribe to "concrete images" and "concepts" the respective underpinnings of savage versus scientific thought.[14] He explained that concrete images were the basic building blocks of myth-based knowledge systems (that is, of "savage thought"), which constructed meaning through associations of resemblance, not on abstractly derived "concepts," as was the case with Western science.[15] Lévi-Strauss described these processes of constructing meaning as intellectual bricolage. Concrete images were, he said, multivalent, lending themselves to diverse configurations under operations of bricolage.

FIGURE 3.1. Independent Group, *Patio and Pavilion* installation in *This Is Tomorrow* exhibition, Whitechapel Gallery, London, 1956. Photograph by John Maltby. Reprinted with permission of the Alison and Peter Smithson Estate.

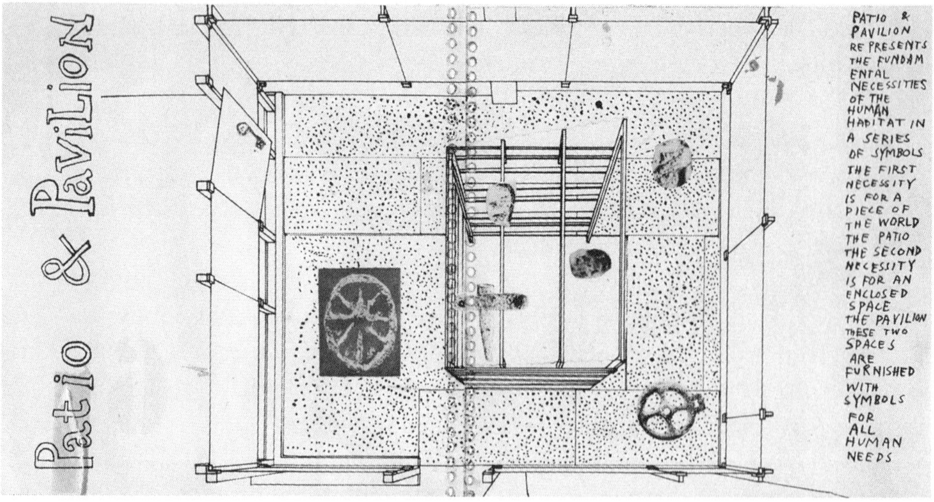

FIGURE 3.2. Alison and Peter Smithson, *This Is Tomorrow* exhibition, Whitechapel Gallery, London, 1956. Cardboard, 2, 405 x 36 cm. Musée national d'art moderne, Centre Georges Pompidou, Paris, France. Copyright CNAC/MNAM/Dist. RMN-Grand Palais / Art Resource, New York.

Art historian Hal Foster has subsequently referred to the Independent Group's installations as perfect examples of bricolage.[16] The same was suggested by Banham's claim that concrete images could operate multivalently while still weighted—constrained—by "the mass of tradition and association." It was precisely the propensity toward multivalency that allowed such images—though seemingly rooted in an autochthonous past—to lend themselves to future adaptations.

Just as the nostalgic primitivist tendencies in Lévi-Strauss's work have caused its cybernetic preoccupations to be sometimes overlooked, the futuristic aspects of *Patio and Pavilion* were ignored by Banham on the basis of the work's presumed nostalgia.[17] Yet Lévi-Strauss's cybernetic anthropology lent itself to the model of Hegelian synthesis, according to which Euro-American subjectivity (qua anthropology) might decode and technobiopolitically reproduce authentically human forms of cultural organization. As such, cybernetics—far from inaugurating a posthumanist rupture, as has been claimed—was framed as a humanist recuperation of autochthonous proclivities, a framing aided by anthropologists' participation in cybernetic discourse.[18]

Patio and Pavilion can be understood in a similar vein, as a prolegomenon to the Smithsons' subsequent installation *House of the Future,* produced the same year. The earlier installation in fact engaged a technological tomorrow in subtle ways.[19] Suggesting an emergent structuralist science of architectural semiotics, the installation proposed primal linkages between the human organism, its environment, and its patterns of thought and communication. These linkages—supposedly lying below the stratum of conscious language or "abstract concepts"—relied on the viewer's cognitive faculty for semiotic arrangement, which could more readily assert itself in the absence of linguistic interference. It should be mentioned that the show's curators had opted not to use explanatory textual captions, allowing the visual–spatial to speak for itself, as it were. *Patio and Pavilion* was a kind of machinery meant to simulate the brain's innate propensities for unconscious semiotic modes of association.

The hut that formed the centerpiece of *Patio and Pavilion* was constructed from loosely spaced boards, providing glimpses through and beyond its three walls.[20] As viewers perambulated the hut's exterior, their shifting perspectives would have fluidly assimilated the installation's strewn artifacts and surrounding environment into different proximities and juxtapositions, and thus into different associations and meanings. Rather than being organized into an a priori order, the sundry things of the world had to be synthesized by the mind into an order instinctively imposed through relationships of visual association, suggestive of the Smithsons' recent gambit to replace CIAM's strict urban zoning categories with "scales of association" based on cognitive, cultural, and environmental linkages.[21]

The group's prior use of surrealist montage and juxtaposition in their show *Parallel of Life and Art* had likewise charged the viewer with the task of forging associations. However, the primitive hut of *This Is Tomorrow* made architecture the specific framework through which diverse "concrete images" were brought into shifting contact. The primitive hut's skeletal form stressed the link between architectural and intellectual structures: architecture as analog to the mind's own facility for sifting the world's abundance into a semblance of order through its primitive means of semiotic production. Moreover, as had been the case with Edward Steichen's recent traveling exhibition *Family of Man*, *Patio and Pavilion* implied a universal, essential humanity, presenting an ur-architecture that was common to all societies. This installation was not about recuperating what Banham had dismissed as "traditional values"; instead, the primitive hut operated as a model for future aesthetic technologies that might subtly meld mind and nature. The primitive hut was the imagined machinery through which modernism could be made into a natural and, thus, universal "language." Team Ten sought to render moot the problem of Babel—a confusion of tongues, or, really, of a confusion of styles and cultures—by proposing magical processes through which the particularities of a given culture could be both conserved and eliminated—rarefied—through their translation into a modernist idiom.

Excursus: The Primitive Hut of Yesterday

How does human cognition transpose itself (magically) into architecture? This question belongs to eighteenth-century Europe as much as it does to the twentieth century. Marc-Antoine Laugier's *Essay on Architecture* (*Essai sur l'architecture*) (1753) presents a lone "savage" who, to shelter himself from the weather, constructs from tree branches the first iteration of human architecture.[22] The essence of this hut—its pure architectureness—was, according to Laugier, subsequently translated into ancient Greek architecture. But why has an essay on the merits of ancient Greek architecture been assigned the canonical status as *the* inaugural text of modern European architectural theory?

In contradistinction to earlier invocations of primitive huts (for example, by Vitruvius), Laugier's essay operates as a guideline for modern modes of architectural translation.[23] Within the cultural terrain of France's inchoate nationalism, Laugier's understanding of Greek architecture as a translation of a more primitive, natural artifact appears as a late postscript to the French Académie's earlier "quarrel between the Ancients and the Moderns." Following the rise of vernacular print in France and the concomitant weakening of the authority of ancient Greek literature, Laugier's allegory reinstates the authority of *both* antiquity and modernity by casting the latter as a translation of the former through their common roots in the vernacular. The fact that this vernacular is of no particular provenance gives it the paradoxical status of a *universal* vernacular. Laugier's text suggests a fundamental kinship between the (nationalizable and also colonizable) vernacular and the imperial lingua franca of Greek antiquity. While the savage is intended to reveal human cognition in its naked unity with the world, antiquity's capture of that naked purity instates a magical authority, conjoining the axiomatic power of the rustic vernacular with all the technical power of empire.

Laugier's concern with the connectivity between cognition and world appears in the preamble to his allegory, where he claims to plunge himself into a Cartesian abyss of doubt from which he might emerge—the reader is led to believe—only through a Cartesian exercise of deducing first principles. However, in the allegory that follows, Laugier immediately abandons any attempt at syllogistic reasoning. With a rhetorical

FIGURE 3.3. Charles Eisen, frontispiece, circa 1754. From Marc-Antoine Laugier, *Essai sur l'architecture,* 2nd ed., 1755.

gesture cruder than René Descartes's theological prestidigitations, Laugier slyly posits savage nature as a kind of axiomatic *eidos* in lieu of the syllogistic method he had seemed to promise the reader. As an analog for cognition in its naked state, divested of any acquired conventions, we have the mythic savage in *his* naked state, exposed to the irksome elements, whereupon there devolves from his brain an originary architecture, as if coaxed from some primeval wellspring of truth. The implication is that this architecture had always-already dwelt in the brain, similar to the Platonic *eidos,* so that—with gentle prodding from sun and rain—it would inevitably spring forth in all its naked purity. To have thus existed always-already in the brain was tantamount to existing always-already as a translation, strung between an endless series of transhistorical reemergences.

By presenting the primitive hut as a reification of primitive thought, Laugier provided an exposition of how to think about thought in its originary condition at the precise moment when it transposes itself magically into architecture.[24] Being a perfect crystallization of thought in its natural state, the primitive hut smoothly elides the division between nature and human representation, disavowing contextual particularities, historicity, or (what we might call) arbitrariness—that is, the contingent circumstances and diverse influences through which the world's architectures develop. The apodictic claim of Laugier's fabled architecture derives from the curious double structure of the Platonic *eidos and the mythical savage,* which suggests a potential reversal between copies and originals, or between the concrete iteration of a thing and its mental representation. In Laugier's account, the mind, in direct contact with the primordial conditions of nature, *builds a copy in the absence of a prior original.* The subaltern aboriginal is always-already displaced by its translation, existing in the form of antiquity's canny divination of the savage *eidos.*

These fabulous foundations of modern architectural discourse, far from collecting dust in the annals of history, were adopted by many of the great fabulists of twentieth-century modernism. Anticipating the mystifications of Critical Regionalist architecture, Team Ten architects implicitly invoked this mythical copy-that-lacked-an-original as the underlying rationale of their quasi-anthropological methods.[25] Whether understood as a kind of *eidos* or according to twentieth-century structuralist understandings of underlying mechanisms, the primitive hut suggested an innate link between cognitive habitus and human habitat, lending itself to an architectural ergonomics of the spirit that was expedient as a device of acculturation in the cases of both Europe's working classes and the former colonies of the global south.

Pattern and Diagram

In postwar Europe, as in eighteenth-century France, a preoccupation with origins belonged to a broader intellectual project that sought apodictic principles underlying the world's myriad iterations of architecture. For the architects examined in this chapter, the architectural *eidos*—that is, naked architectural thought—expressed itself most cogently through the rarefied abstraction of architectural diagrams. Diagrams laid bare the hidden kernel that was secreted within every cultural variation of architecture, the underlying logic of architecture, linked to a notion of pattern. Pattern was understood as innate to both architecture and human culture.[26] Patterns offered a way to copy without really copying: to translate. While abstracting certain existing cultural features of local societies, they also permitted permutation. In this respect, Peter Smithson stressed to his Team Ten colleagues the difference between a "prototype," which is immutable, and an "archetype," which encouraged adaptations (much like the primitive hut).[27]

Peter Smithson, reflecting on Van Eyck's contribution to Team Ten thinking, emphasized that diverse architectural precedents were not to be imitated; rather, they should suffuse the mind, informing its processes:

> When [Van Eyck] talks about all previous language, all previous sensibilities, which run through you, this opens my mind to the fact that academic historic knowledge, and knowledge of earlier sensibilities could *run through you* without having to use the form of these historical styles.[28]

Although Smithson seems to suggest here a transhistorical haunting whereby the architect might inhale the past and then exhale it as architecture, Team Ten members, needing a more pragmatic working method, typically strove to identify underlying patterns manifest in world architectures and cultural habits.[29] Those patterns—often suggestive of programmatic relationships and circulation diagrams—enabled habitus to be translated into habitat, and thus made it possible for patterns of the past to be translated into modernisms for the future.

Implicit to Team Ten's interest in world architectures was a notion of the architect's own epistemic position as distinct from that of the countless anonymous builders whose products served as empirical evidence, even while the architect attempted to *self-consciously* capture the mindset of those same builders. For example, Christopher Alexander, an occasional Team Ten participant who had conducted fieldwork for a year in a Gujarati village, distinguished between the "unselfconscious" architectures of a global indigene and the "selfconscious" architectures produced by professional designers.[30] The former replicated a single architecture within a given context, whereas the latter applied a plethora of diverse architectural types. Alexander argued that a diversity of types rendered it exponentially more difficult to determine an appropriate solution to an urban architectural problem.[31] By contrast, long-standing conventions made occasional adaptation far easier, as fewer variables were involved. For Alexander, the way to handle this complexity was to use computers to process anthropological data, breaking down urbanist systems into component groups so as to render these components more like simple village architectures (that is, "unselfconscious" architectures). As such, a global indigene provided an experimental arena within which the architect could explore the transformation of simple types and, from these studies, develop an architectural grammar (a "pattern language") that could be digitally encoded.[32] While Alexander thus valorized "unselfconscious" architectures, his search for a "pattern language" nonetheless can be construed as an apperceptive posture, transcending the "primitive" through its conscious categorization and synthesis of diverse forms into a universal science of design.[33] The "pattern language" was based on diagrammatic studies of "primitive" villages as well as on medieval urbanisms.

Another impetus for architects' structuralist approach to aesthetic pattern lay in the ideological mandates of the Cold War, prompting Team Ten panegyrics to "freedom" and "choice." Several Team Ten designers proposed decentralized rhizomic patterns (what they called "mat buildings") as an organic form of urban growth that could be freely altered and expanded in different directions as dictated by future needs, unhampered by a rigid compositional order.[34] Candilis-Josic-Woods's campus plan for West Berlin's Freie Universität, sponsored by the Ford Foundation, attempted to express U.S. support of free learning.[35] Foreshadowing twenty-first century neoliberal ideas of higher learning that echoed ideals of consumer freedom, Candilis-Josic-Woods claimed that their design would optimize the brain's learning capacities while conserving the individual's freedom of choice through rhizomic form.[36] University students would not be overregulated by rigid disciplinarity but would instead develop intellectually through spontaneous interdisciplinary encounters among peers, encouraged by the campus's intricate circuit of corridors and courtyards, which wove together disparate departments.[37] The repetitive rhizomic grid thus operates as a double metaphor: on the one hand, for nonauthoritarian social relations, emblematized by the acephalous tentacles of the plan; on the other hand, for the natural circuitry of the brain itself, its myriad pathways and connections permitting a freely associative play of thought. Authority is subsumed within the cybernetic notion of a neurobiological organism.

Structuralist anthropology and cybernetics in this era helped frame the brain as simultaneously universal and culturally specific, insofar as universal semiotic mechanisms were said to give rise to specific cultural patterns, as argued by the anthropologist Ruth Benedict. Benedict was an acquaintance of Van Eyck, and her theories are said to have strongly influenced his ideas of cultural pattern.[38] In ascribing a gestalt-like structure to these "patterns of culture," anthropology naturalized all aspects of a given social order while appearing simultaneously to grant each society a cultural purity and autonomy, it's innate patterns untouched by external influence or contingency. In Team Ten discourse, the invocation of freedom was helpful in masking not only architecture's cybernetic and (at times) neocolonial tendencies but also a few disquieting similarities between fascism's erstwhile evocations of *Volk* and Team Ten's conception of *völkisch* habitus. Even though Team Ten's internationalism distanced the group from the Third Reich's xenophobia, Team Ten discourse nonetheless brought a different form of ethnoracial essentialism to bear upon their ambitions of large-scale urban reorganization.

This can be seen in Alison Smithson's essay "How to Recognise and Read a Mat Building," published in *Architecture Design* in 1974, largely as publicity for the Smithsons' own recent proposal for Kuwait City but also as a retrospective framing of the work of Team Ten architects.[39] The article made use of Team Ten's principle methods of visual rhetoric, combining photographs of medieval Euro-Mediterranean and Islamicate architectural "patterns" with architectural diagrams, models, and photographs, using works mostly by the Smithsons, Candilis-Josic-Woods, and Van Eyck. Mat buildings, "said to epitomise the anonymous collective," were traced by Smithson back to those medieval examples and even to geological formations.[40] Effectively, the tendencies of the "Arab mind" could be encapsulated by an architecture that mimicked that brain's supposed propensity to spontaneous reroutings. Describing the Arab "folk" influences on her and Peter Smithson's mat-building design for Kuwait, she wrote,

> In [Arab] folk-buildings, this [mat-building type] is un-monumental, full of stops and starts and shadow . . . with a high degree of interconnectedness to allow for change of mind and the inroads of time. . . . Arabic cities are full of buildings started and never finished, and then abandoned, for it would seem that the Arabs are more spontaneous, less worldly in the long term that [*sic*] cultures either to the east or west.[41]

The orientalizing gesture offered here—in tandem with Kuwait's transformation by British and U.S. petroleum interests—belongs to a slightly different order of orientalism than that of colonial subjugation, pure and simple.[42] This new orientalism served to justify technocapitalist transformation by its assertion of European architectural expertise as a sophisticated science of cultural translation. According to this science, the Arabic brain is not denied its putative (and admittedly ambivalent) merits—incompleteness and unworldliness. But Arabs must rely on European modernism to translate and conserve the nature of the oriental brain amid techno-economic upheavals.

Smithson continues, "Today space is total and society is universal. These realities must be reflected in our planning and building."[43] In thus claiming to translate ethnocultural specificity into a universally relevant form of modernity, she unwittingly illustrates the way ethnoracial essentialism functions differently in fascist versus neocolonial ideology. If, say, *Heimatkultur* invoked a folk aesthetic redolent of rustic Germanicness, in Smithson's rhetoric, a position of white Christian epistemic privilege is asserted through the translation of the Arabic brain's innate propensities into the infrastructural requirements of a British–U.S. oil protectorate.[44] The structuralist–anthropological hinge between capitalist infrastructure and folk culture is to be found by interpreting the presumed "stops and starts" of Arabic *urbanism* as evidence of the Arabic *brain*'s supposed tendency toward spontaneous caprice. The brain (in its various racialized types) becomes the chiasmus through which "culture" can be converted into high-tech architectural infrastructure. The ergonomics of the spirit work, however, in both directions: architecture is adduced as proof of the (racialized) brain's innate proclivities; conversely, from the resulting understanding of this brain, a new architecture can be addressed to that brain's inner workings.

The Indebted Original: Translation as Epistemic Domination

At the 1962 Team Ten meeting in Royaumont Abbey, a heated argument broke out between the Smithsons and Van Eyck.[45] In the late 1950s and early '60s, Van Eyck had conducted fieldwork on the Dogon in present-day Mali. As editor of the architectural magazine *Forum*, he had then published a feature on architectural, anthropological, and ethnopsychiatric research on the Dogon. By the time of the meeting at Royaumont, two years had passed since his return from Mali, and, hard-pressed to give architectural form to the intellectual structures he had supposedly gleaned there, he exhibited one of his student's design projects as an illustration of Dogon mental processes. Piet Blom's student project, *Noah's Ark,* proposed a city for one million inhabitants, to be built in the Netherlands using an intricately woven arrangement of repetitive building types—essentially a mat building.

Van Eyck presented this work as a demonstration of the Dogons' cognitive penchant for metonymic thought: the scheme's architectural parts are reflected in the form of the whole.[46] He alluded to an article he had authored, inspired by the Dogon (and reacting against Alexander's cybernetic village analyses), describing "the house as a small city, and the city as a big house" and, relatedly, the leaf as a tree and vice versa.[47] The Smithsons took issue with such nonsensical mystifications. And besides, Blom's repetitive pattern looked "fascist," they claimed, precisely the sort of monumental urbanism Team Ten members had repudiated a decade earlier when urging the dissolution of CIAM.

That Van Eyck was taken aback by such criticism (and by the unwonted epithet "fascist") is unsurprising given that the scheme embodied many of Team Ten's pet motifs: mat-building structures, different "scales of association," interlaced courtyard-like spaces, and so on. The problem may have rested within the unasked question of what might be said to constitute "culture" in a middle-class European context, given the tendency in architectural discourse to counterpose "civilization" to "culture."[48] In order to render legible the structuralist logic the Smithsons espoused, repetition and simplification were necessary. However, this process of abstraction had to be based on anthropological context, allowing for the richness of culture to then be sublated: incorporated and, at the same time, transcended through the idiom of modernist design.

Against the Smithsons' criticisms of Blom's design, Van Eyck countered, "This diagram is *a process of mind,* not a city." Peter retorted, "Why should we struggle with this guy's brain?"[49] Why indeed? Because, Van Eyck might have replied, the basic, if unspoken, tenet of all Team Ten discourse was that the diverse contexts in which these architects worked could be rendered into a universal aesthetic grammar by dint of the structures shared by all human brains. Blom's diagrammatic architecture was offered as an analog to the brain's own diagrammatic workings—quite similar, in fact, to Alison Smithson's later analogy between the Arabic brain and the Arabic city. However, in the proposed *Noah's Ark,* the Arabic brain had been displaced by a European one, and this was its fatal flaw: the European brain—especially when not identified with a subaltern European class—was not an evidentiary object from which to extrapolate anthropological truths but, rather, a sovereign subject.

The European brain was flatly unmagical. If one was to produce architectures for Europe, the necessary cognitive magic had to be conjured through reference either to more primeval European architectures or to children (Europe's own little savages), as had been the case with the Smithsons' use of Henderson's street photographs for their famed CIAM grille, a work they had executed years earlier. In case the Smithsons' intended homology between working-class children and savages was not clear enough,

a

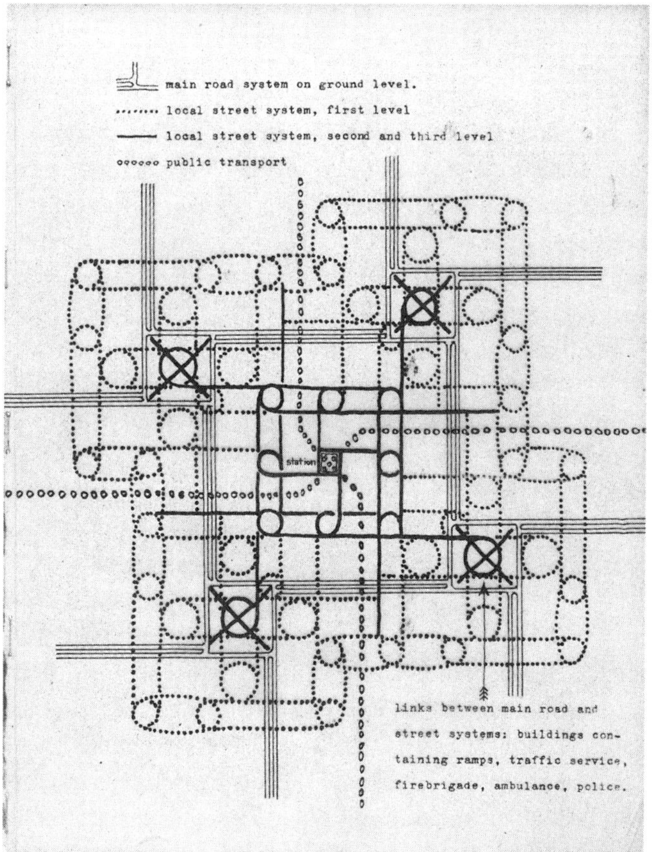

FIGURE 3.4. Piet Blom, *Plan of Noah's Ark (Plan de Ark von Noach)*, a city for one million inhabitants. (a) Circulation system; (b) medium-rise housing complexes, circa 1962. Collection Het Nieuwe Institute/BLOM, Blom_s1–43.4 b and Blom_s1–2.

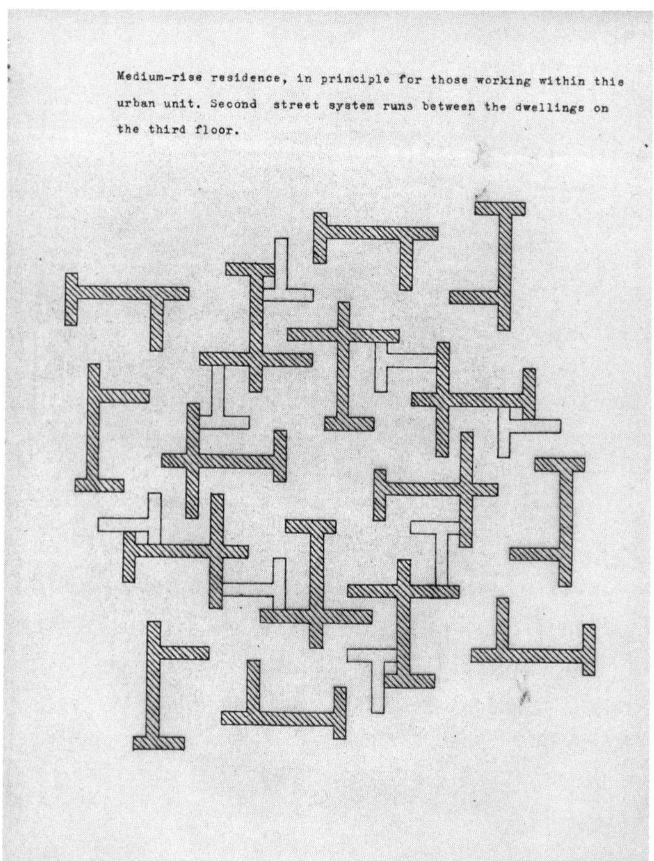

b

the architects had painted over the grille a dancing figure wearing a ritual costume and a horned mask labeled by the word "UR," an abbreviation of "Urban Reidentification" but also probably a pun on the Germanic root *ur-* (aboriginal). The masked figure conjoins the two halves of the grille, serving as the anthropological alembic through which an indigenous habitus (working-class children playing) is transposed magically into architectural form.

Of course, most Team Ten participants framed their work not through an explicit differentiation between the savage and the civilized but, rather, through essentialist notions of human culture. But then, why should not *any* architecture be regarded as symptomatic of cultural proclivities? Why look toward the Dogon or (in the case of the Smithsons) the Scottish peasant croft to derive architectural principles?[50] And, for Cold War supporters of British–American ideology like the Smithsons, why look to the artifacts of noncapitalist architectures to derive the architectures of capitalism? The answer is that modernism's culture of expertise rested on two (neo)colonial constructions: first, that the expert is competent to perceive and diagnose local conditions in a manner unavailable to the locals themselves so as to then translate those conditions into modern solutions, and, second, that the resulting translation belongs to an epistemic order that was not only superior to but so wholly *different from* that of the original as to be incommensurate with it. This incommensurateness took the form of something like an epistemic debt. What rendered the original less valuable than its translation was that its creators were supposedly unconscious of the underlying cognitive

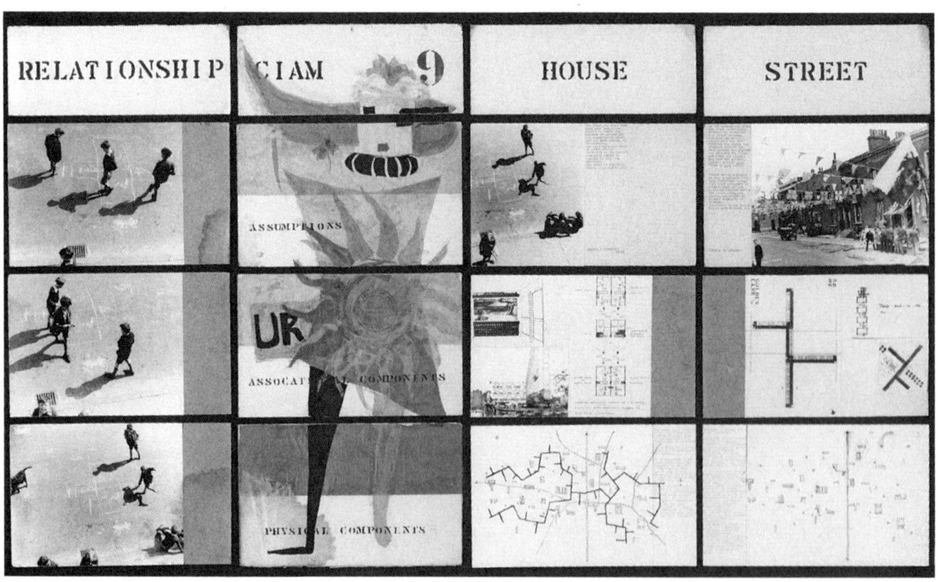

FIGURE 3.5. Alison and Peter Smithson, grid for CIAM from Aix en Provence, 1952–53. Presentation panel: ink drawing, sized papers, 83.5 x 275.5 cm. Inv. no. AM1993-1-688. Musée national d'art moderne, Centre Georges Pompidou, Paris, France. Copyright CNAC/MNAM/Dist. RIHN-Grand Palais / Art Resource, New York. Reprinted with permission from Alison and Peter Smithson Estate.

logic reified in the very architecture produced by that logic. Structuralist comparison revealed those logics, and this diagnosis was key to translating the primitive into the rubrics of modernity. Architectural professionalism was basically a form of apperceptive consciousness.

This construction calls to mind Walter Benjamin's idea of literary translation, according to which an original poem incurs a debt to its translation insofar as the latter reveals—through the process of translation—the fundamental languageness of language, or what Benjamin calls a "pure language" (*reine Sprache*).[51] Although such a debt may be innocent in the case of poetry, in the case of postwar architectural expertise, the notion that a pure language—or what I will call a pure architecture—might produce an unreciprocal debt is suggestive of the linkages between actual debt formation and racialized forms of epistemic domination. What Benjamin describes as the translator's efforts to uncover a "pure language" is strikingly similar to what I am calling savage thought—the deduction of basic structures of human cognition based on the evidence offered by cultural "originals."[52] Benjamin's idea that translation reorients language toward the depths of prelinguistic thought touches on the fantasy of a pentecostal semiosis—of a form of communication that overcomes the arbitrariness of signification, reaching toward the autochthonous depths of consciousness (notwithstanding the fact that Benjamin in *some* respects refutes the very basis of the pentecostal).[53]

The notion of a "pure language" thus cogently captures a burgeoning tendency of early and mid-twentieth-century structuralism in its search for the languageness of languages (including architectural "languages") as a way of rendering up the systematicity of semiotic systems, stripping away the contingencies, such as the arbitrary relationship between signifier and signified, so as to reveal the inner logic of semiotic cognition. It captures, moreover, the surplus value accruing to the pure language relative to the profane vernaculars from which it extrapolates that inner logic. The translation gazes consciously at—rather than swimming within—the semiotic and aesthetic workings of the human brain; therein lies the debt the original owes to the translation. It cannot repay the translation because its very status and value—that of being originary—consists in its not knowing what it is, whereas the currency that structuralism deals in is a mechanistic knowledge of that which lies beneath the surface of things. The original *must* be this thing that does not know itself—for example, a savage that constructs beautiful works unconscious of how or why—so that outsiders' knowledge of that thing can be extracted and cast as a legitimizing form of expertise.

It should be stressed that the value architects extracted from "originals" was, by and large, not in the form of architectural knowledge. Clearly, Van Eyck's Dogon fieldwork did not really transform his design work (and hence he clutched at Blom's design instead); nor did the Smithsons derive any real insights from Scottish crofts. The value they extracted from cultural analysis was in its legitimizing effects, offering a new set of professional trappings. Hence, when the Dutch modernist (and occasional Team Ten participant) Herman Haan traveled to the Dogons (many years before bringing Van Eyck there), his ludicrous performance of "going native" was clearly not intended to strip him of his racial and professional status.[54] Indeed, film footage shows him participating in the most racially degrading forms of anthropometric research, standing before a queue of adult Dogon men, carefully measuring the circumferences of their heads.[55] (It was no doubt practices such as these that led Peter Smithson to admiringly refer to Haan as an anthropologist and an archaeologist.)[56] Haan was famous for designing and manufacturing a special aluminum-frame spherical cage, which was used to lift him up high into the steep uninhabited escarpments of the Dogons' lands where the earlier Tellem society had constructed a small architectural necropolis.

Van Eyck's approach to the Dogon brain was different from Haan's. Following the interpretations of the ethnographer Marcel Griaule, with whom he collaborated, Van Eyck marveled at the structural congruity between different Dogon semiotic forms, such as architecture, myth, dance, and domestic crafts.[57] The interplay between these arts was indicative to Van Eyck of structuring patterns that helped render a given culture legible and decodable. Contemporaneously with Van Eyck's trip to the Dogon, Lévi-Strauss had also noted the "savage" tendency to forge reciprocities between different semiotic forms, ultimately ascribing all human semiosis to binary code. That is, the neurological electric signal (with its on/off or positive/negative charges) gave rise to semiotic and taxonomic systems based on binary oppositions, a theory Van Eyck echoed.[58] In other words, binary code suggested a pentecostal technology, a pure language rooted beneath the arbitrariness of actual languages. In thinking reminiscent of the Bauhaus interest in synesthesia, Lévi-Strauss discussed the brain's capacity to translate between different semiotic modes, using the example of the visual translation of an opera score performed by the set designer and costume designer.[59] The set designer had to root out those presemiotic traces that were embryonically at work within the opera score, aspects of the music that were in fact *prior* to music. Intersemiotic translation is meant to reveal that fleeting moment when inchoate thought, freed from constraining systems of formal language and sense making, stands poised on the brink of the semiotic systems through which it can be expressed, not yet fallen into their profane and arbitrary conventions. To explain how music might carry secreted within itself certain nonmusical elements, Lévi-Strauss invoked the universality of binary code, anticipating the observations Friedrich Kittler would make (albeit as critique) at the end of the twentieth century concerning the ascendancy of binary code over other media: binary code was the universal semiotic system—the "pure language"—into which all other representational systems could be transposed.[60]

A Western translation of foreign knowledge has often appeared to incur a debit rather than a debt vis-à-vis its "original." Accordingly, when Haan built a water reservoir for the Dogon (using his expertise and their labor), the reservoir was proudly proclaimed in Dutch newspapers as a European "gift" from Haan to the Dogon, rather than describing it as a simple reimbursement for the Dogons' assistance in Haan's research efforts, to say nothing of the knowledge Haan acquired from the Dogon, the anthropological trappings that helped boost his professional profile.[61] The "primitive" served as an intellectual commons, since techniques that were particular to a given

FIGURE 3.6. Photographer unknown, Herman Haan with aluminum ball in Mali. *Revue: Nederlands Familieblad* 16 (April 18, 1964). From the Herman Haan archive, Het Nieuwe Instituut.

society could simply be conflated with universal human tendencies and subsumed in the general category of Western science.

Team Ten's endless discussions on how to extrapolate the knowledge embodied by "original" architectures without simply replicating those models must have been motivated by a nagging awareness that the only possible justification for modernist expertise hinged on its claim to be conferring rather than extracting value from the various societies and social classes it studied and built for. Architects would have to tally up the intellectual balance sheets so that whatever architectures emerged from their anthropological efforts would exceed the value of the native models they studied. The balancing act was a delicate one between two extremes: on the one hand, if they strayed too far from native architectures, architects would merely advance CIAM's supposed neglect of local context, thereby making architecture a coercive imposition rather than a gift; on the other hand, if they remained too faithful to existing or native models, they could not really claim to have superseded the original.[62] The trick was to create an architectural language more native to a society than its own native architecture. Translation was to be based on a new model of the gift: not the Maussian gift that demands commensurate reciprocity but, instead, a gift that presumes epistemic incommensurability, thereby rendering reciprocity unthinkable. The point was to establish a relationship of epistemic indebtedness between Western Europe and its former or present colonies.

In Enlightenment-era accounts of the primitive hut, we find an early suggestion of the idea that the translation might indebt the original to itself. The work of Antoine-Chrysostome Quatremère de Quincy on "primitive types" appeared in Bernard Rudofsky's 1964 exhibition *Architecture without Architects* at New York's Museum of Modern Art, in which several Team Ten architects showcased their own studies of world architectures.[63] For Quatremère, world historical progress assumed the form of the civilized translation of primitive architectural types (similar to the *eidos*).[64] In claiming for ancient architects the ability to translate primitive archetypes without actually copying them, Quatremère distinguished between a "type" to be translated and a "model" to be slavishly mimicked.[65]

Against rationalist critiques of Greek antiquity's alleged transformation of the primitive hut's structural wooden elements into nonfunctional stone ornament, Quatremère argued, in line with Laugier, that this translation—although nonsensical from a practical viewpoint—made Greek architecture superior to all other architectures.[66] The conversion of functional wooden rafters into the purely decorative band of stone triglyphs, the conversion of the hut's gabled roof into a false pediment masking a flat roof, and the conversion of a light, tensile wooden frame into massive, brittle stone beams did not, for Quatremère, impute any corruption of the architectural logic of the wooden original.[67] Foreshadowing Benjamin's theory of translation, Quatremère argued against the value of *sensical* translation in favor of revealing the pure (presensical) language of architecture. By rendering the original's simple wooden structure into aggrandized monumental structure and ornament, stone temples supposedly brought into relief the fundamental architectural *eidos* of the wooden hut on which it was modeled. What was formerly pragmatic in terms of construction had become, through translation, a rich semiosis.[68]

The temple's massive monumentality relative to its actual wooden precedent (and to its alleged precedent, the primitive hut) marks its dominance over that precedent (and over whatever social regime had constructed it). In this sense, it is significant that this late eighteenth-century author felt the need to link the temple back to a *primitive* antecedent. Moreover, Quatremère's account helps illustrate the pentecostal powers of pure architecture. The temple's absorption of its presumed signified (the primitive hut) into its own architectural means, seamlessly blending the past with the present, the primordial with the imperial—all this produces a strong affective power, which, in concert with the building's monumentality and ritualistic functions, expresses the magical power of the state without needing to put that power into words. A visitor to such a temple might simply sense subliminally the various ways in which power is expressed.

Unlike linguistic translation, which presumes the dual directionality of the process (that is, that languages are mutually translatable into each other because they are commensurable), the geopolitics of architectural translation appears in the assumption that this process occurs unidirectionally. (Nobody has ever hypothesized that a "primitive" hut might be a translation of ancient Greek temples.) There reigned an assumption that all these "original" (that is, nonprofessional) architectures were not *already* translations or perhaps hybridizations of diverse architectural conventions. Against this assumption, we could point to the ways many world architectures transposed heterogeneous influences into workable constructions for the present.[69] Yet in order to claim the task of translation as their own special purview, modernist architects had to uphold a false division between an unchanging indigeneity and an ever-adaptable modernity. Modernity's putative ability to adapt and translate lay in its special ability to extract general rules from particular examples, an ability that had often been deemed lacking in "primitive" peoples.

Architecture and Words

Each family in the Dogon owned a hut-like granary, and these highly photogenic structures were at the heart of Haan's and Van Eyck's interest in the Dogon. According to the Dogon elder Ogotemmêli, the heavenly spirits descended to earth upon such a granary.[70] The ethnographer Marcel Griaule, hired by the French government to undertake the colonial Mission Dakar–Djibouti (an expedition across sub-Saharan Africa in 1931–33), subsequently returned to the Dogon to expand his scholarship. He transcribed his conversations with Ogotemmêli (conducted with the aid of an interpreter) in a book titled *Dieu d'eau: Entretiens avec Ogotemmêli* (God of water: Interviews with Ogotemmêli, 1948).[71] Van Eyck, who had encountered Griaule's work on the Dogon through the surrealist magazine *Minotaure*, subsequently met Griaule on his trip with Haan to Bandiagara in Mali, and he published some of Griaule's ethnography in the 1961 *Architectural Forum* issue that featured Dogon culture, abundantly illustrated with photographs of the granaries.[72]

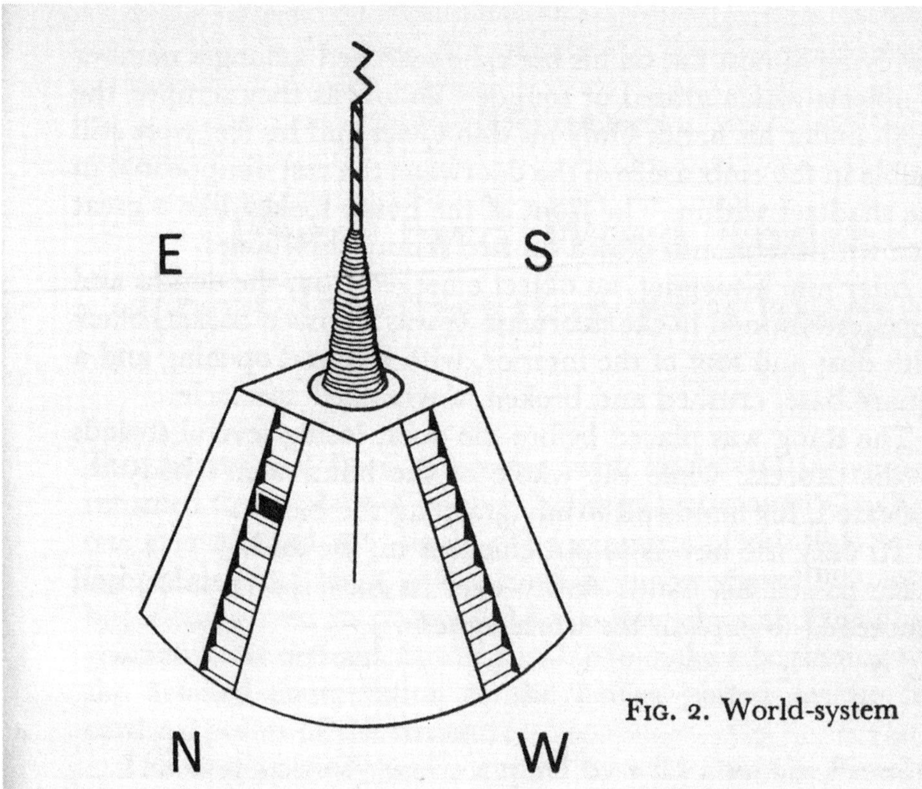

FIGURE 3.7. Marcel Griaule, *Système du monde,* illustrating Ogotommêli's description of a Dogon granary descended from heaven with steps cut into its sides, circa 1948. From Griaule, *Dieu d'eau: Entretiens avec Ogotemmêli* (1948).

In Griaule's interviews, Ogotemmêli offered an account of how the world's onto-semiotic order had been translated from its divine provenance into an earthly taxonomy. The first granary had descended to earth from heaven. Its walls—unlike those of their earthly counterparts—were stepped, forming a steep ziggurat, and upon those terraced steps all the living species of the world were arranged in taxonomic order. When asked how the world's biotic abundance could fit on the walls of the granary, Ogotemmêli explained, first, that only a single representative of a particular species within a larger genre would be visible (for example, a red antelope would stand in front of all other antelope species), and second, that these were not actual plants and animals but rather the "symbols" for them, "the words of this lower world."[73] It would appear, then, that the Dogon acknowledged the relationship between words and things to be debased—deracinated from its divine origin—and that this "arbitrariness" (as we might put it, mutatis mutandis) was in fact integral to the structure of knowledge. There was no "pure language" through which the world might pass directly into human awareness. Rather, the world is given to human knowledge through the translation of things into their debased, earthly symbols. Contrary to the presumed enchantment of primitive semiotics, Ogotemmêli suggested an ontosemiotic order based on a "neutral" spatial logic, not so dissimilar from what Michel Foucault has described as a hallmark epistemic event of early European modernity: the neutral organizational grid said to supersede the erstwhile magical unity between words and their referents.[74]

Van Eyck surely couldn't have hoped to discover a more perfect semiotic role for architecture than this: the granary as the spatial–epistemic scaffold on which things were distributed into taxonomic relationships rendering order—and thus meaning—possible. But Van Eyck never mentioned this account in the 1961 issue of *Forum*. Instead, he focused on a different account by Ogotemmêli (also transcribed by Griaule) of the Dogons' anthropomorphic arrangement of domestic architectures. Apparently, this more blatant use of architecture as a mimetic and thus nonarbitrary form was much more compelling to Van Eyck than the invisible, foundational role of the granary as an abstract semiotic scaffold.

It should be mentioned that Dogon architecture—understood by Van Eyck as a manifestation of autochthonous cultural purity—was hardly indigenous to the Dogon, having probably been adapted from the Tellem, who were already occupying the escarpments around Bandiagara when the Dogon migrated there in the fifteenth century. While some of the Tellem population is believed to have been absorbed within Dogon society, it appears that the majority were probably killed off by the Dogon. Dogon architecture has been interpreted by archaeologists as a likely adaptation of Tellem techniques.[75] The Dogon granary, despite constituting a fairly recent adaptation of heterogeneous influences, nonetheless figures in Dogon narratives as the primordial vehicle of the origins of human knowledge. We could thus understand the granary as an inverse of Laugier's always-already translated hut. Marked by a fundamental contingency and heterogeneity, the granary is placed at the center of the epistemic order, suggesting that this order—however divinely inflected—is subject to a fundamental impurity and arbitrariness, to heterogenous influences and adaptations. It acknowledges the possibility of translation, while still existing as both a concrete particular and a metaphoric abstraction.

This suggestion of epistemic and semiotic impurity reappears in Ogotemmêli's subsequent description of the act of commodity exchange, where he raises an age-old economic question of how two unlike objects can be traded for each other as if they were equivalent.[76] Ogotemmêli explains that twins symbolize the process of trade, suggesting *parity* though not identical unity. Moreover, trade must always be accompanied by words. Words are spoken by commodities, channeled through the mouths of the owners who trade them. "To have cowries," Ogotemmêli explained, "is to have words."[77] Here, a distinction must be drawn between an assumption of the basic *sameness* of human organic processes (which for Marx is implicit to abstract labor) and *parity* enunciated through semiotic performance. Ogotemmêli notes that, apart from physical resemblance, these symbolized twins also possessed "equal speech" (*égale parole*).[78] That is, exchanged objects are deemed fungible not because of some hidden irreducible quality (whether Marxian labor time, Platonic *eidos*, or structuralist structures). What determines the rate of exchange is not a hidden system of translation but, rather, a social–political relationship that grants each party an equal say in negotiating relative values. Epistemic debt does not exist in this version of exchange because commodities on both sides of the transaction must pass through the equalizing alembic of language.

Chapter 4 will recount the thesis forwarded by the ethnopsychatrist John Colin Carothers: that what distinguished Africans from Europeans was the former's inability to comprehend the arbitrary relationship between signifier and signified, leading to the magical belief that words—because of their intimacy with their referents—could exert control over the things they referred to. Ogotemmêli's explanations of Dogon architecture and of commodity exchange point, however, to a different understanding and use of magic: not as a delusional exercise of one's will over inanimate objects but, rather, as a performative mediation of the inevitable rift arising between an object's concrete singularity and its fungibility, a mediation enacted by all forms of representation, taxonomization, and monetization. What is at stake in these conceptions of human representation is ultimately the difference not between magic and nonmagic (since all societies—hegemonic or otherwise—dabble in magic) but between the ways that magic is bound up with different modalities of authority and violence.

Fascism and Its Architectural Other

During Team Ten's Rotterdam meeting in 1974, the group revisited the unhappy incident of the Smithsons' invective against Blom's *Noah's Ark* scheme. Peter Smithson said that he had expected Van Eyck's Dogon research would have led him to represent "a permanent human characteristic, which was to have some sort of animal relationship, one with another. . . . I thought you were saying that these were all symbols of constancy."[79] Van Eyck protested, "Did I speak about constancy? When I see a Bedouin tent I have an enormous feeling of permanence, even if they move somewhere else." This tent was the primitive hut par excellence: a pure, elemental form of architecture, so pared-down as to conserve its meaning intact, uncorrupted, when transposed into different contexts.

The very title of Blom's project, *Noah's Ark,* suggested precisely this "immutable mobility," invoking the Jewish narrative of a family that migrates and reestablishes itself on a foreign soil wiped clean of human and animal life.[80] The mythical ark, capable of transporting and reassembling, piece for piece, a divinely ordained world order turns its shuttered hull to the heterogeneous effects of migration, trauma, and transformation. Clearly born of the recent decade of postwar reconstruction, Blom's *Noah's Ark* project had elicited the accusation of fascism because it appeared as (among other things) too homogeneous, placed outside existing cultural context. Implicitly, Team Ten modernism was supposed to retain a trace of cultural particularity to underscore the essential difference between original and translation, between the debtor and the creditor.

Nonetheless, in seeking such elemental purity, did Blom really deserve the epithet "fascist"? The purity sought by fascism and the "pure architecture" tacitly sought by postwar architects definitely belonged to different orders, the latter depending on class and racial heterogeneity, as distinct from fascist concerns with racial homogeneity. The architects' nonfascist search for what I have called a "pure architecture"—an elemental and universal architecture—belonged to the logic of capitalist democracy with its combined modes of economic exploitation and biopolitical management. Fascist architectures had certainly served as pentecostal technologies, as they produced a unified racial–national self through multimedia spectacle and monumentality, producing the working classes' numinous identification with the sovereign class. By contrast, the pentecostal aspect of many Team Ten architectures lay in the fact that they tended to simultaneously elide *and* construct racial, cultural, and class difference. The idiom of modernism both established the subaltern as a unit subsisting within the state's care and purview and expressed an essential difference between the modern state and its wards (domestic or colonized).[81] As seen with the Nid d'abeille housing project in Casablanca or with Van Eyck's Wheels of Heaven Church—to be described momentarily—a trace of esoteric cultural particularity had to remain legible in the modern architectures intended for a subaltern, even if that esotericism was rendered abstract.

When Van Eyck was tasked with designing a Catholic church in The Hague, he encountered the problem of abstracting from the Christian edifice the pure essence of spirituality untainted by the particularity of Christian rituals and semiotics. Describing himself as a "tourist" in relation to religion, Van Eyck chose to restrict his architectural role to the design of a neutral space within which sacred rituals might take place:

> It is from [my] accumulated secular experience that I started . . . [the church design], confident that specific paradoxes appertaining to the subject could still be translated into architecture. . . . .
>
> Except for the altar . . . all the ecclesiastical objects were introduced by those who believe in them. I just provided the places to receive them. There are also *no built-in sacred signs or symbols* of any kind anywhere.[82]

In other words, modernism might accommodate religion only insofar as religion could be reduced to pure architectural effects and spatial provisions, wresting out of architecture various magico-theological effects. For Van Eyck, this included the use of overhead indirect daylighting to produce an ethereal effect and a dramatic ceiling height change between the areas for congregation and those for sermon and ritual.[83] Van Eyck guarded against being mistaken for one of the church's primitive believers, eschewing culturally specific "signs or symbols" that resisted translation into pure architecture. His objection was not to magic itself but to the subject position of enthrallment to culturally specific forms of magic, as distinct from the subject position of developing a new secular–cosmopolitan magic from a structuralist understanding of the underlying principles of those cultural specificities.

Van Eyck had encountered a similar problem when he went to Mali to document the Dogon granaries: the problem that signification posed to the search for a more transcendent universal semiotics. The profession to respect local particularity in the context of postwar development impelled architects toward contradictory operations of analysis and synthesis, separation and incorporation, such that the ruse of the unreciprocal debt could be concretized as architecture, according to rubrics of both Third

World developmentalism and European welfare. The history of the Smithsons' Robin Hood Gardens public housing project (slated in the early twenty-first century for demolition to make room for private development) underscored that "stealing" from the rich to "give" to the poor (like the legendary Robin Hood) produced a gift that the recipients had no proper rights to, although, framed as a gift, it did render them symbolically indebted to others' largesse.[84]

What this concept of the unreciprocal debt adds to existing scholarship on architecture and the European welfare state is an understanding of the way the welfare state (which was also in many cases a colonial and neocolonial state) was based on a loosely racialized epistemic positioning of the modern state (and its architects and experts) vis-à-vis its governed subjects. Team Ten architecture was conceived as an architecture of inverted debt, demanding not reciprocity but, rather, the perpetual indebtedness of the translation to the original.[85] The "new brutalist" or "structuralist" styles of Team Ten members—appearing as stripped-down translations—arose mostly from projects that were presented as *gifts*—public housing projects, public playgrounds, colonial housing schemes, public schools, orphanages.[86] The affectation of stripping architecture of all that was nonessential and recombining what remained into a pure architectural language reinforced the tacit economic ruse of the colonial "gift" as a precedent for the ideology of state welfare: first, in its claim to confer wealth while disavowing its extraction of the same, and, second, in the suggestion that the gift constituted by the architectural reorganization of wealth (in the form of infrastructures, housing, or public institutions) was nonremunerable because its underlying epistemic order posited an essential incommensurateness between modernity and its other. The architectural diagram as a distillation of comparative structuralist studies was the perfect aesthetic and epistemic support for the production of architecture as unreciprocal gift in colonial, neocolonial, and welfare contexts.

Scholarship has typically characterized Team Ten in terms of contradictory impulses, especially in the case of its primary propagandists, the Smithsons, who are described as torn between nostalgic and progressive tendencies, between their working-class backgrounds and their embrace of U.S.-driven consumerism, or between their "humanist" and technological concerns.[87] I would say that such contradictions result not from the architects' biographical idiosyncrasies but from long-standing disciplinary obfuscations exemplified by the modernist myth of the primitive hut. As the *original copy,* always given over to structuralist translation, the primitive hut allowed an elision between nostalgia and technofuturity, between the "common people" and the culture of professional architecture, and between the prerogatives of capitalist development and local cultures. The hut was a Rosetta stone from which the present would translate the past, indebt "tradition" to "modernity," and extrapolate from the former an aesthetic lingua franca capable of circumventing the world's confusion of tongues.

4

BRICOLAGE, MEGASTRUCTURE, INTERFACE

Yona Friedman and the Humanitarian Machine

Producing the Third World Subject

When the architect Yona Friedman presented his program for *une architecture mobile* (mobile architecture) at the 1956 Team Ten meeting in Dubrovnik, the project was met with antagonism by Alison Smithson, although it aroused the interest of many.[1] Intended to encourage flexibility and adaptiveness in the face of rapid urban growth, Friedman's megastructural space frames largely eschewed Team Ten's mission to translate local conventions into a modernist idiom. The "mobile architecture" offered, instead, merely a skeletal form of modernism—the steel space frame—to organize urban housing into a dense, gridiron pattern, while leaving each housing unit to be designed and built by its inhabitant. Not only would this megastructure help preserve the cultural and personal autonomy of its inhabitants, Friedman claimed, but it would also help preserve cities' existing urban fabric by spanning over and around buildings, parks, streets, and rail tracks. Friedman was taken to task by the Smithsons (among others) for reasons similar to those prompting their earlier censure of Piet Blom's proposed city scheme: Friedman's megastructures were deemed sterile, totalitarian, and blind to the particularities of cultural context.[2]

In light of Friedman's biography, it is not so surprising that he may have preferred to leave the determination of culture up to the urban migrants who were the intended occupants of these architectures. Himself a refugee of European anti-Semitism, he had fled his native Budapest as a young adult, taking sanctuary in Palestine, where he lived for more than a decade. There he drew on his formal training in architecture to develop new forms of low-cost housing in response to the influx of Jewish refugees.[3] In 1957 he moved to Paris, where he founded the Groupe d'études d'architecture mobile (GEAM), and he remained in Paris for the rest of his career.[4] Shortly after settling there, one of his collaborative proposals for prefabricated, low-cost housing units—inspired by his work in Israel-Palestine—attracted the interest of the French state, which entertained it as a solution for temporary workers' housing in North Africa.[5]

Friedman's lifelong interest in low-cost housing was accompanied by an abiding concern for low-tech means of economic survival in the global south, attested by the many didactic *bandes dessinées* (that is, cartoon-style pamphlets) he produced during the 1970s and '80s, primarily for UNESCO but also for Indian magazines on low-tech means of rural improvement. Taken as a whole, his work points to the discursive construction of a new type of subject in the global south, one now familiar in the age of late-capitalist humanitarianism but still quite novel in the 1960s and '70s: that of the resilient bricoleur. This chapter examines how an idiosyncratic paradigm of self-help, which mediated between programs of modernization and local practices, helped sketch out the lineaments of this new adaptive, entrepreneurial figure of the bricoleur, and how this development intersected with conceptions of southern austerity and with related developments in digital technologies—namely, in computer-aided design, graphic user interfaces, and the idea of the "boot," or the initial program load.

As distinct from the architectural programs discussed in chapter 3, which were attuned primarily to the European welfare state, Friedman's work anticipated twenty-first-century modalities of self-help as well as the expansion of urban immigration and in-migration, mostly of rural-to-urban resettlement in the global south. Compared to the fledgling traces of systems thinking detectable in the work of Candilis-Josic-Woods or the Smithsons, Friedman's work directly engaged the question of how systems—both megastructural and digital—could mediate the contact zones between north and south. Moreover, whereas Team Ten architectural methods and discourses suggested the paradigm of debt (the unreciprocal gift of translation), Friedman's work was better adapted to another dominant economic paradigm, that of informality, of activities that—though perhaps impelled by state, UNESCO, and World Bank programs—did not necessarily entail contracts, regular wages, official registration, or taxation. Similarly, "informal" architectures were built outside of legal systems of land titling, building code compliance, permit processes, and taxation. Friedman's work focused on ways to work informal (or autoconstructed) architecture into formal urban organizational schemata and to influence informal economic activities through developmental programs (related to UNESCO- and state-devised economic programs), all the while upholding a kind of laissez-faire approach to the architectures and livelihoods of the global south's indigent. Criticizing professional architectural practices as incompetent to accommodate the changing demands posed by growing urban populations, Friedman insisted on forms of urbanism that could meet basic housing needs without imposing rigidly controlling architectures. Underlying his work was a particular notion of a global indigent, whose material needs were deemed minimal but whose innate capacity for creative, informal adaptation was deemed vast—at least when nudged in the right direction. As such, what was needed in the global south was not fully constructed houses, basic services, formal education, or formal employment opportunities. What was needed were simply the barest of organizational rubrics capable of integrating the bricoleur's natural creativity and survivalist competencies into economic and urban infrastructural systems.

Economic austerity and laissez-faire capitalism in the global south would not, therefore, necessarily entail a lack of organizational intervention on the part of state and international actors. Instead, technologies of minimal intervention—what we could think of as infrastructures of *arrangement*—could instate modes of organization without accompanying forms of welfare provision—that is, without the infrastructural allowances of basic sanitation, nutrition, health, and education. In lieu of what has been referred to as a colonial contact zone, Friedman's work suggests a technohumanitarian zone in which infrastructures and programs intended to leave a southern indigent *free* to cobble together a livelihood and habitation would also interlace those practices into a global economic system.

Megastructures: An Infrastructure of Quasi Contact

Friedman's early conjectural architectures of the late 1950s formed the basis for the megastructural schemes he would sketch throughout the remainder of his career, a career stretching into the twenty-first century. Because the work he produced from the 1950s onward is so internally consistent (most of his basic architectural inventions being simply reiterated in different cities, ad infinitum), I will take the liberty of moving quite freely among Friedman's fragments of design and writing during those decades in order to describe how his skeletal megastructures answered to a particular set of architectural and sociopolitical problems, problems that set the stage for his forays into computer-aided design in the 1970s. The megastructures delineated the preliminary contours of the southern bricoleur, a figure that would be further fleshed out through his graphic propaganda work for UNESCO.

The vast majority of Friedman's architectural work was executed without a client and without any real prospect of being built (a notable exception being his and Eda Schaur's design for the Museum of Simple Technology in Chennai). However, shortly after moving to Paris, he and his collaborator, the engineer Jean-Pierre Pecquet, brought a proposal for low-cost housing to the attention of French administrators engaged in developing extremely low-cost housing for temporary workers in what they called "North Africa," presumably meaning colonial Algeria, although Friedman's and Pecquet's proposal for "Sahara Cabins" never mentions a specific site. Given, however, that the main selling point of the design was that its components could be easily transported by truck and required no foundations or skilled labor for their assembly, there is reason to surmise that the state's interest in the Sahara Cabins was owed to the recent discovery of petroleum fields in the sparsely inhabited deserts of inland Algeria. Indeed, it seems likely that Friedman and Pecquet may have chosen the designator "Sahara" as a way of obfuscating the likely context in which it would be adopted by the French state. Its prefabricated nature lent itself to this open-endedness: Friedman described the project as applicable to "temporary camps in under-developed regions, workers' housing for large *outre-mêr* or metropolitan construction sites, or vacation camps."[6] Similar to "Saharan," *outre-mêr* appears to be an intentionally vague term, as it literally means "overseas" but was in fact an idiomatic term for the colonial territories. Moreover, designed to house one or, at most, two persons in a space that allowed for little more than sleeping, the Sahara Cabins are clearly tailored not for families but for single adults. They were designed to serve solely as labor camps.

FIGURE 4.1. Yona Friedman and Jean-Pierre Pecquet, Sahara Cabins prototype, circa 1958. Yona Friedman Papers, box 60, folder 1, Getty Research Institute, Los Angeles (2008.M.51). Photographer unknown. Courtesy of Getty Research Institute.

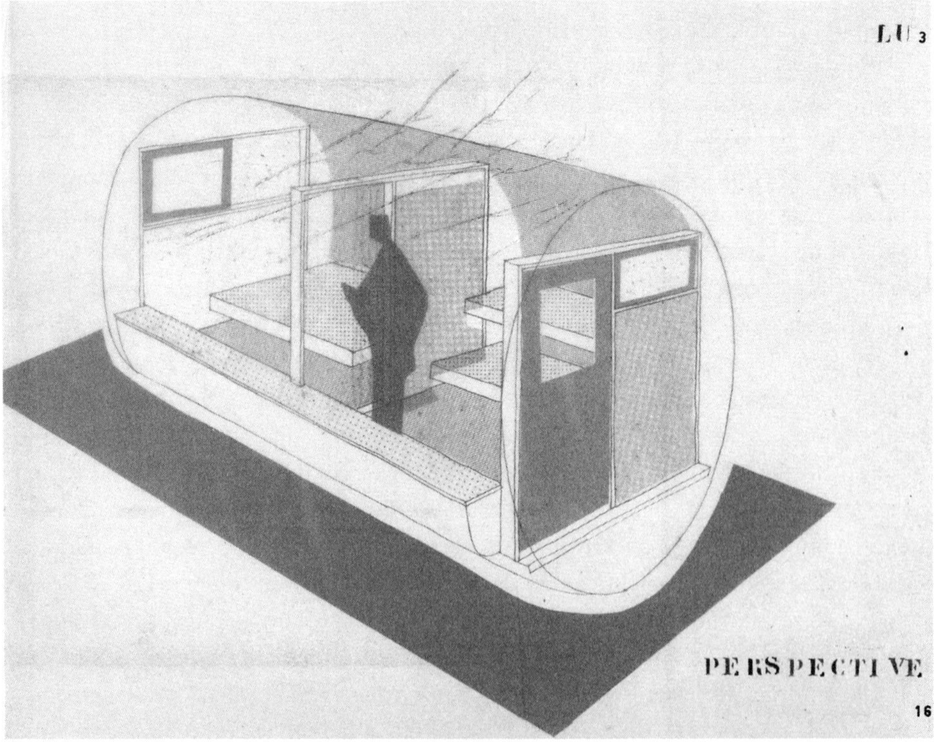

FIGURE 4.2. Yona Friedman (with Jean-Pierre Pecquet), Sahara Cabins axonometric sketch, circa 1958. Yona Friedman Papers, box 60, folder 1, Getty Research Institute, Los Angeles (2008.M.51). Courtesy of Getty Research Institute. Copyright J. Paul Getty Trust.

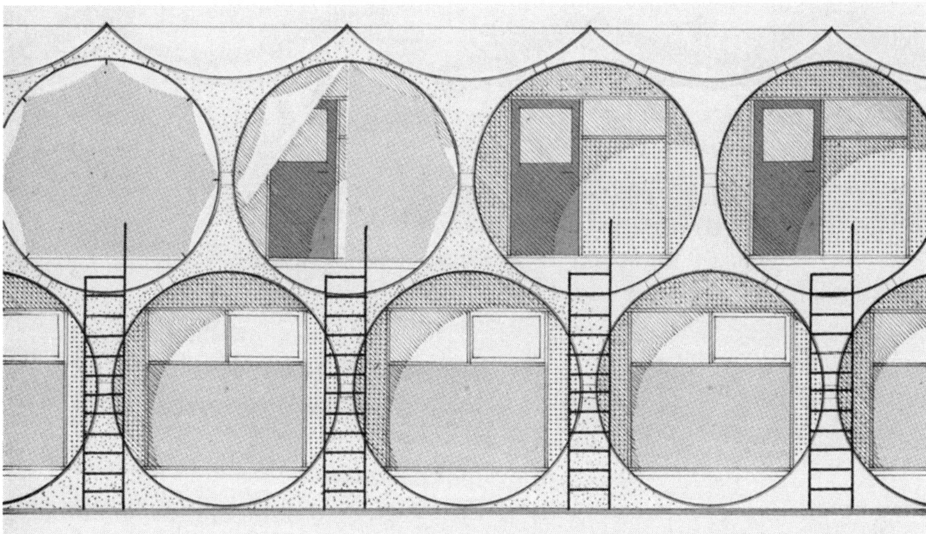

FIGURE 4.3. Yona Friedman (with Jean-Pierre Pecquet), Sahara Cabins elevation, circa 1958. Yona Friedman Papers, box 5, folder 9, Getty Research Institute, Los Angeles (2008.M.51). Courtesy of Getty Research Institute. Copyright J. Paul Getty Trust.

Supported by modest government funds, Friedman and Pecquet oversaw the construction of a cluster of several prototype units. The project did not proceed beyond this prototype for reasons that remain undocumented, though they are probably related to the escalation of Algeria's war for independence. Being the only project Friedman ever designed for a colonial rather than a postcolonial context, the Sahara Cabins were in some ways distinct from—but nonetheless seminal to—the habitational megastructures he would design for the remainder of his career, especially his well-known series of drawings, collages, and models produced over several decades that he referred to collectively as the *Ville Spatiale*. The Sahara Cabins were unique within Friedman's oeuvre in that they were to be completely prefabricated units, leaving no room for autoconstruction by the cabins' occupants, who, as temporary laborers without their families, would feel little personal investment in their accommodations. The architecture consisted of two levels of laterally stacked metal pipes, 2.68 meters in diameter and several meters long, supported by a very light metal frame and protected from solar heat by arced sections of pipe forming a metal roof over the whole structure. Each pipe constituted a dwelling unit—what Friedman called a "cell" for one or two persons; the units ranged from 2.5 meters to 4.4 meters long, thus providing the barest minimum of space needed for a human body, especially since, as the unit was circular in section, much of the interior space was effectively unusable.

The bleakness of the cabins (not only because of their constrained proportions but also because of their regimented repetition) is to be contrasted in some respects with Friedman's later work, which was marked by his penchant for whimsy and his strong conviction that domestic space should be personalized and ornamented according to the dictates of its inhabitants. Nonetheless, this reduction of habitation to the minimal requirements of bed and enclosure was formative of Friedman's ensuing tendencies to reduce the necessities of habitat to the scope of survival, representing this minimal form of existence as an authentic attribute of indigenous culture—an attribute that did not, however, preclude ornamental flourishes. As such, the megastructures Friedman would design throughout his career effectively imagined a form of life that was simultaneously bare *and* adorned. As a kind of prolepsis to Giorgio Agamben's critique of bare life, the image of the southern bricoleur suggested that a life of austere survival could be a thing of rich, whimsical beauty.[7] The latent aesthetic dimension of Agamben's critique (suggested by the terms "bare" or "naked") is significant here because, in potentially conflating aesthetic bareness with his actual object of concern—namely, biopolitical methods of depoliticization—his critique tacitly encourages aesthetic richness to be counterposed against depoliticization, which is precisely what we witness in Friedman's megastructures and his related representations of southern bricolage. Following his design for the Sahara Cabins, Friedman would obsessively produce the massive megastructural grids for which he is best known: sprawling structural scaffolds intended to be filled in by the cultural efflorescence of its autoconstructing bricoleurs.

Yet as Friedman's bricoleurs ostensibly did not require the programs of European urban modernity (such as formal education, formal housing, and formal employment), the question that haunted his life's work was: Why produce the megastructure at all, constraining this presumed bricoleur's creative and adaptative capacities within this sprawling, repetitive grid? The explicit reasons he proffered were not always entirely convincing (yes, the megastructure supported urban density, but the slums were *already* dense). Another reason is to be found within the computational drift of Friedman's thinking. Not only did he seem to detect a fruitful homology between primitive bricolage and computer programming, but the megastructure also presented a peculiar concrete analog for the burgeoning field of computer-aided design, insofar as it offered a supposedly neutral organizational structure within whose parameters a vast number of formal permutations might be explored.[8]

Friedman was one of the first—though not the only—proponents of architectural megastructures, which were explored by several European avant-garde groups of the 1960s and '70s and which had roots in the interrelated colonial urban projects of Le Corbusier, ATBAT-Afrique, and Candilis-Josic-Woods (some of these were described in chapter 3).[9] The genealogical and historical linkages between megastructures and computational frameworks have been noted by various scholars of computation, including Benjamin Bratton (who notes the utopian/dystopian dimensions of those megastructures) and Molly Wright Steenson.[10] What Friedman's work brings to light is the way the specific issue of slum urbanism in the global south informs the megastructure and, consequently, Friedman's and his colleagues' conceptions of computational interfaces. In Friedman's case, the megastructure was conceived as something like a transcriptive device rendering global-southern informality into a formally legible system.

Friedman seemed to regard the slums—or *bidonvilles*—as a site where city residents adapted to twentieth-century capitalism through the putative operations of bricolage.

At least, this is suggested by his consistent presentation of the south's urban denizens engaged in perpetual processes of adaptation to unspecified transformations. In Friedman's written work, one of the first formulations of bricolage appears in his 1978 book *Une architecture de survie: Une philosophie de la pauvreté* (An architecture of survival: A philosophy of poverty), a book based on an earlier educational *bande dessinée* produced for UNESCO, which was intended to encourage habits of self-help and survival in the periurban settlements of the global south. The book proclaims, "The bidonvilles are . . . the atelier of the future."[11] The observation is oddly prescient of twenty-first-century social scientific formulations interpreting various southern practices (mostly related to the informal economy) as sites of fecund social and economic experimentation, predictive of "resilient" modes of survival under austerity measures in the global south. As we see with Friedman's work, southern forms of urbanism have in fact long been regarded as avant-garde (even if by virtue of being simultaneously deemed *derrière-garde*), useful for suggesting how minimal state expenditures might nonetheless give rise to economic and urban practices conducive to capitalism and state power. This work proposed that economic and urban precarity was an essentially sustainable condition.

Referring to the bidonville as a model for future architectures, Friedman proceeded to describe the resourcefulness of its inhabitants:

> The unemployed person transforms himself very quickly into an "urban villager," invents for himself . . . a marginal occupation, useful to the village—and with this we witness the return to the bidonville laboratory. . . . The unemployed-as-bricoleur . . . constitutes a completely natural development.[12]

In regarding the bidonville as a "laboratory" model for the future, Friedman was treating it as an analyzable entity, certain aspects of which were to be replicated. The job of the architect, Friedman said, was to develop modes of self-help urbanism that did not hinder the slum inhabitant's natural vocation of unemployment qua bricolage. In order to devise architectures appropriate to this state of affairs, he said, the architect needed, first of all, to accept the unforeseeable aspect of the future, and second, to realize that the bidonville appeared undesirable to professional architects merely because of the arbitrary biases of their profession. That is, poverty was not a political problem but, rather, a category whose boundaries depended merely on aesthetic and semiotic conventions.[13] On the idea of the bidonville laboratory, Friedman continued, "Anything or anyone can be deemed to emit a message of intoxicating beauty, so long as the person who receives the message is open to that. A natural object or a crafted object becomes an art object from the moment that you esteem it as such."[14] He proceeded to describe how a megastructural scaffolding might accommodate the basic functions of the bidonville.

One purpose of the megastructure, then, was ostensibly to effect a representational shift in how slums were perceived by an international elite. And while those perceptions may certainly have benefited from some amendment, Friedman's corrective (proclaiming the "intoxicating beauty" of bidonvilles in general) veered toward an unwonted fetishism. The futuristic quality of the *Ville Spatiale* and *Architecture Mobile* constitute an acceptance of the slum as a permanent feature of the world's growing metropolises and, moreover, as the logical context for a future organic systematicity. Cybernetics might find its natural landing site in the slums because, for Friedman, they *already* functioned in a self-regulating fashion. The basic structures of creative bricolage already allowed the indigent urban resident to adapt to whatever urban and economic vicissitudes he encountered: "The unemployed person transforms himself very quickly into an 'urban villager,' invents for himself . . . a marginal occupation." Cybernetics is united here with an ideology of laissez-faire with which it always bore a strong kinship.[15] As will be seen with Friedman's interest in global telecommunications, the technologies wiring the cybernetic city were conceived as mere supports to indigenous semiotic tendencies (such as orality), much as megastructural domestic infrastructures were intended to support putatively indigenous tendencies of informal economic subsistence.

In an article published in 1971 alongside various architects' speculations on the technological future of cities, Friedman exhorted:

> We must . . . construct a global infrastructure that will enable any imaginable transformation of a human community. This global infrastructure should also be as unconstraining as possible. All material decisions (such as construction) or immaterial (how it is used) should be made by the occupant.
>
> My proposal thus entails the elaboration of an organizational schema for a process of choice and the elaboration of a *code,* which is to say, a *writing.* . . . Effectively, the infrastructure is nothing more than the support that permits the realization of any term within the repertoire or the transformation of any term within the repertoire into any other term.[16]

In other words, Friedman did not understand his proposed megastructural space frames only as material skeletons for facilitating an indeterminate urban future to which its inhabitants would adapt; he also saw the megastructures as semiotic scaffolding to support the perpetual transformation of "terms." Autoconstructed (or "informal") housing constituted a code waiting to be deciphered, with the megastructure functioning as something like the invisible grammatic and syntactic rules, allowing the "terms" to be recognizable as such, as so many elements within a coherent system that, however, could only be parsed when cast into the putatively transcriptive device of the megastructure. The simple structural systematicity of the latter would apparently clarify the otherwise illegible systematicity of autoconstructed housing. Friedman's description foreshadows the mania among urbanists, architects, and social scientists for deciphering the "logics" of slums, a tendency that would emerge more distinctly in the twenty-first century.

In this passage, Friedman's language strongly echoed Lévi-Strauss's usage of the term "bricolage," developed in *The Savage Mind* (*La pensée sauvage*) to explain the workings of myth and of human cognition in general.[17] Perceiving myths as operating through a flexible structure, which encouraged substitutions and transformations, Lévi-Strauss likened this semiotic malleability to processes of bricolage through which any objects at hand could be cobbled into a new configuration to achieve a desired goal, a process he distinguished from engineered planning in much the way that Marx had distinguished between the instinctual architectures of bees and the architectural plans of humans.[18] What the megastructure sought to instate was a preliminary mechanism through which to incite a natural and systematic process of autoconstruction and subsistence, a mechanism that (thanks to the megastructure's semiotic framing) would no longer be deemed abnormal or entropic. The mechanism would lead to a normalized bidonville that, through its newfound legibility, could be tweaked as needed while leaving the poor more or less to their own devices—that is, allowing the *form* of the informal to be read as such and thus understood as a formal and permissible component of urbanism.

This is not to deny a compelling and utopian aspect to the megastructural proposals, in that they seem to supplant the precarious institution of squatting with an official right to occupation and autoconstruction, although Friedman never explicitly addresses the problem of land rights, which is largely what underlies the precarity of the slums. Indeed, in this respect the megastructures carried certain implications that went well beyond what Friedman probably intended, the gridded demarcation of each occupant's space anticipating the way autoconstructed housing would increasingly be submitted to formal rubrics of property demarcation in the proceeding century. Although this transformation would be effected not through physical infrastructures but, rather, through new technologies and social science–based means of property mapping, Friedman's megastructures, by delineating clear spatial boundaries to each plot, suggest (unintentionally) that autoconstructed houses could be easily integrated into the state's system of private property. Indeed, the megastructural grid—with its uniform dimensions—even hints at one of the cynical rationales underlying the conversion of usufruct properties into state-sanctioned private property: namely, to render more legally viable the displacement of residents to other distant urban sites with identically sized plots. In other words, by so clearly demarcating spatial *quantity*, the megastructural grids seem to support the assumption of fungibility between one autoconstructed site and another, neglecting the varying values and functions accruing to different urban sites. The fact that this fungibility—and the displacement it might facilitate—was not Friedman's intention does not change the fact that the designs lent themselves to such possibilities.

Thus, these imagined structures are ambiguous: on the one hand, they seem to proclaim an urban indigent's right to the city (which was Friedman's likely intention) but, on the other hand, they suggest that this right could only be acknowledged if autoconstructed urbanism was guided by a top-down systematicity and legibility. (This is distinct, however, from James C. Scott's well-known formulation of "high modernism," insofar as legibility and systematicity were intentionally partial operations, meant to minimize interference in the informal, self-reliant practices of an urban indigent.)[19] The megastructure, in enunciating the slum's potential systematic organization, also suggested it as a domain assimilable to burgeoning technological regimes. While Friedman's rhetoric in many ways espouses a respect for the self-determining prerogatives of a postcolonial indigent, there is an uneasy slippage between the concept of Third World *self-determination* and the cybernetic construct of *self-regulation,* the latter appearing in Friedman's work as a kind of neoliberalism *avant la lettre*. The slippage would be all the more evident in Friedman's proposals for modes of global communication that sought to work *around* multilingualism and nonliteracy.

In stressing the adaptive freedom of the global indigent that was to occupy his proposed megastructures, Friedman was unwittingly setting up a representational framework through which conditions of poverty could be construed as having been freely chosen. Friedman's emphasis on the semiotic aspect of the megastructure (that is, as a "writing") revealed the ways in which that global indigent was really being transcribed within a representational system that would enable poverty to be differently encoded (the megastructure being "an organizational schema for a process of choice and the elaboration of a code"). This tendency would come to the fore circa 1973 through Friedman's collaboration with the architect Nicholas Negroponte, who, having mimicked Friedman's megastructural proposals in his own student thesis project, subsequently invited Friedman to work on a project with the Architecture Machine Group, which he had just cofounded at MIT.[20] According to Friedman, the ensuing project was based on his existing architectural self-help proposals; the Architecture Machine Group essentially translated his proposals into computer software. The resulting program, Flatwriter, in aiming to reconcile the self-determination of a global indigent with the formal regimentation of the megastructure, effectively reimagined autoconstruction as a matter of abstract spatial configuration—and thus a problem of geometric arrangement—rather than a matter of social negotiations related to land tenure, economic needs, architectural regulation, and power relations.

Insofar as Friedman regarded the Flatwriter software as simply a scaffolding to support extant practices of autoconstruction (similar to his megastructures in this respect), the software's intended intervention seemed to lie at least as much in the domain of representation as in the domain of urban practice.[21] And, vis à vis MIT research initiatives, the effectivity of this representation had to do less with concerns about urban poverty and more to do with the concerns of computational research. As will be detailed in subsequent chapters, the Architecture Machine Group's efforts to develop computers capable of capturing a southern market helped steer the development of graphic user interfaces, construing the computer as a domain of easy instinctual *play,* thus leading away from the strictures of programming language. A global indigent was thus an inspiration for media developments that were to have a universal appeal, the alleged creative instincts of that indigent being indicative of a global user's underlying psychic proclivities.

Interface

It is not clear what led Friedman, between 1960 and 1963, to propose a collection of unsolicited schemes for postcolonial West Africa in collaboration with the engineer

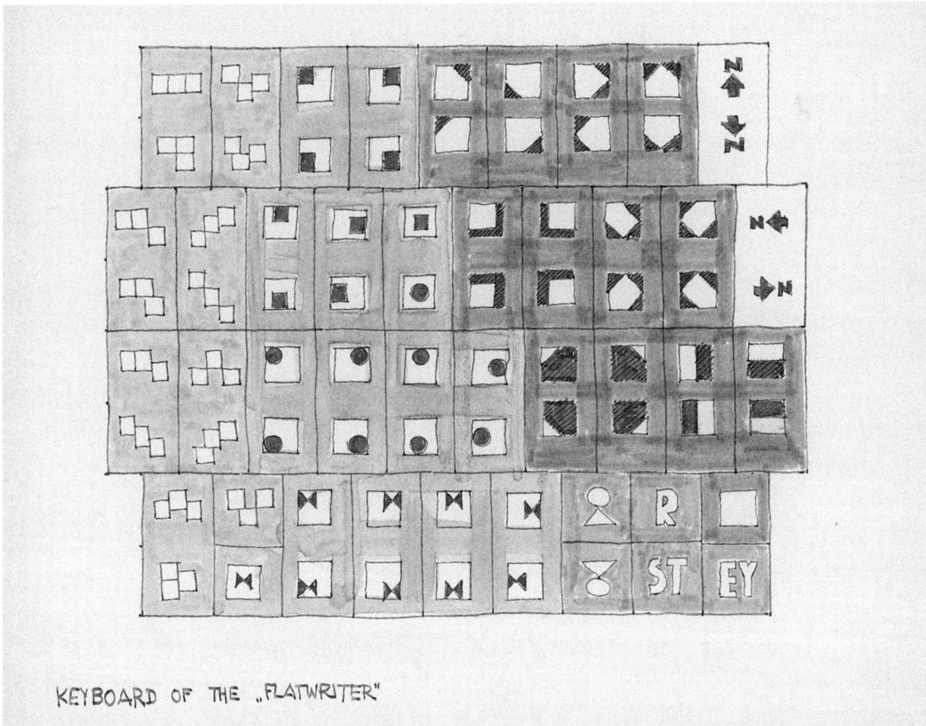

FIGURE 4.4. Yona Friedman, sketch for Flatwriter keyboard, circa 1970. Yona Friedman Papers, box 61, folder 16, Getty Research Institute, Los Angeles (2008.M.51). Courtesy of Getty Research Institute. Copyright J. Paul Getty Trust.

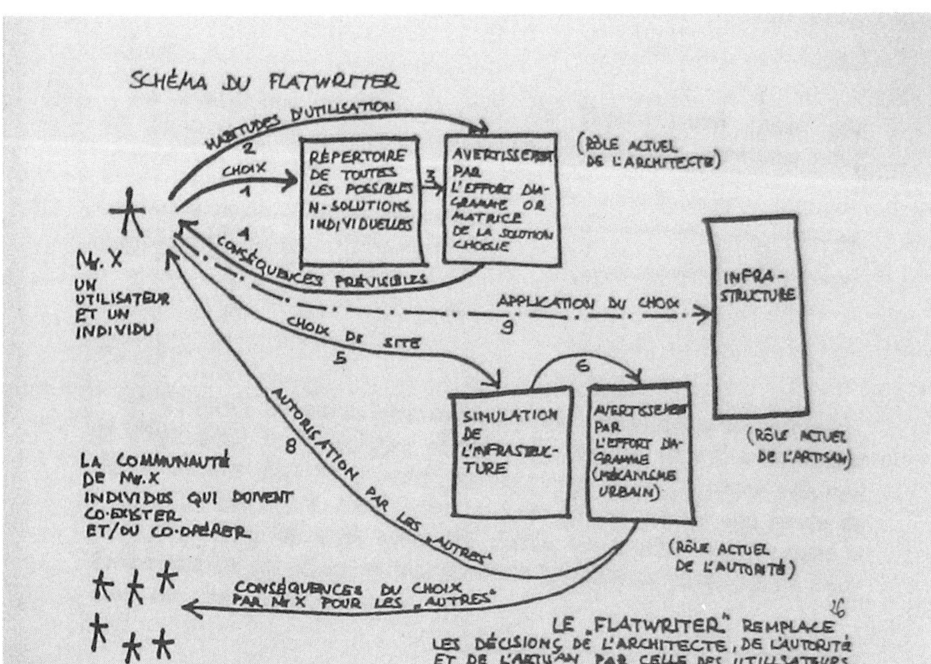

FIGURE 4.5. Yona Friedman, schema of Flatwriter, circa 1971. From *Progressive Architecture* 52 (1971): 98–101. Yona Friedman Papers, box 5, folder 9, Getty Research Institute, Los Angeles (2008.M.51). Courtesy of Getty Research Institute. Copyright J. Paul Getty Trust.

Serge Ketoff and the city planner (and later UNESCO administrator) Roger Aujame;[22] the projects were grouped together in Friedman's records under the designation "African Projects."[23] Whether he was following the lead of his former Israeli colleagues in engaging in opportunities offered by African development or simply wished to participate in the heady context of postcolonial liberation, Friedman proposed several projects: a residential district for Abidjan in 1960 (more or less contemporaneously with the advent of Ivoirien independence); a similar district for Niamey, the new capital of Niger; and a transnational "African Bridge City," which—going beyond Le Corbusier's similar but smaller-scaled scheme for colonial Algiers—combined urban architectures, ports, and highways into a single megastructural network that spanned between several West African coastal cities and the region's interior conurbations.[24] This last project, responding to pan-African calls for massive infrastructural development, never went beyond the most rudimentary schematization. The housing projects were worked out in a bit more detail and offered a fairly novel treatment of the phenomenon of inter- and intranational urban migration in West Africa's rapidly growing cities. They engaged the question of how linguistically and culturally diverse groups, often coming from rural areas, were to cohabit in these dense urban centers and form communities despite their diversity, an issue that reflected Kwame Nkrumah's ambitions that Accra's new satellite city of Tema could be designed to culturally integrate diverse ethnonational groups into modern Ghanaian society.[25] The treatment of this issue by Friedman, Aujame, and Ketoff anticipated the ways new media technologies would come to mediate cultural diversity in the decades to come.

According to Friedman and his colleagues, the main question driving the Abidjan project was how to "rationally regroup" the inhabitants in such a way as to "represent the beginnings [*amorce*] of a neighborhood." In 1960, when this proposal was drafted, the term *amorce* had not yet come to refer to the self-booting mechanism of a computer, although, in a related usage, it did refer to an ignitable fuse and to specific devices for initiating more complex processes. In many respects it is simply an etymological coincidence that the designers should employ a term that would soon come to refer to the mechanism by which a personal computer reinitiated its programs. Nonetheless, there is a genealogical linkage between the way Friedman conceived of the architectures of the global south and the way issues of computer programming were contemporaneously thought of at the time, both being characterized by cybernetics and systems thinking. Friedman's collaborative Africa Projects set the stage for his subsequent forays into computer programming roughly five years later. The *amorce* suggested a mode of interfering without interference, of booting up a system through a program that let the system effectively reboot itself, that allowed for self-initiative and autonomy *within* a defined program.

The housing proposals for Abidjan and Niamey conceived of postcolonial independence as requiring two contradictory conditions: on the one hand, the freedom to pursue cultural practices that eschewed the homogenizing tendencies of modernization; on the other hand, the organization and structuring of that freedom so that it would self-regulate, thus systematizing society in a way that relied on foreign expertise and

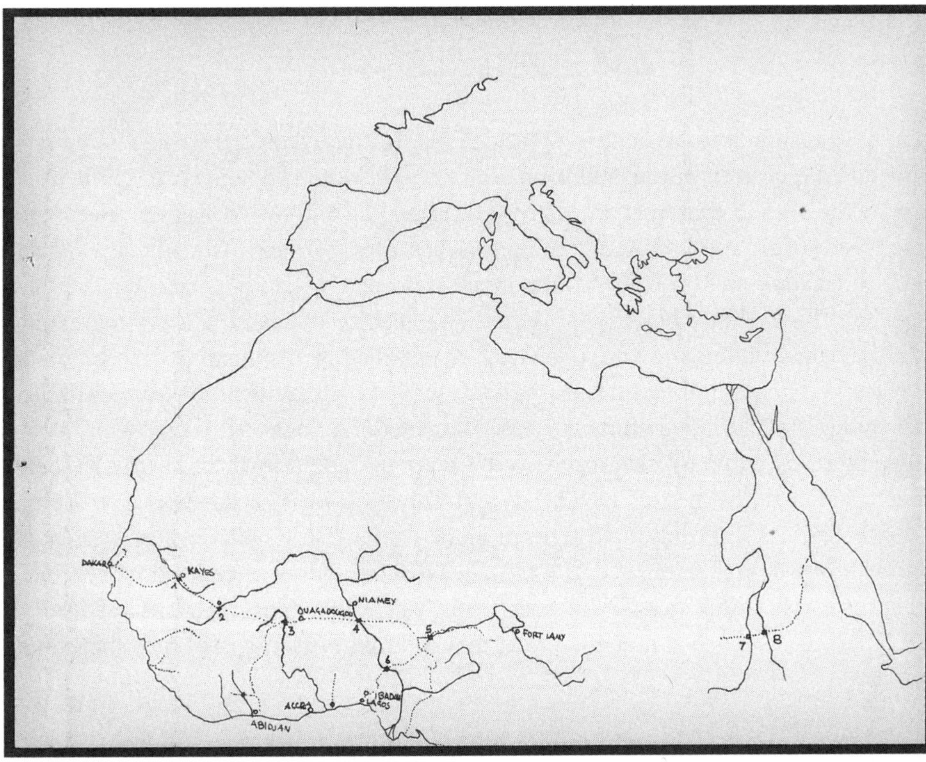

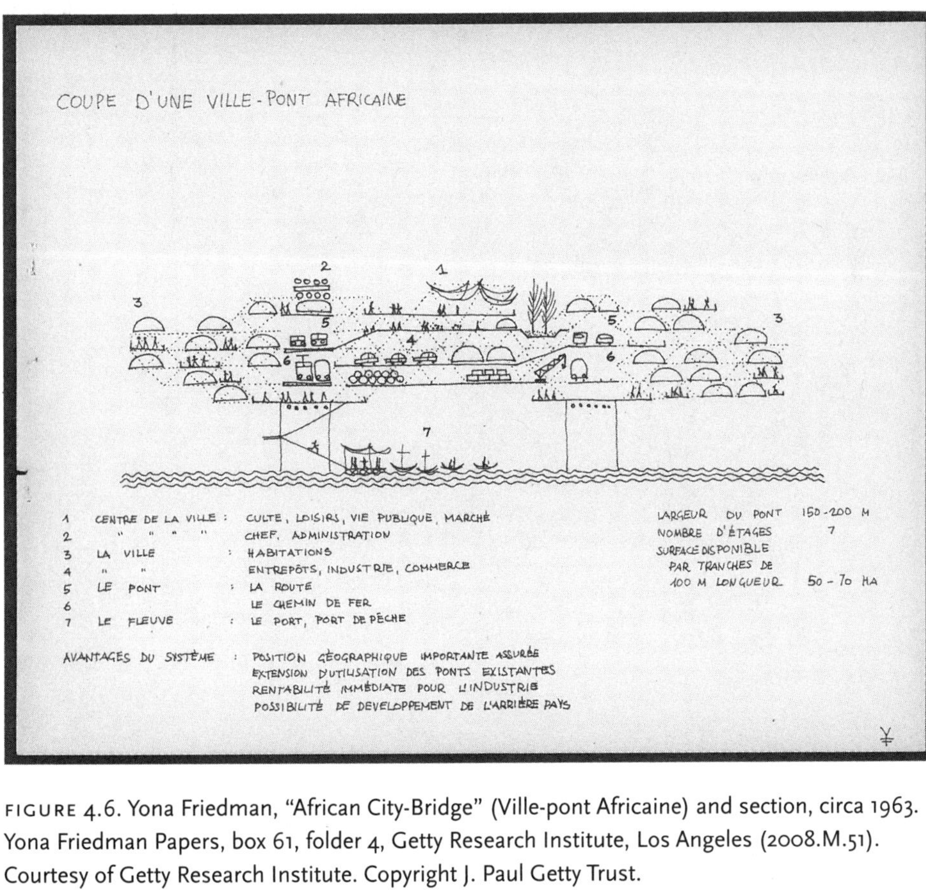

FIGURE 4.6. Yona Friedman, "African City-Bridge" (Ville-pont Africaine) and section, circa 1963. Yona Friedman Papers, box 61, folder 4, Getty Research Institute, Los Angeles (2008.M.51). Courtesy of Getty Research Institute. Copyright J. Paul Getty Trust.

techniques for its deep, structuring foundations. In this respect, the usage of *amorce* in the domain of beekeeping is illuminating: it refers to the slip of wax or fabric used to incite the bees to construct a hive. In fact, Friedman and his colleagues referred to these West African megastructural designs as beehives, perhaps in a nod to the earlier European scheme in North Africa discussed in chapter 3, Candilis-Josic-Woods's Nid d'abeilles ("bees' nest") housing project.[26] The beehive epitomized a self-regulating system of construction and social behavior. As clarified by his ensuing description of the Nigerian Home in Abidjan, Friedman was indicating that the proposed megastructure would establish the rudimentary mechanisms of a construction program to be subsequently taken up by local residents, built upon, transformed, and expanded over time, "adapted to [the inhabitants'] needs and truly evolving."[27]

Regarding the concentration of immigrant workers in Abidjan's port district of Treichville, Friedman, Ketoff, and Aujame noted that the convergence of a dozen ethnicities in the dense slums around the docks gave Treichville a "cosmopolitan and impersonal character."[28] Their scheme for what they referred to as a "spatial neighborhood"

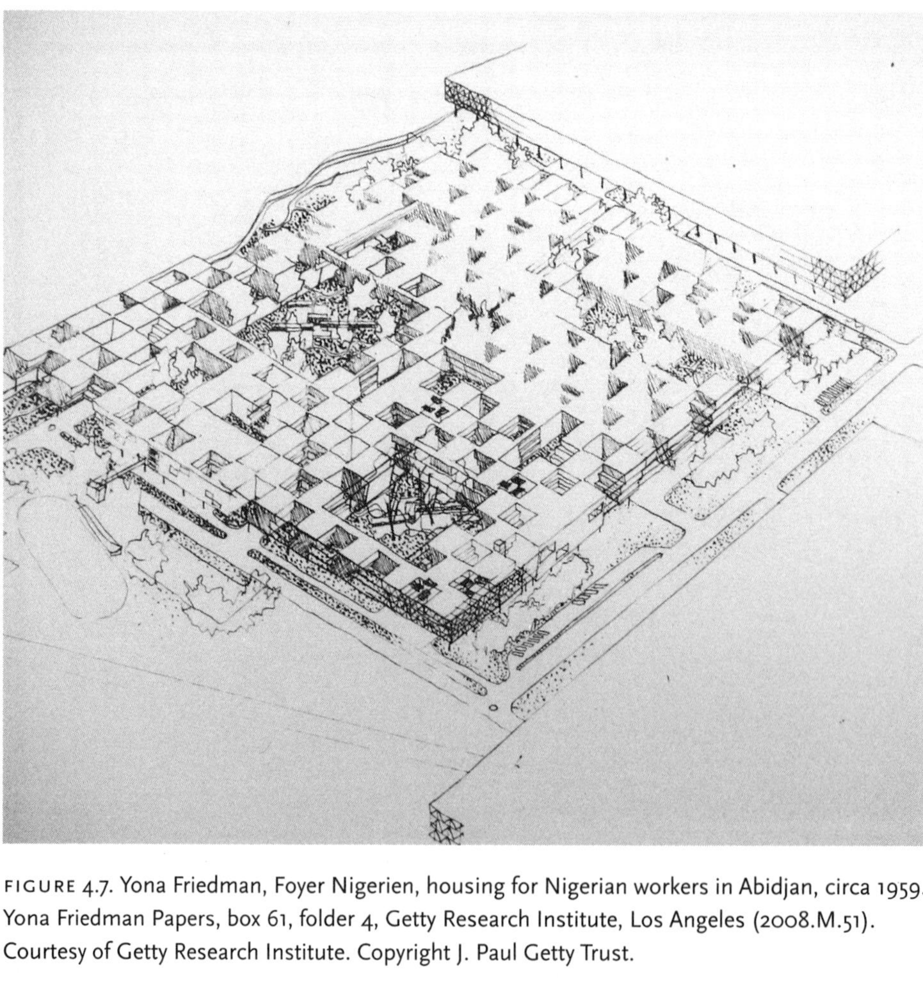

FIGURE 4.7. Yona Friedman, Foyer Nigerien, housing for Nigerian workers in Abidjan, circa 1959. Yona Friedman Papers, box 61, folder 4, Getty Research Institute, Los Angeles (2008.M.51). Courtesy of Getty Research Institute. Copyright J. Paul Getty Trust.

for Niamey also grappled with the cosmopolitan aspect of West Africa's cities, proposing a dense pattern of interlocking ethnolinguistic groups. Rather than designating a single area for each ethnolinguistic group, the design fragmented each group into smaller clusters and then dispersed these ethnolinguistic microclusters throughout the proposed megastructural block. The scheme thus struck a middle path between integration and ethnic ghettoization, as it negotiated between an agenda of cultural preservation and the production of a more globalized, cosmopolitan urban culture.

The authors of the design did not explicitly address the problematic status that the colonial lingua franca would have surely played in these urban conditions, but the status of French (and to some extent English) seems implicit to their scheme. In fragmenting the linguistic groups so as to encourage sociability across linguistic differences, the likely emergence of a local dominant language is diminished, albeit with the probable effect of exacerbating the continued reliance on French. The authors did, however, propose a *nonlinguistic* device for bringing people together. One of Friedman's sketches shows a large community space accommodating a few large and mysterious mobile elements. These include a rotating *tableau* (indicating either a "panel" or a "painting," thus leaving open the question of medium), a sliding *tableau,* and a "flashing reflector" (also a large rotating architectural element). Friedman shows these devices distributed along the perimeter of a sixteen-square-meter open space, functioning as spectacular screens producing an array of shifting effects. Striving against the creation of ethnolinguistic enclaves, the authors of the scheme broke up these linguistic communities

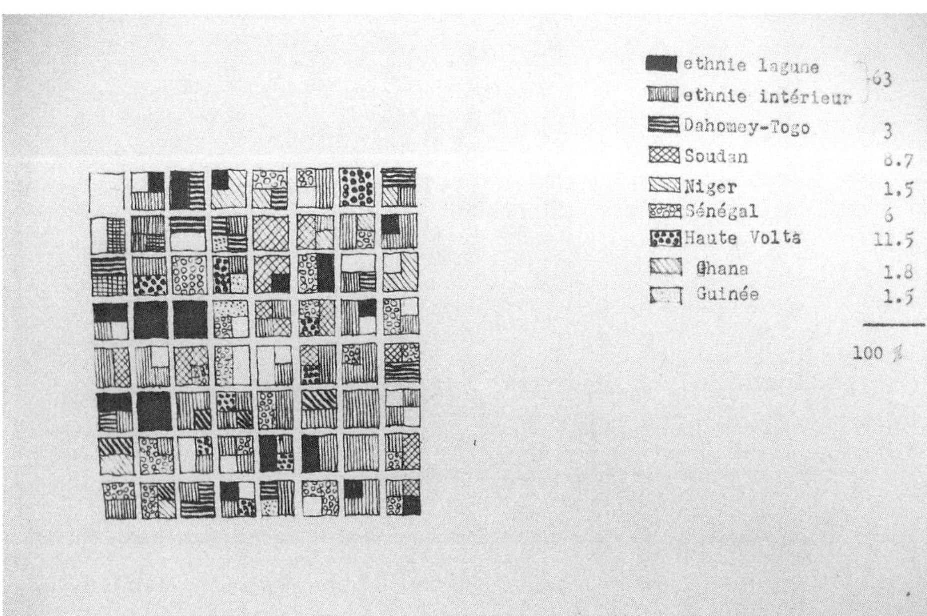

FIGURE 4.8. Yona Friedman, Housing for Niamey, circa 1960. Yona Friedman Papers, box 60, folder 7, Getty Research Institute, Los Angeles (2008.M.51). Courtesy of Getty Research Institute. Copyright J. Paul Getty Trust.

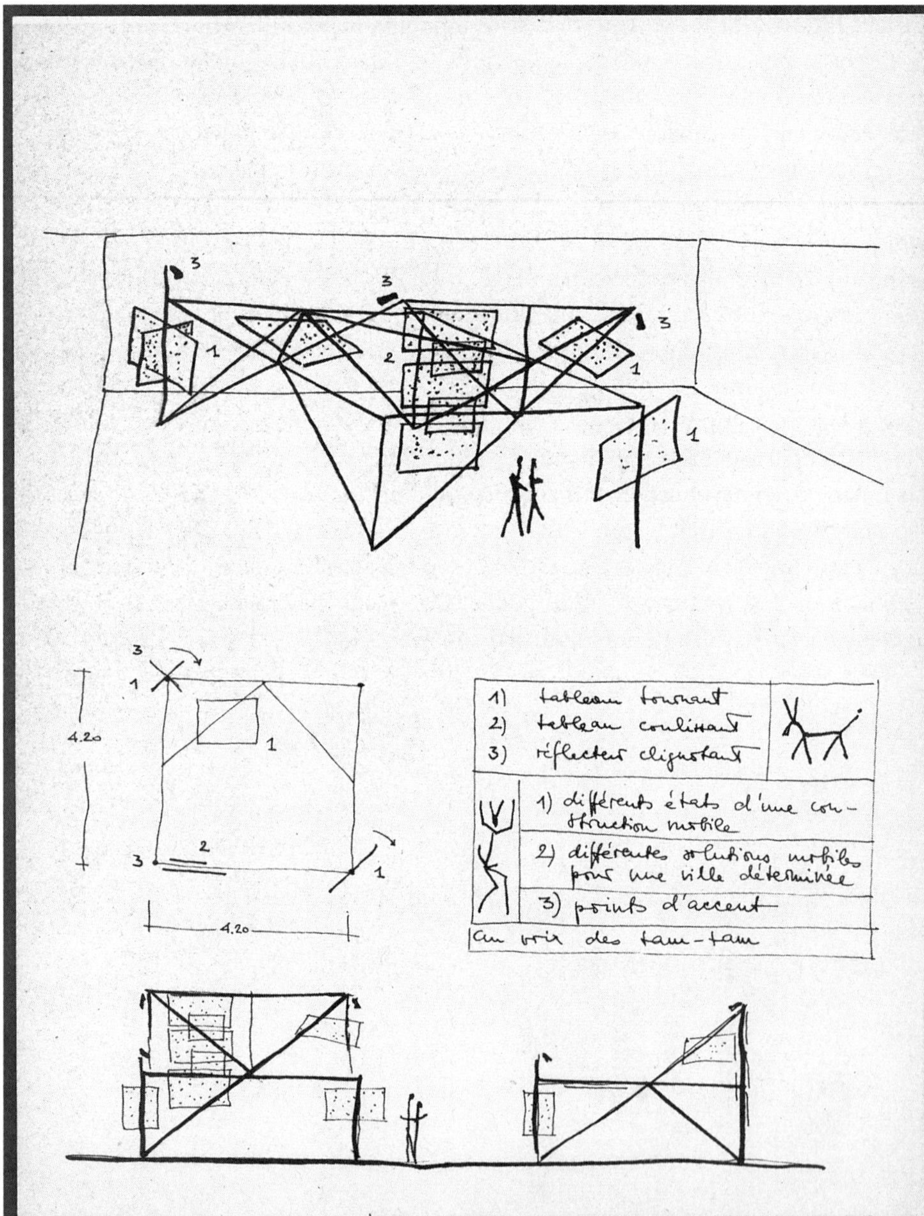

FIGURE 4.9. Yona Friedman, mobile *tableaux* and flashing reflector, Housing for Niamey, circa 1960. Yona Friedman Papers, box 60, folder 7, Getty Research Institute, Los Angeles (2008.M.51). Courtesy of Getty Research Institute. Copyright J. Paul Getty Trust.

and—presumably in an effort to address the ensuing linguistic diversity—instated an immersive visual environment of revolving, flashing imagery, suggestive of electronic media (notably, in a city where no substantial electronic infrastructure yet existed). Eschewing the problematic issue of the colonial lingua franca, Friedman and his colleagues proposed a new quasi lingua franca, a pentecostal technology for supplanting language with visual spectacle.

The shift from print media to visual and audio media had for decades at this point constituted a strategy of colonial governance in contexts of linguistic diversity and nonliteracy.[29] (In sub-Saharan Africa especially, colonial administrators and settlers had actively and often violently suppressed education and literacy.) Friedman was hardly sympathetic to colonial governance (the Sahara Cabins notwithstanding); however, at the intersection of his cosmopolitan leanings and his romantic conception of indigenous cultural authenticity can be detected a belief in the special appropriateness of electronic media for the global south, insofar as those media were deemed akin to oral culture, and insofar as they represented a common aesthetic and semiotic mode cutting across residents' different languages. In his ensuing career, Friedman would often focus on mediatic methods to conserve cultural "tradition" amid globalization, anticipating late twentieth-century proposals for the design and marketing of digital interfaces, as will be discussed in the book's final chapters.

In 1969 Friedman's erstwhile collaborator, Aujame, joined UNESCO, where he worked on educational programs primarily in the global south. Within a few years of Aujame's appointment, Friedman began to produce for UNESCO a series of didactic educational *bandes dessinées* for distribution among communities with low rates of literacy. This medium, which would later be replicated in some of Friedman's own architectural publications, foregrounded the reasoning subsequently applied (by Friedman's protégé Negroponte, inter alia) to the development of the digital graphic user interface. The pamphlets generally explicated the virtues of various low-tech means of habitation and subsistence intended to improve the lives of rural or peri-urban communities, bearing titles such as "Modest Program for Surviving in a World in Crisis," "Weeds into Wealth," "Wasteland into Farmland," and "Simple Technology."[30] The goal of reforming local practices without offering any material incentives placed on the pamphlets the burden of not just explanation but, above all, seduction, a burden that—given the pamphlets' rather mundane didactic content—would have to be carried largely by the medium itself.

To give some historic context here: mid-twentieth-century projects of agricultural and economic reform initiated by colonial officials had often transpired through the vehicle of demonstration farms (where, for example, agricultural officers would show to the colonized new techniques of cultivation or soil conservation). However, because such demonstrations often failed to convince their audiences, colonial officials—and subsequently developmental regimes—explored the attractions of other media (such as film), at times citing the need to replicate "native" media.[31] At the same time, a lack of communications and transportation infrastructures in the areas targeted by such programs constrained the viability of employing various popular media, such as radio, television, and film. Read against this background, Friedman's low-tech medium—that is, the pamphlets, along with another media innovation he suggested, the wall journal—can be seen to correspond closely to Friedman's computational work with MIT's Architecture Machine Group. The eventual shift from alphanumeric keyboard input to indexical input and from programming language to graphic user interfaces answered to an explicitly articulated demand on the part of digital researchers to capture a growing southern market for computer exports, as well as to a more implicit demand to render computer use into a compellingly easy and instinctually pleasurable activity instead of a disciplined task—essentially, to make the experience of using computers more like the experience of watching television.

Friedman's written work throughout the 1970s and '80s repeatedly referred socioeconomic problems back to the issue of communication. In 1978, he prepared for UNESCO the proposal "UNESCO for All: Project for Vernacularizing UNESCO's Works Sectors." In it he described the potential uses for a low-cost "wall journal," a large mural-sized poster affixed to an exterior wall in a visible, public area, using cartoons to depict useful information on what Friedman referred to as the "science of survival."[32] According to Friedman, the medium answered the need for a nonliterate medium but, more generally, it was addressed simply to "the man on the street," who might be literate or not. The goal was to "transform his behavior," and as that man tended to be distrustful of the kinds of reforms UNESCO was advocating, it was important that he be given "proof" in lieu of mere abstractions. As proofs of the efficacy of the proposed reforms, Friedman suggested that drawings could translate mere abstractions into the domain of personal "experiences."[33]

This is a trick of the medium. What was being offered to "the man on the street" was not "proof" but, rather, the translation of international developmental programs into a kind of pseudovernacular, intended to speak implicitly to its audiences' "personal experiences" (even though intended for global distribution). The proposed *bandes dessinées* were to *nativize* UNESCO's developmental programs in order to overcome distrust. This was not to be effected only through the (pseudo)folksy idiom of stick-figure imagery (designed, Friedman wrote, to be easy to copy, though also surely intended to *look* nonexpert); distrust was also to be overcome by dint of an imagistic power to create fictional identifications between the reader/viewer and the depicted human figures. Such fictional identifications are not to be confused with Benedict Anderson's "imagined communities" produced largely through fictional literature, as the whole point was to short-circuit both the literary medium and the social entity of "community" (national or otherwise) in the interests of rapidly implementing international developmental initiatives.[34] This identification, then, was to be far more simple than that of an imagined community: in lieu of the grammar of instruction—be it in the form of "Do this" imperatives or technical drawings—the *bande dessinée* offered a playful rendition of people engaged in the proposed activity. The point was not, as Friedman claimed, to *prove* the efficacy of that activity; it was to render that activity in a pleasurable light through the ludic aspect of the graphic style.[35]

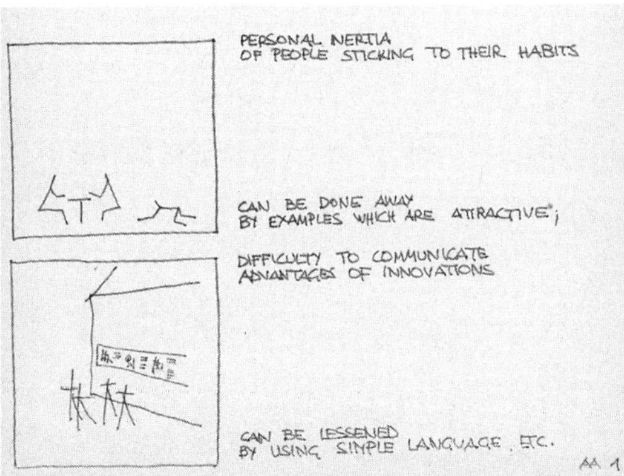

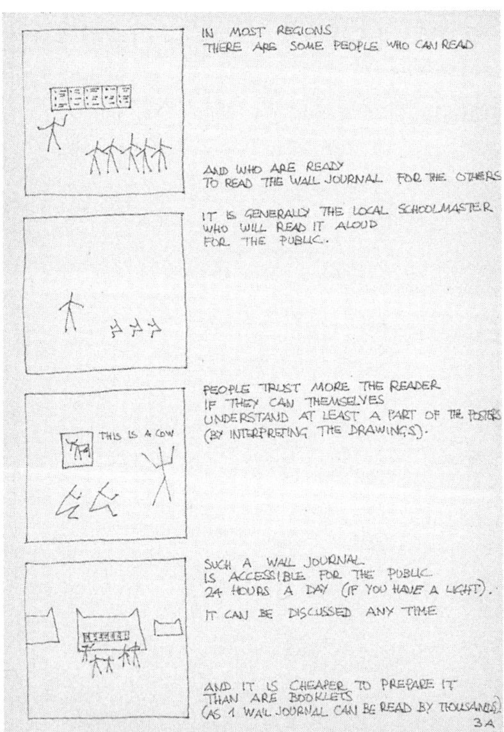

FIGURE 4.10. Yona Friedman, excerpts from UNESCO pamphlets, 1976. *(Top and right) A Modest Program for Survival in a World of Crisis,* Yona Friedman Papers, box 21, folder 5, Getty Research Institute, Los Angeles (2008.M.51). *(Bottom) Manual for Inducing Popular Creativity into Science,* Yona Friedman Papers, box 21, folder 10, Getty Research Institute, Los Angeles (2008.M.51). Images copyright J. Paul Getty Trust.

After all, the need for literacy was minimized, not wholly eliminated, by the medium of these *bandes dessinées,* for each frame bore a textual caption without which it would be quite impossible to make sense of the pamphlet. Friedman acknowledged as much, advising that nonliterate consumers of the *bandes dessinées* would require a literate person's assistance. Friedman explained that as the literate person read to the nonliterate majority, the imagery would allow the nonliterate viewer to detect any serious discrepancy between the interpretation and the image, thus preventing the reader from "abusing the ignorance of the illiterate."[36] Although displacing the real object of distrust (from the authors of international development programs onto the local literate

FIGURE 4.11. Yona Friedman, excerpt from *Inducing Popular Creativity into Science,* UNESCO pamphlet, circa 1976. Yona Friedman Papers, box 21, folder 10, Getty Research Institute, Los Angeles (2008.M.51). Courtesy of Getty Research Institute. Copyright J. Paul Getty Trust.

reader of the text), Friedman's words nonetheless reveal that the main efficacy of the visual medium lies in its ability to dispel distrust. The proposed *bandes dessinées* and wall journals were to function as Trojan horses, delivering within a playful and seemingly unexpert idiom the transformative agenda of international expertise. In fact, what these colloquial media generally promoted were methods of living under programs of severe economic austerity, an important detail to which I will return momentarily. In this respect, there was a strong kinship between Friedman's megastructures and his propaganda work for UNESCO, as both sought to intervene and organize without *appearing* to impose European programs and objectives onto postcolonial societies.

Friedman's preoccupation with media in relation to the livelihoods and habitations of a southern indigent found its most cogent architectural realization with a project sponsored by the United Nations University (UNU) for the Museum of Simple Technology in Chennai, designed jointly with the Austrian architect Eda Schaur. In 1983, shortly after conceiving of the project, Friedman and Schaur cofounded the Communication Centre of Scientific Knowledge for Self-Reliance (CCSK) under UNU. Schaur's expertise was in lightweight constructions, and she was engaged at the time as an architecture instructor at India's National Institute of Design in Ahmedabad, where she developed an interest in the use of locally available construction materials, following state initiatives to identify alternatives to steel.[37]

Drawing on that knowledge, Schaur and Friedman designed for the museum a series of bamboo dome structures supported on timber columns with brick-infill walls. The bamboo mats draped over the roof structure were built by local basketmakers and, like the bamboo structure, were wrapped in aluminum foil. Bamboo had a special significance here as it was, on the one hand, a cheap and ubiquitous material (a material Friedman promoted for diverse economic and architectural applications in his UNESCO work), while, on the other hand, its sparkling aluminum wrapping made it difficult to identify as bamboo. The museum complex looked something like a village of modest brick huts topped by a glittering sculptural filigree. This rather surreal effect seemed to derive from the mediatic program of the architecture.

In a short article, "Why a Communication Centre," published in India's *Journal of Extension Systems,* Friedman states that the mission of the Centre was to

> make accessible for the disfavored such knowledge of scientific origin which might enable them to improve their life conditions, making use . . . of those means they can dispose of without cash expense. . . .
>
> The staff animating the [CCSK] must combine competence about new scientific achievements with substantial sociological experience in order to guess what innovations might be accepted by the target public. Besides that, the same team has to be expert in communication techniques and in media, sophisticated or simple.
>
> The communication techniques implemented by the Centre include inexpensive presentations like wall-journals or posters, more sophisticated ones like animated cartoon features, and finally, some highly complex operations like the Museum of Simple Technology.[38]

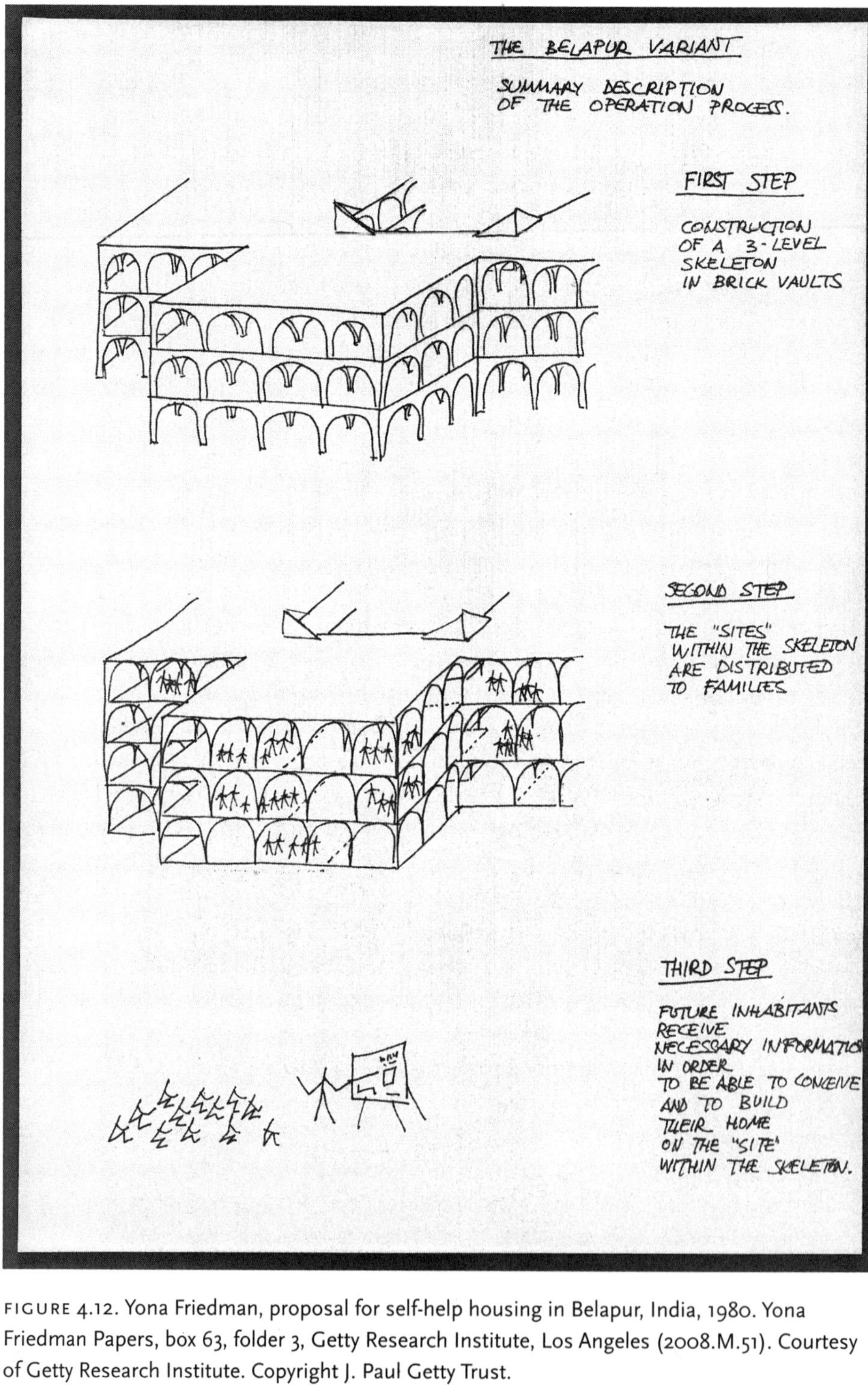

FIGURE 4.12. Yona Friedman, proposal for self-help housing in Belapur, India, 1980. Yona Friedman Papers, box 63, folder 3, Getty Research Institute, Los Angeles (2008.M.51). Courtesy of Getty Research Institute. Copyright J. Paul Getty Trust.

In its roles as a medium of demonstration—that is, a life-size exposition of "simple" architectural techniques—and as a platform for other exhibitions, the museum's architecture had to perform a difficult double function, similar to what Friedman had described as UNESCO's general semiotic challenge in converting a global indigent to its programs. The museum's architecture had to seduce while simultaneously presenting itself as a humble extension of existing local practices. Hence, it had to act as the material counterpart to the disciplinary hybridity required of the CCSK's staff, combining technoscientific expertise with a locally attuned anthropological discernment of native proclivities. "The presentation," Friedman continued, "has to appeal to knowledge already possessed by the target public."[39] This mandate to *appear* to tell the locals what they already knew (while in fact instructing them in programs of modernization) anticipated developmental initiatives in decades to follow, including the spread of digital media.

The requirement that the museum demonstrate easy replicability while also communicating its own superior status—that it be both accessible and seductive, familiar but transformational—effectively meant that the museum had to appear simultaneously cheap and ostentatious, a trick accomplished by the tinseled bamboo. There is a temporal sequence to the way the eye is drawn in by this architecture, the design making strategic use of the primordial lure of metallic luster. First, the eye is seduced

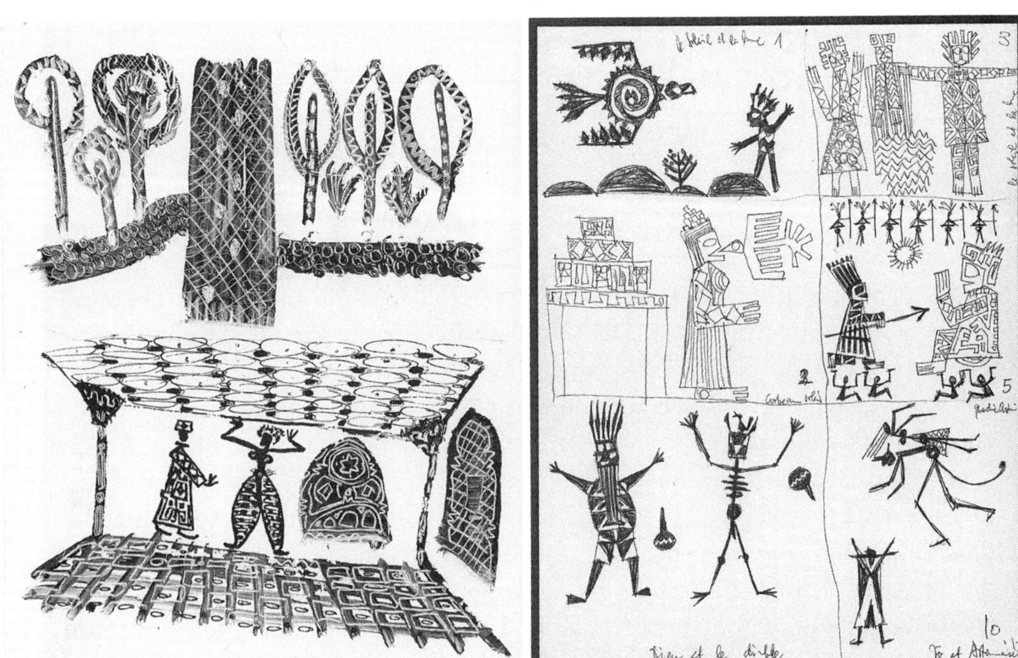

FIGURE 4.13. Yona Friedman, puppet sketches related to popular demonstration media for the Museum of Simple Technology, Chennai, circa 1984. Yona Friedman Papers, box 93, folder 6, Getty Research Institute, Los Angeles (2008.M.51). Courtesy of Getty Research Institute. Copyright J. Paul Getty Trust.

FIGURE 4.14. Museum for Simple Technology, Chennai, 1986. Designed by Yona Friedman and Eda Schaur. Photographer unknown. Courtesy of Foundation Yona Friedman.

by the glittering filigree; then the eye travels to the homely brick base. The indigent are to be baited with the shimmer of material plenitude before being resolved to the more parsimonious materiality of brick. Friedman specified that the Centre's proposed self-improvement methods should cost no money, a theme repeated in various UNESCO pamphlets such as "Weeds into Wealth."[40] In discussing the self-help agenda of the Communication Centre, Friedman explained that the capital India saved through impoverished populations' "subsistence efforts" could then "be invested into the development of more sophisticated means of production" in other areas of the economy.[41] That is, a subsistence economy for the subaltern would enable industrial development for wealthier segments of society. Modernization is imagined as coexistent with its opposite—indeed, as dependent on a nonliterate subaltern living in conditions of mere subsistence. As such, the semiotic interfaces anticipated by *bandes dessinées* and wall journals are complemented by the fabrication of a southern subject appropriate to those interfaces: the subsistence bricoleur who is oriented toward a realm existing in the interstices between modernity and "tradition," where she or he is to imaginatively enfold the glittering detritus of late capitalist consumerism into the mundane business of daily survival.

Bricolage as Structural Adjustment

In the early 1980s, Friedman collaborated with the conceptual artist Jean-Pierre Giovanelli on an art project he called "an intervention on the scrap" (*une intervention sur le déchet*).[42] The project entailed a four-phase process: First, during the "Phase of Accumulation," the artists amassed what they described as scrap parts from "our sophisticated technologies." During the subsequent "Phase of Transformation," these scraps were distributed among "artisanal populations" in Africa and were there subjected to a process of "free transformation." For the subsequent "Phase of Recuperation," the altered detritus was shipped back to Europe. And finally, during the "Phase of Reinjection," the resulting art objects were exhibited and sold at a Parisian gallery, with the financial proceeds remitted to Africa. The project suggested an ambivalent economic model, anticipating new paradigms of self-help architecture and labor. Although the project presupposed a global division of labor based on global economic inequality, it also offered the potential to lessen this inequality, stipulating that the financial profit gleaned from the north–south economic differential would be directed back to Africans instead of remaining within Europe.

The project reiterated many tropes of Friedman's career—in particular, his notion of southern bricolage. However, the collaboration with Giovanelli added to this trope the structure of economic exchange and, as such, can be read vis-à-vis the contemporaneous debt crises throughout the global south, which hit Africa with especial severity. In the early 1980s, economists warned that financial instability in the global north might follow on the heels of the south's epidemic of debt defaults, and new methods for restructuring debt were subsequently proposed. The Republic of Zaire was used as a primary testing ground, starting with the massive devaluation of its currency. Amid these events, Friedman and Giovanelli's project can be seen as an artistic analog to the methods of restructuring debt that were being contemporaneously pioneered in Africa by the Paris Club, the International Monetary Fund, and the London Club. As these syndicates sought to render southern debt crises financially viable for northern investors, the art project suggested a way to stabilize capitalism by tinkering with its underlying conditions of instability.

Taking advantage of the different values that had historically accrued to African versus European creative labor (that is, to African "bricolage" versus European "conceptual art"), the art project made this system of economic imbalance serve as a basis for profit (hence mirroring the ongoing shift of northern manufacturing concerns to cheaper labor pools in the global south). The technological scrap's transmutation from dross into lucre generated profit not as much by dint of the African artisans' *specific* physical transformations as by dint of Friedman and Giovanelli's general conceptualization of the project as a work of fine art. However, the artists stipulated that the resulting profit would be returned to Africa. In other words, African artisans stood to profit from the long-extant devaluation of African intellectual labor. Legacies of racism could be turned to these Africans' financial advantage because economic inequality between Africa and Europe would be recast as the essential ingredient within an alchemical system. The long-standing devaluation of African technical proficiencies would be turned to African profit when passed through the alembic of European conceptual art, an alembic that magically transposed the products of mere tinkering into the putative domain of European apperception, a domain of structuralist consciousness, of consciousness over larger underlying *systems*—in this case, a consciousness of a capitalist system of inequitable valuation and exchange, which the artwork arguably attempts to subvert (*détourner*).

There is an ambiguity concerning whether the artwork's presentation of a global division of labor is being critiqued or naturalized. In fact, the two interpretations are not mutually exclusive, as global inequity is an object of critique but also a condition to be transformed and improved through some proposed structural adjustments. These adjustments, intended to lessen global inequity (by converting European dross into African lucre), do so by naturalizing that division of labor, ascribing it to the allegedly innate proclivities of southern versus northern skill sets. The artists' belief in indigenous capacities for creative bricolage provoke their glibly optimistic proposal for how to alleviate southern debt and dearth. Their reasoning is suggestive of incipient modes of neoliberal humanitarianism, according to which seeming self-determination is conflated with a form of artisanal creativity (that is, "free transformation"), the latter being prodded by northern economic programs, whether the imports of technological detritus or other technological initiatives.

As such, humanitarianism could increasingly direct itself toward supporting a southern indigent's entrepreneurial capacities, the presumed existence of such capacities serving as a vague promissory note for the (ever-deferred) restitution of political and economic parity between north and south. The cybernetic aspect of laissez-faire ideology, seen earlier in Friedman, Ketoff, and Aujame's African Projects, provides a schematic program—that of technological recycling—through which conditions of massive debt might ultimately self-correct.

The art project relied on the discursive formulation of an exemplary southern subject who was to possess both a dearth and an excess of self-determining capacities, including the basic (in)ability to eke out a habitation and livelihood. Even though artisanal technical skill is a precondition for the art project, the centuries of technical knowledge undergirding that skill are cast as mere spontaneous creativity, a kind of primitive surrealist encounter with unfamiliar detritus or found objects. This devaluation results less from the artisans' personal anonymity (though that too is noteworthy) and more from the anonymity of the African city, village, nation, or region that was selected for the project. We can only guess that the project's Phase of Transformation was probably undertaken in Francophone West Africa (perhaps in one of the West African cities for which Friedman had previously proposed architectural projects) because of the region's expertise in iron and bronze work and its deep economic and social connections to France. What is erased in the project are long-extant societal modes of transmitting knowledge, including, for example, the centuries-old guild systems that cultivated metallurgic expertise throughout much of West Africa. In the erasure of that context—marked by the erasure of any geographic nomenclature beyond the signifier "Africa"—there emerges the ingenious bricoleur whose self-determining entrepreneurialism appears to rely less on his locally derived expertise than on the ingenious structuring system established by European conceptual art.

It seems likely that under the economic regime of structural adjustment first promulgated in the early 1980s, the presentation of southern creativity and entrepreneurship as instinctive and untrained—encouraged by the conditions of the informal economic sector—helped exculpate financial actors from their imposition of austerity measures (since the bricoleur's creativity emerges ex nihilo, requiring no formal education or employment). Friedman and Giovanelli's project did not merely reflect the economic processes instated by debt restructuring; it also, through its re-presentation of these processes, offered terms and categories—essentially, a conceptual framework—through which drastic austerity measures could be rendered unexceptional, normalized, even idealized. As such, *une intervention sur le déchet* anticipated the vast expansion of self-help technics that would occur decades later, including the recent rise of maker culture in Africa—promulgated by Silicon Valley corporations—as well as the practices of participatory mapping and land titling that now form the basis of slum-upgrading programs throughout the global south. Those practices are indebted to a trope of southern bricolage that Friedman helped establish, probably inspired by his reading of Lévi-Strauss.

Lévi-Strauss had stipulated that the (implicitly brown or black) bricoleur—though similar in some respects to Western engineers—lacked a *design* and worked not with a planned set of raw materials but with reused materials, constrained by whatever was available. "The characteristic feature of mythical thought," wrote Lévi-Strauss, "is that it expresses itself by means of a heterogeneous repertoire which . . . is . . . *limited*. It *has* to use this repertoire . . . whatever the task at hand, because it *has nothing else* at its disposal."[43] For Lévi-Strauss such material was a metaphor for the elements of mythic thought and was thus not synonymous with actual physical detritus. In Friedman and Giovanelli's project, however, modern bricoleurs work with the material wreckage wrought by capitalism and thus seem to make some good the same modernity whose fruits are largely denied to them. The bricoleur can turn to the good the effects of austerity measures because the nature of bricolage is not to turn *something* into something, but to turn *nothing* into something. This *nothing* would come not only in the form of austerity but also, as Friedman and Giovanelli had divined, in the form of industrial (and, later, electronic) pollution, which, within a decade or so of "an intervention on the scrap" would indeed become the principal ingredients for southern bricolage.

In consistently blurring boundaries between playful creativity and programs of economic austerity and international intervention, Friedman's oeuvre—despite its utopian, critical, and occasionally Marxian aspects—sketched out the rough contours of the global-southern bricoleur as a necessary actor in neoliberal economics, also entailing the conversion of a southern indigent into both a consumer base and a database for the high-tech economy. Such a conversion owed something to mid-twentieth-century experiments in pseudovernacular media, as exemplified by Friedman's wall journals and graphic pamphlets. The final chapters of this book will resume the thread of a history foreshadowed here, whereby the pseudovernacular became a way of conceiving of digital interfaces. However, before delving into that history, there is another cultural construct to be explored, also related to the construction of a global-southern subject, specifically as regarded that subject's supposed semiotic constitution. Moving away from modes of transnational practice that were largely European in their conception, the next chapters examine an enabling semiotic construct assisting the U.S. transnational sovereignty in the decade following World War II and related to a notion of magical semiotics: that of the global environment.

PART III

THE ENVIRONMENT

It has been noted by various scholars that only quite recently has the word "environment" come to refer to a global model of ecological systems. This development, dating roughly to the last years of World War II, has been regarded as marking a distinctly new definition of "environment," no longer referring to an organism's perceptory milieu but referring, rather, to a global system (or a set of interlocking global systems); in other words, no longer *an* environment but *the* environment. Chapters 5 and 6, concerned with the development in the United States of this latter concept of the global environment, nonetheless argue that the incredible potency of this new environmental construct—its relevance to burgeoning regimes of global power—derived in part from a furtive retention of the term's earlier meaning (that of an organism's perceptory and semiotic milieu) within the same disciplinary frameworks responsible for the discursive construction of *the* environment. This scalar linkage reflected the way the burgeoning U.S. means of global governmentality depended on mediatic strategies that operated on a human subject's immediate perceptory and semiotic environment. That is, influence over individual brains was a key component of global governmentality.

The sequence of chapters 5 and 6 follows a transition from one disciplinary cosmography to another—from the world as conceived by Western humanism to the world as conceived by environmental design—showing that a transcendental humanist subject remained implicit to the supposedly posthumanist paradigm of environmental thinking. The global environment was an object deemed discernible only by cognitively transcending one's immediate semiotic environment, a feat that depended on one's ability to grasp the inherent structuralist systematicity of that semiosis as well as the systematicity of a global resource ecology. Corresponding to the continuities between the humanist and environmental paradigms was the development of a new environmental subject roughly analogous to the "savage" of earlier eras, still allegedly captured in the semiosis of magical thought. This environmental subject was to become the object of the new discipline developed in the 1960s of environmental design, which sought to redesign environments according to psychological understandings of various aesthetic effects on human disposition. Focused primarily on American urban ghettoes, this discipline effectively positioned the population along a continuum from the designers to the designed.

As was the case in the preceding chapters, there are numerous historical actors that could be used to sketch the contours of this new environmental disciplinarity. I have homed in on the Aspen Institute of Humanistic Studies and its related International Design Conferences at Aspen as a historiographic strategy for giving some narrative coherence to the widespread emergence of environmental thinking out of an earlier Western humanist world view. I suggest that this shift is seminal to the later rise of design thinking. Examining several spatial and semiotic paradigms through which environmental subjectivity was formulated, these chapters suggest that environmentality was heavily reliant on visual–spatial (rather than linguistic) means of representation, as these contributed to the understanding of the world as a set of systems.

5

THE EARTH UNFOLDED

Aspen, Africa, and the Geopolitics of Environment

To Make the Earth Speak: From Humanism to Environmentalism

In 1954 in a derelict mining town in Colorado, a seemingly primitive earthwork appeared. Almost thirteen meters in diameter, it consisted of a grassy bermed circle inside of which were three primal elements: a large stone evocative of prehistoric menhirs, a semispherical depression, and a larger circular mound. Although the work has been interpreted as a precursor to the land art movement, the piece engaged a set of themes quite different from those associated with land art.[1] Designed by former Bauhaus student and instructor Herbert Bayer with the collaboration of architect Fritz Benedict, *Earth Mound* belonged to Bayer's broader interest in developing what he called a "pure, essential graphic" (*reine gebrauchsgraphik* [*sic*]), linked to a "universal writing" (*Universalschrift*). At the Bauhaus Bayer had designed "the basik alfabet" to render writing more intuitive and natural.[2] Now, invoking primordial forms of human architecture (mounds, menhirs, and bermed enclosures), Bayer and Benedict suggested the earth itself as a natural medium of nondenotative communication. Whereas the basik alfabet had been bound to the arbitrary forms and phonetics of roman script (even if its orthography was rendered internally consistent), the earthworks suggested a more essential link between representation and the earth itself.

The work was conceived during Bayer's tenure as the director of design at the newly founded Aspen Institute of Humanistic Studies. Highly accomplished in graphic design, architecture, painting, exhibition design, and photomontage, Bayer had moved from Berlin to New York in 1938 after having intermittently lent his talents to the Third Reich.[3] In New York, he began designing exhibitions for the Museum of Modern Art, and several years later he was hired by Walter Paepcke to assist with advertising and product design for the latter's Chicago-based Container Corporation of America.[4] Shortly thereafter, Paepcke purchased the former silver-mining town of Aspen, Colorado, intending to transform it into a leisure destination. Strapped for initial investors to back the resort, Paepcke turned to the Ford Foundation with a proposal for the Aspen Institute of Humanistic Studies (AIHS), a non-degree-granting liberal arts "university" for businessmen. With funding from Ford, Paepcke was able to revamp Aspen's basic

FIGURE 5.1. Herbert Bayer and Fritz Benedict, *Earth Mound*, 1954. Photograph by James Milmoe. Copyright 2020 Artists Rights Society (ARS), New York / VG Bild-Kunst, Bonn.

infrastructure and attract press coverage to make the remote mountain town more attractive to private investors.

Under the guidance of his wife Elizabeth Paepcke, who had studied at the Art Institute of Chicago, Paepcke had become an enthusiast of modernist design and had hired several ex-Bauhaus immigrants, including László Moholy-Nagy. Paepcke designated Walter Gropius as the lead planner in redesigning the town of Aspen and appointed Bayer as the AIHS director of design, responsible for the institute's graphics. Bayer also designed several buildings and a sculpture garden for the AIHS complex, and from 1951 to 1965 he chaired the board of directors for the yearly International Design Conference in Aspen (IDCA).[5] In addition to their support of modernist art and architecture, the Paepckes were great patrons of the humanities and of U.S. global cultural ambitions following World War II. The concept of the AIHS stemmed from Walter Paepcke's involvement with the University of Chicago's recent Great Books program under the presidency of Robert Hutchins, a close friend whom Paepcke would later hire to chair the inaugural opening event of the AIHS.[6] In the following years, the AIHS would expand from an institution whose original mission was to provide American businessmen with the ornaments of a humanist education into a large interdisciplinary research center concerned primarily with strategies of liberal global governance and environmental management. The logic underlying Paepcke's interest in the Great Books programs—namely, that literacy in what he called "the Western classics" was prerequisite to U.S. management of international business and geopolitics—evolved into an ethos linking Western humanism to the control of "the environment" as the latter term gained currency throughout the decades following World War II.

The program of the AIHS, read in conjunction with that of the IDCA, exposes a certain tension between Paepcke's interest in Great Books and the IDCA's explorations of nonverbal means of communication rooted in psychological and environmental theories. The logical problem implicit to the discourses charted in this chapter was how to conserve a centuries-old European humanist subjectivity (with its racial, epistemic implications) amid a burgeoning construct of environmental subjectivity that was emerging at the nexus of the social sciences and systems thinking. Whereas humanism, broadly speaking, had conceived of the world as knowable by dint of a transcendental epistemology, the new environmentalism represented humans as cognitively and semiotically formed by—and engulfed in—environments and therefore not in a position to objectively know the world. Thus, to perpetuate a privileged objectifying epistemic relationship toward the globe, U.S. environmental discourses and aesthetic practices subtly implied the existence of two distinct forms of semiotic subjectivity: one that was enthralled by its environmental surround, and another capable of transcending that environment by virtue of a particular understanding of global communications and language. It was no longer the trick of the Kantian sublime but rather a host of new spatial and visual modes of representation—as we will see in this chapter—that would enable an aporetic construction of "Western" subjectivity as *both* environmental and humanistic while at the same time relegating the great portion of humanity to the position of merely environmental subjectivity.

During the decades leading up to the environmental movement of the 1960s and '70s, the conception of the environment prevailing within architectural and urban discourses was linked less to ecological concerns than to geopolitical, psychological, and semiotic ones, related to a growing interest in new audio and visual media. As we will see in chapter 6, which turns to the 1970 IDCA, "Environment by Design," this earlier figuration of the environment as a psychosemiotic sphere remained subtly interpolated within many architects' responses to the environmental movement. Instead of focusing, then, on something now referred to as "sustainable design," this chapter questions how "the environment" in the postwar decades mapped particular forms of semiotic subjectivity onto Cold War geopolitics. Whereas there had previously existed *environments*—signifying the immediate surrounds or environs of a particular place—*the* environment referred to a nonbounded system of global interactions.[7] The difference between—and conflation of—these two definitions was crucial to how the term was leveraged as an instrument of both psychological and economic world governance.

To willfully imbricate and conflate the two defining scales of "the environment" (one corresponding to the terrestrial planet, the other to the individual organism's semiotic sphere) required a magical visual–spatial reimagining of the earth.[8] Artists and architects abetted this transformation by presenting the environment as an ambivalent spatial construct that, depending on one's subject position, could appear either as a sensory enclosure or as an object—sometimes in the form of the terrestrial globe—to be cognized from a transcendent position.[9] This often entailed a spatial operation of eversion—of literally turning inside out the environmental or global sphere such that the environmental subject could become a humanist subject, viewing the world from a more omniscient position.

The operation of eversion that enabled an elision between environmental and humanist subjectivity was symbolically suggested by one of the first architectural works commissioned by the AIHS. The office of Saarinen and Saarinen was commissioned to design an open-air auditorium for the AIHS's inaugural convocation, the 1949 Goethe Bicentennial. In honoring Johann Wolfgang von Goethe, that paragon of European humanism, the bicentennial was intended to mark the continuity of Euro-American humanism despite the damage done to that construct by recent wars, the Holocaust, and anticolonial independence movements.[10] The large tent designed to accommodate the bicentennial's lectures and musical performances represented a corresponding effort to conserve some basic structures of a humanist episteme amid the world's reconfiguration as "environment."

Saarinen and Saarinen's tent consisted of four main architectural elements. The most visually dominant was the canvas roof, whose circular base converged toward its top into a square supported by four masts, thus forming a complex curving membrane. The audience seating was arranged in a circle and was sunk into the earth. The performers' podium took the unconventional form of a triangular wedge jutting sharply into the circle of seating, its shape emphasized by a triangular canvas suspended above.

FIGURE 5.2. Goethe Bicentennial at Aspen, 1949. Photographer unknown. Walter P. Paepcke Papers, Special Collections Research Center, University of Chicago Library.

Finally, in the center of the auditorium, a large circle of "wild" vegetation created a space between audience and performers. Considered in section, a light atmospheric membrane encloses a group of listeners and speakers communicating across a vegetal mound. In plan, this sphere of communication was composed of a wedge inserted into the receiving crescent of the audience, the two components completing each other and forming a continuous circle. As we will see, this circle of communication resembled the cybernetic conception of the environment emerging during this era: a communicative feedback loop of signals and receivers.[11]

Most striking, though, is the fact that the tent everted one of the paradigmatic forms associated with so-called Western humanism: the pendentive domes characteristic, inter alia, of Italian Renaissance churches.[12] Pendentive domes had been used to structurally negotiate the geometric transition from a square distribution of columns to a circular dome above. Conversely, Saarinen and Saarinen used four masts arranged in a square to suspend a canvas that transitioned to a circular floor plan. The tent's structure anchored a light membrane back to a terrestrial base, counteracting not gravity as much as the upward thrust of air currents. This earthward vector was underscored by the vegetal earthen mound around which the four masts were arranged. The circular roof, which in Renaissance churches had represented the dome of heaven, was here not heavenly but, rather, environmental: it delimited a sphere of sensory cognition,

FIGURE 5.3. Aspen auditorium tent at the 1949 Goethe Bicentennial. Photographer unknown. Walter P. Paepcke Papers, box 130, folder 7, Special Collections Research Center, University of Chicago Library.

filtering what could (and could not) be perceived by its human occupants. Yet despite the way the tent functioned as an environmental sensorium, it conferred to this particular sensorium a privileged position insofar as it translated a trope of Renaissance humanism into a sphere of audio reception.

To thus evert the pendentive dome form spoke to a double epistemic project: on the one hand, to understand human subjects as captured within an environmental sensorium in which there was no epistemic position external to human perception, and on the other hand, to uphold a humanist paradigm in which a certain class of humans might maintain a privileged epistemic externality from the sensory environment that engulfed them. The tent presents a certain malleability between these two otherwise antithetical positions. The interiority of environmental subjectivity could be everted to allow the humanist subject to assume a privileged external vantage point.

The construct of the environment as a sphere prone to eversion would be underscored by the two foremost celebrities chosen to speak at the Goethe Bicentennial. The first of these, José Ortega y Gasset, had recently published an essay, "In Search of Goethe from Within" ("Pidiendo un Goethe desde dentro"), which reinterpreted Goethe's ideas of *Bildung* and *Ur*-forms into the idea that a person's originary, embryonic destiny could only be fully determined through its interaction with an external world.[13] As keynote speaker, Hutchins had invited the missionary doctor Albert Schweitzer, who entertained his own conception of global insides and outsides. Schweitzer had long directed a missionary hospital in the small village of Lambaréné in French Equatorial Africa, described in his famous missionary memoirs, *On the Edge of the Primeval Forest* (1921).

There is a peculiar inversion between Lambaréné and Aspen, the two being linked through the chiasmus of the forest as an environmental category: in the case of Aspen, a regenerating forest described as postindustrial and functioning as an aesthetic asset in the town's economic redevelopment; in the case of Lambaréné, a forest described as "primeval" and functioning as a different kind of economic asset, through its proximity upriver from the French timber-exporting town Port-Gentil. As will be explained over the course of this chapter, the sensory environment of Africa's "primeval forests" was said to give rise to nonliterate forms of magical thought. By way of contrast, Aspen's sparse forests, creeping over former sites of resource extraction, figured as the proper "postindustrial" domain of leisure, visual knowledge, and literacy, as suggested by a photomontage Bayer would produce during his years in Aspen. In this work, *In Search of Times Past,* a forest of birch trees appears as a field of watchful, knowing eyes.

Aphasia: "He Who Lives in Africa . . . Can Give No Message to the World."

> That extraordinary missionary, Albert Schweitzer . . . epitomizes the ambivalence [between political liberalism and racism]. In a comment which has often been quoted Schweitzer says: "The African is indeed my brother but my junior brother." . . . Naturally he became a sensation in Europe and America. Pilgrims flocked . . . to witness the prodigious miracle in Lambaréné, on the edge of the primeval forest.[14]

FIGURE 5.4. Town of Aspen in promotional brochure for the Aspen Institute of Humanistic Studies, circa 1949. Artist unknown. Walter P. Paepcke Papers, box 130, folder 7, Special Collections Research Center, University of Chicago Library.

FIGURE 5.5. Herbert Bayer, *In Search of Times Past,* 1959. Copyright 2020 Artists Rights Society (ARS), New York / VG Bild-Kunst, Bonn.

In June 1949, amid much fanfare and curiosity, Schweitzer traveled by boat from western equatorial Africa to New York on his way to Aspen. Upon landing, he was asked by reporters to assess current prospects for world peace. "No," he demurred, "he who lives in Africa *can't speak about the outer world* . . . can give no message to the world—just as those who come to us can give us no message."[15] His words were hailed as the sort of aphorism befitting a humanist sage. No one apparently thought to ask what caused this alleged semiotic impasse between those living in Africa and their counterparts in "the *outer* world." (Nor did they remark on the fact that the speaker who claimed an incapacity to speak was being paid a $6,000 honorarium for his talk.)

This purported aphasia between Africans and non-Africans had long formed a motif within European colonial discourse, one rivaled, however, by colonial reports of the wild cacophony of African speech. The semiotic impasse, then, was obviously not owing to silence; nor was it due to linguistic difference, given that many Africans spoke and read European languages, nor even to putative racial difference, given that a white colonist like Schweitzer claimed to be unable to bring messages to non-Africa. Rather, this chasm between Africa and non-Africa had been dreamed up as a circumstance of the environment: of the irremediably different environments of "pre-" and "postindustrial" worlds.

On his own experience of reading in Lambaréné, Schweitzer had noted, "Newspapers one can hardly bear to look at. The printed string of words . . . seems here, where time is . . . standing still, positively grotesque."[16] Decades prior to Marshall McLuhan's ideas of the cognitive habits arising from literacy and orality, Schweitzer avowed that "the negroes are deeper than we are . . . because they don't read newspapers." And yet his reports of nonliteracy appear exaggerated, given that he also mentioned hiding newspapers from Africans during World War I, "lest the boys, who can read, should *absorb* both text and pictures."[17] Whereas Europeans—as McLuhan would later say—detachedly filtered words and pictures through the sieve of analytical thought, Africans who were literate nonetheless *absorbed* text and image as a direct, numinous experience—that is, as though it were electronic multimedia.

Yet, apparently, there was an exception to the communicative rift sundering Africa from non-Africa. Schweitzer had commissioned a piano with an organ pedal to be specially made for the humid tropics and brought to Lambaréné.[18] While working in "the primeval forest," he observed that there were "many of J. S. Bach's organ pieces into the meaning of which I can now enter with greater ease and deeper appreciation than ever before."[19] Bach could, seemingly, give a message from "the outer world" to Africa through the enchanted semiosis of nonlinguistic music. In fact, Schweitzer had argued in a two-volume book on Bach that the composer's work was less purely abstract than it was pictorial.[20] Although, he conceded, mathematical patterns underlay much of Bach's music, the semiotic *effect* of these patterns was to convey imagistic impressions verging on narrative. This, then, was an autochthonous form of communication that did not depend on signifiers. Bach's music was mathematically coded according to nature's own rationale (Schweitzer mentioned Bach's use of the golden ratio). Yet by virtue of this *mathesis universalis*, listeners experienced something quite different from mathematics.[21] They experienced a synesthetic confluence of sound and vision. Bach spoke to Africa because the score's authorial, rational *encoding* was not apparent in the sensory message *experienced*. What the listener cognized was an effulgent flow of sound and vision, not likely to encourage analysis or discourse.

The "basik alfabet" and the *world geo-graphic atlas*

> The revitalization of typography will come . . . from the increased demands made on the psychophysiologic apparatus of our perceptive senses. . . .
>
> for a long time to come we will accept the existence of different languages now in use. this will continue to pose barriers to communication, even after improved (possibly phonetic) writing models have been adopted within all the languages. therefore, a more universal visual medium to bridge the gap between them must eventually evolve. . . .
>
> exploration of the potentialities of the book of true text–picture integration has only begun and will, by itself, become of utmost importance to universal understanding.[22]

Bayer worked with Moholy-Nagy while at the Bauhaus on developing a "pure essential graphic" that would purge typography and orthography of all idiosyncratic elements. The resulting "basik alfabet" would provide a more rational phonetic code into which all the languages of the world could supposedly be transcribed.[23] If the arbitrary relationship between alphabetic signs and phonemes and likewise between signifiers and signified was ineradicable, these codes could at least be rendered more internally consistent and legible, thus giving rise to a more natural semiosis. But Bayer's ambitions went further. In a later lecture, "Design and Industry," Bayer speculated that in the future,

> we will write and read less and less, and the book will perhaps entirely disappear. Likely, there will come a time when we no longer need to learn to read and write; when we will instead *absorb* and *convey* information not through eyes, mouth, and ears but rather through *supernatural means*.[24]

Bayer's oeuvre should be read according to this fantasy of a magical semiosis, evident not only in his and Benedict's 1954 earthworks but also in his design of the *world geo-graphic atlas: a composite of man's environment* (the title's lower-cased letters conform to the syntax of the basik alfabet). The work had been commissioned by Paepcke in 1949 to be produced by the Container Corporation of America. Intended for private distribution only, the atlas served to garner support for the newly founded AIHS. It can be read, then, as a map of what was meant by "man's environment" within the context of Paepcke's new institute of "humanistic studies." Comparing the wealth, population, industry, racial composition, and material and intellectual resources of nations and colonies, the atlas might be construed simply as a more graphically virtuosic compendium of the kinds of studies undertaken in the eighteenth and nineteenth centuries, which assessed the material resources of colonies and nations. What makes the atlas different, however, is first, its global scope; second, its preoccupation with the earth as a unified object bound by layers of atmosphere (as depicted in the book's opening spreads); and finally, its data-based stratification of this object into First and Third Worlds (with the communist "Second World" legible largely through the absence of available data).

How do we make sense of these two tendencies within the atlas: to present the globe, on the one hand, as a unified object and, on the other hand, as a bifurcated entity? The *world geo-graphic atlas* rendered the earth's bisection into First and Third Worlds as a scientific fact of nature so self-evident as to require little verbal language to elucidate it. In lieu of language, mimetic icons and swaths of color segregated the world into vivid hierarchical strata. Yet to conceive of this "geo-graphic" entity as a single object of sovereignty, a magical elision was necessary: that of environmentality, which magically bridged the rift between these two worlds. Aphasia—figuratively speaking—is promulgated here through an almost "supernatural" means of graphic communication. The atlas presented information so that it could be absorbed with a mere glance, with almost no need of language or analysis on the part of "readers."

Cybernetics and the Jungle: The Problem of "Noise"

In 1953, the same year as the *world geo-graphic atlas* was published, another book, *The African Mind in Health and Disease: A Study in Ethnopsychiatry*, happened to forward a noteworthy theory on "the environment." As part of Britain's ongoing war against Kenya's anticolonial movement, the book's author, John Colin Carothers, had been sent to Nairobi to diagnose the psychological constitution of Kikuyu society.[25] While Carothers's various anthropometric experiments had failed to adduce persuasive proof of intellectual difference between blacks and whites, his subsequent theory that the African environment must render "the African mind" different from its European counterpart was highly influential to McLuhan's theory of media. An article by Carothers based on his Kenyan research was cited copiously in the opening sections of McLuhan's *The Gutenberg Galaxy: The Making of Typographic Man* and then again in his *Understanding Media: The Extensions of Man*.[26] Drawing on Carothers's conflation of race, environment, and semiotics, McLuhan suggested that the aural semiosis of what he called the nonliterate "tribal world" offered evidence of how electronic media might obviate the need for language.[27] "From the current example of Africa," he wrote,

> we can observe how very much visual processing of the human psyche by alphabetic means will be needed before any appreciable degree of homogenized social organization is possible. . . . The phonetic alphabet has no rival . . . as a translator of man out of the closed, tribal echo-chamber into the neutral visual world of lineal organization.[28]

Carothers had linked nonliteracy to the environment, explaining that the jungle's darkness had formed the African psyche by obscuring visual information, thereby compelling greater attentiveness to sounds and ultimately encouraging oral versus written means of communication. Claiming that speech links word to object in an immediate and present way, Carothers argued that nonliterate societies thereby remained ignorant of the *true* arbitrary relation between sign and signified.[29] He contended that Africans' sense of an unmediated unity between words and things was related to a host of other traits, including the tendency toward magical thought, or what Freud called "omnipotence of thought," and toward blind submission to charismatic authority and a subsequent inaptitude for rational problem solving. All of these traits allegedly culminated in Africans' psychological unfitness for industrial urbanization and self-rule.

Carothers and McLuhan both claimed that the phonetically printed word revealed the mediation between signifier and signified, leading to rational, independent thought, in contradistinction to the delusions of magical thought encouraged by aural societies' supposed belief in the unity of words and things. For Carothers and McLuhan, *truth*—far from being logocentric in nature—lurked in the yawning chasm between words and their referents. For "tribalized" societies, however, a different truth must hold sway: not *true* truth (that is, analytic, structuralist truth) but the more primordial truth binding word to world and thereby speaking directly to the savage mind.

Concomitantly with the conceptualization of the environment as a unified global system, the ideological tendency described by Jacques Derrida as logocentrism splintered in two opposite directions. *True* truth would belong not to *logos* but to structuralist semiotics, while another, more primordial and magical truth (which circumvented the arbitrary relation between signified and signifier through aesthetic communications) would be deployed toward managing the subaltern classes of the world. *Logotechnics* would leverage structuralist knowledge toward the techno-aesthetic production of "the environment" as a magical media sensorium capable of binding words to things. McLuhan built on Britain's Colonial Film Unit's recent activities in Africa, arguing that electronic media should be instated as the basis of governance in the global south.[30]

The idea that a nonlinguistic semiosis—indeed, an environmental semiosis—might work toward the management of humans is shown in an example Schweitzer offered in *On the Edge of the Primeval Forest.*[31] At Lambaréné Schweitzer often conscripted Africans to the grueling task of forest clearance required for his improvement schemes and—we might speculate—for timber export. Frustrated by the conscriptees' tendency to lapse into discussions with each other about how to best proceed with their work, Schweitzer eventually came to perceive an ideal symphonic scheme to the men's labor. He detected within the working day four distinct orchestral "movements," each with its respective rhythm and sound. So long as the workers moved under the sway of this orchestral scheme, they unflaggingly persevered in their efforts. However, any acoustic interruption—birds, thunder, and especially speech—would break the symphonic spell.

Noise acted as a trigger provoking workers' sudden arousal to consciousness and discourse—that is, their tendency to transpose what should have been rote manual

FIGURE 5.6. Forest clearance in Lambaréné under the direction of Albert Schweitzer, n.d. From Albert Schweitzer, *Zwischen Wasser und Urwald: Erlebnisse und Beobachtungen eines Arztes im Urwalde Aequatorialafrikas* (1921). Photographer unknown.

labor into deliberate intellectual labor. To short-circuit consciousness—in the interests of a racialized division between manual and intellectual labor—it was necessary to short-circuit the space between signified and signifier, the space that demanded the intervention of conscious interpretation. Language would be preempted by a form of music that, as we recall from Schweitzer's interpretation of Bach, might conjure forth meaningful imagery without the use of signifiers. A protocybernetic system (in the form of this imagined "symphony") invoked a nonlinguistic semiosis as a means to the self-regulation of menial work. Flowing, mesmeric forms of communication would allow conscious, linguistic thought to be circumvented. Aphasia could be maintained by drowning any noise that might provoke language within a music that directly orchestrated the unconscious movements of labor.

The literary theorist Roman Jakobson had noted that in one common form of aphasia, a person is unable to distinguish phonemes as referent-bearing components of speech and instead perceives them merely as noise.[32] Aphasia thus derived from a malfunctioning of the basic operations of encoding or decoding signs. Around the time that Jakobson wrote his essay on aphasia, the problem of noise formed one of the central concerns of communications scientists such as Warren Weaver, whose research into "noise" (that is, the electronic degradation of messages) would become an important foundation for the interdisciplinary project of cybernetics.[33] Cybernetic theorists, in fact, had many concerns in common with European doctors and psychiatrists living in Africa, such as the problem of organizing production in such a way as to preempt labor politics, problems of communication and translation, and, related to these latter, the problem of how noise disrupted the transmission of coded information.

Within the field of cybernetics, minimizing noise relied on statistical analyses of information, filters, and deconvolution processes; for the likes of McLuhan, Schweitzer, and Bayer, the problem of noise (within a system of production or communication) could be resolved by replacing language with other forms of semiotic organization. "The African mind" served as an exemplar of how communication might transpire with minimal interpretation or decoding: that mind's alleged belief in the unity of signifier and signified indicated that while a sender might artfully encode a message (we might think of Bach's golden ratio), the receiver would not need to decode anything but could simply "absorb" the message into the unconscious. Media then would need to be conceived as something like environments, something that could engulf a message's sender and receiver in a semiotic nimbus.

Some years after writing *The Gutenberg Galaxy* and *Understanding Media*, McLuhan served as guest editor for *Aspen* magazine (a publication that had spun off from the IDCA's). The magazine's opening pages bore McLuhan's assertion that "any understanding of social and cultural change is impossible without a knowledge of the way media work as environments."[34] McLuhan's keen interest in how media could be leveraged by the global north in the form of propaganda for the global south drove him to cite from social scientists working in Africa and Asia. But the nonliterate cognition he ascribed to the "tribal world" (for him, basically the non-West) also offered clues as to how the West was at risk of being "re-tribalized" through new semiotic technologies.

In his introduction to *Aspen* magazine, he proposed, "Electric circuitry is Orientalizing the West. The contained, the distinct, the separate—our Western legacy—are being replaced by the flowing, the unified, the fused."[35] What the preindustrial jungle had purportedly accomplished toward shaping the methods of magical thought of "the African mind" was being reproduced on a global scale (in the absence of jungle) through the analogous environmental sphere of electronic multimedia. For McLuhan, the inheritance of "Gutenberg" humanism might rescue "Western man" from the environmental subjectivity that described the condition of "the tribal" world.[36]

The Environmental Sphere: Unfolded, Everted, Refolded

In the latter half of the twentieth century, "the environment" may have become synonymous with "global system," but its thicker sedimentation of meanings implicitly linked that globality to the more minute sphere of perception. Spanning these two disparately scaled environments required spatial and graphical constructions capable of articulating the planetary sphere and the organism's sensorium as fungible terms. For example, the prevalent modeling of the organism's environmental interactions as a feedback loop rendered the immediate environment in terms akin to those in which global systems were being articulated—namely, as feedback loops and as cycles. Conversely, the terrestrial globe itself could be modeled as a perceptory milieu that could be unfolded and refolded in relation to the perception and knowledge of a human subject.

In 1943, Bayer had first attracted Paepcke's attention with an exhibition he had designed with curator Monroe Wheeler at New York's Museum of Modern Art. *Airways to Peace: An Exhibition of Geography for the Future* informed many of Bayer's later designs for the 1953 *world geo-graphic atlas*. Conceived as wartime propaganda for envisioning a postwar America, the show drew on cartographic warfare technologies to demonstrate a burgeoning conception of the globe as simultaneously an object of sovereignty and a sphere of communications.[37]

During the planning phase for *Airways to Peace*, Wheeler accumulated clippings from various newspapers and magazines that denounced the outdatedness of the Mercator map in this new era of air travel. The Mercator, linked to nautical travel, produced the greatest spatial distortion around the North and South Poles, and yet, Wheeler stressed, "the most populous nations of the world are clustered about the North Pole, within easy flying distance of each other."[38] Wendell Willkie, a proponent of what he called "one world" for purposes of "free trade," authored the exhibition catalog, stressing the importance of non-Mercator geographic relations, ones that situated the North Pole as the world center (essentially, the configuration the United Nations would use on its logo).[39] Yet Willkie's catalog failed to address the resulting problem: spatial distortion toward the equator was increased, and the southern hemisphere was either omitted altogether or else depicted on a separate map. This new global bifurcation, inherited from the wartime mapping of air routes, graphically enabled a rethinking of geopolitics—amid decolonization movements—in terms of north–south divisions.

When designing *Airways to Peace* and later the *world geo-graphic atlas*, Bayer referred to Richard Buckminster Fuller's cartographic techniques, such as the Dymaxion map he had designed while serving on the Board of Economic Warfare to present strategic geospatial contiguities.[40] A Dymaxion map published in *Life* magazine in 1943 placed the North Pole in the middle of the map, from which concentric bands of "isotherms" radiated. Distinct from zones bounded solely by latitude lines, Fuller's "isotherms" banded together swaths of land according to their shared seasonal temperature ranges, thereby allowing almost all of the United States, Europe, Japan, Korea, and northern China to be banded together, while much of the Soviet Union and the global south were relegated respectively to polar and tropical isotherms. Declaring that "zones of temperature influence history," the article asserted that because the temperate isotherm was deemed "the optimum temperature zone for the well-being and efficiency of human beings," its nations had succeeded in controlling "84% of the world's mechanical horse-power and, in consequence, dominating the territories and people outside [that zone]."[41] Like Carothers, Fuller invoked climate as the justification for the global north's stewardship of the world's resources.

Bayer's move was to represent the globe as being itself an environmental medium for communicative systems. Suggestive of the cybernetic-related discourse of biosemiotics, which construed an organism's environment as an extension of its own being, and anticipating McLuhan's concept of media as "extensions of man," Bayer depicted the world as a vast geocentric envelope of media transmissions of which the earth itself was merely a small nucleus. In a series of five drawings titled *Nature of the Air,* Bayer treated the earth and its atmospheric strata as media-specific substrates; the outermost layer, the ionosphere, was, according to the drawing's captions,

> the radio-roof because radio-waves bounce back from it. The Stratosphere is a layer of air too thin for human life but navigable and sensitive to radio-electric communication. . . . The Troposphere is the air we breathe, the layer in which we live.[42]

While the troposphere was thus conducive to material existence and immediate communication within a local milieu, the strato- and ionospheres enabled the mediated interactions of what McLuhan would later call "the global village," resembling, at blown-up scale, the perceptory sphere of a single organism.

The twentieth-century biologist Jakob von Uexküll had recently described any given organism as being "captured" in its environment. Uexküll modeled the environment as a feedback loop between an organism's inner and outer environments (*Innenwelt* and *Umwelt*).[43] The organism is "captured," according to Uexküll, because of the ways its faculties and its specific biological functions have coevolved, determining which aspects of that world are available to perception. Environment thus describes not a spatial area, much less territory, but, rather, a particular semiotic sphere delimited by the perceptory possibilities available to a given organism.[44] An organism is little more than the signals that bind it to its environment. If Bayer's *Nature of the Air* drawings could redefine the earth as "a ball of gaseous fluid with a solid center," it was because the earth qua environment could be understood as a sphere of communications. The human subject was "captured" in this vast, superterrestrial field, according to Uexküll, as surely as a small blind tick is captured in its tiny world of crude environmental signals.

As distinct from constructs of knowledge such as episteme, paradigm, or habitus, the reimagining of the globe *spatially modeled* a new mode of knowledge and correlative forms of political subjectivity. It thus enabled a seeming fungibility between an abstract geopolitical "sphere" constituted by global exchanges (semiotic, human, and material) and a less abstract sphere of individual perception. This was not a synecdochal relationship, for, despite the movement from one scale to another, a part was not being substituted for a whole. Rather, a homology between the global environmental sphere and the personal perceptual environmental sphere encouraged a slippage between them. The environment as global ionosphere, as "radio-roof," would support global governance by operating on the perceptory environments of individuals. That this environmental sphere was indicative of a particular kind of subjectivity has been suggested by Beatriz Colomina in her account of Ray and Charles Eames's film installation *Glimpses of the U.S.A.*, which was projected on multiple screens within a domed pavilion designed by Fuller, essentially enclosing spectators in a mediatic nimbus. Speculating on the cognitive effects of this installation, Colomina notes the disappearance of a "privileged point of view" as well as the sensory overload that would short-circuit conscious processes of thought.[45]

Yet there was another model of globality presented at *Airways to Peace*. The show's main attraction, Bayer's *Outside-In Globe*, treated the earth as a skeletal, architectural enclosure. Visitors could enter the scaffolding of the globe and view its geographic configurations in a quick sweeping glance rather than having to perambulate the outside of the sphere. The everted globe thus amended Renaissance techniques of representing scenes as if from the vantage point of a single stationary viewer. Bayer's sphere took what could not in reality be seen from any viewpoint and rendered it within not a single *frame* of vision but a single *sweep* of vision. The terrestrial sphere was thus captured by the viewer even while the viewer was, in turn, captured by it. In other words, the viewer was neither entirely inside the globe nor entirely outside it.

Many years later, in his guest-edited issue of *Aspen* magazine, McLuhan included a poster with his 1967 essay, coauthored with Quentin Fiore, "The Medium Is the Massage." The essay contrasted the effects of Renaissance perspective painting to the effects of electronic media: whereas the former situated the world "outside the frame of experience," the latter "involves all of us. . . . No detachment or frame is possible."[46] The everted globe, however, attempted to elide the inside–outside distinction. While, on the one hand, the world/environment was rendered quite literally as bounding "the frame of experience," it conversely could be modeled, objectified, and comprehended as bounded by perception itself, an orb to be viewed from all sides. Against the dichotomy drawn by McLuhan, the subject of the *Outside-In Globe* was at once detached and involved, framing and enframed. The ability to stand *outside* one's own captivity *within* a global sphere pointed toward a paradoxical form of hegemonic subjectivity in which humans were simultaneously humanist agents and environmental subjects.

FIGURE 5.7 Herbert Bayer, *Outside-In Globe.* Installation views of the exhibition *Airways to Peace,* 1943. Museum of Modern Art Archives, New York. Photographer unknown. Copyright 2020 Artists Rights Society (ARS), New York / VG Bild-Kunst, Bonn, and copyright The Museum of Modern Art. Licensed by SCALA / Art Resource, New York.

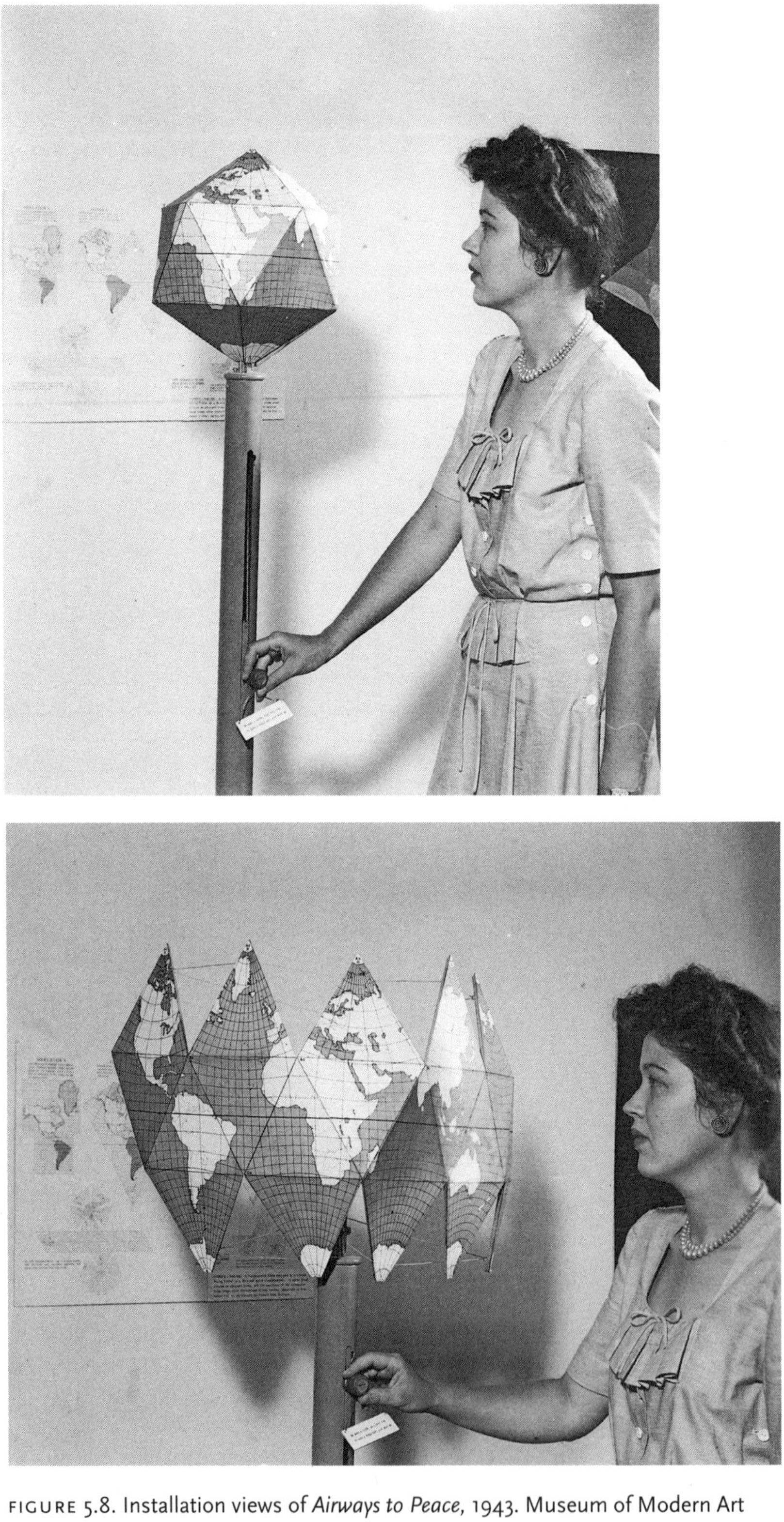

FIGURE 5.8. Installation views of *Airways to Peace,* 1943. Museum of Modern Art Archives, New York. Creator and photographer unknown. Copyright 2020 Artists Rights Society (ARS), New York / VG Bild-Kunst, Bonn, and copyright The Museum of Modern Art. Licensed by SCALA / Art Resource, New York.

In the previous chapters, I showed that the "primitive hut" had figured for European architects as a model of the "primitive mind." In the United States, in the decades following World War II, architectures reduced to roof membranes figured as semiotic-environmental spheres in various exhibition pavilion architectures.[47] The idea of an architecture that could mimic the function of a mediating interface between an organism's inside and outside worlds was described succinctly years later at the 1970 IDCA, "Environment by Design." A professor from Berkeley's new College of Environmental Design, Sim van der Ryn, discussed the archetypal form for an environmental architecture:

> The metaphor for the tribal form is the circle. In tribal times people lived in a condition we now call mythic unity. It is a state of *total participation between self and surroundings. The boundary between man's interior ecology inside his skin and the exterior ecology of the surrounding world is thin indeed.*
>
> ... The current mystique about domes that is growing up among many young people, I think, is related to their attempt to get back to the unity and simplicity of the tribal form.[48]

Whereas Team Ten architects viewed the structure of the primitive hut as analogous to the brain's processes of associative construction, domes and membranes demonstrated the brain's immersion within an environmental-media sphere.

The spatial construct of a globe that could be flipped inside out and objectified can be seen in the cut-out patterns for icosahedron globes that *Life* magazine had published in a 1943 issue largely devoted to Fuller. The globes' foldable, geodesic surfaces encouraged children to manipulate and reconfigure them as playthings. As with Bayer's *Outside-In Globe,* environmental insides and outsides could be flipped in relation to the postindustrial, humanist subject, whereas it was assumed that for the preindustrial environmental subject, in McLuhan's words, "no detachment or frame is possible." While Bayer dreamt of a not-so-distant day when humans would "absorb and convey information ... through supernatural means," a prevailing Eurocentric notion of literacy as the special purview of the white race afforded the latter the potential to step outside—even if perhaps only momentarily—the supernatural ambience of electronic communications.

From Liberal Arts to Environmental Arts

As organizer of the 1956 IDCA, "Future of Man and Design," the architectural historian Robin Middleton invited Mortimer Adler to speak. While at Columbia University in the 1920s, Adler had become involved with John Erskine's development of the Great Books of the Western World courses, which became the basis for a host of programs and publications, such as Columbia's core curriculum, the University of Chicago's Great Books course, the Great Books of Western Civilization series, Hutchins's Great Books for Business Men, and, stemming from this last, Paepcke's initial conception for the AIHS. For the 1956 IDCA, Adler delivered a talk, titled "Some Philosophical

Questions about Design," focusing on the question of whether design fell solely into the category of what he called the "servile arts" or whether it might, in some of its "higher" forms, be counted among the liberal arts. The distinction between servile and liberal arts depended on whether a given art tended toward serving merely "biological" needs or was associated with leisure. Architecture, Adler avowed, was first and foremost a servile art insofar as it served the biological need for shelter, but the question remained whether, to some degree, it attained to the liberal arts, given that it also adorned and beautified. Yet ultimately, the question was not about beauty per se but about a certain communicative intelligibility:

> But . . . do works of predominantly servile art ever *have anything at all to say*? The question is not whether they have something important or profound to say. It is simply whether they have any message at all, any truth to communicate, any instruction for the human mind.[49]

Architecture apparently inhabited a position oddly similar to that occupied by Africa in Schweitzer's recent formulation: architecture's alleged aphasia would be taken as proof of its inherent servility (Adler having finally concluded that indeed architecture had no "message" or "truth to communicate"). Adler apparently remained blind to the fact that architecture, as a nonlinguistic semiotic system, also held out the possibility of a quasi-semiotic meaningfulness, its aesthetic effects requiring no decoding, much like Schweitzer's conception of music in Lambaréné. Implicit in Adler's distinction between the liberal and servile arts was these terms' origins in ancient Greece, where they had designated the areas of knowledge befitting citizens and slaves, respectively. Hutchins had published in 1952 *The Great Conversation,* a work arguing that a liberal arts education need not be the special purview of an elite. Asserting that "the dominant element [of Western civilization] is the *Logos,*" Hutchins claimed that in the West "everybody is to speak his mind. . . . The exchange of ideas is held to be the path to the realization of the potentialities of the race."[50] "If leisure and political power are a reason for liberal education," wrote Hutchins, "then everybody in America now has this reason." However, in the same passage, Hutchins seemed to ascribe a lack of education to people's own lack of initiative, claiming that "if the people are not capable of acquiring this education, they should be deprived of political power and probably leisure."[51]

Indeed, Hutchins conceded that a nation's lack of industrial development would probably preclude the equitable distribution of leisure necessary to pursuing the liberal arts and suggested that a "universal liberal education" need not constitute an immediate agenda for all nations but only an ideal to which they might strive. In line with 1950s developmental theory, such as promoted by economist Walt Rostow, Hutchins insisted that the impoverished nations of the world must industrialize *before* they could approach the ideal of liberal arts learning: the "mechanization which tends to reduce a man to a robot also supplies the economic base and the leisure that will enable him to get a liberal education and to become truly a man."[52] The implicit division here—between the class of robot-like laborers and the class thereby afforded leisure time to pursue the liberal arts—is slyly elided by the implication of a universal "man" who is *both* the robot-like laborer *and* the bearer of leisure and liberal arts. While Hutchins was espousing an ideal of universal equality through liberal arts education, African American researchers at the University of Chicago's sociology department were taking his administration to task for its direct involvement in racial covenants intended to keep the vicinity around the campus reserved for white tenants and landlords.[53]

At the same time as the Great Books were being promoted among an educated elite, the United States and Great Britain were exploring modes of communication intended to supersede writing, precisely for purposes of warfare and propaganda in the arboreal tropics, first with Britain's wars in Malaya and Kenya and subsequently with the U.S. wars in southeast Asia.[54] Promoting the liberal arts as a form of verbal literacy and denigrating architecture and other visual media as "servile arts" helped guarantee that these servile arts would *not* be decoded; they would capture subjects while remaining nonetheless illegible.

Given that the first few IDCAs had been themed on the relationship between corporate business and design, it is not surprising that many IDCA topics throughout the 1950s and '60s dealt with design's potential for psychological persuasiveness. Perhaps bearing in mind Adler's designation of design disciplines as mute and therefore servile, the IDCA's advisory committee formulated their 1959 conference with the title "Communication: The Image *Speaks*" (emphasis added). That Adler should have failed to perceive how design did, in a sense, "speak," albeit in a manner that could not be reduced to signifiers and signifieds, testified to a certain obdurateness against acknowledging the rising power of visual and spatial media, increasingly developed for purposes of Cold War propaganda. A subsequent IDCA in 1963 was explicitly themed on the potentials of propaganda, titled "Design and the American Image Abroad." The AIHS and the IDCAs, having been born of two quite disparate frameworks—those of the text-based humanities and of the propagandistic potentials of design (whether for military or corporate purposes)—were symptomatic of the split construction between humanist and environmental subjectivity, an aporia supported through spatial and visual sleights of hand.

Inner Environment / Outer Environment: The 1962 IDCA

The 1962 IDCA, titled "Environment," included in its roster of speakers a scientist, a theologian, a philosopher, and an anthropologist in addition to several architects and designers. Although the term "environment" meant somewhat different things to the sundry disciplines represented, the talks were assimilated by a recurring theme—namely, the distinction between inner and outer environments. Most of the topics dealt in some way with the problem of how human subjectivity was to be formed in relation to both its cognitive–semiotic sensorium and the larger world around it.

Oscar Lewis, an anthropologist of Mexican lower-class communities, delivered a talk on one particular "environment" that he regarded as structurally similar throughout vast parts of the world: "the culture of poverty" whose "universal characteristics . . . transcend regional, rural–urban, and even national distinctions."[55] The globally dispersed societies constituting the culture of poverty were purportedly united by their nonliteracy. Lewis claimed, for example, that "the Jews of Eastern Europe . . . are a group, who, because of their cultural traditions and literacy, do not show many of the traits associated with the culture of poverty." The culture of poverty was characterized by its lack of a "great native literature" comparable to the "outpouring of a universal literature" occurring with Euro-American industrialization and urbanization. He added that the culture of poverty "can also occur in the process of detribalization such as is now going on in Africa, where tribal cultures are developing what have been called 'courtyard cultures' which are remarkably similar to the *vecindades* of Mexico City."[56]

As courtyard housing was common in many parts of the world, it is difficult to understand why it should have been singled out as pertaining to a culture of poverty and, more specifically, to African "detribalization." The answer resides in an ambiguity between interiority and exteriority that occurs with this domestic type, an ambiguity reflective of the problem that the concept of environment posed at this moment in history: if the environment was simultaneously external and internal to the human organism, how could one affect the organism's internal constitution through interventions into its external environment? Courtyard housing rendered this problem all the more difficult by creating an exterior milieu *within* an interior space that was invisible—or perhaps mute—to outside observers.

The most significant discursive shift detectable at this IDCA, however, was the reimagining of the humanist subject as an environmental *operator* rather than an environmental subject. The historian Herbert Muller (a recent signatory of the Second Humanist Manifesto), ranted against anthropologists' questioning of their own subjective cultural biases: "These anthropologists were *not* strictly culture-bound. . . . They were trained observers, who had achieved at least a measure of objectivity, of detachment from both our culture and the cultures they were studying. . . . With such knowledge men are no longer slaves of custom, no longer mere creatures of the environment." Distinguishing between the abilities of primitive versus advanced societies, Muller claimed that the latter "has meant a more conscious, less purely tribal culture."[57]

The notion that consciousness, in contradistinction to unconscious or habit-based behavior, could interject a wedge between the otherwise perfectly imbricated systems of inner and outer environments implied a triangulation of the tightly bound dyad proposed by Uexküll. The cybernetic physicist Heinz von Foerster, in his IDCA talk on the "structure of the environment," followed in the vein of Uexküll by describing "the totality" of the relationship "Environment–Environmentee" as one in which the neural–sensory system of an animal was formed in specific relation to its particular material needs. The environmentee's external world was translated into "symbols" the brain could process. Foerster noted, however, that there always lurked the question of knowing whether the perceived environment might not in fact be "the sole product of the environmentee's imagination . . . an illusion."[58] Uexküll had described such productions of the imagination as "magical environments," giving examples of animals that projected a traumatic memory onto the external world.[59] In other words, since the model of a semiotic feedback loop between environment and organism did not readily permit the interjection of a *nonenvironmental signal* into the organism's cognitive world, magic was necessary to explain the possibility of the environmentee's creative (rather than receptive) constructions.

Foerster seemed determined to conserve a more humanist element within the new model of environmental subjectivity. To distinguish between illusion and empirical knowledge, Foerster explained that two observers were needed to confirm each other's perception. Yet the "two elements observing the environment" need not be two discrete persons. "Environment," Foerster continued, "can be called 'together-knowledge' . . . namely, *conscientia,* from which, of course, our word 'consciousness' is derived."[60] As such, a nonmagical, empirical knowledge of the environment arises from consciousness as a form of "conversation" (or "great conversation"), crucial to preserving a humanist subjectivity within a movement converting much of humanity into environmental subjects.

According to Foerster, the individual organism verified the objectivity of the environment through a conversation between multiple sensory perceptions: "In order that these senses may compare their various experiences, it is necessary that they translate these into the same language."[61] The language was, he elaborated, the binary code of the neural system's on/off signals. Semiotics was thus bound to nature's codes, but at the same time, a structuralist understanding of that code allowed privileged subjects to overcome environmental subjectivity.

In the context of a conference that included a military intelligence expert, a virologist, a psychiatrist who invented "milieu therapy," a cyberneticist, a theologian patently dismissive of non-Judeo-Christian religions, and a propaganda designer, conferees' recurring motif of inner/outer environment seems to suggest a form of pastoral power scaled up to the field of geopolitical strategy. A transference between self and global power was effected through psychologically binding forms of communication. However, the liberal arts available to a white postindustrial subject were to be a safeguard against total environmental capture, allowing recourse to text-based consciousness and thus lifting white postindustrial subjects out of the aphasic thralls of magical semiotics. The environment was construed by many at the 1962 IDCA as a semiotic interface typologically akin to the model of the environment as a global system of interactions.

On the other hand, a political and cultural movement focused on material ecology was also given impetus that same year by the publication of Rachel Carson's *Silent Spring.* The book opens with a description of a bucolic town "in the heart of America" and proceeds to describe the town's total blight some years later as pollution poisons its children and wildlife and fires devastate its homes. The town, Carson wrote, did not actually exist, but it easily could. While her vision was compelling, the imaginary town seems slightly misconstrued. In the years after the book's publication, city neighborhoods across the United States would indeed be set ablaze, first during the civil rights riots of the midsixties, then through the scourge of arson in places, like the Bronx, that had deteriorated from decades of redlining, landlord neglect, and invasive infrastructures. These sites of post-Fordist disinvestment were *actually* ecologically ravished, unlike the quaintly bucolic towns of the sort imagined by Carson.

Without denying the value and courage of Carson's work, one can nonetheless question the georgic bias that seemed to render her blind to the racial politics underlying environmental injustice. Whose actual "silence" is concealed by her invocation of the imminent silencing of birdsong? Given the incipient civil rights movement forming concurrently with the publication of *Silent Spring*, the seeming aphasia of the subject of urban blight is striking. Having dedicated *Silent Spring* to Albert Schweitzer, Carson prefaced her book with his words: "Man . . . will end by destroying the earth." One pictures Schweitzer in the village of Lambaréné, musing about the great achievements of Western humanism and the tragedy of the world's possible destruction, all the while overseeing his conscripts clearing the preindustrial forest in a magical symphony of orchestrated labor.

Coda

The 1962 IDCA, titled "Environment," was not hosted in the tent designed by Saarinen and Saarinen; that had been replaced several years earlier by another tent, designed by Bayer and Benedict, which served exclusively as an auditorium for musical performances. AIHS conferences—"great conversations"—took place in a quite different architecture, a building also designed by Bayer and located immediately next to the auditorium tent. The Koch Seminar Building consisted primarily of two hexagonal rooms in each of which discussions took place around a large hexagonal table, with additional seating radiating hexagonally outward along the room's periphery. The Seminar Building thus distinguished the kind of architecture proper to academic lectures and conversations from the kind of architecture appropriate to the auditory enchantments of music. The environment had been formulated as a new model of economic and psychological interaction governed, on the one hand, according to an increasingly global division of labor and the expansion of global finance and debt and, on the other hand, according to growing networks of communications media. The strengthening grasp of these mechanisms allowed AIHS speakers to model themselves explicitly as humanist rather than environmental subjects. Music was for AIHS participants to enjoy in their leisure hours, not for coordinating their bodies in physical labor.

The new tent by Bayer and Benedict was suited to the purposes of leisure, to letting listeners lose themselves momentarily in sound. As such, the tent was modeled on the image of an environmental sensorium: a single sphere atmospherically suffused with indirect light that cast no sharp shadows by which to differentiate self from nonself. In this tent there would be no conversational exchanges, no parsing of language; there would be only listening and luminosity. The hexagon, by contrast, created a "circle" of communicative exchange, but its sharp corners emphasized the breaks and facets of this exchange, the different positions assumed by its speakers, and their ability to step outside the exchange, to evaluate and judge rather than be captured in a seamless merging of mind and sensory signals. But the construct is not quite so simple. After the Seminar Building's completion, Bayer designed a sculpture garden that resembled the earthwork piece executed a year earlier, insofar as it expressed the pure and elemental: a square terrace composed of white slabs interspersed with a few squares of green

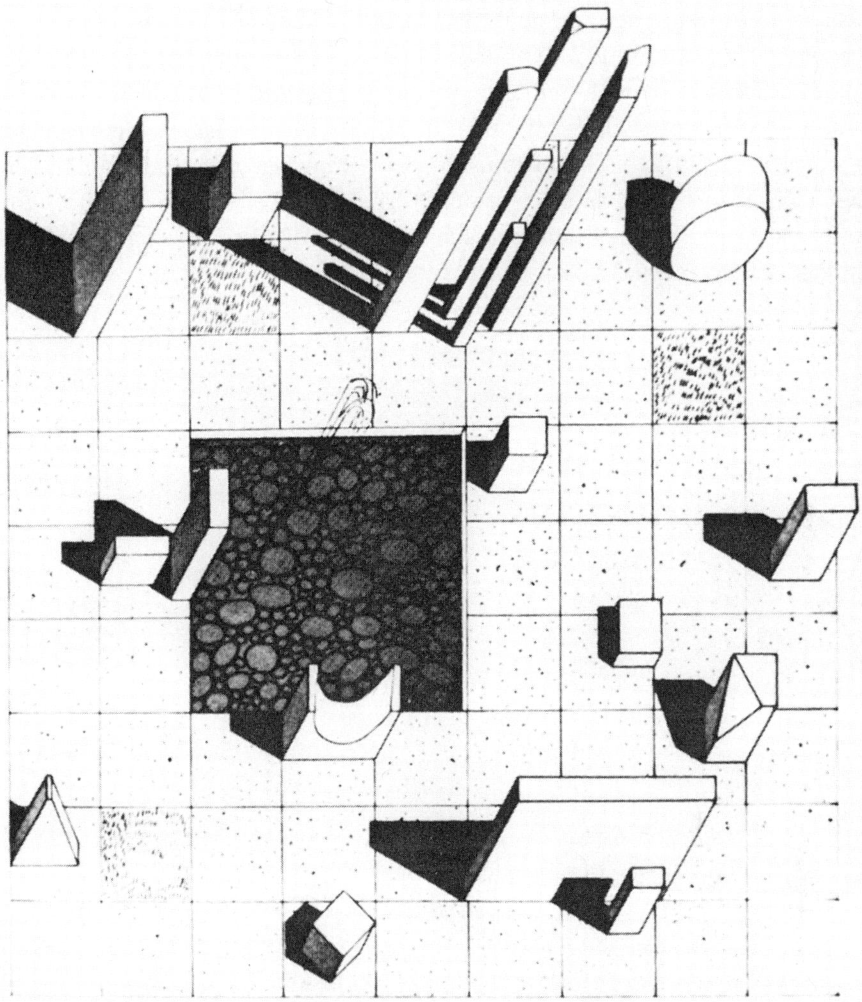

FIGURE 5.9. Herbert Bayer, design for *Marble Garden* at Aspen Institute of Humanistic Studies, 1955. Copyright 2020 Artists Rights Society (ARS), New York / VG Bild-Kunst, Bonn.

grass, a square fountain placed slightly off center in the composition, and a dozen or so geometric forms carved from white marble. The fountain, the white marble, the simple forms, and the patches of grass evoked the Italianate classicism of humanist culture. At the same time, the garden's modernist idiom seemed to reveal representation's primordial nature, something belonging less to humanism per se than to environmental subjectivity, to the workings of primitive thought.

Bayer later designed one last landscape work at the AIHS, a park dedicated to Robert Anderson, heir of ARCO (a vast petroleum concern) and chairman of the AIHS for many years. The park was similar to Bayer's earlier *Earth Mound,* though it covered a much larger area. Perhaps he had this park in mind when he later drafted an essay titled "future lecture on environment," which proclaimed that art would soon come to "assume terrestrial, even cosmic dimensions. It will again assume meaning for the majority."[62] If art was to attain this universal relevance through, on the one hand, its conflation with the "terrestrial" and "cosmic" and, on the other hand, its invocation of the "primitive" forms of menhirs, mounds, and berms, then perhaps the putative humanist subject was not to differentiate from the environmental subject after all. Perhaps these participants in "great conversations" were, like their "environmentee" counterparts, also in the thralls of nonlinguistic semiotics, also enchanted and captured in a semiotic–environmental haze.

6

HARLEM SPEAKS TO ASPEN

Environmental Politics versus Environmental Design

> "Environment," says [Richard Buckminster Fuller], "is everything but me." . . . I would say that a more workable way to think about this infinitely complex subject can be found if we turn the Fuller aphorism around. . . . Why not describe it as the *me* in everything else?
>
> . . . I have often found it handy to consider environment anything that gets processed through those incomparable computers—the human mind, the heart, and the spirit. . . . As most of us flew or drove over the Front Range of the Rockies on our way here to Aspen, I think we transformed the natural world through our perception into environment.
>
> —WILLIAM HOUSEMAN, introductory remarks to the International Design Conference at Aspen, 1970

At the 1970 IDCA, titled "Environment by Design," conference participants found themselves caught between two contemporaneous movements, each leveraging different concepts of the environment: on the one hand, the environmental movement linked to U.S. countercultural and ecological concerns, and on the other hand, the interrelated development of environmental design and environmental psychology as new academic disciplines.[1] The conference organizers were concerned primarily with the discipline of environmental design, which, without wholly excluding ecological concerns, generally attempted to depoliticize the ecological. On the other hand, the busloads of protesters—mostly students—who descended on the conference came to agitate in the name of ecological concerns, staging their own counterconference events.

It is not the purpose of this chapter to examine the standoff between the invited conference participants and the protesters, as recent scholarship has addressed this history in detail.[2] Instead, this chapter concerns itself with how the discourse surrounding the standoff managed to entirely eclipse a landmark event in the IDCA's history and, indeed, in U.S. architectural discourse more generally—namely, the talk delivered by Cora Walker, a Harlem-based lawyer and community activist. The conferences' yearly rosters had almost never included women, and the only African American to have been invited to an IDCA prior to Walker's inclusion was Gwendolyn Brooks, who had been asked to recite one of her poems at the 1961 conference. Walker's presentation on a Harlem cooperative moment was certainly relevant to the political dissensus staged by conference protesters, given her pointed critique of the conferees' framing of the environment. Yet Walker's contribution received scant attention either during the conference or retrospectively. Her strong political position was not noted in the conference's summary comments (which addressed the event's contentious politics in reference only to the student protestors and the lecture delivered by "the French group," led by Jean Baudrillard). Unlike the French group's contribution, Walker's talk was not among the many published in the official conference proceedings. Reyner Banham's edited volume of IDCA presentations included a section, "Polarization," in which were reprinted the presentations by the French group and the architect Peter Hall but not Walker's, although Banham briefly paid tribute to her contribution in his introductory remarks on the 1970 conference.[3] Subsequent journalistic and historical analyses, in describing the political stakes of the event, omitted any description or analysis of Walker's contribution.[4]

Relevant to Walker's positionality vis-à-vis the IDCA's discursive framing of the environment was the fact that, since the IDCA's last environmentally themed conference in 1962, a crop of environmental programs related to both psychology and architectural design had sprung up in North America and Britain.[5] Two of the IDCA speakers were affiliated with the University of California at Berkeley, where in 1959, William Wurster, a former member of the group Telesis, had overseen the unification of the architecture, city planning, and landscape programs under the new umbrella of the College of Environmental Design (CED). Into the 1960s and '70s, the CED became known for its focus on environmental psychology. At the Graduate Center of the City University of New York, a program in Environmental Psychology was founded in 1959, focused largely on the psychological effects of the physical environment at institutions of detention and rehabilitation. More recently, the architectural critic Reyner Banham, who delivered a talk at the conference, had just been appointed head of the new School of Environmental Studies at the University College of London (UCL). And finally, another invited speaker at the conference, Richard Farson, had recently become dean of the new School of Environmental Design at the California Institute of the Arts.

The purpose of this chapter is to ask how the disciplinary lineaments of environmental design served to secure Walker's silencing—to the extent that even while she was given an audience, she was not heard. (Or, to be accurate, she was not *written*.) This entails discerning how the disciplinary goals and assumptions of environmental design (including environmental psychology) lent themselves to projects of urban renewal at the expense of urban residents and how a construct of semiotic cognition implicit to this new disciplinary configuration was implicated in the architectural processes of depoliticization that were branded as postindustrial urban renewal.

The ways that a cybernetic vision of environmental design were used to circumvent urban politics have been noted in various scholarship, including Yates McKee's analysis of post-Katrina redevelopment in New Orleans and Felicity Scott's and Orit Halpern's respective studies on MIT's School of Architecture and Planning.[6] This chapter supplements this line of critique by examining how the discipline's neglect of the urban reforms led by city residents such as Walker was supported by the contradictory framing of the environment as both enveloping and enveloped (described in chapter 5). According to this framing, humans were construed as "environmentees" (to use the word of one 1962 IDCA participant), characterized by their cognitive capture within a given environmental-semiotic milieu, but a certain class of humans were simultaneously construed as what Banham described at the 1970 IDCA as "environmental operators."[7] The latter notion was heir to a humanist figment of sovereign cognitive subjectivity that had shaken off the shackles of enthrallment to its immediate environmental milieu. The contradiction was not recognized as such because it was—by turns, explicitly and implicitly—enabled by a split conception of humanity itself.

Although the notion of environmental operators was not explicitly racial, the discipline of environmental design—as we will see with the IDCA proceedings—promulgated techniques of urban and psychological transformation, typically directing such techniques against the urban poor. The contradictory framing of the human subject as simultaneously humanist (cognitively transcending environmental capture) and posthumanist (not transcendent) was enabled by class- and race-based exceptionalism, tacit or otherwise. What we might think of now as a posthumanist condition—the state of cognitive capture within a semiotic milieu—was formulated in the middle to late twentieth century less as a posthumanist than as a *pre*humanist condition, the latter being an essentially racial designation. Hence, Walker's instantiation of forms of cognitive subjectivity that might easily qualify her as an "environmental operator" could not be processed by an ideological system that designated black persons as environmentees, cognitively captured in environments that had (incidentally) been economically blighted by racial covenants, urban disinvestment, and the post-Fordist evisceration of industrial jobs.

In recounting the events of the 1970 IDCA, it is tempting to represent the protesters and the French group in a heroic light while casting the official conference as a monolithic agent of hegemony. Yet, though I do not discredit the political import of the protests, it is telling that the counterconference proceedings did not pause to acknowledge Walker's significance. Granted, the protesting groups were heterogeneous and included some people agitating on behalf of civil rights movements, such as Stephen Frazier's group of minority students from Chicago.[8] Nonetheless, the version of the environment advanced by many countercultural protestors—though in some instances overlapping with those of civil rights and anti-imperial movements—had their georgic biases.[9] Even while repudiating some key fundaments of U.S. settler colonialism (such as the sacrosanctity of private property), strains of countercultural utopianism nevertheless involved a peculiar rehearsal of settler colonial dependence on a "frontier" of available land. This repetition of white flight to agrarian regions—despite its counterhegemonic impulse—placed the environmental movement in an awkward relationship to issues of urban justice, even though its participants might be sympathetic to those issues. Walker's urban interventions—to be described shortly—were not easily categorizable within the strain of environmental activism that tended to enframe environmental politics through an anti-urban cultural aesthetic. Even if the countercultural movement often involved a more benign form of urban neglect than that promulgated by conservative political interests, it still unintentionally lent itself to a subject positionality external to urban blight. Such blight, as shown by some of the conferees' architectural projects, was a prelude to urban redevelopment.

Postindustrial Bridge

The conference was chaired by the architect William Houseman, whose own urban redevelopment work dealt with conditions described by the euphemistic neologism of the time as "postindustrial." One of the participants he invited, Carl Koch, presented his plan for redeveloping the derelict warehouses of Boston's Lewis Wharf into condominiums and leisure venues for the "creatively inclined."[10] An early example of repurposing a defunct industrial site for luxury habitation (although not so early as Paepcke's postindustrial redevelopment of Aspen), Koch's Lewis Wharf project posited the rightful subjects of postindustrialism as the creative class, the humanists par excellence, whose urbanity and consumer tastes would render desirable the site's immediate proximity to downtown Boston. Jutting into Boston Harbor yet directly adjacent to downtown, the wharf gave its postindustrial residents the luxury of being in a sense both inside and outside the city.

At the time of the conference Houseman was involved in organizing a community-design charrette for the development of the Harlem River Yards in the South Bronx, a long swath of land lying across the Bronx Kill from Harlem, which had been cordoned off from the rest of the Bronx by a rail line to the suburbs many decades prior. Later, one of Robert Moses's projects, the Major Deegan Expressway, further severed the Yards from the surrounding city. Then, throughout the 1970s, following years of urban disinvestment, rising unemployment, and architectural neglect, an epidemic of arson—many of the fires were landlord instigated—swept across the South Bronx, leading to massive depopulation. With the city of New York on the verge of bankruptcy throughout the 1970s, city administrators began a campaign of redevelopment entailing different strategies for cultivating a tax base, now all very well known: attracting artists into downtown ethnic and industrial ghettos by excusing them from rent or property costs, using tax incentives to refashion downtown business districts into centers for the investment of global finance, and, on the other end of things, seeking new industrial tenants for sites that, because of their locations, would be unlikely to attract other types of profitable investors.

The Harlem River Yards fell into this last category. Its waterfront position at the conflux of massive infrastructures was a potential asset for factories, whereas its distance from downtown and proximity to urban blight made it unsuitable for other profit-generating enterprises. The city's Economic Development Commission had managed to attract the interest of an Italian real estate developer who imagined that an industrial park at Harlem River Yards could draw tenants from Europe "escaping higher corporate taxes at home in favor of an acceptable cost of doing business in the South Bronx." According to Houseman, "little mention was made, however, of how an industrial park might affect the surrounding community."[11] Consequently, the Wave Hill Center, an endowed estate located in a more affluent part of the Bronx, secured funding from the National Endowment for the Arts to investigate redevelopment strategies for the Yards and recruited Houseman's involvement.

Wave Hill Center assembled a committee that included the director of the new Environmental Psychology program at the City University of New York, as well as developers, planners, and architects (including Steven Holl). The project was couched in terms reminiscent of U.S. discourse of nineteenth-century westward conquest and infrastructural development. A representative from the British architecture firm Llewelyn Davies declared that the Yards could "lie fallow for a period of time, until something major happens in the South Bronx." In the meantime, he said, a design charette could produce "the perception that something positive is going to happen—the creation of a plan, and making people believe that this plan is going to happen."[12] This ruse was to be produced in part by gesturing toward assets well beyond the actual site.

The deputy borough president of the Bronx proposed "bridging the Harlem River Yards . . . physically and psychologically," suggesting the area might serve as a connector between the burnt-out South Bronx and the recreational parkland of Randall's Island. Wave Hill Center impressed upon the charrette teams that they should "consider the Harlem River Yards an *environmental bridge* to Randall's Island."[13] In other words, Wave Hill Center regarded these two geographic entities not as distinct urban districts or neighborhoods but, rather, as distinct environments, whose difference required a form of architectural elision. Economic profitability thus depended on a conceptual splitting of the notion of "environment," such that ecological and socioeconomic degradation could be cast as surmountable not by addressing the root causes or even the effects of degradation but by making strategic infrastructural connections that could cast a site within a different frame of reference than that of the immediate neighborhood community. This strategy of urban recontextualization depended on the involvement of what Banham referred to as "environmental operators," trained to conceive of the environment in terms of macromanagerial strategic planning. Against an assessment of local socioeconomic concerns, the postindustrial site could be reborn by dint of a more omniscient, transcendent conception of environmentality, linked not only to humanist aesthetic tropes but also to practices like infrastructural planning and real estate financialization.

For the sake of brevity, I will focus on just one of the Harlem River Yards design proposals, developed by a team of architects, planners, and representatives from the South Bronx community organization.[14] The two dominant features of the scheme were a "gymnasium bridge" and a "checkerboard site plan," intended, in combination, "to signal hope and despair." Stylistically, the team employed a formally austere and monumental architectural style made popular by the Italian architect Aldo Rossi, a style that translated an Italianate classicism into a modernist idiom. The team proposed a gigantic pivoting building-cum-bridge they referred to as a "payroll gymnasium bridge," thus named because its interior program would serve the double purpose of providing jobs to the underemployed residents of the South Bronx while also providing spaces for leisure and recreation. The second element was a vast checkerboard field in which other programmatic elements might eventually be distributed. Alternating with

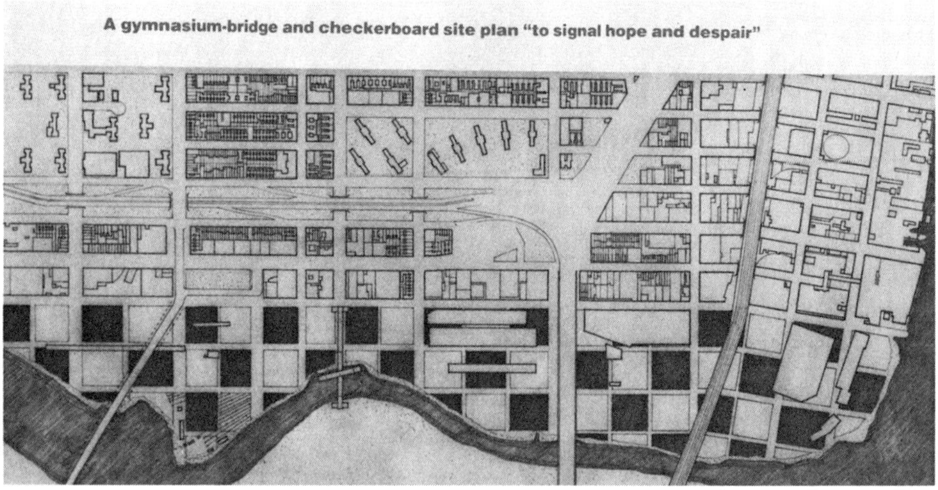

FIGURE 6.1. "Checkerboard pattern . . . signaling hope and despair" for proposed Harlem River Yards redesign, circa 1977. Artists unknown. From William Houseman, *The Harlem River Yards: Bridging a South Bronx Community Need* (1978).

FIGURE 6.2. "Environmental bridge" for proposed Harlem River Yards redesign, circa 1977. Artists unknown. From William Houseman, *The Harlem River Yards: Bridging a South Bronx Community Need* (1978).

squares of newly planted grass, black squares were to be filled with ashes taken from the burnt-out buildings throughout the area. Given the vast scale of the pattern, the checkerboard would be "clearly visible from airplanes passing directly over the site as they come and go from the airport." Remnants of older infrastructures were to remain on the site; for example, old boxcars from the rail yard were to be "incorporated in a kind of railroad graveyard and recreation area." In one corner of the site, as a gesture to postindustrial georgics, hydroponic towers would grow "Manhattan tomatoes and exotic fruits such as balloon figs."[15]

The design proposal was notable for a certain heightened ambivalence, not simply between hope and despair but also between legibility and muteness. The massively monolithic concrete bridge, sublime and cryptic, inspired silent solemnity more than it issued a sense of welcome. Yet this silence was counterposed by the potent symbolic function of the checkerboard, whose legibility, however, was intended to speak to those who might fly above the "environmental bridge." Unlike residents of the South Bronx, they could come and go from the city as they pleased and could observe the entire postindustrial city: from downtown, where depopulation and disinvestment were leading to intensified financialization, to the South Bronx, where reinvestment was as yet merely a vague promissory note taking the form of a bridge. The environment—in the sense of its structural workings—could only be *read* from the stratosphere. For those who remained captured inside the environment, its strange, sublime forms offered no legibility. Rather, they communicated in a more haunting, numinous manner, better suited to maintaining the imagined aphasia of the poor.

"An Environmental Revolution": From the Slums Outward

The projective aspect of the Harlem River Yards charrette stands in contrast to Walker's project for Harlem. Walker had probably become known to Houseman through his involvement with the South Bronx, leading to Walker's unlikely inclusion in the conference events. Before describing the project she had helped organize in Harlem, Walker began by noting a communicative impasse between Aspen and Harlem, implying the inadequacy of *the* environment as a conceptual category. In Harlem, she said, an idea of environmental justice was inflected by the fact that people "must struggle constantly for mere survival," whereas those gathered at Aspen "live in another world . . . a dream world."[16]

At an environmental conference funded by major aluminum and petroleum corporations (a fact that had never been questioned by IDCA conferees), Walker pointed out that those sponsors were appropriating the nation's resources without "putting what they take out back into the ghetto communities" and that in light of such sponsorship, she was compelled to "question whether you are serious in this group as to your intention to make a contribution to change of the environment by design for all the citizens of this country."[17] Walker remarked that the kind of environmental movement suggested by the conferees would be unrecognizable to poor blacks, Puerto Ricans, Mexicans, and Indians, who, thanks to economic injustices, were still focused on the environment as it related to their day-to-day abilities to survive. An "environmental revolution," she argued, must begin in the slums and then move outward from there.

Walker's proposed model of environmental politics implied a very different spatial–political construct than the everted globe presented decades earlier at *Airways to Peace.* The latter had afforded its viewers the illusion of transcending capture within an environmental surround by allowing them to view the entire global sphere as if it *were* an environmental perceptory sphere. By contrast, Walker was proposing not a transcendent form of subjectivity through which one's immediate environment might be overcome but, rather, a movement that would engage immediate environmental and social politics, moving outward from there. Her framing suggested that a local movement could form alliances with other movements or organizations so as to critically address the larger legal frameworks, institutions, and corporations affecting urban and ecological conditions. In other words, Walker suggested political negotiation (rather than, say, psychological design) as a way to effect change. The difference between grassroots politics and professional architectural design was underscored by Walker's reproach to the conferees: "You have the arrogance to feel that you can solve vast national problems simply by remaining in your own comfortable world of design."[18]

Walker then offered an example of what sorts of political activities an "environmental revolution" might entail, describing a project she had helped organize in Harlem starting in 1967. Protesting against a proposed low-income high-rise project whose construction would exclude local labor, neighborhood residents organized their own housing council to participate in City Planning Commission meetings. The council subsequently oversaw the creation of a cooperative supermarket to redress Harlem residents' lack of access to quality food. They also launched a cooperative housing development company, which, by the time of Walker's presentation to the IDCA, had secured most of the funding to build hundreds of housing units, drawing largely on local labor skills. Walker insisted to her Aspen audience that positive environmental transformation "must enable people to become a part of their own designing process. They must become self-determining and self-directed."[19]

The environment was thus understood as an object that must be politically approached, whereas the discipline of environmental design—with its pet projects of prisons and psychiatric wards—was conceived of as a substitute for politics. It was this latter configuration of the environment as a disciplinary apparatus of control that the French group's critique completely overlooked. Their contribution, credited to Baudrillard's authorship, entailed a brief but scathing denunciation of the way the concept of the environment had been ideologically conjured in order to mask socioeconomic conditions that were causing widespread civil unrest in the United States, particularly its wars in Southeast Asia.

The French group was correct to point out that the environmentalist cause risked deflecting attention from U.S. imperial wars. Nonetheless, it was misleading to reduce the environment's ideological powers (to say nothing of actual ecological problems) to the powers of mere distraction. The environment was not simply a conspiratorial ruse conjured to mask social injustices; rather, the environment constituted a formative disciplinary rubric *and* an actual aspect of social injustice. So there was not just the problematic ambivalence of the environmental concept—which could be invoked in the name of both hegemonic and antihegemonic politics. Dominant conceptions of the environment—far from being a mere ideological veil draped over the real and ongoing catastrophes of economic inequality, racism, and proxy wars—in fact helped aesthetically and epistemically configure and perpetuate those catastrophes.

In its function as a transcendental spatial and semiotic mechanism, "the environment" ascribed racial and economic difference to climatic causes (such as theories described in chapter 5) while, at the same time, couching various forms of neocolonial governance as natural extensions of environmental stewardship. Falling within the purview of such stewardship was the management of brains and the environments that shaped them. The environment was not only ideology in the traditional Marxian sense; it was a flexible set of spatial and semiotic concepts that helped naturalize racial injustices, while at the same time mobilizing environmental design as a biopolitical device used to circumvent urban politics.[20] The disciplinary development of environmental design did not only mark a shift toward a posthumanist construct of environmental subjectivity (that secreted within itself a humanist exceptionalism); it also helped lay the ground for an understanding of architectural education as a design of perceptory systems, lending architecture to the growing domain of digital aesthetics.

"Environmental Operators"

> This setting is far removed from the dirt, the grime, the poverty. . . . Many of the conferees whom I have met here in Aspen live in another world. . . . They have lulled themselves into a dream world and a false sense of inner security.
>
> —Cora Walker, "Pioneering in Co-Op Programs"

At the 1970 IDCA, an unprecedented number of talks focused on design education. Banham, now director of the program of Environmental Design at the UCL, delivered a characteristically gnomic talk entitled "The Education of the Environmentalist," which described how his school had decisively parted ways with its eponymous predecessor, the College of Environmental Design at the University of California at Berkeley (the latter derided by Banham as the "Great Berkeley Disaster"). Rather than simply reassembling the traditional design disciplines under the conceptual umbrella of "environmental" and assuming that they must thereby be environmentally oriented (although this was not an adequate description of Berkeley's program), the UCL, Banham boasted, offered not a basic design curriculum but, rather, a "degree in environmental studies, a general degree with no necessary linkage to any professional destination that a student might have in mind." The environmental design degree, according to Banham, should confer neither professional training nor expertise in a particular craft (an echo of the Bauhaus *Vorkurs*). "If," Banham proposed, "to quote Bucky again, everything is environment which is not me, then environmental education is the study of the whole damn universe." Far from training students in "the servile arts" (to use Mortimer Adler's words, discussed in chapter 5), the degree in environmental studies would constitute a revision of liberal arts in the curriculum, preserving all the latter's claims to universalism, albeit now with a stronger emphasis on crafting the world's technopolitics. What the school would produce, claimed Banham, although he couldn't be sure of precisely what this new occupation would entail, were "environmental operators."[21]

Banham was also vague about what the education of an environmental operator might consist of, although he mentioned that the broad options available to design students within the larger university might lead them to pursue courses as disparate as "Futures and Forecasting," symbolic logic, and urban geography, thus suggesting interests in finance, semiotics, and urbanism. He proclaimed that students were not to become "environmental know-alls," nor simple problem solvers. His disciplinary ambitions seemed to imply a question of epistemic scale and positionality: to take a perspective of the world so macroscopic as to lead to detachment (as the humanities are often accused of doing) would impede the ability to intervene, to design. But conversely, to simply solve problems would relegate environmental designers to merely tinkering with microscopic details in lieu of revealing and producing larger systemic frameworks for environmental intervention. In other words, Banham seemed to be conceiving of a version of the humanities and social sciences that would become instrumentalized through techniques of design.

To illustrate the difference between environmental operators and crude problem solvers, Banham described the studio assignment given to first-year students to design a "portable photographic dark room that could be built and used by eight-year-old school children during their field trips." When students and critics from the neighboring Architectural Association showed up to survey the results, a number of them, according to Banham, snidely demanded whether UCL students had ever heard of the Polaroid. The question exemplified for Banham the mentality of mere problem solving in contrast to the complexity and creativity demanded by the darkroom project. What Banham was getting at lay close to the old Bauhaus pedagogical exercise of designing "useless machines" (described in chapter 2) as an important exercise for transitioning from a conception of arts pedagogy to one of media pedagogy. The point of the darkroom exercise was not to produce a machine with any use value per se (since, yes, there existed Polaroids) but, rather, to have students consider the relationship between world and representation through the rubric of cognitive instruction, that is, addressed to an eight-year-old human brain.

The darkroom exercise was based on the agenda of environmental design, insofar as it engaged not questions of material ecology (much less those of ecological justice) but, rather, technologies of perception, representation, and reproduction. Moreover, it did so while addressing specifically the little savage minds, for whom the darkroom construction drawings had to outline a set of discrete operations presuming no architectural knowledge or skill. In some ways, the education of environmentalists was the education of education itself, insofar as the environment was conceived of as the interface through which the brain understood the world beyond. Thus, it is telling that the only UCL faculty member Banham mentioned by name was the psychologist and zoologist Jane Abercrombie, claiming that the Environmental Design program was deeply indebted to her research on education. Further demonstrating the developmental–psychological orientation of environmental design, the architect Paul Friedberg, who had recently designed a nursery school, claimed in his talk, "Energy of Communication: Tools of the Design Process," that the conference might have better addressed issues of environmental design had it actually had education as its theme.[22]

The conferee who most insistently stressed the connection between the changing nature of education and the burgeoning conceptualization of the environment was Walter Orr Roberts, who was not a design educator but an atmospheric physicist. Roberts's talk began by predicting the imminent development of technologies for suppressing hail and deterring hurricanes from reaching land. He pointed, furthermore, to accidental "weather modification experiments" that might already be underway, and he used the example of airplanes' production of contrails, which turned into tropospheric clouds with the potential to affect weather patterns. He went on to forecast a bright future for cities, a future in which the quality of life would be so improved as to reverse the ongoing exodus to the suburbs. In addition, there would be great improvements to waste recycling and a general perfection of resource management. But what would, above all else, "characterize life in the revolutionary times of the year 2000" would be the computer. And the "educational uses of the computer," Roberts mused, "are going to be the greatest part of this revolution of all." Roberts described education as already being the "biggest and probably most important business" in the United States. By the year 2000, however,

> with the vast leisure that can be available, the largest number of hours of a student will be spent in a computer-based multi-media carrel talking with the computer. . . . The use of the computer, moreover, will be highly individual. . . . The wider use of computers in education is going to make it possible for our teachers to cease being machines and [instead to] be humans in interaction with people.[23]

Whereas nineteenth- and early twentieth-century machine fantasies had promised the liberation of people from rote physical labor, the dream of the post-Fordist age was, apparently, for machines to liberate people from various forms of intellectual labor—such as teaching—as well. If on the one hand, as Hutchins had argued, machine production had enabled the possibility of universal liberal arts education, on the other hand, the machine was now being said to usher in a new model of education, one in which the student, instead of interacting with a teacher, would be absorbed in a sphere of "multi-media." The question was whether one would remain inside the multimedia carrel—the darkroom of the twenty-first century—or whether one would attain the status of environmental operator and help design the darkrooms of the digital age.

The environment had long been conceived of in conjunction with computational developments, both at the scale of global systems management, as exemplified by Fuller's World Game, and at the scale of electronic media environments, as articulated by McLuhan. The environment was a construct that permitted new computational technologies to elide the disparate scales of the individual's perceptual milieu and the global sphere. This elision would take on a new idiomatic charge in the decades to come with the idea of global interconnectivity via electronic media. Chapters 7 and 8 look at the beginnings of the MIT Media Lab in the 1970s and continue through the turn of the twentieth century, when its researchers' goal of developing creative, thinking machines to assist in global-southern development shifted gradually toward questions of the kinds of interfaces and operations through which human brains and machine brains might best engage with and transform each other. In this endeavor, the "savage mind" of childhood intelligence became central to the Media Lab's experiments with machine and human learning.

Aphasia

When Eliot Noyes delivered a summary address of the conference's events, he made many specific references to particular talks and to the dramatic commotion caused by the French group's presentation. No mention, however, was made of Walker's talk, as if it had apparently provoked little reaction despite its pointed critique and the positive model it advanced of urban improvement. Later, the conference papers were published with a preface consisting of Houseman's pithy notes, which included brief quotations and summaries of the speakers' most salient points. For Walker, however, Houseman chose a rather odd passage to cite, one that hardly conveyed her main arguments. Houseman quoted Walker as saying, "I must agree that Aspen is a garden spot of the world. I was asked on my arrival here whether I had even been to Aspen before. I openly admit that I had never *heard* of it before."[24] The critical insights formulated—and written—by the New York lawyer were neglected by focusing on her aural disposition—that is, what she knew through hearing, rumor, reputation. In citing this introductory comment instead of the substance of Walker's presentation, Houseman inverted Walker's own self-proclaimed subject position vis-à-vis Aspen. Her provincialization of Aspen (relative to, say, Harlem) was converted into Aspen's provincialization of her and, by extension, Harlem. Houseman went on to assert that Walker's unawareness of Aspen "spoke volumes."

However, in mentioning her ignorance of Aspen, Walker had been making a point (which perhaps Houseman was honoring, but the brevity of his citation makes it unclear). Calling Aspen "fabulous," Walker played with the word's double meaning to insinuate that the town's beauty rested on a certain fictiveness. Here, she was not so much trivializing the self-aggrandizing pretensions of this bucolic/cosmopolitan institution as she was speaking of epistemic problems of distance and framing:

> This setting is far removed from the dirt, the grime, the poverty, and the problems of the ghetto community. . . . Many of the conferees, whom I have met here in Aspen, live in another world. They have no concept of what this other side of life in America is like. They have lulled themselves into *a dream world and a false sense of inner security.*[25]

The criticism might appear fairly mundane. However, in ascribing these men's ignorance to epistemic seclusion within a limited and even illusory sphere, Walker pointed to the contradictions and phantasmagoric qualities of the postwar U.S. environmental construct. She suggested that the sovereign, transcendent form of cognition implicit to this concept was in fact a finite cognition, constrained not only by its limited vision but indeed by its delusional character. To put this another way, the outside-in globe described in chapter 5 could be understood very differently from its implied intentions: not as enabling the environment to be comprehended as *both* a cognitively structuring perceptory surround *and* an object of sovereign understanding—that is, as *both* circumscribing *and* circumscribed. Instead, through Walker's words, the outside-in globe was re-everted, revealed as a delusional "dream world" that merely provided a "false sense of inner security." Walker's words turned would-be "environmental operators" into the "environmentees" they really were—at least to the extent that all humans are equally formed by their semiotic and perceptory environments.

If Houseman had wished to more justly paraphrase Walker's comments concerning Aspen, he might have pointed to her converse remarks: not that she had never heard of Aspen, but that Aspen had never heard of Harlem (and apparently still didn't hear it even when it came all the way to Aspen to speak). In the reception, or lack of reception, of Walker's talk, race was operating not overtly—not through outright dismissals of what African America had to say—but, rather, through semiotic and disciplinary barriers willed into existence by the other conference participants. On the one hand, Walker was doubtless understood as an *environmentee* whose activities, though laudable, remained within the realm of bricolage, as she and her collaborators tinkered with their immediate neighborhood surrounds unguided by a more cosmographic vision, design, or theory. (In other words, to act locally was presumably to act in a state of environmental capture, ignorant of macroscopic systems.) On the other hand, Walker lay outside the purview of what passes aesthetically and genealogically as theory or avant-garde politics.

Indeed, Walker posed a greater epistemic threat to the IDCA's status quo than did the French group or even the conference protestors. The French group, in treating the environment as a fabricated conspiracy that might be ripped away to reveal the truth of U.S. imperialism, still allowed the possibility of recuperating a sovereign position by coming into consciousness of the truth. Walker's talk, however, implied something more profoundly destabilizing—namely, the irrelevance of such a sovereign position, given that the world might be more effectively transformed by first engaging local knowledge, concerns, and agency and, from there, perhaps moving outward. Walker's proposal for politics rooted in local dissent and action against urban redevelopment schemes is to be distinguished from the Wave Hill Center's proposed "environmental bridge." The latter served as an aesthetic strategy for attracting investment precisely by making the local point to something more distant—the recreational pleasure grounds of Randall's Island. Walker, instead, showed how local investment could resist external design proposals and turn urban improvement into a political process so as to better serve disenfranchised communities.

Concurrently with the 1970 IDCA, however, another form of "environmental bridge" was being coaxed into existence, this time through the apparatus of computation, which was intended to serve as a connective interface between local needs and sovereign knowledge. One of the aims guiding the development of graphic user interfaces at this time was its potential to reach nonliterate users and, moreover, the potential for computer interactions to adapt to the personal inclinations of individual users. In other words, computational design offered a way to secure a notion of knowledge as bound by the immediacy of a perceptory environment (this time, a media environment) while nonetheless operating on that environment from the outside in.

PART IV

MEDIA ARTS

The final two chapters show how international competition to capture markets in the global south influenced the design and marketing of personal computers in the 1970s and '80s. Focusing mostly on the development of the Media Lab out of the Architecture Machine Group at MIT, these chapters highlight the importance of several actors that have been largely missing in accounts of MIT's early research on personal computing technologies. The mutually formative relationship between the MIT Media Lab (still in its initial stages of development) and France's new Centre mondial informatique et ressource humaine (CMI) helped carve out a potential consumer market for personal computing in the global south—namely, in the domain of primary and secondary education. This was at a time when social services like education and state programs of import substitution were being decimated by austerity measures imposed by international creditors. The promotion of computer use for educational purposes in the global south gave impetus to a growing area of research on the relationships among child cognition, machine intelligence, and graphic user interfaces. Effectively, educational pilot programs in the global south became an experimental arena for research into personal computing interfaces more generally, contributing to the development of machines that would require minimal literacy (if any) to operate.

The early interest in educational machines, pursued by the CMI in conjunction with MIT's Seymour Papert and Nicholas Negroponte, helped stage personal computing as part of a north-to-south humanitarian project focused largely (though not exclusively) on Africa. The burgeoning field of technohumanitarianism served as a supplement to structural adjustment programs (SAPs), providing consumer products (at a cost) to fill the vacuum in social services that SAPs created in many states. The effort to supplant typical classroom pedagogy with computer-based learning led Media Lab researchers to discredit intergenerational human-to-human forms of group learning by pointing to the machine's ability to individuate—to adapt its pace and content to a given user's learning needs—and to capture a child's attention (this last point helping justify the development of addictive interfaces). Personal computers were subsequently designed and marketed as devices intimately attuned to individual needs. This strategy built on the earlier efforts of the Architecture Machine Group and Yona Friedman to develop architecture software that would enable users in the global south and in ghettoized neighborhoods in the United States to individuate units within mass-housing schemes. Thus, tracing the entwined emergence of child computing, global-southern austerity measures, graphic user interfaces, and technohumanitarianism, these chapters show how the spiritual ergonomics of personal computing—its focus on individualized human–machine intimacy—endeavored, first, to displace forms of language-based political negotiation and, second, to create new forms of global-southern economic dependency. These efforts were supported by a structuralist understanding of the human brain, guided by Jean Piaget's structuralist theories of child cognitive development and by fieldwork in the global south.

7

PENTECOSTAL TECHNOLOGIES

The Architecture Machine (Again)

> The [CMI's] work focused on the use of computers for primary education in developing nations. The first site was a school outside Dakar, Senegal. This small experiment was just terrific. . . . Kids from the jungle learned faster than kids from the city.
>
> —Nicholas Negroponte, *Wired* (1997)

Education, "The Oil of the Future"

In 1982, Nicholas Negroponte, the founding director of the new Media Laboratory at MIT, stood before the audience assembled at the thirty-first IDCA to deliver a lecture titled "Micro-Electronics and Human Development." He opened with an emphatic pronouncement:

> Education, in the broadest sense is clearly, if you will, the oil of the future. And in fact, the entire future of mankind clearly rests on education, and by that I don't just mean the education we know in schools, but the education that is appropriated personally, mostly through computation. My first encounter with this group interested in personal computation and education was in November at the OPEC meeting . . . to set the price of oil.[1]

The metaphor of petroleum did not seem to indicate simply that education constituted a kind of fuel for impelling other economic activity. The metaphor was in fact suggesting a paradigmatic shift in geopolitical power from a fossil fuel–based economy to an economy in which educational technologies would become a major exportable commodity. Following the previous decade's shifts in international power related to the control of petroleum (including events such as the 1973 oil embargo and the 1979 Iranian Revolution), the framing of educational technologies as "the oil of the future" constituted a bid for securing U.S. economic domination. To focus on digital exports was by the 1970s a fairly orthodox strategy in U.S. efforts to strengthen its economic position. The innovation voiced here by Negroponte was to regard education as the most lucrative area for technological exports, an idea that would have implications not only for education around the world but for the design and global marketing of digital technologies.

At the time of Negroponte's presentation at Aspen, he and his colleague Seymour Papert had recently taken leaves of absence from MIT, where they had begun developing the Media Laboratory ("the Media Lab") as a new program within the School of Architecture and Planning. They had been recruited, along with computer scientist Raj Reddy, by the French politician Jean-Jacques Servan-Schreiber to help direct his new Centre mondial informatique et ressource humaine (CMI), headquartered in Paris. The CMI, sponsored by François Mitterrand's government, sought to develop France's computer sector, in tandem with spreading computer literacy throughout the global south.[2]

Servan-Schreiber had just published *The World Challenge* (*Défi mondial*), a book that traced a history of global economic shifts from World War II through Japan's recent transformation into a leading exporter of digital technologies.[3] The book took the United States and Europe to task for their contempt of Third World leaders' demands for a new international economic order and praised OPEC nations, particularly Kuwait and Saudi Arabia, for their expressed commitment to eradicating economic inequalities between First and Third Worlds. Optimistically, Servan-Schreiber declared that the universal diffusion of personal computing and data-bank networks would spell "the end of imperialisms and neo-colonialisms" throughout the world.[4]

Yet Servan-Schreiber also reminded his readers of another historic precedent, explaining that the Marshall Plan had been conceived not altruistically but as a way to ensure future markets for U.S. products. The Third World, he added, represented three billion people with a potential purchasing power that might far exceed that of Europe in decades to come.[5] To educate these masses in basic computer skills should thus form a priority of international development projects. A corollary initiative would be to make France competitive with the United States and Japan in high-tech exports by targeting the largely untapped consumer markets of the global south, including (but not limited to) France's former colonies. In effect, Servan-Schreiber believed that the only way for France to avoid economic domination by U.S. technological imports would be for France to become a rival technological superpower.

Officially established in 1981, the CMI was housed in Paris's eighth arrondissement in a building well suited to Servan-Schreiber's intentions to welcome passersby to enter and play with the center's computers. Originally designed for a U.S. advertising agency in the early 1970s, the building at 22 avenue de Matignon was notable for its postmodernist facade.[6] A jagged section of masonry curtain wall protruded into an otherwise-glass facade, evoking an antique ruin crumbling to give way to a gleaming futurist architecture. The masonry section of the curtain wall presented in relief classical European architectural forms. The glass portion of the curtain wall was composed of shifting recessed and protruding planes. The linear and curvilinear aluminum frames around the glass panes played on some of the classical forms of the masonry facade. However, the sinuous tracings of these aluminum frames also looked like circuit wiring, a resemblance augmented by the play of receding and projecting surfaces, making the entire facade look like a circuit board, a likeness that may or may not have been noted by its future tenants.[7] In any case, the expansive glazed facade allowed passersby a view of the building's ground-floor computing activities, in this sense anticipating Apple's glass-box stores developed in the twenty-first century (perhaps not just coincidentally, as Steve Jobs had been invited to the CMI in 1984). The building's exhibitionary qualities allowed pedestrians to glimpse France's high-tech future. Offering a slight deviation from the mirrored curtain wall that Fredric Jameson has regarded as emblematic of late-capitalist postmodernity, the relatively transparent facade of CMI's headquarters blurred the distinction between private and public spaces and between spectacle and education, producing an ambiguity that would be repeated in the CMI's and the Media Lab's conceptualization of computing technologies. As a didactic medium of technological proselytization, the building's postmodernist architecture conveyed an easily legible image of a nation emerging from the ruins of a glorious past to reclaim its global economic dominance.

The CMI's proposed global network of centers for education and research recall Le Corbusier's colonial cartographic sketch that traced a line from Paris across the Mediterranean though Algiers to Gao (in modern-day Mali). In 1984, the CMI opened a center in Marseille (Centre pour l'intégration en Méditerranée) in an effort to revitalize the ailing industrial port city. Envisioned as a point of connection to France's former African colonies, the center was intended to produce "data banks of information about trade in the Mediterranean and North Africa."[8] Much as French colonial urbanism had relied on architecture as a mediating device between colonized populations and French "modernity," the CMI saw personal computers as a new means of economic and cultural integration, believing they could be designed—like colonial architecture—to negotiate cultural differences. Negroponte, Papert, and Reddy were hired to help with this initiative to make computer technologies readily adoptable by societies in the global south. Negroponte mentioned as an example the CMI's social scientific research in Senegal, a history that will be addressed in chapter 8.[9]

It is uncertain how much this interest in the global south may have influenced the design and marketing of personal computing technologies, given that the areas of research undertaken by Negroponte and his MIT colleagues—in graphic user interfaces, for example—predated the MIT faculty's involvement with the CMI and had long been pursued by other actors. For example, the Xerox Star's graphic user interface (the first to employ the desktop idiom) was launched in 1972. However, whereas Xerox PARC's research was largely directed toward business activities, the CMI and the Media Lab were oriented toward childhood education, leading to different implications for interface design. Whereas Xerox PARC designed its machines to minimize the costs of human capital by reducing the technical expertise required of its users, Papert and Negroponte were interested in interfaces that could capture children's attention. In both cases, the goal was to develop a user-friendly platform, but business-oriented technologies—unlike child-oriented ones—did not really need to *mesmerize* their users.

In seeking to develop technologies of entrancement, Negroponte's deployment of anthropologists in the global south followed a tradition (as seen in chapter 4) of identifying possible points of connection between indigenous practices (such as music, theater, and rituals) and new media. In late-colonial tradition, such media would *build on* native structures of authority and communication. Hence, when computers running on Papert's LOGO operating system were implemented in a pilot program in Dakar, it

FIGURE 7.1. Vittorio Mazzucconi, eventual headquarters and storefront for the Centre mondial informatique et ressource humaine, designed and built 1972–76. Front view and facade detail. Photographer unknown. Courtesy of Vittorio Mazzucconi.

was said that the system would "respect and build on the Senegalese traditional oral culture," while also conforming to traditional modes of intergenerational knowledge transmission (despite the fact that the older generations were deemed almost entirely irrelevant to LOGO-based education.)[10]

This chapter and the following one will show how different research projects at the Architecture Machine Group (from 1967 until circa 1980) and the Media Lab adopted Servan-Schreiber's strategy of presenting children in the global south as the most logical subjects and beneficiaries of personal computing technologies. Such technologies were described as tools of liberation and human development that would inculcate self-sovereignty at the scale of the individual user. Proclaiming the "birth of the first truly human society," Servan-Schreiber rehearsed the same claims made regarding industrial technologies a century earlier: that whereas the human being had "always been a slave," now "the computer society will, for the first time, make man capable of fulfilling his own personality."[11] Servan-Schreiber insisted that computer literacy in the global south could support the sovereignty of not just the individual but also the nation-state by providing a path to economic solvency, effectively allowing states to overleap industrialization and partake instead in the fruits of a high-tech economy. This claim must be considered in relation to the CMI's own nationalist ambitions, sponsored by Mitterrand, to treat computer exports to the global south as part of France's own Marshall Plan of the digital age.

These final chapters therefore examine how claims of fostering independence through personal computing were undermined by various research policies and design agendas intended to create cognitive and economic dependencies (at the scale of both individuals and nations), while computers became increasingly central to international economic competition. The racialized figure of the global-southern child was key in this respect, given its equivocal status, being cognitively independent (or so it was said) while economically dependent. Inherently both dependent *and* free (free in the sense that their future remained undetermined), children were metonymic for the position of the global south in the age of structural adjustment programs—dependent on the global market through debt-restructuring schemes and liberalization measures but supposedly freed from the protectionist and dirigiste economic programs characteristic of the early postcolonial decades. This putative freedom was exemplified by the claim that microcomputers would enable an entrepreneurial form of bricolage.[12] In chapter 4, we witnessed how Yona Friedman's encouragement of global-southern bricolage and the arts of survival gained currency with the rise of debt-restructuring following the debt crises of the early 1980s. (Negroponte, remember, was a collaborator with Friedman and an ardent enthusiast of his work.)

The metaphor of educational technologies as the "new oil" did indeed suggest globalizing relationships of dependence. Just as a natural disequilibrium between petroleum-poor and petroleum-rich nations had been a necessary condition for the lucrative international trade in oil, maintaining an imbalance in educational resources was presupposed by the production of education as a major world export. As such, efforts to bridge the digital divide always threatened to simultaneously deepen digital dependencies, creating a different kind of digital divide: not in personal *access* to computers but in digital-import versus digital-export economies. For educational exports to be sustained (and to justify the investment poured into their development), global educational imbalances would need to be perpetuated even while the very purport of educational exports was to redress those same imbalances. That is, educational technologies would have to produce educated people who, despite their education, would be unable to educate others without the perpetual import of new technologies, following a logic analogous to Monsanto's contemporaneous development of terminal seeds.

Papert, too, was focused on the use of computers for childhood education. Prior to the formation of the Media Lab, he had worked at MIT's Artificial Intelligence Laboratory and had then joined Negroponte's and Leon Groisser's Architecture Machine Group (a precursor to the Media Lab) to lead its Epistemology and Learning Research branch. Raised in South Africa, Papert was dismayed by the racial and economic segregation he now witnessed in the U.S. school system. Regarding technology as a solution to this problem, he argued that the use of personal computers in the classroom could help instate high-quality education in underprivileged schools; it could also, he believed, redress what he perceived as the stultifying authoritarianism inherent to classroom structure.[13] Papert ignored the fact that a similar reasoning was contemporaneously driving the expansion of computer-based learning in South Africa, where repeated civil unrest over educational inequalities led apartheid schools to implement U.S.-manufactured microcomputers in several townships and Bantustans.[14] In contrast to the satellite network the United States had developed to integrate the Indonesian Archipelago into its Open University system, educational technologies in South Africa were implemented to accommodate racial rather than strictly geographic divides—that is, it was a way of maintaining racial divides through infrastructures that brought state services across racial boundaries while keeping races separate.

Similarly, in Boston, Papert's efforts to improve ghettoized schools, coming at a time of intense local protest against forced school desegregation, could have easily contributed to justifications against desegregation, as computers were intended to redress differences in educational quality between segregated schools, not to address the fact of racial segregation itself. Chapter 8 will delve further into Papert's work, looking at his programming environment LOGO, his collaboration with the MIT-based psychiatric researcher Sherry Turkle, and the CMI's and the Media Lab's forays into educational technologies in the global south, including the Media Lab's One Laptop per Child project. The current chapter foregrounds these developments by examining how architectural disciplinary concerns contributed to a notion of digital interfaces as means of circumventing negotiation, political process, and dissensus in the global south (including in U.S. urban ghettos). Negroponte, who had received both his bachelor's and his master's degrees in architecture from MIT (before being hired there as a member of the architecture faculty in 1966), focused his early career on the argument that computers would be more competent than human architects at designing mass housing because of their ability to process complexity. The early efforts of the Architecture Machine

Group were in many respects heirs to Team Ten modernism—to its systems thinking as well as to its humanist critiques of CIAM urban principles.

The Architecture Machine Group's work could in fact be thought of as an alternative to mainstream architectural postmodernism, sharing the latter's concern with semiotics, although not in exactly the same way. Whereas Charles Jencks's *The Language of Postmodern Architecture* argued for a communicative architecture, the Architecture Machine Group sought to develop an architecture of communication. The distinction is less stark than it might appear. For example, the slippages between architecture *of* communication and architecture *as* communication were clearly evident in the systems-oriented work of architects and urban planners like Kevin Lynch, Donald Appleyard, John Myer, and Christopher Alexander.[15] For example, Alexander shifted from computation research in the 1950s and early '60s to a nostalgic new-urbanist cataloging of architectural typology. Postmodernist efforts to derive a language of architecture looked to eighteenth- and nineteenth-century French academic treatments of architecture as a system of discrete elements that could be cataloged and then arranged, similar to some early approaches to computer-aided design. With the Architecture Machine Group we see how a semiotics of architecture was in fact bound up with an architecture of semiotics, as the task of programming a machine to design intelligently turned increasingly to issues of machine communication.

The semiotic instincts of childhood cognition—especially nonliterate forms of cognition—were instructive in this regard. The protean learning capacities of young children offered hope that computers, too, could acquire the demiurgic ability to learn: to organically advance in a self-guided manner from a state of basic programmed operations to a state of semiotic complexity and nuanced understanding of human and nonhuman input. In the years preceding the Architecture Machine Group's metamorphosis into the Media Lab during the early 1980s, Negroponte and his colleagues would turn gradually from ideas of computer-designed architecture toward the problem of the computer interface, a semiotic problem that had both psychological and architectural dimensions. As John Harwood has shown for the mid-twentieth-century design of workplace computers, those computers possessed an architecture in the form of the interface, which materialized certain conceptions of human–machine relations.[16] In the late twentieth-century history examined here, the architecture of the interface was specifically oriented toward eliding class and racial differences—as manifested in differential access to education and literacy. Hence, the modernist aesthetic project of transcending the arbitrary relationship between signified and signifier here assumed a practical purpose. For personal computing technologies to find a wide market in the global south, they would need to supplant the requisite knowledge of a programming language with more intuitive ("user-friendly") semiotic means, as represented by the development of graphic user interfaces.

The computer interface was now assigned the task Team Ten had pursued through architectural design: that of translating between modernist and indigenous semiotics. Like Friedman, Negroponte saw an opportunity for computers to become devices for adapting rural people (or rural-to-urban migrants) to the exigencies of a global, urban-oriented economy.[17] Just as many of Friedman's megastructural schemes were intended to spatially integrate rural migrants into urban contexts while still conserving the migrant's putative habitus, so, too, would computers mediate between the cognitive and cultural habitus of the rural and urban. If rural denizens of the global south were to become computer consumers, the computer would have to become more like them, addressing them through the simplified semiosis of the interface.

In the decades to come, the development of graphic interfaces was crucial in producing semiotic subjectivities, exemplified by the growing semiotic distinction between computer programmers and computer consumers. The increasing sophistication and elegance of interfaces touched on an aporia lying at the heart of modernity's enduring technopentecostal search—its search, that is, for a technological lingua franca that might eliminate the arbitrariness between signifier and signified in order to communicate *around* language. Graphic user interfaces, by dint of the various ways they have come to mediate the mutual unintelligibilities among user, software, and hardware, have effectively enabled the babel of the actual computer operating system to persist beneath the pentecostal magic of the interface. The Pentecostal—according to Christian gospel—suggests a mystical communal intelligence that circumvents the need for translation. Under the spell of pentecostal understanding, signs are magically effervesced into the substrate of pure thought or spirit. There was a proselytizing dimension to pentecostal technologies, insofar as the circumvention of semiotic difference would recruit new users to a global market and to a new technosensory ambit, regardless of users' levels of education or literacy. This project echoed an architectural one discussed in earlier chapters: the idea of a nonreciprocal translation. Machines would translate users' inchoate impulses into design solutions, without the users being able to translate the workings of the machine.

From Architecture Machine to Interface

> Any design activity is characterized by intelligent behavior in that there must exist an understanding of goals, purposes, and meanings, and that this understanding can only follow from a more primitive understanding of the world. . . . We are at such an early stage of understanding the ingredients and motivations of intelligent behavior that we must of necessity work at this most primitive end of the scale of knowledge.
>
> —Nicholas Negroponte, *Soft Architecture Machines*

Negroponte is not the first person encountered in this book to have speculated on the uses of an architecture-making machine. On the cusp of the twentieth century, Charles Godfrey Leland had suggested that such a machine might allow the Tower of Babel to be completed, this time untroubled by the confusion of tongues. "As the method once acquired was inexpensive and easy," he wrote, "the poorest people, and even boys erected at will houses or huts as they pleased."[18] That "*even* boys" should wield these machines lent a misleading nuance to Leland's prophesy, for his pedagogical theories suggest that it was *specifically* children (and especially poor ones) who could best adapt to new technologies of design and production. It was not, therefore, *even* children who would wield the architecture machine. The technological transposition of inchoate creative impulses into refined material constructions would be effected by dint of an implicit intellectual kinship between the simple, uneducated intelligence of the child and the intelligence of machines. This same assumption would prevail toward the end of the twentieth century at the Architecture Machine Group.

There is an ample literature on the Architecture Machine Group, literature that often examines the influence of military-related funding and Cold War agendas in the group's research.[19] As these critiques have already been well articulated, I will be focusing on the intersection between the semiotic aspects of the group's research endeavors and the various capitalist motivations (broadly speaking) driving those aspects, with capitalism in this case including formations such as Cold War strategy in Latin America, the ghettoization of U.S. cities, the privatization of university research, and the Marshall Plan strategy (to borrow Servan-Schreiber's metaphor) to make the global south dependent on U.S. technologies.

The Architecture Machine Group's initial purpose was to develop a computer that could design architecture in response to users' input. It would rescue slum residents from monolithic, top-down planning solutions, casting the residents, instead, as collaborative agents of urban transformation. In developing this project, Negroponte was savvy about funding opportunities, as his senior colleagues at MIT's School of Architecture and Planning, such as those involved with Harvard and MIT's Joint Center for Urban Studies, knew that the Ford and Rockefeller Foundations readily awarded money to projects based on both their technological innovativeness and their promise to combat communist sympathies.[20] Not surprisingly then, Negroponte's first book published on the Architecture Machine Group's research, *The Architecture Machine: Toward a More Human Environment* (1970), refurbished one of the key formulations of the early Cold War decades, namely "the human" as the implicit subject of capitalist freedom, to be distinguished from the statistical units of population governed by communist regimes. Similar to postwar architects' claim to respect individual difference (against modernist aspirations to universality), the Architecture Machine Group's research focused on how individualism could be addressed by machine-generated urban designs. Even if capitalist societies had hitherto failed to accommodate "human needs"—as exemplified by the bleak, undifferentiated forms of urbanism decried decades earlier by Team Ten—this glitch was presumably correctable within the framework of capitalism, which was often defined as a dynamic, self-correcting system (to be contrasted with both the rigidity of Soviet planning and the economic sluggishness of the global south). This notion of self-correcting logic appears in Lévi-Strauss's and Friedman's respective conceptions of the savage mind and the slum inhabitant as natural bricoleurs. That is, if capitalism's wont was to naturally correct its own crises, the bricoleur's intellectual tendency was likewise to perpetually invent, adapt, and recalibrate according to the nature of the objects and systems encountered.

Indeed, the expansion of technologies mandated a more adaptive kind of human. Negroponte's undergraduate design thesis, "Systems of Urban Growth," was premised on projections of unprecedented Third-World population growth, in response to which he proposed a megastructural housing skeleton of the sort Friedman had made famous. As a nonviolent weapon against the spread of communism, this architecture had to noncoercively modernize a peri-urban indigent. Even before his turn to research in machine intelligence, Negroponte was considering how humans had to be differently designed in order to accommodate industrial urbanism, implying that architecture could mediate and assist in human assimilation to machines. In his prefatory remarks to "Systems of Urban Growth," he mused,

> With instantaneous communication one runs into further danger of alienating direct human experience. Implicit in technological revolutions is . . . the creation of a society which can assimilate a world controlled by remarkably advanced inventions. Can man in fact adapt physically and emotionally to the future world? One thing does seem obvious: even though we can imagine startling technological advances, some even in the immediate future, it will take much longer for men to assimilate these advances into his culture and his past way of life.

There is, Negroponte continued, the "need for sudden adaptiveness."[21] The theme of mutual adaptation between machines and humans would be prevalent in the Architecture Machine Group's orientation toward the global south, as intelligent machines were seen to mediate the alienation characterizing human relationships to the machinery of the industrial era and to the industrial metropolis.

The preface to Negroponte's first book, *The Architecture Machine,* opens with a series of images. First, a juxtaposition of two aerial photographs of La Paz, one showing the affluent district whose Spanish colonial grid, according to the caption, was intended for infinite expansion regardless of context, and the other showing a poor district stretching up the hillsides of La Paz and demonstrating how "growth beyond the Spanish colonial plan has forced a 'pebble-oriented architecture.'"[22] By "pebble-oriented," Negroponte meant that the tiny individual unit expressed its uniqueness even amid the vast urban conglomeration. On the facing page, he wrote of the need to concentrate on the local, exceptional, and particular, for, as he quoted from *Brave New World,* "particulars . . . make for virtue and happiness; generalities are intellectually necessary evils."[23] Negroponte was apparently blind to the irony of Aldous Huxley's words, uttered by the director of a human cloning hatchery who was admonishing his new interns to concern themselves only with the *particular* rote tasks assigned to them and not with the general social system their labor contributed to. (It is "not philosophers," says the director, "but fret-sawyers and stamp collectors" that "compose the backbone of society.")[24] Negroponte's captions thus unwittingly likened the role of the Architecture Machine to that of totalitarian biopolitics—that is, a system in which the public was not to concern itself with the larger political implications of its activities. Orit Halpern's assessment of this passage rightly links Negroponte's discourse to the burgeoning conceptualization of "smartness" (as in "smart cities"), a discourse that "assumes that many different agents making minute decisions can, collectively, produce an intelligent or 'smart' environment. This smartness can emerge without consciousness."[25]

The next page in Negroponte's book showed four more images: a photograph of newly constructed apartment towers in Brasilia, two photographs of medieval Mediterranean hill towns (borrowed from Bernard Rudofsky), and a computer-generated linear diagram showing an ideal urban pattern.[26] The image of Brasilia was meant to represent the totalitarian solutions Negroponte deemed typical of modernist architecture, linking modernism to communism, given the communist leanings of architect Oscar Niemeyer, who had been heavily involved with Brasilia's design.[27] It was a peculiar moment to accuse Brazil of authoritarian forms of planning, as the United States had just helped replace Brazil's democratically elected government with a military junta. However, as a planned tabula rasa city situated within a vast jungle, Brasilia presented the direct inverse to the "natural" development of La Paz's poor districts. The latter represented the ideal of the city-*like*-a-jungle: one whose growth occurred spontaneously according to the nature of the available means. That is, La Paz's poor districts were constructed through the bricolage of inhabitants with limited material means. These bricoleurs are racialized figures in that they supposedly performed by instinct processes that would be *consciously* harnessed by the designers of the Architecture Machine and reified within a technological system. The Architecture Machine was to be a technological instantiation of the racialized split between presumably unconscious and conscious modes of habitation and urbanism.

To understand La Paz's under-resourced neighborhoods as expressions of individual preference, freed from the constraints of top-down planning, does not only naturalize poverty while neglecting the mutually formative relationships between the planned and unplanned parts of the city; it also displaces a politics of negotiation with a non-politics of assimilation—that is, assuming that a degree of individual choice could be preserved within a larger assimilatory system, such that no negotiation of difference was needed. At the time, Bolivia had been embroiled for more than a decade in leftist revolutionary and counterrevolutionary politics. The national regime, supported by the United States, had since the 1950s placed a strong emphasis on mestizoism as a form of racial and cultural assimilation between indigenous and white populations, privileging indigenous integration within European-derived forms of modernization.[28] As a technological corollary to mestizoist programs of assimilation, the Architecture Machine was designed to permit a degree of personal difference, such that larger differences between societal factions need not come into conflict.

The figuring of the Architecture Machine as a device of assimilation presupposed the research and design problem of assimilating computer technologies to individual human users. Alongside the images of La Paz and Brasilia, Negroponte included an image of a computer-drawn line pattern that he likened to the finely nuanced variation of the Mediterranean hill towns, saying both were characterized by a certain *systematic* irregularity, "attainable in high-density urban life, now that the serial, repetitious, and generalized aspects of the industrial revolution can be superseded."[29] Whereas architects of the industrial era could never, according to Negroponte, mimic the minutely scaled variation of homes conceived by nonprofessional architects, an Architecture Machine could, in theory, reproduce the hill town's piecemeal accretion of individuated units.[30] Whereas Brasilia was solely "the result of the global and general," the variation within repetition seen in the hillside town of Mojácar in Spain demonstrated a certain "unity, which results from more global causes."[31] Indeed, what the Architecture Machine should be uniquely able to accomplish, Negroponte explained, was detection of a *pattern* of variation, such that the production of *difference* could henceforth be automatized. In a sense then, the indigenization of media (as seen with Friedman's work) was being replaced or perhaps supplemented by the individuation of media. The ergonomics of the spirit in this case was about circumventing the question of culture (to say nothing of circumventing political discourse) by developing a direct relationship between the architecture machine and the individual human occupants.[32]

Decades earlier, in their *Dialectic of Enlightenment,* Theodor Adorno and Max Horkheimer had criticized the homogeneity of city housing projects, as found in the commonalities between the domestic sphere and the forms of cultural consumption offered in cities' downtowns. This "striking unity of microcosm and macrocosm" (that is, between the domestic unit and the downtown, commercial city) led, they argued, to "the false identity of the general and the particular."[33] However—as Negroponte's ambitions demonstrate—capitalism, aided by personal computing technologies, could also preserve individualism as a strain *within* the homogenizing substrate of mass-consumer culture. In the same IDCA speech in which he proclaimed education to be "the new oil," Negroponte spoke of the potential for personal computer–based news platforms to tailor to a given reader the kinds of news and information that reached that reader, as the computer would incorporate a person's extant reading habits into a feedback loop that would effectively obscure any news not likely to elicit her or his personal interest.[34] As such, preferences a user evinced at one point in time would circumscribe the information later presented. In other words, to make the machine pander to a user's preferences, the user would need to be arrested at a certain level of intellectual development and political affiliation. Although Negroponte often advocated the mutual coevolution between human and computer habits, the proposed mirroring of the user's preferences did not offer much opportunity for long-term transformation of the user's interests and beliefs. As we know, in the twenty-first century this problem has made itself felt in the canalization of political beliefs into specific channels carved out by the mutual reinforcements between advertisers and content providers, a relationship in some respects entwined with racial, class, geographic, and gender profiling.

With the design of an architectural machine, the challenge was to establish an architectural system that was universal but somehow tailored to the individual, which meant that a basic pattern of commonality had to be gleaned from myriad individuals' preferences. In his book *Soft Architecture Machines* (1975) in a section titled "Indigenous Architecture as a Model," Negroponte explained the need for a common "'infrastructure,' a mix of conceptual and physical structures, for which we all have a different definition or interpretation." He explained that this infrastructure would require "a machine intelligence acting as a personal interface (not translator) between this infrastructure and my ever changing needs." In other words, the computer interface was to serve as the alembic through which personal cognitive habitus was filtered into the infrastructures of a technologizable pattern—in Negroponte's words, "the basis of a 'vernacular' . . . what Friedman calls the 'alphabet' of the [architectural] language."[35]

The detection of pattern held a significant place in the human sciences, especially with structuralism's efforts to detect elemental commonalities underlying disparate languages and societies. Because the Architecture Machine Group intended their machine to glean knowledge of various slum inhabitants' particular architectural desires and then construct these differences into an overall pattern, the machine was something of a technological instantiation of structuralist anthropology. Claude Lévi-Strauss and Ruth Benedict alike (despite their disputes) had written of the brain's innate propensity to pattern. The Architecture Machine would sense patterns of indigenous habit so as to translate them into urban habitation. That is to say, "the jungle" would be transposed naturally and fully intact into the city.

John Colin Carothers and Albert Schweitzer had characterized the jungle (and the global south more generally) as producing in its inhabitants a magical, nonliterate semiosis. Negroponte's work, however, situated the arboreal in harmonious conjunction with the urban, this nexus serving as the ideal locus of a new digital semiosis. It was through his work with Servan-Schreiber and Papert that the paternalistic aim to interpolate the south's slums within modern architectural systems evolved into a more eccentric view, as he came to regard the rural population as *more* readily adaptable to computer technologies than urban populations.[36] This viewpoint was developed several years prior to the founding of the Grameen Bank, which similarly offered mechanisms for integrating impoverished populations into rubrics of capital. The Architecture Machine Group's orientation toward global-southern slums thus anticipated a growing interest in the distinct economic potentials of the frontiers of capital. Pentecostal technologies, intended to dispense with written language in favor of more subliminal means, were now to be developed in close relationship to their ideal subject user: a nonliterate, quasi-urban indigent whose entry into modernity could bypass formal education, yet without sacrificing education's economically assimilative effects. In this respect, the Architecture Machine Group's thinking echoed Servan-Schreiber's insistence that the spread of computer technologies in the global south would allow the south to overleap the process of industrialization and move straight into a post-Fordist economy.[37]

Thus, what Ijlal Muzaffar has described as the intentionally partial modernization of Third World denizens in the decades following World War II takes a turn in the age of personal computing technologies.[38] In the work of the Architecture Machine Group and the CMI, the slum inhabitant was poised at the *forefront* of technological modernization while being *simultaneously* relegated to nonmodernized forms of urban and economic existence. That is to say, slum inhabitants were conceived as simultaneously behind *and* ahead of their more affluent counterparts. With one foot thrust into the digital age as computer consumers and the other foot planted firmly in the mythic jungle, the slum inhabitant was to overleap all the transformations associated with industrialization, such as literacy and formal education. Increasingly with the development of the Media Lab, the urban indigent—especially of the global south—would figure in this dual role of technological vanguard and quasi-urban indigent.

The Architecture Machine project, described at length by Negroponte in two successive books, made no mention of the possibility of educating the machine's intended users about architecture's social ramifications, its histories and theories, or its constructive processes. Obviously, such an agenda would have been highly inconsistent with the Architecture Machine Group's concerns, which were precisely to smooth out the ambivalent effects and implications of architectural projects by offering a pure and direct transposition of users' desires into architectural form. The whole point was to render textual analysis obsolete, as text-based education constituted a disruption—a kind of noise—within the process of transposing human desire into architecture. As with the group's proposed software program URBAN5, machine technologies would allow slum inhabitants to retain their vernaculars, as if a presumed semiotic difference—rather than different class interests—was at the root of social conflict. Conceived amid continuing civil unrest in U.S. cities, URBAN5 was intended as a computer platform for channeling urban residents' concerns directly into design solutions. Suggesting implicitly a communicative impasse between black urban residents and white architects and planners, the machine was to interact with urban denizens *by speaking their own language,* thereby obviating the politics involved in residents' translation of their concerns to planners and city officials.[39] Described by Felicity D. Scott as an "eavesdropping device," the machine was, as she writes, intended to produce consensus by encouraging conflict resolution.[40] Indeed, in a putative gesture of redressing racial prejudice, the program in fact produced race, insofar as it produced and reinforced an assumption of insurmountable semiotic difference, which lay at the basis of racial designations. This presumed difference thereby necessitated mediation to occur outside of the realm of human-to-human discussion, since such discussion was presupposed, by definition, to be impossible.

In describing URBAN5, Negroponte alluded to a prior experiment conducted by the computer researcher Richard Hessdorfer for a "machine conversationalist" that could take into account different local inflections of speech. The "machine tries to build a model of the user's English and through this model build another model, one of his needs and desires."[41] As such, "needs" are diagnosed not according to what the user consciously claims to need but, rather, according to what his or her unconscious linguistic idiom reveals. As the requisite language translation technologies did not yet exist, Hessdorfer brought a mere teletypewriter into Boston's South End ("the ghetto area," Negroponte explained) allowing a concealed human researcher to transmit and receive messages to test subjects. Led to believe they were interacting with an intelligent machine rather than a fellow human, "three inhabitants from the neighborhood were asked to converse with this machine about their personal desires."[42] Negroponte asserted that the men felt at ease communicating with the machine in a way that they would not have felt in talking to an urban planner or architect, as the machine, he alleged, "was not black, was not white, and surely had no prejudices."[43] In fact, "the machine" (that is, Hessdorfer) did have a racial affiliation, as did the Architecture Machine Group.

To add to Scott's critique of the depoliticizing tendencies of URBAN5, I would stress the importance of long-standing concepts of language (and especially textual language) as an imperfect facsimile for thought. This formulation allowed URBAN5's curtailing of language-based politics to appear as a corrective to language's inadequacies. It essentially claimed to restore to a racial subaltern a primitive unity of thought and expression. This is evident in Negroponte's assessment of the experiment. As evidence of the freedom and authenticity of expression URBAN5 would grant its test subjects, Negroponte adduced a photograph of one of the men in Hessdorfer's experiment wearing a button with the words "Tenant Power." Making the baseless assumption that the same test subject, in the company of human planners and architects, would have timidly removed such a political statement, Negroponte ignored the fact that URBAN5 in any case would not have registered this item of evidence. More important though, Negroponte's conceptualization of politics as tantamount to pithy assertions appended to one's apparel underscored the project's implicit diagnosis that the test subjects were semiotically incompetent. For URBAN5 to be relevant, Negroponte *had* to assume that its test subjects could not speak for themselves, and accordingly his summary of the project avoided citing any of the responses offered by those men. The proposed machine recast class politics as an innate semiotic incompatibility between presumed racial-urban vernaculars and the technical languages of experts, such that this difference must be bridged through pentecostal technologies rather than negotiated by those involved.

Perhaps anticipating such criticisms, Negroponte assured his readers that

> [what] will remove [URBAN5 or intelligent machines in general] from a 'Brave New World' is that they will be able to . . . search for the exception (in desire and need), the one in a million. In other words, when the generalization matches the local desire, our omnipresent machines will not be excited. It is when the particular varies from the group preference that our machine will react, not to thwart but to service it.[44]

Yet the gratification of exceptional needs and desires was hardly tantamount to the version of politics suggested by the expression of "Tenant Power," an allusion to forms of community organization in which political processes of dissensus and consensus were paramount.

The vision of the city suggested by *The Architecture Machine* was one whose opacity could only be penetrated by science and its related technologies, not by city residents. (After all, the human inability to grasp such complexity was, according to Negroponte, what mandated the invention of an Architecture Machine.) Relatedly, Negroponte's graduate thesis adviser, Lynch, had recently coauthored with Stephen Carr an article, "Where Learning Happens," calling for ways to render cities into didactic expositions of themselves.[45] The work Lynch was best known for—interpreting people's "mental maps" of the cities they lived in—sought a semiosis or coded "pattern" of urban form, so that cities could be planned in such a way as to be more easily usable by residents.[46] The device of mental mapping sought to establish how residents perceived and experienced the city, circumventing language so as to extract unconscious perceptions, disregarding the possibility that residents might directly, linguistically articulate their conceptions and critiques of the city.[47] The semiotic chasm supposedly existing between planners and residents was to be overcome with devices for tunneling under residents' conscious analyses to uncover deep, prelinguistic perceptions. Lynch's influence on Negroponte's early research appears in Negroponte's master's thesis on machine vision, which was clearly indebted to the book Lynch had coauthored with Appleyard and Myer, *The View from the Road*. This work imagined a multimedia system installed along U.S. highways educating motorists about the localities they traversed.[48] A later Architecture Machine Group project, the *Aspen Movie Map*, was an antecedent to Google Earth and related technologies of cartographic representation.[49] Critiques of this project have emphasized its creation of a private experience of the city, safely navigated in virtual space rather than in the potentially confrontational space of actual urban sidewalks.[50] While such technologies supposedly rendered the city more legible to civilians (while also assisting military intelligence and global strategies of financial investment), legibility in such cases did not lie within the city itself but within the graphic reduction of the city to a simplified spatial rubric through which to navigate among proliferating sites of consumption. The magic of the interface was that it enabled consumption without comprehension, navigation without interpretation.

The technological navigation of the city could serve as a model for personal computing technologies more generally. The Architecture Machine Group's metamorphosis into the Media Lab in the early 1980s was supported by cybernetic discourses that had for decades represented cities as complex cybernetic organisms. Urban architectural idioms overlapped with those used by computer designers and researchers in several crucial respects. Just as the city could be simultaneously inscrutable *and* usable, providing a working platform for a host of very different but interrelated activities, so too would personal computers be at once inscrutably complex and perfectly simple to operate. It is already evident with *The Architecture Machine* that behind the specific aim of developing a machine capable of designing mass housing, a more expansive area of research had been discovered in the problem of the computer interface. Although only the book's penultimate chapter was devoted to questions of the interface, most of the book's contents implicitly referenced this topic insofar as they dealt extensively with a twofold problem of communication: first, between machine and user, and second, between machine and the environment. Negroponte understood the relations between user consciousness and machine consciousness through a view of language as a poor facsimile to thought, one unable to rival thought's supposedly more direct relation to sensory perception (as input) or to graphic means of communication (as output):

> So-called computer graphics has popularized the architect–machine dialogue by affording a *natural language*—the picture—where the designer can talk to the machine graphically and the machine can graphically respond in turn. This congenial technique is surely a natural way for architects to express their thoughts.[51]

When Negroponte discussed the need for an architect engaging in an "architect–machine dialogue" to express his or her "concerns in a natural vernacular," the vernacular he meant was not that of language but of drawing.[52] Negroponte's subsequent book, *Soft Architecture Machines,* described experiments the Architecture Machine Group undertook in the early 1970s following the group's previous assertions that machines would need to learn to see so that they could bypass human linguistic input as their primary means of acquiring environmental information.[53] However, despite various experiments with photographic input, the machine remained unable to spatially interpret photos depicting even the simplest configurations of white-painted blocks.[54] The Architecture Machine's newfound "softness," then, seems to have consisted not only in its researchers' interest in the heuristic, creative aspects of intelligence (which had, after all, interested them from the start), but also in the softness of the interface: soft because, rather than seeking an exact analogue of human intelligence, it would instead seek a mediating platform between human intelligence and the complexities of digital code.

However, at stake here was the human ability to comprehend not only machine codes but, more importantly, written language. According to Servan-Schreiber, one advantage of computer education was that future computers would not necessarily require keyboard input. "Thus, a person who cannot read and write, can learn to operate a computer and, through it, have access to all the power of the electronic age."[55] Corroborating this position, Negroponte explained to his audience at the 1982 IDCA how Ahmed Yamani, the oil minister of Saudi Arabia, had inspired him at the OPEC meeting:

> *You gentlemen* [said Yamani] *believe that computers are going to help the Third World, and that computers are in fact going to move education in the Third World. Have you thought about the difference between primitive man and illiterate people?* And clearly I hadn't, and the question was incredibly good. . . . And, thank goodness, Yamani answered it himself: *Well, primitive man is in fact a very literate man, and yet his literature and his culture is passed through media—through storytelling, through all sorts of channels—which you guys know nothing about. And that in fact this primitive man is a very literate person in a way that you don't understand literacy; whereas an illiterate person, particularly in an industrialized society, has a problem of being in that industrialized society and not knowing very much, and if you are going to in fact apply computation to helping that person . . . you know what you have to do first, you have to spend time pulling things out of their heads before you put the new stuff in.* This is incredible! Here's this bastard who's raised the price of oil for all these years, and he's so incredibly smart and understanding, and isn't [OPEC] a neat operation to get involved with.[56]

Negroponte interpreted Yamani's words less as an admonition against ethnocentric assumptions and more as a hint for a new direction of research. Computer technologies might employ more "primitive" semiotic means to reach a wider consumer base rather than presuming that literacy was a prerequisite for computer education. People without access to formal education could still have access to (and purchase) computer technologies. As international lending policies were just starting to impose structural adjustment programs, resulting in cuts to education budgets in many countries, Negroponte's discovery of "illiterate" media was appropriate to burgeoning conditions in much of the global south. That is, the expansion of personal computing in the global south would occur in tandem with the erosion of the liberal ideal—the postcolonial ideal—of universal literacy.[57] This was paralleled in the United States with attacks on efforts to redress educational apartheids.

Into this picture enters the child. If Papert's background in child developmental psychiatry had initially seemed a promising foundation for instilling machines with the capacity to learn, the strenuous difficulties of this endeavor now placed children in a somewhat different role vis-à-vis personal computers—effectively, as ideal consumers of computer technologies. Childhood intelligence would still serve in certain respects as a model for machine intelligence, but as focus shifted toward the design of the interface, the distinction between children as consumers of computers and children as analogous to computers became fuzzy because the interface had to become *like* a child if it were to be consumed by children. This had various ramifications not only for how childhood itself would be conceptualized and configured in the decades to come, but also for how computer consumers more generally would be conceived. A claim central to Papert's promotion of computer-based education was that working with computers would encourage cognitive apperception—an awareness of how human intelligence worked. At the same time, however, the design of computer interfaces, along with various international policies of technology transfer, seemed to discourage precisely this kind of intellectual skepticism in regards to computer use, seeing such skepticism instead as something that must be overcome in order to integrate computers fully into children's daily habits. In chapter 8 I examine the way epistemic and racial inequities produced microscopically through the design of computer interfaces as addictive media were also being produced macroscopically through the uneven international ownership of technical knowledge. All this spoke to Negroponte's ambition to turn educational technologies into the "oil of the future." That is, it spoke to his desire to maintain the distinction between computer-importer and computer-exporter economies and thus to maintain a distinction between global south and north, even while the stated purpose of those technologies was precisely to eradicate those distinctions. Computers would be promoted as tools of developing literacy while being designed in many respects to discourage literacy and uphold racialized categories of human cognition.

8

TECHNOLOGICAL SOVEREIGNTY AND THE GLOBAL SOUTH

The Flea's Jump

> Several days ago four mini-computers were delivered [to Taroudant, Morocco]. Since then there has been great excitement among the upper-year students. There are the enthusiasts ("It's cooler than a motorcycle"), the skeptics ("Will the West really agree to yield its manufacturing secrets? Instead, we will get its gadgets"), the worriers ("They condemn us to laziness: I'm told to press a button to get the answer, but I'd like to know how this answer was elaborated").
>
> . . . Seen from Africa, the diffusion of computers does not present itself with the simplicity close to the evidence that M. Jean-Jacques Schreiber demonstrated in October 1980 in his *Défi mondial* (*The World Challenge*).
>
> —PIERRE DROUIN, "Le saut de la 'puce'" [The flea's jump]

In his 1982 op-ed piece "Le saut de la 'puce'" (The flea's jump), Pierre Drouin, an editorialist for *Le Monde,* assessed a pilot project to introduce computers in Moroccan schools using the LOGO operating system developed by MIT's Seymour Papert, Wally Feurzeig, and Cynthia Solomon. The project was undertaken by the CMI, which at the time was directed by Papert in conjunction with Jean-Jacques Servan-Schreiber.[1] Drouin punned on the two meanings of *puce* (flea and microchip), implying that the distance covered by a flea's jump was a fitting metaphor for the way personal computers might transform the global south. What worried Drouin—in the case of a large jump for the global south—was not that technology transfer might exacerbate economic dependencies but that grafting computer technologies onto societies would lead to a rejection, as was sometimes the case, he said, in botany when grafted elements were too dissimilar.[2] Contrasting Morocco and Senegal with India and Brazil, Drouin asserted that while the latter two countries had taken steps toward developing their own means of computer production, Morocco and Senegal were incapable of such a smooth transition into what he called "self-development."

It is not clear why Drouin perceived a nation's computer production capacities as a precondition for its citizens' psychological adaptation to computing technologies or "self-development," although he seems to have been suggesting a teleological schema of evolution. Whatever his reasoning, Drouin declared that for these African nations, "the 'jump,' the rupture with many habits," prompted by computation would be inevitable.[3] He cited Mahdi Elmandjra, founding chairman of the Moroccan Futurology Association and an active member of the Intergovernmental Bureau for Informatics, who had helped organize this technological collaboration between Morocco and its former colonizer and who appears to have been well aware of Papert's ideas of cognitive development. "Piaget has certainly shown," Elmandjra was quoted as saying, "that the child does not learn in a linear manner, that ruptures are necessary. It is the same for the transition to new technologies."[4] That is to say, the imminent technocultural rupture in France's former African colonies—though inevitable—could be elided, its effects buffered, thanks to this *other* rupture, one that was structurally integral to children's natural cognitive development. So long as children were placed at the forefront of African computer consumption, computer dependency need not be regarded as a threat to tradition. Elmandjra appears to have been borrowing here from Papert's theories of the cognitive effects of computation on children. Having trained in Switzerland with the developmental psychologist Jean Piaget, Papert translated Piaget's structuralist understanding of childhood development into questions of how to assimilate computers into childhood education. He hypothesized that computers might bring about a change in cognitive developmental sequence, such that children would advance to abstract thinking without having first passed through the stage of concrete reasoning in which the brain begins to intuitively grasp basic principles governing physical matter.

At the same time as Papert was speculating on possible cognitive alterations effected by educational computing, Servan-Schreiber was hypothesizing that the spread of microcomputers in the global south could allow nations to bypass the phase of industrialization and move directly into a high-tech economy.[5] In both cases, what would be overleaped had to do with the manipulation of physical matter. In this sense, both men's arguments constituted a departure from long-standing racially biased postulations that non-Europeans were best suited to rote physical labor rather than intellectual labor. However, their hypotheses need to be considered in the larger context of several developments—the recent debt crises crippling much of the global south, the expansion of intellectual property law, the development of data-collecting technologies throughout the world, the respective bids by the United States and France to dominate the high-tech economy, and the burgeoning design of graphic user interfaces. In other words, we should consider how computers—and the specific forms they would take—would dovetail with programs to maintain and deepen economic domination and thus help produce epistemic apartheids.

Papert's and Servan-Schreiber's interest in designing computers to accommodate cultural and economic contexts in the global south—including rural areas—often contradicted their professed agenda of using computer literacy to catapult nations of the global south into a high-tech, postindustrial economy. In answer to the question of what economic relevance computers might have for the global south, strategies of technological implementation often favored agricultural applications, an approach arguably ill suited to creating more-prosperous, equitable societies. While prosperity and greater economic self-sovereignty for global-southern states was often cited by Papert and Servan-Schreiber as the reason to implement computer use, French and U.S. efforts at international implementation focused more on issues of cultural assimilation than of economic equality. For example, Drouin's editorial, echoing late-colonial and developmental discourses, cautioned that in societies characterized by illiteracy, agrarian production, and "vivid" traditions, it was important that the computer not overhaul conventional beliefs and practices. Advising that computers should be used primarily for agricultural purposes in such societies, he argued that they would need to be designed in such a way that they would not only obviate the need for literacy but also mesh with those "vivid" traditions (that is, magical thought and ritual). Computers would need to be vernacularized, much as architectures in the mid-twentieth century were pseudo-indigenized in efforts to (partly) modernize the urban poor. As Drouin described the situation, the computer could thus be highly useful in the global south "despite [its] economic lag and slow progress in literacy."[6]

In 1982 Edward Ayensu, a London-trained Ghanaian scientist who served on various technology advisory committees, noted a mediatic kinship between new cordless electronic technologies and the talking drums conventionally used in parts of West and Central Africa to communicate between adjacent villages.[7] (This kinship would be invoked again less than three decades later with the expansion of cell-phone use in Central Africa.)[8] Ayensu pointed to this supposed cultural predisposition for wireless technologies when asked to testify before the U.S. Congress's Committee on Science and Technology (along with Servan-Schreiber, Negroponte, Papert, and Reddy) concerning the CMI's work. (Congress was weighing how much cooperation with the CMI would benefit the U.S. high-tech economy rather than France's.) Asked by the members of Congress about the feasibility of implementing widespread computer literacy in Africa, Ayensu explained, alluding to the talking drums, that regardless of a lack of necessary electric infrastructure, "the new technologies that are totally wireless are much more compatible with *our sociology* than you may actually believe."[9] The emphasis on "sociology" (along with his colleagues' interest in anthropology and child psychology), to the neglect of physical and educational infrastructure and economic resources, helped skirt issues of equitable distribution and national sovereignty that were at stake in the deployment of digital technologies. Prominent in the CMI's and Media Lab's ethos was the insistence on identifying a native link between indigenous cultures and new technologies, often leading back to conceptions of nonliteracy as an essential cultural and mediatic feature of much of the global south. Computing technologies were framed by the CMI and Media Lab as continuous with nonliterate traditions and other local practices. Writing of the CMI's pilot project in Senegal, a social researcher discussed the way the hands-on learning approach encouraged by Papert and by the LOGO platform in fact mimicked a local tradition of emphasizing "learning by doing," a claim no doubt made by Papert himself in introducing LOGO to the Senegalese educators.[10]

An article in *Le Monde* in 1983 on the training of computer technicians in Africa stressed the importance of considering African modes of thought. African technicians would have to possess a "primordial" quality, explained the author, "for in countries where magical practices are still very developed, a machine of this sort can constitute a formidable instrument of power."[11] But the Moroccan students cited in Drouin's editorial seemed concerned less with the conservation of Africans' presumed modes of "primordial" thought than with the contractual terms of international technology transfer: "'*Will the West really agree to yield its manufacturing secrets? Instead we will get its gadgets'* . . . '*They condemn us to laziness: I'm told to press a button to get the answer, but I'd like to know how this answer was elaborated*'" (emphasis added). Apprehensive of becoming a pool of captive consumers for global-northern products, the young students regarded economic imperialism, not cultural incompatibility, as the primary threat posed by a costly technology that did not readily lend itself to reverse engineering and import substitution. At the congressional committee meeting mentioned above, Representative Albert Gore, Jr. questioned Servan-Schreiber and his colleagues on the issue of generating economic dependencies. For example, he asked, if CMI's pilot project in Senegalese schools proved successful, wouldn't the Senegalese government proceed to "buy the equipment that they were used to?" Servan-Schreiber dismissed the question by asserting that Senegal was "not a colony anymore" and could do as it wished.[12]

Papert's philosophies of computer learning would prove strategic in orienting discussions of global technological expansion away from questions of economic imperialism and instead toward questions of psychological adaptation and epistemic subjectivity. Drawing on Piaget's theories and on the psychiatric studies of his close colleague Sherry Turkle, Papert was a key contributor to a burgeoning humanist conception of personal computing, as he and Turkle aligned these machines to Enlightenment ideals of inquisitiveness, creative experimentation, and apperception. For Papert and Turkle, the computer was an instrument through which the naturally interrogative and creative proclivities of childhood intellect could be recuperated. Effectively, an idea of cognitive self-sovereignty—of consciousness over consciousness—was to be cultivated by personal computing, thereby displacing questions of political and economic sovereignty.

LOGOcentrism

> The Wild Child was human, yet he had lived apart from culture and language. He walked out of the woods to enter history and, what is perhaps more to the point, to enter modern mythology as someone with a secret to tell. As a human being who had lapsed back to the animal condition, he was thought to embody the "natural." His way of thinking, if he could be taught to communicate, would testify to the condition of "man in nature."
>
> —Sherry Turkle, *The Second Self*

Personal computation—which, for most users, involves little comprehension of how computers really worked—might certainly stir up anxieties about Marxian alienation, anxieties about the world's growing social economic dependence on a tool of production that eluded epistemic mastery over its inner workings. Although personal computers clearly posed a threat to the Enlightenment notion of a predicative sovereign form of cognition, proponents of graphic user interfaces argued otherwise: computer intelligence need not cognitively alienate; rather, human–computer interaction might act as a provocation to the imagination, helping children ponder the nature of human thought and emotion. So argued Turkle, a professor at MIT's Science, Technology, and Society program who studied the psychological dimensions of computer use in collaboration with Papert, with whom she embarked on an initiative to launch a program of Humanistic Computer Studies.[13] Her interest in the psychological and affective relationships between humans and computers helped provide a social and theoretical scaffolding for the Media Lab's early research endeavors. Against the threats personal computers posed to long-standing Enlightenment notions of cognitive mastery (as most users were largely ignorant of complex coding), she and Papert argued that interaction with computers at all levels could be regarded as a stimulus to epistemological reflection.[14] In Papert's words, "As more complex and varied uses of the computer are developed the distinction 'programming vs. using' will slip away into a complex of richly variable possible relationships between people and machines."[15]

However, Papert had proposed elsewhere that all children must learn to be programmers so as to undo existing educational disparities resulting from economic (and therefore educational) inequities.[16] Yet in developing various applications for the computer language LOGO, Papert and his colleagues Cynthia Solomon and Wally Feurzeig had sought to create a platform for simple, intuitive interaction with computers that would obviate users' need for first-order computer coding. Papert wrote later that computer use in the classroom would diminish the relevance of reading and writing, which could thereby be reduced in school curricula.[17] Designed especially for children, LOGO used a cursor shaped like a small turtle to execute graphic operations following simple navigational commands based on geometric coordinates. LOGO became the CMI's initial platform of choice and was implemented, among other places, in the CMI's pilot education programs in the suburbs of Dakar. Papert also implemented LOGO applications in several of Boston's elementary schools, as discussed in chapter 7.

The term "LOGO" comprehended the polyvalence of the ancient Greek root, *logos*, which included notions of logical reasoning and innate truth or essence/*eidos*. Papert argued that LOGO could help reveal the inner truth of the universe—its mathematical principles—thereby lending itself to philosophical and scientific reasoning.[18] LOGO's visual and spatial basis granted child computer users access to the truth of pure, geometric reasoning in a Cartesian sense, exposing students to "*real mathematics* instead of *denatured mathematics*."[19] Papert's descriptions of LOGO were thus symptomatic of an ideological convergence of *eidos* and *ratio* within the scope of semiotic technologies, which I call LOGOcentrism. This convergence had been long in the offing but was honed with the development of personal computer interfaces. LOGOcentrism consists of the contradictory proposal that visual–spatial indexicality—because of its proximity to mimesis—might inscribe within a dominant *medium* of representation (the graphic user interface) the essential, *unmediated* truth of things. The phantasmagoric task—the pentecostal fantasy—of collapsing the difference between signified and signifier was recast as a desire to render more seamless the relations among nature, computer code, and the cognitive habitus of the computer user.

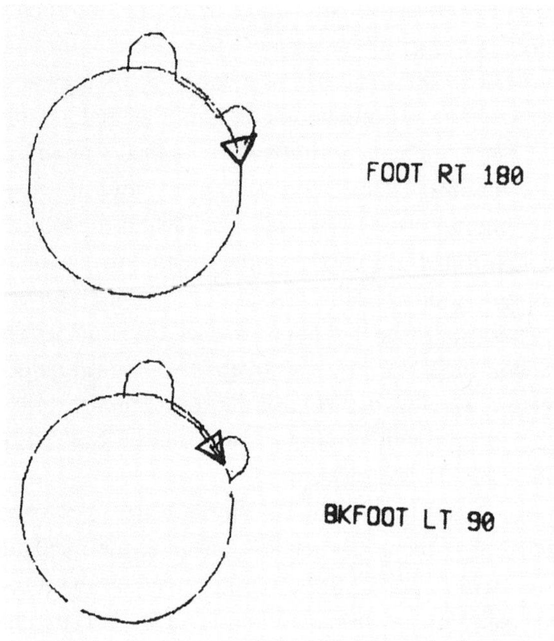

FIGURE 8.1. Programming a LOGO turtle to move, 1978. From Papert et al., "Interim Report of the LOGO Project in the Brookline Public Schools," Artificial Intelligence Memo, no. 484, Massachusetts Institute of Technology.

Papert's and Turkle's claims about the epistemological education conferred by computer use presumed that computer operations were sufficiently akin to thought that a child programmer could be said to be reflecting on the nature of human thought when programming. Recalling John Harwood's critique of the Turing Test, it would be more accurate to say that LOGO programming involved reflection on an extremely specific form of thought: the sequential operations required to program a robotic turtle to move.[20] The tendency to conflate thought in general with specific programming problems rested on an idea that thought—when disentangled from language—existed in an unmediated state. This supposedly unmediated state was conflated with imagistic representation. Papert's colleague Negroponte had claimed during his years in the Architecture Machine Group that "so-called computer graphics has popularized the architect–machine dialogue by affording a natural language—the picture—where the designer can talk to the machine graphically and the machine can graphically respond in turn. This congenial technique is surely a natural way for architects to express their thoughts."[21] Negroponte concluded his argument by advocating, first, that architects return to a natural semiosis in the form of intuitive sketches that a computer would be able to translate and reproduce, and second, that computers acquire the capability to see so as to bypass the inadequacies of language.[22] Negroponte seemed to assume that architectural sketches were absolutely intuitive, not an acquired skill guided by representational conventions such as plans or axonometric and perspectival projections.

The ideology guiding the development of personal computing was that through electronic media humans could finally transcend mediation. Toward this end, computers would need to become like "primitive people," for whom there allegedly existed no distinction between signifieds and signifiers. Rather than expecting children to master the complexities of first-order computational code, children were asked to do what came more naturally to them: to manipulate visible objects through a system of graphic coordinates and simple commands and to focus on concrete particulars rather than on semiotic abstractions.[23] (Hence, Papert described LOGO programming as involving the use of "primitives.") A long line of nineteenth- and early twentieth-century educational theorists, including Friedrich Fröbel, Charles Godfrey Leland, Johannes Itten, and Rudolf Steiner, had made similar arguments about the importance of the concrete and the spatial in childhood learning. In contexts of industrialization, education for the masses was to involve the physical manipulation of objects. In an era of computation, education was to involve imagistic manipulation. In both cases, the object of manipulation was believed to be linked to the primal truth of things, in contradistinction to linguistic description.

For Turkle, personal computers raised the specter of primitive, autochthonous thought. She observed that explorations in computer intelligence recalled the story of the Wild Child—Victor d'Aveyron—the aphasic orphan captured in the French forests in the early nineteenth century.[24] She explained that the question of the child's mind in a state of nature—having not yet acquired the mediation of language—corresponded to similar questions now provoked by human–machine communication. In fact, Victor's semiotic dysfunction improved, after years of education, only in two very minor respects. He learned to identify likenesses between household objects and the simple silhouettes of those objects drawn in chalk, and he learned to communicate his desires by gesturing toward associated objects—for example, pointing to his milk bowl to indicate his thirst for milk.[25] That is, his semiotic means remained indexical, lacking the linguistic mechanism of more advanced symbolic displacement. Although Turkle did not mention these details, Victor's semiotic limitations seem indeed prescient of the direction taken in the design of personal computers in the 1970s and '80s.

During that era indexical graphic user interfaces became central to research in personal computing, constituting a clear direction for the late Architecture Machine Group as it transitioned into the Media Lab. The design of the interface was to curtail the need to know programming languages by offering spatial, graphic environments that relied on icons and pointing devices. In the early 1970s Xerox PARC had developed the programming language SMALLTALK under the guidance of Alan Kay (a former LOGO collaborator) and, subsequently, the Xerox Star system, a graphic user interface based on the desktop metaphor, relying on icons and a pointing device rather than typographical input. It was largely the work of David Canfield Smith, whose dissertation, "Pygmalion: A Creative Programming Environment" (sponsored by the Advanced Research Projects Agency [ARPA] via Stanford University's Artificial Intelligence Laboratory), had called for an interface that would more closely resemble the authentic nature of human thought. Invoking the myth of Pygmalion (in which the chasm between representation and nature is magically effaced), Smith claimed that thought was primarily a matter of visual rather than verbal cues.[26] Citing Papert, he privileged the "concreteness" of the graphic over the abstractness of language, regarding words more

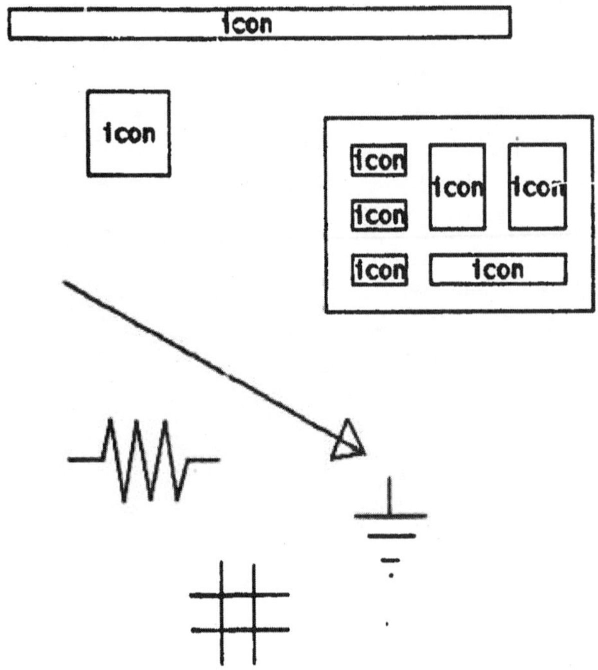

FIGURE 8.2. David Canfield Smith, examples of icons, 1975. From "Pygmalion: A Creative Programming Environment" (PhD diss., Stanford University, 1975).

as being flawed "indices, pointers to concepts" than as actually constituting a form of thought in their own right.[27]

Early twentieth-century psychological discourse had held a somewhat different view on the hierarchy between linguistic and more mimetic and indexical forms of representation. Freud, it will be recalled, had maintained that savages were so ignorant of semiotic abstraction that they believed signifiers to be concretely bound to their signifieds, such that the former could magically influence the latter.[28] The semiotic immaturity of savages was also symptomatic, he claimed, of European psychological disorders such as narcissism and schizophrenia.[29] In fact, a rising interest in schizophrenia—a disorder that tends to be characterized by semiotic dysfunctions—had reigned in the decades leading up to the technological development of indexical, graphical interfaces. Definitions of schizophrenia varied, but the one offered by Jacques Lacan was particularly relevant to the subsequent technological turn from the lexical to indexical. Schizophrenics, according to Lacan, could not understand signs in relation to each other (that is, in their grammatical relations, as structuralist analysis would emphasize) but could comprehend them only as isolated referents of particular objects.[30] Unable to adapt to the symbolic order of language, schizophrenics perceived an immediate, indexical connection between words and things.

"Schizophrenia" was a fluid term throughout the twentieth century, as recounted in Jonathan Metzl's study of how its meaning transformed during the U.S. civil rights movement. Whereas prior to this period, diagnoses of schizophrenia in the United States had mostly been applied to despondent bourgeois housewives, during the civil rights era the diagnosis came to be applied primarily to black men, often men arrested for civil rights activities.[31] Cases of allegedly schizophrenic persons included black men who, incarcerated during civil rights demonstrations, allegedly commenced speaking in tongues, ranting in what were described as made-up *African* languages (as if a made-up language could have a geographic provenance different from that of its speaker).[32] Thus diagnosed as a *semiotic* pathology, the inherently (if not exclusively) semiotic nature of civil rights could be discredited. Simply put, this was a cunning way to *silence* such politics. Shortly following the political activities of the 1960s, Gilles Deleuze and Félix Guattari had likened the schizophrenic's penchant for destroying codes and signifiers to capitalism's own tendencies.[33] Fredric Jameson, years later, interpreted schizophrenia (in a metaphoric sense) as symptomatic of the "cultural logic" of late capitalism; schizophrenia for Jameson was evinced in the form and content of postmodern art, which, he argued, offered too little symbolic—critical—displacement between artistic and capitalist production.[34] For these various authors, schizophrenia constituted a negation of the abstractly symbolizing function of the signifier. In other words, the LOGOcentric ideal of circumventing symbolic displacement—linked to the arbitrariness of the signified/signifier relationship—was viewed elsewhere as pathological, whether in a psychological or an economic and cultural sense.

In fact, personal computing ushered in a semiotic culture that was not simply an artistic *expression* of capital (as described by Jameson). Semiotic dysfunction was to be instated in and through the semiotic technologies crucial to capitalist globalization, technologies conceived by their developers as supplements to childhood intelligence and nonliteracy and thus working against advanced literacy and maturation. As Bernard Stiegler persuasively argues, computer technologies do not infantilize only by forming their users into consumers rather than investors (that is, investment in the Freudian sense of cathexis).[35] They also infantilize, very simply, both through the use of simple, visual icons to which a user points (as a child or aphasic might) and through the use of "primitive" behavior-reward systems (triumphant ding tones and the like). That is, they infantilize by actualizing the myth of "primitive thought," the myth of an idealized form of cognition that dispenses with symbolic displacement.

Interface design in the early 1980s was clearly guided by the goal of capturing the elementary education market, which was not only a sizable market in and of itself but would also ensure a future market of technology consumers. As the CMI and Media Lab endeavored to make personal computers foundational to primary schooling in the global south, researchers focused on capturing children's attention (often in contexts of overcrowded classrooms, poorly trained teachers, and perhaps nutritional deprivation). Thus, rather than cultivating acquired habits of attentiveness (as with reading), the computer would better prove its effectiveness by meeting children at their own level of psychic immaturity. It is unsurprising that in the late 1980s Papert would seek out funding from the video-game corporation Nintendo, obtaining from them a three-million-dollar grant for directed research at the Media Lab. Papert argued that video games' addictive qualities were not a bad thing, as they apparently gratified some intrinsic psychological *need* and, at any rate, could be put to beneficial use if applied to educational purposes (leaving aside the issue of addiction as a problem in and of itself).[36] What the anthropologist Natasha Schüll has called "ludic loops" (in reference to the cognitive manipulations of electronic gambling-machine interfaces) could be designed into educational technologies to make them more appealing to children.[37] In other words, Papert's lifelong insistence that childhood education should privilege the child's natural self-directed curiosity ultimately amounted to little more than the claim that cognitive manipulation by machines was better (because tailored to the individual learner) than cognitive guidance offered by human teachers.

As discussed in chapter 7, educational technologies were being promoted by Papert to redress race- and class-based educational inequalities in the United States at a pivotal moment of intense debate over recent policies of school desegregation.[38] The same educational technologies that could be used to justify educational apartheids (because they would supposedly uplift under-resourced schools in the ghettoes, thereby making them "equal" though still separate) were also designed to replace intergenerational means of knowledge transmission with devices that played on subconscious psychic instincts. As such, discourse was being supplanted at two levels: at the level of national and municipal political discussions around the crucial issue of school segregation and at the personal level of cognitive development, where "ludic loops" could prove more effective than the kinds of intergenerational care typical of teacher-led instruction. By making learning dependent on infantile gratification triggers (such as the aural and visual reward indicators common to most video games, gambling machines, and educational software), the educational approach promulgated by the Media Lab's partnership with Nintendo suggested that a certain kind of cognitive immaturity—a dependence on primitive psychic reward systems—would be sustained throughout the child's education. The preservation of childhood immaturity and dependence by the very system—education—intended to inculcate habits of maturity and independence was especially troubling given the CMI's and Media Lab's orientation toward the global south and underprivileged schools in the United States.

As mentioned earlier, Papert and Turkle proposed that computer education might occasion a radical change in children's natural sequence of cognitive development by allowing them to overleap what Piaget had called the "concrete operational stage" and move directly into abstract, self-conscious thinking (a key component of Piaget's "formal operational stage").[39] What this meant was that children who learned computer programming would effectively leap directly from the preoperational stage, characterized by what Freud would have called magical thought (symptomatic of both narcissism and savagery) into the highest stage of cognitive development, which involved both hypothetical, complex thinking and the ability to consciously reflect on and correct one's own processes of thought. This last stage of cognitive development was said by many followers of Piaget to be unavailable to people lacking higher education, whereas the other stages of development were deemed more or less universal categories, independent of formal education.

Turkle and Papert don't mention if and when the concrete operational stage would, according to this new developmental sequence, ever be mastered.[40] It seems likely that child computer users, in overleaping the concrete operational stage, would thereby in some respects defer transitioning out of the habits of magical or "primitive" thought that characterized the preoperational stage. Indeed, Turkle and Papert noted the similarity between Piaget's preoperational stage and Lévi-Strauss's notion of bricolage:

> Jean Piaget recognizes in young children ways of thinking that do not conform to the canon but that are too coherent and efficacious to be branded simply as "wrong." He casts children's concrete thinking as a stage in a progression to a formal style. Similarly, Claude Lévi-Strauss recognizes "bricolage," a "science of the concrete," but relegates it to primitive societies, a manifestation of the "savage mind."[41]

For Piaget, the concrete operational stage *corrects* the fallacies of the preoperational stage, including its egocentric and animistic tendencies. Thus, despite advancing to sophisticated abstract reasoning, child computer users might, at the same time, retain the basic lineaments of magical thought. By preserving the habitus of magical thought *while* moving into the most sophisticated intellectual phase—in which consciousness of consciousness (apperception) develops—child programmers would effectively attain the ideal creative state that had long been sought by the avant-gardes, such as those at the Bauhaus. Recalling Hegelian notions of cognitive synthesis, the child would be *both* "primitive" and advanced.

An analogy can be drawn between the child computer user, as envisioned by Papert and Turkle, and Negroponte's Senegalese "kids from the jungle," who, he claimed, learned [to use computers] faster than kids from the city." As the Senegalese children were learning through LOGO platforms in a project initiated by the CMI under Papert's direction, Negroponte's claim attested to a presumed affinity between graphic interfaces and the "primitive" cognitive habits of nonliterate children.[42] The CMI's work in Senegal also appears to have left a strong impact on Papert's thinking about the environmental formation of intelligence. In applying for a grant to launch a center for Humanistic Computer Studies, Papert explained, "The differences between the intellectual environments of the USA before and after the age of the personal computer are . . . very much bigger and more significant than the differences between the USA today and *pre-urban jungle villages*."[43]

Why should "the jungle" have indicated intellectual backwardness to Papert while representing for Negroponte a preserve of intellectual suppleness? Clearly, Papert was pointing to a jungle not *yet* infiltrated by computers. This predigital jungle resonated with the descriptions offered by Carothers and McLuhan: its thick vegetation warded off the illuminating effects of the printed word. For the Media Lab, what was to illuminate the jungle was not the printed word but the glow of personal computers. This jungle was a metaphor for a cognitive condition believed to exist in any underprivileged area, whether Boston's South End or the rural outskirts of Dakar.[44] Collapsing these geographies, Papert explained that LOGO was specifically directed toward alleviating cognitive blockages shared "between city children in Europe or the United States and tribal children in African jungles."[45] By conflating the educational contexts of global north and south, Papert minimized questions of global competition and economic imperialism that in fact placed different countries in very different circumstances vis-à-vis the use of computing technologies.

The Privatization of Knowledge

In the 1970s and early '80s, the Intergovernmental Bureau of Informatics (IBI) provided a forum at which nations could debate the international regulation and trade of digital technologies. The IBI had formed around 1974 under the aegis of UNESCO, although by the 1980s relations between the IBI and its parent organization had begun to sour, as global-southern priorities came into conflict with UNESCO's aims.[46] With the exception of France, Italy, and Spain, the IBI membership was made up of nations from the global south that sought a greater role in determining how technologies would be globally diffused. The organization added questions of economic and technological parity to UNESCO's goal of spreading technological education in the global south. Influenced by dependency theory and Latin American structuralist economic theory, Colombian president Belisario Betancur reminded IBI representatives that "political independence [in the Third World] has been achieved, but [these nations] do not have real economic independence."[47] IBI member nations thus sought to broaden their import-substitution programs to include computer production and to establish regional and transregional cooperation for sharing technology and implementing telecommunication networks. Questions of education were also paramount. Finally, a recurring theme was the tension between, on the one hand, promoting an open global exchange of data and technical knowledge and, on the other hand, preserving national sovereignty against the use of data for international espionage and economic infiltration.

Thus, while the tenor of IBI conferences tended to be optimistic, discussions were also pervaded by anxiety that extant models of economic dependency were at risk of worsening with technological globalization. As noted by Marius Franciscono, who directed Benin's Informatics Office, "billions of dollars are going to be placed at our disposal to establish *their* banks for *our* data." Data, Franciscono pointed out, helped "any industrialist in Europe . . . penetrate a market [in Africa]."[48] In other words, data constituted a new kind of raw material to be extracted from Africa for other nations' enrichment. The technological facilities, infrastructure, and knowledge that African nations developed ran the risk—much like colonial transportation systems—of serving first and foremost as vehicles of wealth extraction.[49] The French term for data, *données* (literally, "givens"), even hinted at the long-standing construct of savage thought: data was assumed to be a raw, natural *given,* free for the taking, as well as apodictic in its epistemic status. However, in its processed—that is, consciously analyzed—form it became the intellectual property of others. Like the Team Ten discourse discussed in chapter 3, global-northern technological discourse was often suggestive of the unreciprocal gift, since data extracted from the south was seen as always-already "given" and thus not really ever "taken." In response to this looming crisis of sovereignty, members of the IBI proposed control over national data and the cooperative creation of their own shared data networks. State-centralized import substitution provided a model that had been fruitful in many Asian and Latin American countries during the preceding two or three decades. India, moreover, had developed a large computer-manufacturing sector.[50] However, emerging international battles over intellectual property law and the debt crises of the early 1980s would weaken the potential of such models.

For example, during the 1960s, tensions had escalated between the Indian government and the two foreign corporations manufacturing most of its computers, IBM and Britain's International Computers Limited (ICL). The two firms granted little equity to their host country and tended to recycle obsolete parts from the global north into refurbished models, recalling Charles and Ray Eames's suggestion that cardboard computers could be manufactured in India.[51] Hence, a technological lag was maintained through corporate modes of technology transfer.[52] In the late 1960s, as India issued stronger demands for equity and knowledge transfer, IBM began to withdraw its operations, finalizing its departure in 1973 when India passed the Foreign Exchange Regulation Act, requiring foreign companies to cede majority control to Indian partners. As a result, by the early 1980s almost all computer components and subsystems consumed in India were being fabricated by its own companies. However, after enjoying a few years of tremendous growth in computer knowledge and production, India was compelled by the oil crises of the 1970s to allocate 40 percent of its import budget to petroleum, drastically reducing research expenditures and thereby paving the way for the neoliberal economic reforms ushered in following Indira Gandhi's return to power.[53] The situations in Latin America and Africa were still more dire, given the severity of debt crises and foreign economic domination.

Demands for greater technological parity by global-southern states were waged contemporaneously with battles over intellectual property law. Between 1980 and 1984, diplomatic conferences were held in response to international pressure to reform the Paris Convention for the Protection of Industrial Property of 1883, intellectual property laws that had been signed by merely eleven nations. At the first diplomatic conference, the nations constituting the Group of 77 identified abuses and areas of possible reinterpretation stemming from the Paris Convention codes and its subsequent amendments.[54] These specific legal grey areas were distinct, however, from the more general differences in agenda between the Group of 77 and the computer-exporting nations, especially as manifested by some of the more radical proposals being made contemporaneously at the IBI conferences. For example, "technology transfer" had been defined by some IBI members as the free, unremunerated sharing of technical knowledge, whereas technology-exporting nations typically understood technology transfer as either the international sale of technological products or the establishment of overseas manufacturing facilities, whereby host countries were compelled to uphold the foreign corporations' domestic patents. Some voices at the IBI meetings called for the abolishment of intellectual property altogether, but for those Latin American nations whose call for freer technology transfer had been accompanied by strong leftist political movements, the 1980s debt crises, combined with U.S. military interventions, undermined efforts to redefine technology transfer. Following the IMF's increasing imposition of economic liberalization, the south's formerly assertive demands for the free sharing of technical knowledge gave way to various concessions to accommodate foreign manufacturing enterprises on the latter's own terms.

Intellectual property law was important to the fortunes of the Media Lab, as its expansion intersected with several developments under the Reagan administration. The first of these was the passage of the Bayh–Dole Act, enabling universities and private corporations to hold private intellectual property rights over a patented invention whose development had been funded by public research grants.[55] The second of these was the diversion of funds away from open-ended scientific research and toward military funding, along with stepped-up efforts to halt international technology transfer owing to fears that digital technologies would find their way to the Soviet Union. Against backlash from the scientific community, the Reagan administration emphasized the funding of what they called "dual-use technologies," technologies that might lend themselves to both military and commercial, civilian uses. The innovation that helped launch the Media Lab to prominence during the last decades of the twentieth century was largely to take advantage of these developments. Negroponte developed a system whereby separate laboratory groups within the Media Lab would offer two levels of sponsorship to external funding agencies (both private and public). The more popular one granted the sponsors shared intellectual property in any research undertaken by a particular laboratory; the other allowed a corporation exclusive intellectual property rights to a particular research endeavor they helped direct. Under the Bayh–Dole Act, generous research funding from government-related bodies such as the Defense Advanced Research Projects Agency (DARPA), when pooled with corporate funding, allowed federal tax dollars to be directed toward research leading to private corporate intellectual property. As the Architecture Machine Group transitioned into the Media Lab, it homed in on the idea of dual-use technologies, which encouraged joint sponsorships between private industry and federal military on Media Lab research.

The concept of dual-use technologies could be applied retrospectively to the longer twentieth-century history of savage thought and savage machines, as it suggests a structuralist approach to research and technological invention. As common denominators of diverse applications, such technologies were intended to be generative of manifold possible configurations, much as structures—linguistic, cognitive, cybernetic—were understood by the structuralist sciences and human sciences. A structuralist approach to technological research had long been foregrounded by European notions that all knowledge was reducible to common mechanisms. As becomes especially legible with the advent of the Media Lab, a structuralist approach to technology was suited to burgeoning capitalist forms of knowledge production, insofar as pooled investments could yield results for diverse commercial and military needs. Moreover, the idea of dual-use technologies lent itself to the techno-utopian notion of digital technologies as universally available, insofar as code was, in theory, open to all and flexible to diverse uses. While access to computers would, indeed, become globally widespread (though hardly universal), persistent digital divides were not only about whether a given village did or did not have access to computers, but also about *how* they accessed computers (toward what ends, with what applications, and through what costs) and, most importantly, about how computers accessed them.

Savage Data

In the early 1980s, following global economic recessions and southern debt crises, the IBI's journal *Agora* devoted one of its semiannual issues to advocating the dissemination of computer technologies among rural populations of the global south for purposes of assisting agricultural production. Attempting to address how the growing epidemic of food shortages could be mitigated through better agricultural methods, IBI members proposed that computer data be employed by farmers so they could follow shifting supply–demand relationships for particular crops. Such technologies—which would soon come to undergird global futures trading on agricultural products—were initially touted (and continue to be touted) as technologies that would assist small farmers, whereas in fact giant agribusinesses and financial speculators stood to gain windfall profits from networking small farmers into the data banks on crop production. Microcomputing technologies were to bring to fruition the physiocrats' dreams of a self-regulating harmony between agricultural prices and production by placing the data pertaining to each of these realms into real-time contact with each other, provided that microcomputing technologies would somehow be made available to small farmers throughout the global south. The role farmers had long played in shouldering a heavy burden of economic risk could, with the aid of personal computing technologies, be reconfigured as independent financial entrepreneurship, with every farmer becoming a self-directed agent of financial risk vis-à-vis the global market for agricultural products, communing directly with it.

In other words, the pentecostal condition of direct communion envisaged by McLuhan was materializing as a new form of electronic agrarian subjectivity to be realized in the twenty-first century with the spread of personal cell phones in rural parts of the global south (cell phones that would be likened in Central Africa to indigenous talking drums). Farmers, by dint of these technologies, could become the channels through which speculative financial markets were placed in direct communication with small-scale agricultural production. Formal education and literacy could be sidestepped—as proposed by early programmers and designers of digital interfaces—through these personal electronic economic infrastructures. In the 1980s, IBI participants fell in step with this vision of small farmers' greater integration into the global market, a relationship they described—as did their computer-exporting counterparts—as *communication* (a more palatable designator than "globalization"). As such, the idiom of communication deferred the question of who was really to profit from the farmer's input of agricultural data. IBI representatives of nations that had formerly mounted trenchant critiques of north–south economic relations began to embrace the adage that personal computing technologies, by virtue of uniting geographically distant people, somehow created a global democracy, or what was often called, after McLuhan, a "global village."[56]

Invoking this idiom, Colombian president Belisario Betancur proclaimed at the 1984 IBI conference "Informatics and Sovereignty" in Cali, Colombia, "We must . . . understand that it is necessary to educate society to this new phenomenon of life and to familiarize it with the new languages which, unlike the languages of the Tower of Babel, can create a sense of community at higher levels."[57] IBI literature—as in its journal *Agora*—now showcased technopastoralist imagery and discourse that suggested that the travails of agrarian and urban poverty alike might be redressed by technologically bridging rural and urban forms of livelihood. The director general of the IBI, Fermín Bernasconi, said in his opening address at a 1982 intergovernmental conference, "Strategies and Policies on Informatics" (SPIN), that the "socio-cultural impact of Informatics must be reviewed in light of this new reality [the microchip], which could permit a return to life in small communities, retaining all the advantages, without the disadvantages of the large urban conglomerations."[58] IBI discussants in the 1980s often echoed ideas generated in computer-exporting nations about a new kind of cyberpeasantry to emerge through the use of (what we could call) pentecostal technologies. *Agora* illustrations showed, for example, electronic networks penetrating and merging with tropical jungle growth and crops being tilled by robots. The phantasmagoria of global villages, electronic jungles, and cyberpeasants implied an elision in the order of knowledge. An intermediary state of knowing and empowerment—literacy—could be overleaped by dint of digital technologies' ambiguous status vis-à-vis literacy. The chasm of technical knowledge lying between agricultural knowledge and computational technologies was to be elided by virtue of interfaces that made computers simultaneously comprehensible and incomprehensible to their users.

The epistemic chasm between forms of nonliterate production and computer use was encouraged by the CMI's and Media Lab's philosophy of educating children rather than adults in computer use. An article in *Agora* in 1983 reviewing the implementation of computer education in Morocco described how the importance of age hierarchies in the transmittal of knowledge was being destabilized by childhood computer education.[59] What Bernard Stiegler has described as a crisis of perpetual psychic immaturity (brought about by the ways electronic media have come to replace education and parental guidance) was to some extent the result of technological policy, especially in the global south, where higher rates of nonliteracy meant that some of the functions of personal computing that were most widely used by adults in the global north at the end of the twentieth century—such as email and word processing—were not so widely used in the south.[60] The author of the 1983 *Agora* article expressed unease concerning this breakdown in the existing chains of knowledge transmission, fearing that elders would no longer be able to serve as sources of knowledge, that teachers would be replaced by machines, and, more generally, that personal computers would "become a source of *incommunicability* among individuals."[61] Contrary to optimistic claims made at IBI's SPIN conference regarding the pentecostal effects of computer dissemination, this author seemed to suggest that a semiotic apartheid was in the offing.[62]

FIGURE 8.3. *Electronic Circuitry and Jungle Vines* 1, 1982. Artist unknown. From *Agora* 1, no. 7 (1982).

The Media Lab did not abandon its interest in the global south even though dreams of digital democracy and egalitarianism seemed increasingly tenuous, thanks to corporate monopolies and states' loss of economic sovereignty under structural adjustment programs, with a subsequent undermining of social services such as public education. Around this time, technohumanitarianism came to displace a potentially more democratic and politically engaged negotiation of technology transfer—that is, a version in which polities might effectively contest how and with what aims computers might (or might not) be integrated into society. At the same time as the Media Lab aggressively pursued corporate partnerships, its showcase piece became the One Laptop per Child (OLPC) project, which aimed to produce a cheap, easy-to-use laptop to be distributed for educational purposes in the global south at a price allegedly affordable to national governments (aiming at a price tag of one hundred U.S. dollars).[63] National governments were asked to sign contracts to purchase a laptop for every school-age child, leading some critics to decry the relative costs of purchasing so many laptops versus

FIGURE 8.4. *Robotic Agriculture*, 1982. Artist unknown. From *Agora* 1, no. 7 (1982).

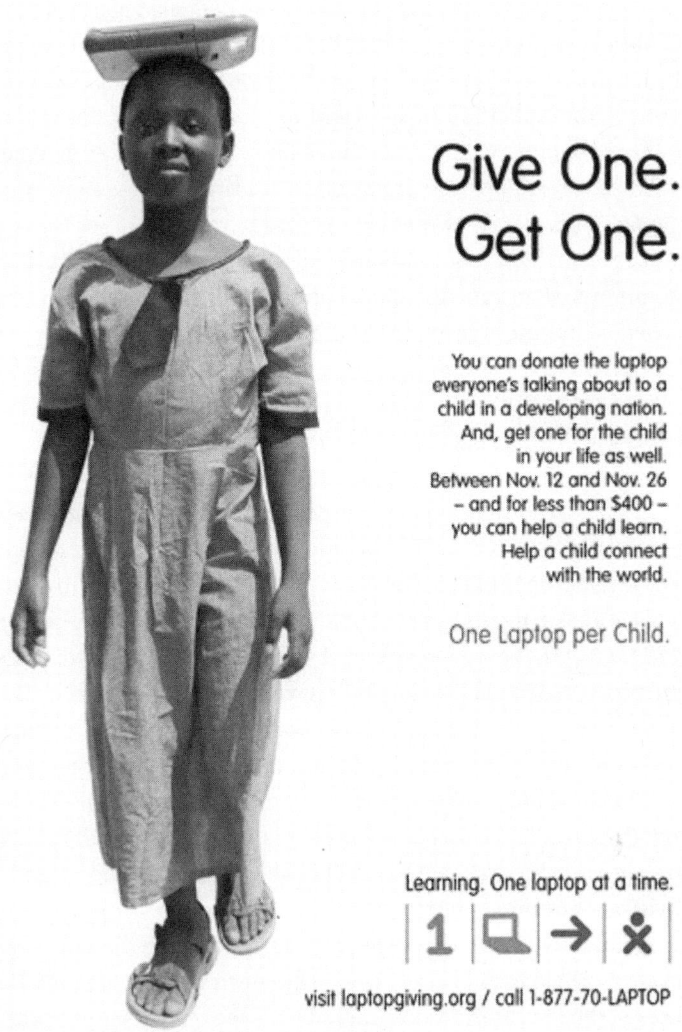

FIGURE 8.5. Promotion for One Laptop per Child, circa 2008.

investment in sharable resources such as libraries, teachers, computer labs, and school buildings.[64] Because the cost of the laptop at the time of its launch was roughly double the target price, the Media Lab turned to a system of consumer philanthropy with its "Give one, get one" campaign, selling laptops in the global north at above-market price to partly subsidize their export to the global south.[65]

The various failures of the OLPC project have been documented elsewhere and are less important here than how the media attention accorded to the OLPC project helped nourish a growing culture of technohumanitarianism. This paradigm mobilized various unspoken rationales that would gain currency in the twenty-first century: first, that overcoming the digital divide (by whatever means and with whatever aims) was somehow tantamount to overcoming economic divides, regardless of the complex factors contributing to the latter; second, that state actors, foreign corporations, and high-profile international research institutions would usher in major technological transformations in the global south, often without serious public discussion in the host states; third, that programs would sometimes be implemented in diverse contexts on a vast scale without any trial period or any effort at critical assessment; and finally, that technology *guided by good design* would be cast in a heroic role of rescuing a global indigent. Thus presented in technohumanitarian discourse as *dependent* on global-northern technological imports, that same indigent would simultaneously be represented as having been granted economic and intellectual independence through such technologies, as if self-sovereignty were a simple matter of owning gadgetry.

Design played an important role in this new technohumanitarian paradigm. For example, in the case of the OLPC, the laptop's special graphic interface, named Sugar, was visually appealing, while reducing the computer's functions to a few child-friendly applications, denoted by conventionally European icons, such as musical notes and paint palettes. The "Help" page on the OLPC's official website stated that any programmers "interested in developing OLPC software at the system-level, the important backend stuff that the user doesn't really see," could find the necessary documentation through the website.[66] The fact that even experienced software developers would need substantial written guidance to decrypt the underlying workings of the machine was hardly surprising given the complexity of computer software, but it does run counter to Papert's earlier insistence that computer use would naturally yield computer-programming abilities. Moreover, the machine's effectiveness as an educational tool was compromised by its extremely low-resolution display, which was much better suited to simple visual graphics than to text, which was reportedly almost impossible to decipher.[67] The object's aesthetically virtuosic design—sturdy (at least by laptop standards) but also delightfully toylike—did not merely make the object appealing (despite the engineers' questionable decision to sacrifice textual readability); the design also conveyed the sense that all such choices had been carefully considered with the child user in mind—that is, the design aesthetically conveyed a sense of anthropological appropriateness.

In the early 2000s the OLPC splintered off from the Media Lab, becoming an independent nonprofit group directed by Negroponte. Shortly thereafter, Negroponte announced his new promotional stunt to drop laptops by airplane into rural African and Asian villages.[68] Delivering no user instructions, these airdrops were meant to demonstrate the ease with which children (many of them basically unschooled and nonliterate) could learn to use the machines.[69] Thus seeming to corroborate Negroponte's long-standing claims of a natural kinship between computers and "primitive" intelligence (that is, the unschooled intelligence of children), media coverage of the stunt (mostly OLPC's own coverage) failed to take into account that any such kinship was not "natural" but had been strategically *designed* by whittling away the importance of language and literacy as means of learning and communication. These computers had been designed to feed into children's innate psychic drives. They were savage machines designed in the image of "savage minds."

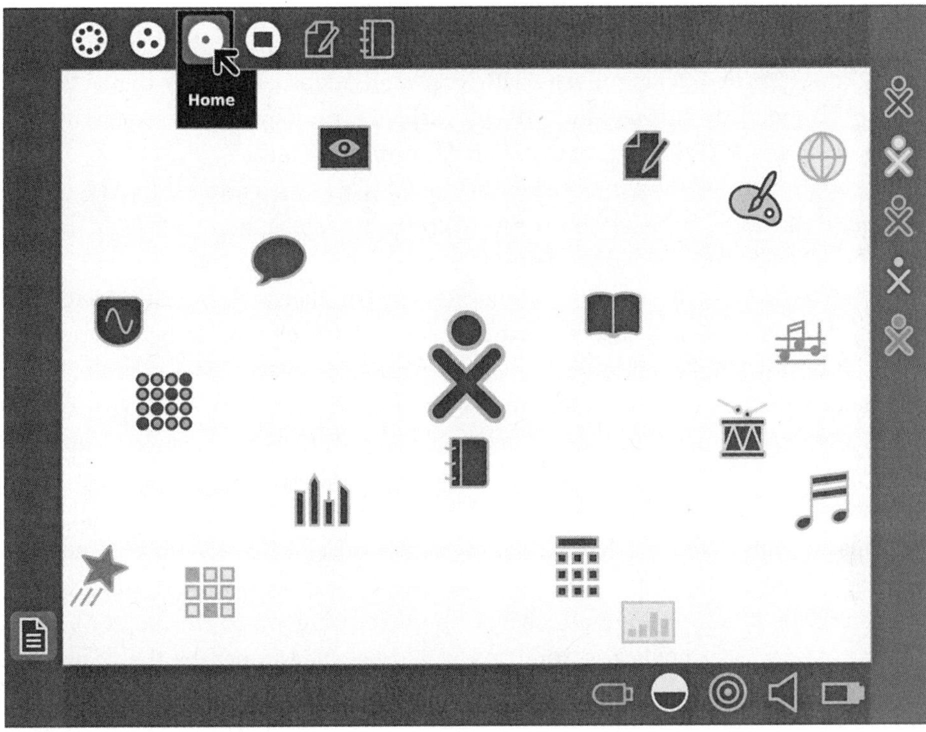

FIGURE 8.6. Sugar interface in promotion for One Laptop per Child, circa 2008.

There are some historical homologies to be drawn between Negroponte's airdrops and mid-twentieth-century colonial military strategies of distributing propaganda in rural areas, often in the form of leaflets dropped from planes with images and slogans discouraging anticolonial and communist movements.[70] The homology comes not so much from the shared device of the airdrop but from the efforts in both cases to "indigenize" a patently nonindigenous medium. Whereas in the case of military propaganda, this entailed a localizing impetus (adopting local visual tropes and languages), in the case of OLPC, the basic universality of children's unschooled cognitive mechanisms was seen to largely obviate any pseudovernacularization of the machine. Yet despite this suggestion of universality, racial difference was nonetheless implied by the entire premise of the project, which was directed toward the global south and which also aimed for personal computing to displace national and international efforts to make print matter more readily available to impoverished schools and children. (It could be argued that erstwhile efforts to democratize print culture had made little headway in the global south, although there are cases to the contrary, such as in Tanzania under Julius Nyerere's socialist regime.) The fact is that by appealing to "primitive" drives and by minimizing the importance of textual input, graphic user interfaces would indeed be easily implemented throughout much of the globe, at least as regards semiotics (not electrical infrastructure). This did not mean that all applications were well adapted to different local contexts, but this issue of adaptation would be tackled in the twenty-first century by collaborations between U.S. corporate actors and local African citizens. For example, the Facebook-sponsored business Andela trains young Africans without a college education to develop software with local applications.[71] Similarly, digital "maker culture" has recently and rapidly spread in urban Africa, sponsored largely by U.S. corporations and MIT, in conjunction with African universities.[72]

Although the initiatives undertaken by the CMI and the early Media Lab cannot be held responsible for the specific forms of economic exploitation that would develop with the global spread of digital dependencies, data collection, and data mining, it must be recalled that the model guiding Servan-Schreiber and the early Media Lab was the Marshall Plan, a scheme that had disguised economic imperialism as an act of heroic salvation leading the world to a perpetual peace. Underlying the CMI's and Media Lab's burgeoning paradigm of technohumanitarianism was a basic contradiction. On the one hand, imports of personal computing technology were supposed to instate in the global south forms of apperceptive self-sovereignty, as indicated by Papert's and Turkle's insistence that computer use pushed children toward epistemic self-consciousness. On the other hand, this presumed self-sovereignty would not only be undermined by digital invasions of privacy or by increasing digital dependencies and addictions (often relying on global-northern software and hardware). More fundamentally, forms of political sovereignty would be undermined by the basic logic of spiritual ergonomics: personal computing would aesthetically, technologically, and rhetorically privilege an infantile semiosis that sought to reduce language and literacy in order to enmesh brains more directly and affectively within digital systems.

CONCLUSION

The Present and Future of Spiritual Ergonomics

This book began by challenging accounts that have linked European modernity to a disenchanted understanding of language premised on a rupture between words and things. I argue instead that a persistent strain of modernist design has lain in the impulse to overcome the nonidentity between signified and signifier, replacing the alienation between words and things with an aesthetic semiosis rooted in an autochthonous nature. The arc this book traces, from the late nineteenth-century industrial arts to the design of graphic user interfaces in the 1970s and '80s, shows a historic development from the idea of the "primitive" as a model for a renatured aesthetic semiosis to the idea that the "primitive" (instantiated by a rural or quasi-urban, nonliterate, global-southern denizen) constituted the ideal *user* of such a semiosis, seemingly because that semiosis had been crafted in that user's likeness but in fact because she or he represented the frontiers of the global market.

The conquest of that frontier promised not only to expand the market of technological consumers but also to serve as a tremendous wellspring of economic data, related to both agricultural production and informal urban and peri-urban economic activity. Digital technologies increasingly allow subaltern (or formerly subaltern) classes to be partly interpolated into global circuits of data and finance without requiring them to be formally educated or literate. In many respects, twentieth-century development and implementation of non-language-based media in economically marginalized communities has been premised on certain conceptions of media (including architecture) as means of integrating and organizing subjects through an intimacy between those media and users' unconscious psychological habits and cultural practices.

The movement from colonial to neocolonial techno-aesthetics has involved the creation of an elision whereby the "primitive"—which was formerly abstracted into *aesthetic* rubrics, or "generative grammars," by dint of ethnographic interpretation, psychoanalytic theory, and structuralist architectural diagramming—could now be more directly abstracted into *economic* rubrics thanks to personal computing technologies that obviated the intermediary step of aesthetic or anthropological interpretation.[1] By this point, savage thought has been enfolded into savage machines, such that an ethnography of the primitive might eventually be altogether bypassed in efforts of rural and quasi-urban governmentality. The same aesthetic technologies that emerged from twentieth-century notions of the primitive have enabled the erstwhile objects of ethnographic analysis to participate directly in data-based technologies, such that digital data has become the new ethnography. The savage machine of the twenty-first century—that is, the realization of capital's technopentecostal fantasies—entails the merging of the "primitive" with the machine. And it should be stressed that we are all, in this respect, primitives, immersed in magical exchanges of data, although, of course, the elite classes remain the beneficiaries—directly or indirectly—of that magic.

The early stages of this book's research and writing transpired concurrently with the rise of electronic social media and smartphones and with the consequent intensification of intimacy between human beings and machines. Subsequent revisions to this book's chapters (circa 2017) were written contemporaneously with the upsurge in ethnonationalist politics throughout much of the world. It has become commonplace to note how such politics are facilitated by the semiotics of electronic media, including media that predate the internet. For example, it has long been acknowledged that the profit-oriented structure of most television networks tends to privilege sensationalist news, polarizing commentary, gnomic utterances, and comic relief (as with the twenty-first-century proliferation of comedy "news" shows). Such forms of televisual programming not only captivate audiences but also lend themselves to recirculation via social media. While many critiques (with good reason) thus focus on how *content* is affected by media platforms, the question of mediatic effects in and of themselves remains somewhat less explored. How have specific designs of human–machine relations helped form cognitive and semiotic habits contributing to the polarized and often fascist-leaning political cultures prevailing in much of the world today? And to what extent are these media tendencies new?

This book has endeavored to show that for more than a century, designers pursuing spiritual ergonomics have struggled to efface the difference between human cognition and systems of representation, designing machines to be so intimately entwined with the psyche as to obviate the need for linguistic discourse. Drawing on Jacques Rancière's views on dissensus, I have emphasized that the medium of language—premised on the imperfect correspondence between signified and signifier—lends itself to nuanced interpretation, questioning, and debate precisely because of that imperfect correspondence.[2] This position should not be mistaken as an echo of McLuhan's and Carothers's assertion that alphabetic-based print naturally gives rise to a democratic, introspective, and dynamically transformative culture. Antiauthoritarian skepticism encouraged by language is not the exclusive purview of print culture; it is also potentially enabled by spoken language and a host of political and micropolitical practices. The point is that the dissensus facilitated by a language-based public sphere has become threatened by pentecostal technologies that privilege consensus insofar as their deep intimacy with users is generally premised on an essential agreement: between innate cognitive proclivities and various mediatic stimuli, between specific users and individually tailored media content, and among members of a social media group (for example, among Facebook friends). McLuhan's adage "The medium is the message" proves relevant especially in cases where the message does not hold up well to intellectual scrutiny, whether that message is tailored toward product advertising, colonial propaganda, entertainment, or fascism. In those cases, the medium's power lies in the aesthetic and absorbing effects that render the message into a form of phatic communication, unrelated to its content.[3]

The racialized character of spiritual ergonomics, which this book has attempted to bring into relief, has not proven easily definable by a single formulation, as this racial character has assumed multiple forms, evolving according to specific economic and geopolitical circumstances throughout the long twentieth century. Nonetheless, this book has identified two primary forms of racialization that often inflect the language, design, and applications of spiritual ergonomics. The first has to do with the basic aims and means of the technopentecostal project, which are to supplant discourse with technoanthropological and technopsychological means of channeling the (presumed) desires of various communities into systems that manage, train, and/or quasi-modernize those groups. This has led to racialized misrepresentations of those groups as innately prone to apolitical modes of interaction—whether by pointing to alleged primitive means of communication, to magical understandings of language, or to the supposed importance of culture over politics, ritual over discourse. The second racializing tendency of spiritual ergonomics, as examined in this book, is more akin to modernist primitivism, insofar as a racialized "savage" was regarded as an open archive of the basic mechanics of semiotic and aesthetic cognition. These two tendencies were often intertwined. The strains of modernist primitivism described in this book—far from remaining in the domain of the fine arts—in fact informed the designs of widely used media and technologies such as architecture and computer interfaces. They were often intended to interpolate subaltern groups into the programs of colonialism, modernization, and development. Thus, a subaltern was often the immediate target and experimental subject of pentecostal technologies, although ultimately we are all targets (and experimental subjects) for those technologies and their depoliticizing effects.

Savage Thought in the University and Beyond

Architecture and related forms of design might seem to be disconnected from the recent rise of electronic social media. This book has shown ways that architecture served the field of interface design as a conceptual precedent insofar as architectures were designed to function as an intimate and transformative technology attuned to the putative mechanisms of human cognition and culture. More recently, however, hints of savage thought in the realm of architecture appear primarily in burgeoning technohumanitarian culture and practices. During the past decade or so, Euro-American architecture schools have taken an increasing interest in global-southern slums, which faculty and students approach in a variety of ways. Some projects respectfully interrogate residents' views; more often, however, students visit these sites only fleetingly, interact minimally (if at all) with residents, and—not surprisingly therefore—offer overly simplified architectural and technological solutions to complex urban social conditions, rarely exploring or critiquing the underlying causes of urban economic and social inequality.[4] Such projects often repeat Yona Friedman's modeling of architecture as a large-scale organizational scaffold to be filled in by the creative bricolage of a global-southern indigent.

Furthermore, data mining has expanded in global-southern slums. A good deal of cell phone–based data is mined for private commercial purposes unrelated to architecture, but in many cases, data analysis and remote satellite sensing help shape and justify redevelopment and slum-upgrading projects.[5] The point is not that such projects are necessarily detrimental to their residents—indeed, they can provide much-desired services, although many projects also seek to contain, economically manage, or displace residents. The point is that data is often made to speak for residents, as if they were unable to speak for themselves. Curiously, this presumption of slum residents' aphasia is tacitly contradicted by the fact that slum-upgrading projects and forced relocations often implement consensus-building initiatives in one form or another. Such initiatives, designed to stave off future noncompliance while also gathering vital information, are described in UN-Habitat literature as a necessary step to any slum-upgrading project.[6] In outlining possible methods of consensus building, this literature seems to assume that the only possible outcome to consensus-building exercises is, in fact, consensus, making no provision for the possibility that residents may *not* be persuaded of the proposed project and that it might therefore be advisable in some cases to rescind or drastically reorient such a project. One advisory pamphlet states:

> By the end of the support and consensus building activities the task force should find that key stakeholders have grasped the issues involved in the future CWSU [Citywide Slum Upgrading] programme, cleared up any misunderstandings and misgivings and have committed themselves in principle to the project.[7]

While most global-northern architectural professionals and academics remain aloof from *actual* slum-upgrading initiatives (as distinct from the imaginary initiatives explored in architecture school studios), the profession is nonetheless complicit with the logic of slum development insofar as the basic premise of design is that it can fix the world's ills without the need for political process. As such, the only seeming obstacle to design solutions lies in the possibility of human noncompliance. Hence, it is unsurprising that the design discourses examined in this book from chapter 3 through chapter 8 have, with varying degrees of explicitness, been focused on the issue of persuasion, of achieving consensus, generally by suppressing the likelihood of dissensus. Architecture itself was often conceived as a device for producing compliance with the programs of modernity.

Although the issue of generating consensus was not a central concern of the late nineteenth-century and early twentieth-century industrial designers discussed in the first two chapters of the book, their widely shared aim of reconciling the masses to mechanized forms of production laid the groundwork for conceiving of design as a way of mediating the antinomies of political positions. In those histories, purportedly holistic approaches to design were to heal the forms of social alienation arising with mechanized production. That is, political reform over the conditions of production would be obviated by designers' own magical integration of machines with human bodily and spiritual practices. In contemporary architectural culture, the rise of what is often called "postcritical" architecture is heir to a long disciplinary tradition of circumventing dissensus and silencing critique of architecture's political consequences. Regarding academic critique as an irksome impediment to architecture's alliance with capitalist development, proponents of a postcritical position advocate for "smartness" and "speculative" forms of design that integrate new technological methods.[8] The histories narrated in this book are forerunners in many respects to this postcritical discourse and to the turn to smartness more generally.[9]

It is not only in the fields of architecture that we witness the persistence of savage thought and savage machines—that is, the technological short-circuiting of politics. The disciplines of digital design and product design have given rise to the new professional domain—and even an academic discipline—of design anthropology. Exploiting the underemployment of PhDs, private corporations now hire PhD-holding anthropologists to help tailor products toward potential consumers. One design anthropologist explains that her discipline offers knowledge "about the everyday practices, symbolic meanings, and forms of sociality with which a successful new product would need to articulate."[10] Supporting the field of research referred to as "UX" or "user experience," design anthropology is premised on the presumed inability of persons to correctly articulate their own interests and opinions. In the words of one design anthropologist consultant:

> We all know that users often misreport when asked questions, not because they are looking to intentionally deceive us, but because they are human. . . . More often than not, they will lack the vocabulary of the discipline [of design], tell you what they have come to believe, or say something incorrectly because they simply can't remember after the fact.[11]

The growing tendency for product and app design to make use of anthropological methods cynically aligns itself with ideas of respecting local culture (as we have seen was also the case with postwar modernist architecture). This obfuscates the fact that such concern for the local belongs to a globalizing project, whether it makes use of anthropologists or direct native informants, as we see with the Facebook-funded corporation Andela (headquartered in New York City but operating throughout Africa) and with General Electric's sponsorship of African maker culture. These ventures seek to adapt digital applications to African consumer markets, using African programmers to conduct local design and research initiatives.

One final disciplinary development presaged by the history chronicled in this book is the rise of both the digital humanities and neuroscientific research in the humanities, often offering the prospect of technological applications deriving from humanities research. The use of neuroscience in the fields of art history and visual studies in many respects rehearses the assumptions of 1970s environmental design (to say nothing of Bauhaus Theosophical aesthetics), albeit employing a more sophisticated scientific apparatus. Zeynep Çelik Alexander has aptly referred to this disciplinary development as constituting a "neo-naturalism."[12] She notes that the discourse on neuroscience in the arts has aimed precisely at eliminating signification and, along with it, the role of critical theory and politics within institutions of higher education.[13] Whereas throughout the twentieth century structuralist anthropology and psychology were expected to disclose the workings of cognition, now it is increasingly the neurological examination of axons that is deployed in the quest for pentecostal technologies. The art historian Norman Bryson writes of Ludwig Wittgenstein, Martin Heidegger, Jacques Derrida, and Jacques Lacan:

> All are committed to a radical, counter-intuitive and disquieting understanding of consciousness as being never in direct communication, in terms of mental contents, with the reality that surrounds it. Yet, as our new century advances, it becomes increasingly evident that despite this shared thematic of groundlessness that runs throughout linguistic philosophy—the insistence that what we take to be reality is only a construction, without foundation in an absolute—what resecures the subject's place in the world is the primacy of the signifier, and the shared semiotic conventions that anchor the subject in the world, giving the world its solidity, coherence, and substantiality. The radicalism of neuroscience consists in its bracketing out the signifier as the force that binds the world together: what makes the apple is not the signifier "apple" (though this, too, may play an important role in the process of reality-building), but rather the simultaneous firing of axons and neurons within cellular and organic life. The level of the ground of being, or of the real, shifts from the signifier to the neural configuration, the orchestration of myriad plays of lightning across the ramifying branches of the brain.[14]

Although I tend to agree with Bryson that Heidegger assigns language the task of resecuring a privileged and "anchored" role for human subjectivity, the same cannot readily be said of the other authors mentioned; their deep attentiveness to language is not tantamount to endowing the signifier with powers to restore humanist precepts or render the world coherent. Moreover, neuroscience's alleged "radicalism . . . in . . . bracketing out the signifier as the force that binds the world together" is—as this present book has endeavored to show—neither new nor radical. The fields of cybernetics, structuralist anthropology, psychology, architecture, and the media arts have long sought to displace the primacy of the signifier. Conversely, it is the signifier's instability—the fact that language calls for our interpretive intervention—that has allowed it to be a crucial terrain on which (and through which) we might engage the world politically. To the extent that savage thought was always-already tending in the direction of a neurology that did not yet fully exist, it bore this agenda of depoliticization.

All this is not to say that savage thought or savage machines always and only bear depoliticizing effects. This book is a critique of aesthetic and mediatic power, examining how such power has been supported by a twentieth-century structuralist approach to human cognition and design. As a negative critique, it has focused on excavating some persistent racial, capitalist, and ideological strains of savage thought or savage machines. Alternative accounts could surely be written highlighting histories of contestation, moments when the power of savage thought was challenged and defused. That being said, the present dangers posed by mediatic cultures of linguistic impoverishment—seen, inter alia, in today's Twitter politics—are acute enough (with, for example, the planet's ecological survival hanging in the balance) that moments of contestation need to be weighed against the special logic of twentieth-century spiritual ergonomics. The fact is that the binary of "above" and "below," now commonly used in the humanities and social sciences (that is, as in "histories from below"), is shown to be completely inadequate in relation to spiritual ergonomics, whose entire thrust is to account for the quotidian habits and cultures of myriad instantiations of humanity and, through this localizing or "indigenizing" method, interpolate people into technological and administrative systems of global capitalism. That is to say, savage machines are directed toward overcoming the putative distinction between "above" and "below." While there is nowadays some excellent scholarship—such as with many anthropologies of infrastructure—that challenge this binary (a binary that nonetheless remains largely in place in academic discourse), this book has adopted the strategy of a prolegomenon to such work, essentially attempting to understand some disciplinary assumptions and logics through which spiritual ergonomics gained impetus over the course of the twentieth century, becoming an integral apparatus of capital.

Acknowledgments

Many people and institutions helped bring this book into existence over the many years during which it has taken shape.

Subventions for the research, writing, and publication of this book were generously provided by many institutions, including the Graham Foundation for Art and Architecture; the Social Science Research Council; Columbia University's Institute of Comparative Literature and Society; the Canadian Centre for Architecture; Basel University's Urban Studies Program through the professorship of Kenny Cupers; the Deutscher Akademischer Austauschdienst (DAAD); the Terra Foundation for American Art; the Buell Center for Art and Architecture in conjunction with Columbia University's Oral History program; and Columbia University's Institute for Social and Economic Research and Policy.

I'm indebted to the patient assistance of many archivists and librarians at the Bauhaus-Archiv, the Bibliothèque Kandinsky, the Getty Research Institute, the Historical Society of Pennsylvania, the Massachusetts Institute of Technology's institute archives, the Museum of Modern Art, the Netherland Architecture Institute (now Het Nieuwe Instituut), the University of Chicago Special Collections, and the University of Illinois, Chicago, Special Collections. The librarians at Columbia University's Avery Library and the University of Southern California's Architecture and Fine Arts Library also deserve recognition for their help.

Several professors during my doctoral studies helped guide the direction of this book. Mabel Wilson challenged me to theoretically engage the issue of race, advice that has been formative to the book's arguments. Reinhold Martin was a mentor who opened up for me new ways of thinking about relations between media and architecture. Paul Kockelman read multiple chapter drafts and was always a generous, insightful reader and teacher, showing imaginative ways to engage with semiotic theory. Ijlal Muzaffar offered valuable constructive criticisms, and his own dissertation has deeply informed my thinking about twentieth-century histories of development. Most of all I am grateful to Felicity Scott, my former dissertation adviser, who has supported me through thick and thin and whose own pioneering work has helped make books such as this one possible in the field of architecture history and theory. Along the way, many other scholars offered excellent advice on the manuscript, chapter drafts, or related article drafts, including Zeynep Çelik Alexander, Tony C. Brown, Charles Davis II, Arindam Dutta, Anooradha Iyer Siddiqi, Catherine Liu, Lydia Liu, and Cécile Whiting. Although they remain unnamed, the anonymous peer reviewers for this book offered brilliant, cogent suggestions.

Throughout the peer review and the entire editing and publication process, Pieter Martin and Anne Carter at the University of Minnesota Press expertly shepherded both me and the manuscript. Kathy Delfosse performed the herculean task of copyediting the book, rendering it far more readable. The book features illustrations from a wide range of designers and archives, and I am thankful for Pieter's help and patience and for the assistance of three PhD students, Henderson Beck, Chi Chia Hou, and Shota Vashakmadze, who assisted in the grueling process of obtaining image reproductions and permissions.

Many former colleagues and friends at Columbia University and other institutions are to be thanked for their collegiality, advice, and support, including Ayala Levin, Diana Martinez, James Graham, Hollyamber Kennedy, Andrea Merrett, Peter Minosh, Remei Capdevila, Daniel Talesnik, Alexandra Quanrill, Leslie Klein, Maria Pendas-Gonzales, Marta Caldeira, Daniel Barber, Irene Cheng, Helen Gyger, Ralph Ghoche, Erik Carver, Addison Godel, Manuel Shvartzberg-Carrió, Eszter Polonyi, Abraham Rubin, Gabriella Szalay, Meredith TenHoor, Olga Touloumi, Alla Vronskaya, and Sarah Williams. I also extend thanks to several friends and family members who generously hosted me and helped me get my bearings during research trips—my sister Tam Mengine, Véronique de Patteuw, Nadya Nilina, and Jennifer Donnelly.

During and after my doctoral studies I was supported by many scholarly groups and academic institutions that served as platforms for intellectual exchange and sounding boards for this work, and I accordingly thank my colleagues associated with Aggregate's Systems and the South group, including Ateya Khorikiwala, Ana María Léon, Fabiola López-Duran, and Nikki Moore; my cohort at Columbia's ISERP/INCITE program under the direction of Bill McAllister; the Global Architectural History Teaching Collaborative under the direction of Mark Jarozombek and Vikram Prakash; the Mellon-funded seminar "The Problem of Translation," directed by Emily Apter and Jacques Lezra; my cohort of art historians at the Terra Foundation, along with Jennifer Ann Donnelly; and Basel University's program in Urban Studies (with Marie-Laure Allain Bonilla, Kenny Cupers, Manuel Herz, Maren Larsen, Sophie Oldfield, Remo Reginold, and Giulia Scotto, as well as Adam Jasper, who was then at Eikones). Finally, many people at my current institution, the University of Southern California's School of Architecture, have provided a supportive and intellectually stimulating environment, including (but not limited to) the dean, Milton Curry, and my history–theory colleagues Kenneth Breisch, Vittoria di Palma, Diane Ghirardo, and Faiza Moatasim.

My deepest personal gratitude is reserved for two people close to me: Sydell Chou, who has had to endure not only my frequent research trips but also the draconian anti-screen policies inspired by this book's thesis, and Jerome Chou, who has provided an endless fund of emotional support, material support (in the form of cooking), and comic relief, and who has made so many generous sacrifices in support of my career, moving across seas and back again.

Notes

All translations by the author unless otherwise indicated.

Introduction

1. Adrian Forty, "Primitive: The Word and Concept," in *Primitive: Original Matters in Architecture,* ed. Jo Odgers, Flora Samuel, and Adam Sharr (Abingdon, UK: Routledge, 2006), 9.

2. Literature exploring the relationship between the colonial and architectural primitivism includes Anthony Vidler, *The Writing of the Walls: Architectural Theory in the Late Enlightenment* (Princeton: Princeton Architectural Press, 1987), part 1. See also John Lagae, "Reinventing 'Primitiveness': Henri Lacoste and the Belgian Pavilion at the 1931 International Colonial Exposition in Paris," in Odgers, Samuel, and Sharr, *Primitive,* chapter 9. In the same volume, Steven Cairns provides a succinct summary of critiques of primitivism in postcolonial studies and looks at how these impinge on architectural evocations of the primitive. See Cairns, "Notes for an Alternative History of the Primitive Hut," in Odgers, Samuel, and Sharr, *Primitive.*

3. Some of the key literature on this topic, which explores the trope of the primitive hut as a (nonracialized and noncolonial) trope, includes Joseph Rykwert, *On Adam's House in Paradise: The Idea of the Primitive Hut in Architectural History,* 2nd ed. (Cambridge: MIT Press, 1981); Forty, "Primitive"; and Michaelangelo Sabatino, "The Primitive in Modern Architecture and Urbanism: Introduction," *Journal of Architecture* 13, no. 4 (2008): 355–64.

4. Miller argues that the fragmentation of contemporary life—and especially the contradiction between art as a highly specialized profession and art's holistic function—gives rise to art's primitivist efforts to recuperate a kind of holism. Daniel Miller, "Primitive Art and the Necessity of Primitivism to Art," in *The Myth of Primitivism,* ed. Susan Hiller (London: Routledge, 1991), 35–52.

5. The art historical literature on modernist primitivism is too large to enumerate. An especially useful collection of essays can be found in Hiller, *The Myth of Primitivism.*

6. On the technological uncanny in Dadaism and surrealism, see Hal Foster, *Compulsive Beauty* (Cambridge: MIT Press, 1993), chapter 5.

7. There exist, of course, art historical accounts of primitivism in the latter half of the twentieth century. However, the general framing of modernist primitivism tends to focus on the first half of the twentieth century, often bookending primitivism with the rise of abstract expressionism. See, for example, Jack Flam and Miriam Deutch, eds., *Primitivism and Twentieth-Century Art: A Documentary History* (Berkeley: University of California Press, 2003).

8. This is a very different framing of the "long twentieth century" than that proposed by Giovanni Arrighi in *The Long Twentieth Century: Money, Power, and the Origins of Our Times* (London: Verso, 1994).

9. Claude Lévi-Strauss, *The Savage Mind,* translator not identified, The Nature of Human Society (Chicago: University of Chicago Press, 1966), 3.

10. This linking of cybernetics to the structures of human cognition, myth, and culture appears throughout Lévi-Strauss's oeuvre, but he offers his most explicit explanation of this relationship in his *Myth and Meaning* (New York: Schocken Books, 1979), chapter 3.

11. As an early example of the governmental implications of cybernetics, see Norbert Wiener, *Cybernetics, or Communication and Control in Animals and Machines,* 2nd ed. (Cambridge: MIT Press, 1965).

12. Scholars have also argued that computing technologies were useful in contesting the apartheid regime in South Africa. See Paul N. Edwards and Gabrielle Hecht, "History and the Technopolitics of Identity: The Case of Apartheid South Africa," *Journal of Southern African Studies* 36, no. 3 (2010): 619–39. See also Richard Knight, *U.S. Computers in South Africa* (New York: African Fund and American Committee on Africa, 1986); Ginger Nolan, "The Pharmakon and the Machine," *Thresholds* 42 (2014): 38–49.

13. Jacques Rancière, *Dissensus: On Politics and Aesthetics,* ed. and trans. Steven Corcoran (London: Continuum, 2010).

14. Aggregate, *Governing by Design: Architecture, Economy, and Politics in the Twentieth Century* (Pittsburgh: University of Pittsburgh Press, 2012).

15. Louis Althusser, "Ideology and Ideological State Apparatuses" (1970), in *Lenin and Philosophy and Other Essays,* trans. Ben Brewster (New York: Monthly Review Press, 1971): 1–31; Guy Debord, *Society of the Spectacle,* trans. Ken Knabb (1967; repr., Berkeley, Calif.: Bureau of Public Secrets, 2014).

16. I'm referring to the work and influence of Friedrich Kittler, especially his *Gramophone, Film, Typewriter,* trans. Geoffrey Winthrop-Young and Michael Wutz (1986; repr., Stanford: Stanford University Press, 1999).

17. Marshall McLuhan, *Understanding Media: The Extensions of Man* (1964; repr., Cambridge: MIT Press, 1994), 80; emphasis added.

18. On McLuhan's race-based theories, see Ginger Nolan, *The Neocolonialism of the Global Village* (Minneapolis: University of Minnesota Press, 2018).

19. By magical thought, I'm referring to Sigmund Freud's definition, elaborated in "On Narcissism." He writes, "In [primitive peoples] we find characteristics which, if they occurred singly, might be put down to megalomania: an over-estimation of the power of their wishes and mental acts, the 'omnipotence of thoughts,' a belief in the thaumaturgic force of words, and a technique for dealing with the external world—'magic'—which appears to be a logical application of these grandiose premises." See Freud, "On Narcissism," trans. James Strachey, in *On Freud's Narcissism: An Introduction,* ed. Peter Fonagy (1914; repr., London: Taylor and Francis, 2018), 5. Highlighting the semiotic aspect of magical thought, Freud writes of the processes of association involved in magical thought: "Association by contiguity is contact in the literal sense; association by similarity is contact in the metaphorical sense." Freud understands the processes of magical thought as inimical to the "structural conditions" of the mind, which, for "primitive man" become projected onto the world through magical praxis. See Freud, *Totem and Taboo: Some Points of Agreement between the Mental Lives of Savages and Neurotics,* trans. James Strachey (1913; repr., London: Routledge, 2001), 99, 106.

20. The original use of the term *architecture parlante* has been ascribed to the nineteenth-century architect Léon Vaudoyer in his discussion of Claude-Nicolas Ledoux's work. See Anthony Vidler, *Claude-Nicolas Ledoux: Architecture and Social Reform at the End of the Ancien Régime* (Cambridge: MIT Press, 1990), ix. Subsequent to Vaudoyer, the term was applied to

French Enlightenment architects by the architectural historian Emil Kaufmann in his *Architecture in the Age of Reason: Baroque and Post-Baroque in England, Italy, and France* (Cambridge, Mass.: Harvard University Press, 1955).

21. Although there have been few claims of a structuralist movement within architecture, Herman Hertzberger identified structuralist tendencies in many of his contemporary practitioners. I am referring, though, not to a self-identified movement but, rather, to the significant influence of the structuralist social sciences on architectural theories and methods of research and design. See Herman Hertzberger, *Architecture and Structuralism: The Ordering of Space,* trans. John Kirkpatrick (Rotterdam: NAi, 2015).

22. On Christopher Alexander's contributions to computer research, see Molly Wright Steenson, *Architectural Intelligence: How Designers and Architects Created the Digital Landscape* (Cambridge: MIT Press, 2017), chapter 2.

23. Mary Louise Pratt, *Imperial Eyes: Travel Writing and Transculturation,* 2nd ed. (1992; repr., New York: Routledge, 2008), chapter 2.

24. Nicholas Negroponte, "2B1," *Wired,* no. 5.06 (June 1997).

25. Freud, "On Narcissism."

26. For examples on the linking of enchantment and modern science and technology, see Joshua Landy and Michael Saler, eds., *The Re-enchantment of the World: Secular Magic in a Rational Age* (Stanford: Stanford University Press, 2009). See also John Tresch, *Romantic Machine: Utopian Science and Technology after Napoleon* (Chicago: University of Chicago Press, 2012).

27. Among this literature, Zakiya Hanafi's work on monsters, magic, and machines is especially relevant to this book, although her work focuses on an earlier time period. See Hanafi, *The Monster in the Machine: Magic, Medicine, and the Marvelous in the Time of the Scientific Revolution* (Durham, N.C.: Duke University Press, 2000), especially chapter 3. On the relationship between technology and the unconscious, see Foster, *Compulsive Beauty,* chapter 5; Maria Fabricius Hansen and Camilla Skovberg Paldam, "Grotesque! Strategies of Figurative Genesis in the Sixteenth Century and in the Surrealism of the 1920s and 1930s," in *Art, Technology and Nature: Renaissance to Postmodernity,* ed. Camilla Skovberg Padam and Jabob Wamberg (London: Routledge, 2016), 81–103; Penille Leth-Espensen, "The Microscope as Musical Instrument: Art, Hermeneutics and Technoscience," in Padam and Wamberg, *Art, Technology and Nature,* 147–61.

28. Much of the literature that presumes primitivism to be a gesture of escape from "civilization" and its related technologies belongs to an older generation of scholarship. For more recent examples of this hypothesis, see Frances Connelly, *The Sleep of Reason: Primitivism in Modern European Art and Aesthetics, 1725–1907* (University Park: Pennsylvania State University Press, 1994).

29. Denise Ferreira da Silva, *Toward a Global Idea of Race* (Minneapolis: University of Minnesota Press, 2007); Tony C. Brown, *The Primitive, the Aesthetic, the Savage: An Enlightenment Problematic* (Minneapolis: University of Minnesota Press, 2012), 75.

30. On otherness, see, inter alia, Homi K. Bhabha, "The Other Question: The Stereotype and Colonial Discourse," in *Twentieth-Century Literary Theory: A Reader,* ed. Newton K. M. Newton, 2nd ed. (London: Palgrave, 1997), 293–301.

31. I am wary here of a tendency to turn a colonial discourse of fetishism against itself by switching the respective roles of the protagonists, as Hal Foster does in his seminal essay "The 'Primitive' Unconscious of Modern Art," *October* 34 (1985): 45–70. On the concept of the fetish, there is a growing body of literature. See, for example, William Pietz's trilogy: Pietz, "The Problem of the Fetish, I," *RES: Anthropology and Aesthetics* 9 (1985): 5–17; Pietz, "The Problem of the Fetish, II: The Origin of the Fetish," *RES: Anthropology and Aesthetics* 13 (1987): 23–45; and Pietz, "The Problem of the Fetish, IIIa: Bosman's Guinea and the Enlightenment

Theory of Fetishism," *RES: Anthropology and Aesthetics* 16 (1988): 105–24. See also William Pietz and Emily Apeter, eds., *Fetishism as Cultural Discourse* (Ithaca, N.Y.: Cornell University Press, 1991); Charles de Brosses, Rosalind C. Morris, and Daniel H. Leonard, *The Returns of Fetishism: Charles de Brosses and the Afterlives of an Idea* (Chicago: University of Chicago Press, 2017).

32. Tony C. Brown has also pointed out this aspect of an aesthetic discourse on the primitive. Brown, *The Primitive, the Aesthetic, and the Savage,* 42–43.

33. Forty, "Primitive," 9.

34. Michel Foucault, *The Archaeology of Knowledge and the Discourse on Language,* trans. A. M. Sheridan Smith (New York: Pantheon, 1972).

35. Mary Poovey, *A History of the Modern Fact: Problems of Knowledge in the Sciences of Wealth and Society* (Chicago: University of Chicago Press, 1998), xiii–xv.

36. Michel Foucault, *Introduction to Kant's Anthropology,* ed. Roberto Nigro (Cambridge: Semiotext(e), 2008), 123.

37. Tony C. Brown has discussed this Enlightenment problematic in terms of the challenge of describing the "relation between an atemporal faculty [i.e., the aesthetic imagination] and temporal experience," a problem he sees as generative to the imbrication between the "primitive, the aesthetic, and the savage." Brown, *The Primitive, the Aesthetic, the Savage,* 75.

38. I have written of the geopolitics of southern bricolage elsewhere. See Ginger Nolan, "Bricolage . . . or the Sudden Impossibility of Pollution," *e-flux,* July 26, 2018, https://www.e-flux.com/architecture/structural-instability/208705/bricolage-or-the-impossibility-of-pollution/. See also Patricio Del Real, "Slums Do Stink: Artists, Bricolage, and Our Need for Doses of 'Real' Life," *Art Journal* 67, no. 1 (Spring 2008): 82–99.

39. In contrast to the horror story of the slums painted by Mike Davis, there has been for at least a decade a surge of interest within architectural discourse and practices in the "logics" of the slums, often understanding these as expressive of organic, cultural modes of development. As an example of the kind of rhetoric that accompanies this particular approach to the slums, see Francesca diFilippi, ed., *Slum[e]scape: A Challenge for Sustainable Development Projects; Echoes from the XXIII UIA Congress of Architecture, Torino 2008* (Florence: Alinea editrice, 2009). See also several contributions in *Lessons of Informality: Architecture and Urban Planning for Emerging Territories. Concepts from Ethiopia,* ed. Felix Heisel and Bisrat Kifle (Basel, Switzerland: Birkhäuser, 2017).

40. This includes work by Elizabeth Grosz, Manuel De Landa, and Brian Massumi. See E. A. Grosz, *The Nick of Time: Politics, Evolution, and the Untimely* (Durham, N.C.: Duke University Press, 2004). See also Manuel De Landa, *A Thousand Years of Nonlinear History,* Swerve Editions (New York: Zone, 1997); Brian Massumi, *Parables for the Virtual: Movement, Affect, Sensation,* Post-contemporary Interventions (Durham, N.C.: Duke University Press, 2002).

41. See Bryan T. Stinchfield, Reed E. Nelson, and Matthew S. Wood, "Learning from Levi-Strauss' Legacy: Art, Craft, Engineering, Bricolage, and Brokerage in Entrepreneurship," *Entrepreneurship Theory and Practice* 37, no. 4 (July 2013): 889–921.

42. Matt Artz, "Contextual Inquiry: Navigating the Politics of User Research," Matt Artz (website), accessed December 18, 2019, https://mattartz.me/contextual-inquiry-navigating-the-politics-of-user-research/.

43. There is a large scientific literature on neurological reward systems and behavior patterns that is linked either explicitly or implicitly to the design of human–machine interfaces. See, for example, Brandi T. Marsh et al., "Toward an Autonomous Brain Machine Interface: Integrating Sensorimotor Reward Modulation and Reinforcement Learning," *Journal of Neuroscience* 35, no. 19 (May 13, 2015): 7374–87.

44. Michael Speaks, Robert Somol, and Sarah Whiting have been the most well-cited proponents of the "postcritical" position in North America, articulated in articles too numerous

to cite. Especially noteworthy, though, is Michael Speaks's series of short articles on "design intelligence" published in various architecture magazines.

1. The Architecture Machine

1. Charles Godfrey Leland, "1936," in "Prophesies for the Twentieth Century" (1899), in Charles Godfrey Leland Papers, Collection 363, box 3, Historical Society of Pennsylvania, Philadelphia, n.p.

2. Leland, "Prophesies for the Twentieth Century."

3. It seems likely that Leland, who was acquainted with Herbert Spencer in London, may have drawn heavily on Spencer's ideas concerning the basic mechanisms of human cognition. See Spencer, *Principles of Psychology* (London: Longman, Brown, Green, and Longmans, 1855).

4. The school also seems to have been known by an alternate name, the Public School of Industrial Art in Philadelphia. Little has been published on it except for an account in David Baker, "J. Liberty Tadd: Who Are You?" *Studies in Art Education* 26, no. 2 (Winter 1985): 75–85. Tadd himself, who succeeded Leland as director of the school, published a book on its methods. James Liberty Tadd, *New Methods in Education: Art, Real Manual Training, Nature Study* (New York: Orange Judd, 1899). See also Ákos Moravánszky, "Educated Evolution: Darwinism, Design Education, and American Influence in Central Europe, 1898–1918," in *The Education of the Architect: Historiography, Urbanism, and the Growth of Architectural Knowledge*, ed. Martha Pollak (Cambridge: MIT Press, 1997).

5. While Leland's design program drew from precedents in England, his ethnological and psychiatric understanding of world crafts distinguishes his work from that of figures like Henry Cole.

6. Charles Godfrey Leland, "The Coming Race, or The New Man of Cromagnon" (n.d.), in Leland Papers, Collection 363, box 7; Leland, "Colonisation" (n.d.), in Leland Papers, box 7.

7. Leland, "Colonisation."

8. See, for example, Charles Godfrey Leland, "The Folding Mirror, or Pocket Kaleidoscope and Its Use in Art" (n.d.), in Leland Papers, box 6; Charles Godfrey Leland, "The Photograph or Helioeidolon of the Future" (n.d.), in Leland Papers, box 6.

9. Frank Lloyd Wright, *The Art and Craft of the Machine*, ed. Henry-Russell Hitchcock (Chicago: Chicago Architectural Club, 1901).

10. Charles Godfrey Leland, *The Mystic Will: A Method of Developing and Strengthening the Faculties of the Mind, through the Awakened Will, by a Simple, Scientific Process Possible to Any Person of Ordinary Intelligence* (Chicago: Yogi Publication Society, 1907).

11. Georg Wilhelm Friedrich Hegel, *Lectures on the Philosophy of World History*, trans. H. B. Nisbet (Cambridge: Cambridge University Press, 1975); Hegel, *Phenomenology of Spirit*, trans. Arnold V. Miller and J. N. Findlay (Oxford: Clarendon Press, 1977). For Carlyle's notion of world history, see Thomas Carlyle, *On Heroes, Hero-Worship, and the Heroic in History*, ed. David R. Sorensen and Brent E. Kinser (New Haven: Yale University Press, 2013).

12. Leland, "Prophesies for the Twentieth Century."

13. Leland specifically mentions Hegel in his literary diary and in his memoirs and also uses the phrase "world spirit" when describing historical progress. He presumably encountered Hegel through his studies in German philosophy at both Princeton and Heidelberg Universities. See Charles Godfrey Leland, "Diaraium litterarium" (n.d.), in Leland Papers, box 24; Leland, notes on "Commencement Speech for Women's School of Design" (n.d.), in Leland Papers, box 24; Leland, *Memoirs* (London: William Heinemann, 1894), 158. See also Elizabeth Pennell, *Charles Godfrey Leland: A Biography*, 2 vols. (London: A. Constable, 1906), 1: 71, 92, 95–96, 104. Leland mentions Herbert Spencer in Leland, *Memoirs*, 389.

14. In Leland's *Memoirs*, he discusses Carlyle's work in relation to transcendentalism, expressing deep admiration for Carlyle's writing but also faulting him (and Ralph Waldo

Emerson) for a lack of truly mystical pantheism. Leland also recounts his surly meeting with Carlyle during which the latter accused him of being descended from the Irish and also insulted the United States. In response, Leland accused Carlyle's "historical criticism" of being "theatrical," but the two men soon reconciled. See Leland, *Memoirs,* 77–87, 429–32. On Conway's procuring Leland an introduction to Carlyle, see Moncure Daniel Conway, *Autobiography: Memories and Experiences of Moncure Daniel Conway* (Boston: Houghton Mifflin, 1905), 400. See also Pennell, *Charles Godfrey Leland,* 10.

15. Moncure Daniel Conway, *Travels in South Kensington; with Notes on Decorative Art and Architecture in England* (London: Trübner, 1882).

16. From an affluent Virginian family, Conway came to repudiate the deeply racist views he had expressed as a young adult. Though clearly objecting to Carlyle's reactionary and extreme racist views, he nonetheless took a paternalistic attitude toward non-Anglo-Saxons. See Conway, *Autobiography.*

17. Leland argues that northern whites should colonize the southern states, while allowing emancipated slaves to colonize westward territories in the United States. See Leland, "Desperation and Colonization," *Continental Monthly* 1, no. 6 (June 1862): 657–62; Leland, "Our War and Our Want," *Continental Monthly* 1, no. 2 (February 1862): 113–17. See also Edward B. Freeland, "The Great Riot," *Continental Monthly* 4, no. 3 (September, 1863): 302–11; David R. Roediger, *The Wages of Whiteness: Race and the Making of the American Working Class* (London: Verso, 2007), chapter 8.

18. Apart from being involved in programs at Harvard University and MIT and in summer programs for training secondary school teachers in biology, Agassiz may have also influenced Boston's school programs indirectly through his deep influence on the abolitionist Samuel Gridley Howe, who worked on educational reforms with Horace Mann, the central organizer of Massachusetts's public school program. Mann, like Howe, was an abolitionist, but, also like Howe, he argued against slavery not only because it was unjust to black persons but because slave labor economically threatened the viability of the white freehold farmer. See Mann, "Speech Delivered in the House of Representatives of the United States, June 30, 1848," in *Slavery: Letters and Speeches* (Boston: B. B. Mussey, 1851), 83. On the educational exchange between Howe and Mann, see R. A. Reid-Edwards, *Words Made Flesh: Nineteenth-Century Deaf Education and the Growth of Deaf Culture* (New York: New York University Press, 2012). On Agassiz's racial theories, see Edward Lurie, "Louis Agassiz and the Races of Man," *Isis* 45, no. 3 (September 1954): 227–42. On Agassiz's involvement in education reforms in Boston, see Christoph Irmscher, *Louis Agassiz: Creator of American Science* (New York: Houghton Mifflin, 2013).

19. See Lurie, "Louis Agassiz and the Races of Man." Agassiz's theories of race, climate, and degeneracy echoed those of Georges-Louis Leclerc, comte de Buffon, among others. On Thomas Jefferson and Buffon, see Lee Alan Dugatkin, *Mr. Jefferson and the Giant Moose: Natural History in Early America* (Chicago: University of Chicago Press, 2009); Matthew Furrow, "Samuel Gridley Howe, the Black Population of Canada West, and the Racial Ideology of the 'Blueprint for Radical Reconstruction,'" *Journal of American History* 97, no. 2 (September 2010): 344–70.

20. A successful push for de jure school integration was led by Boston's black Garrisonian abolitionists in the antebellum years. Horace Mann—celebrated for his abolitionist politics—attempted to quell the Garrisonian boycotts used to force the issue of integration. See Carleton Mabee, "A Negro Boycott to Integrate Boston Schools," *New England Quarterly* 41, no. 3 (September 1968): 345–46. See also Robert L. Osgood, "Undermining the Common School Ideal: Intermediate Schools and Ungraded Classes in Boston, 1838–1900," *History of Education Quarterly* 37, no. 4 (Winter 1997): 375–98.

21. Leland, "The Coming Race"; Leland, "Colonisation."

22. Leland writes, for example, "But the study of these overgrown children is interesting and profitable, as is that of their congeners, the savages, because we learn from them that a certain kind of shrewdness and quickness may be developed in all men. . . . In fact there is not one child in a hundred who, under the pressure of necessity as a gypsy or street arab, would not develop a quickness of observation in certain directions which would seem miraculous in a well-bred nursery child." Charles Godfrey Leland, *Practical Education* (London: Whitaker, 1888), 170. See also Charles Godfrey Leland, "Profitable Work for Poor People" (n.d.), in Leland Papers, box 3.

23. On Leland's acquaintance with James, see Robert D. Richardson, *William James: In the Maelstrom of American Modernism* (Boston: Houghton Mifflin, 2006), 330. On James's ideas of unconscious automatism, see William James, *The Principles of Psychology* (New York: Henry Holt, 1890), chapters 5 and 6.

24. In his prophecy for 1975, Leland described a machine that, through a chemical process, would be able to transcribe thought in the form of images directly onto a screen. Leland, "Prophesies for the Twentieth Century."

25. Leland was living in and around Florence during the years that "Prophesies for the Twentieth Century" was written, and during this period he received countless visits, manuscripts, and letters from Maddalena, his informant on methods of magic and prophesy. Leland describes Maddalena as possessing greater powers than Helena Blavatsky. See Charles Godfrey Leland, *Legends of Florence, Collected from the People and Re-told by Charles Godfrey Leland* (Florence, Italy: B. Seeber, 1910), vii–viii; Pennell, *Charles Godfrey Leland,* 2: chapters 12 and 13.

26. See Charles Godfrey Leland, *Etruscan Roman Remains in Popular Tradition* (London: T. Fisher Unwin Paternoster Square, 1842). See also Leland, *Aradia, or the Gospel of Witches* (London: D. Nutt, 1899); Leland, *Legends of Florence* (London: D. Nutt, 1910). On arguments concerning the authenticity of Leland's transcription of the Tuscan *Vangelos,* see Chas Clifton, "The Significance of Aradia," in *Aradia, or The Gospel of the Witches, A New Translation,* ed. Mario Pazzaglini (Blaine, Wash.: Phoenix, 1998).

27. Pennell writes of Leland's and Maddalena's collaborations. See Pennell, *Charles Godfrey Leland,* 2: 350–422.

28. See Leland's preface to *Aradia.* It is unclear whether Maddalena translated these fragments from a Tuscan dialect into modern Italian prior to Leland's translating them into English.

29. See Leland, "The Coming Race."

30. Charles Godfrey Leland, *Practical Education,* 12; emphasis added.

31. Pennell, *Charles Godfrey Leland,* 2: 71–74, 89–94. See also Paul Larmour, "The Art-Carving Schools in Ireland," *GPA Irish Arts Review Yearbook,* 1989, 151–57. On Leland's influence on Besant, see Walter Besant, *Autobiography of Sir Walter Besant, with a Prefatory Note by S. Squire Sprigge* (London: Hutchinson, 1902), 254–55.

32. Charles Godfrey Leland, *Industrial Art in Schools* (Washington, D.C.: Bureau of Education, 1882), 215.

33. Charles Godfrey Leland, "An Opening for the Unemployed in Ireland," *Longman's Magazine, 1882–1905* 3, no. 13 (November 1883): 44–51.

34. Leland, "An Opening for the Unemployed in Ireland," 47.

35. See Roediger, *The Wages of Whiteness.*

36. See, for example, Charles Godfrey Leland, "Eye-Memory: A Lecture Delivered before the Franklin Institute March 29th, 1880," *Journal of the Franklin Institute,* May 1880, 327–36.

37. On the role of design pedagogy in Massachusetts's public school system, see Mary Ann Stankiewicz, *Developing Visual Arts Education in the United States: Massachusetts Normal Art School and the Normalization of Creativity* (New York: Palgrave Macmillan, 2016). Walter Smith was recruited from the South Kensington circle and appears to have perhaps shared some of

Leland's interest in the design aptitudes of "savages." He writes of Persians making beautiful rugs despite the fact that they were "little better than half-dressed savages." Walter Smith, *Industrial Art Education: A Lecture Delivered in Philadelphia,* April 23, 1875 (Boston: L. Prang, 1875), 21. Smith was trained at the South Kensington School, an institution whose conceptions of industry and craft training appear to have influenced Leland's pedagogical philosophies. See Harry Green, "Walter Smith: The Forgotten Man," *Art Education* 19, no. 1 (1966): 4.

38. The beginnings of compulsory education in the United States were imbricated with the movement to culturally assimilate American Indians and render them industrially or agriculturally productive. On craft pedagogy at the missionary schools on Native American reservations and at the Carlisle school and other compulsory boarding schools, see Kevin Slivka, "Art, Craft, and Assimilation: Curriculum for Native Students during the Boarding School Era, *Studies in Art Education* 52, no. 3 (2011), 225–42; Jacqueline Fear-Segal, "Nineteenth-Century Indian Education: Universalism versus Evolutionism," *Journal of American Studies* 33, no. 2 (1999): 323–41; Donald A. Grinde Jr., "Taking the Indian out of the Indian: U.S. Policies of Ethnocide through Education," *Wicazo Sa Review* 19, no. 2 (2004): 25–32; Robert A. Trennert Jr., "Selling Indian Education at World's Fairs and Expositions, 1893–1904," *American Indian Quarterly* 11, no. 3 (1987): 203–20; Siobhan Maureen Wescott, "Educate to Americanize: Captain Pratt and Early Indian Education," *Change 23,* no. 2 (1991): 45–46.

39. Leland was not resident in Philadelphia at the time of the exposition but was in continual correspondence then and later with Philadelphians who were involved in educational reform. On Booker T. Washington, see Ellen Weiss, *Robert R. Taylor and Tuskegee: An African American Architect Designs for Booker T. Washington* (Montgomery, Ala.: New South Books, 2012), 16, 37.

40. Leland poses this question of universality versus practicality in Leland, *Practical Education,* 2.

41. Horace Mann, based in Boston, was known as "the father of the common school movement" and was also an avid abolitionist. See footnote 20.

42. See Karl Marx, *Capital,* vol. 1, *A Critique of the Political Economy,* chapter 1. See also Marx, "Estranged Labour" in *Economic and Philosophical Manuscripts of 1844,* trans. and ed. Martin Milligan (Mineola, N.Y.: Dover, 2007), 67–83.

43. The ideal of spiritual–corporeal unity is a theme repeated throughout Fröbel's writings. See Friedrich Froebel, *A Selection from His Writings,* ed. and trans. Irene M. Lilley (Cambridge: Cambridge University Press, 1967): 162–63. See especially Froebel, "Outline of a Plan for Founding and Developing a Kindergarten," in Froebel, *Writings,* 118. See also Froebel, *The Education of Man,* trans. Josephine Jarvis (New York: A. Lovell, 1886).

44. Leland, "Eye-Memory." On Fröbel's notion that things must be learned from the inside out rather than only by their names, see Froebel, *Writings,* section 6.

45. An article published under Leland's editorship of the *Continental Monthly* addressed the idea of a universal language: "The Scientific Universal Language: Its Character and Relation to Other Languages," *Continental Monthly* 6 (October 1864): 456–68.

46. Fröbel writes, "True elementary education for the poor must first of all be based on the cultivation of the land, for here the child sees how material is transformed first in form and shape and then along the lines of its essential character; it also promotes and extends his manual skill. When the child observes Nature and cultivates the earth and its products he begins from and is led back to a consideration of God. . . . The aspiration for close unity with God is part of the life of man, and so it is there in the child's disposition and quickens the child's mind." Friedrich Froebel, "Plan of an Institution for the Education of the Poor in the Canton of Berne," in Froebel, *Writings,* 162–63.

47. This quotation is ascribed apocryphally to Hampton's founder, Samuel Armstrong. Whether or not he said these precise words, they were certainly implicit in various aspects of

the school's philosophy. See Paulette Fairbanks Molin, "'Training the Hand, the Head, and the Heart': Indian Education at Hampton Institute," *Minnesota History* 51, no. 3 (1988): 82–98. See also James D. Anderson, *The Education of Blacks in the South, 1860–1935* (Chapel Hill: University of North Carolina Press, 1988).

48. See Leland, *Practical Education.* See also Leland, "The Coming Race"; Leland, "Colonisation."

49. See Leland, *Practical Education,* 3. Leland mentions both Fröbel and Johann Heinrich Pestalozzi without citing these authors' specific works. See Leland, *Practical Education,* 198, 244, 255. Decades later, John Dewey would similarly conclude that structural commonalities between different disciplinary specializations could allow for a shared curriculum that lent itself to diverse vocational pursuits. Dewey, *Democracy and Education: An Introduction to the Philosophy of Education* (New York: Cosimo Classics, 2005).

50. Charles Godfrey Leland, "Ought Elementary Instruction in Drawing to Be Made Part of the National Education?" (n.d.), in Leland Papers, box 5.

51. Tadd, *New Methods in Education,* 6–7, 13–14.

52. Tadd, *New Methods in Education,* 4.

53. Apart from the translation of Tadd's book into German, following his and Leland's various lecture tours there, Leland noted in 1888 during a visit to Hungary that his "system of the Minor Arts" had been implemented in fifty public schools, where "it is usually recognized as mine." Charles Godfrey Leland to Elizabeth Pennell. See Pennell, *Charles Godfrey Leland,* 2: 308. On further explanation of the influence of PIASP pedagogy in Europe, see Moravánszky, "Educated Evolution," footnote 3. See also Zeynep Çelik Alexander, *Kinaesthetic Knowing: Aesthetics, Epistemology, Modern Design* (Chicago: University of Chicago Press, 2017), 156–58.

54. Leland, "Profitable Work for Poor People."

55. Leland, *Practical Education,* 23.

56. Charles Godfrey Leland, "The Inner Life of Nature" (n.d.), in Leland Papers, box 6.

57. The use of directed dreaming as a pedagogical device was also taken up by Rudolf Steiner in the Waldorf schools.

58. Leland, *The Mystic Will,* 72–73, 109–15.

59. Leland, "The Coming Race."

60. Leland, "The Coming Race."

61. Tadd includes in *New Methods in Education* a photograph of a Germantown public school in Philadelphia showing what seems to be an exclusively black student body, although it is not entirely clear from the photo. Tadd, *New Methods in Education,* 51.

62. Leland's biographer recounts Leland's respect for the carpentry instructor, expressed in his correspondence. See Pennell, *Charles Godfrey Leland,* 1: 101, 255.

63. Leland, "Colonisation." On Tuskegee's programs in West Africa, see Andrew Zimmerman, *Alabama in Africa: Booker T. Washington, the German Empire, and the Globalization of the New South* (Princeton: Princeton University Press, 2012).

64. On this critique of Tuskegee, see Anderson, *The Education of Blacks in the South.* Anderson views Washington as completely servile to southern white objectives, which were inculcated in him through his education at the Hampton Normal School.

65. The Atlanta Compromise effectively obtained a modicum of resources for African American higher education by conceding to uphold racial segregation and training blacks only in nonprofessional capacities. See Kenrick Ian Grandison, "Negotiated Space: The Black College Campus as a Cultural Record of Postbellum America," *American Quarterly* 51, no. 3 (September 1999): 529–79. See also Zimmerman, *Alabama in Africa,* chapter 3.

66. Weiss, *Robert R. Taylor and Tuskegee,* 40.

67. Weiss, *Robert R. Taylor and Tuskegee,* 38–40.

68. Weiss, *Robert R. Taylor and Tuskegee,* 38–40.

69. On Du Bois's critique of Washington, see W. E. B. Du Bois, *The Souls of Black Folk* (New York: Dover, 1994); Du Bois, *Dusk of Dawn* (Millwood, N.Y.: Kraus-Thomson, 1975).

70. W. E. B. Du Bois, *The Souls of Black Folk: Essays and Sketches* (Chicago: A. C. McLurg, 1903), 3, 202. Also on Du Bois and double consciousness, see Paul Gilroy, *The Black Atlantic, Modernity, and Double Consciousness* (Cambridge, Mass.: Harvard University Press, 1993), chapter 4. W. E. B. Du Bois, *The Star of Ethiopia* (New York: Negro Universities Press, 1915).

71. W. E. B. Du Bois, "The Strivings of the Negro People," *Atlantic*, August 1897. See also Du Bois, *The Souls of Black Folk*; Adolph Reed, *W. E. B. Du Bois and American Political Thought: Fabianism and the Color Line* (New York: Oxford University Press, 1999), chapter 7.

72. Owen Jones, *Grammar of Ornament* (London: Day and Son, 1856).

73. On the technologization of ornament, see Arindam Dutta, *The Bureaucracy of Beauty: Design in the Age of Its Global Reproducibility* (New York: Routledge, 2007).

74. Susan Buck-Morss, *Hegel, Haiti and Universal History: Illuminations* (Pittsburgh: University of Pittsburgh Press, 2009).

75. Georg Wilhelm Friedrich Hegel, "Appendix 1," in *Lectures on the Philosophy of World History*, trans. Hugh Barr Nisbet, introduction by Duncan Forbes (Cambridge: Cambridge University Press, 1975), 190; emphasis added.

2. The Bauhaus and the Aura of Authorship

1. See Christopher Wilk, "Marcel Breuer and Gunta Stölzl: 'African' Chair. 1921" in *Bauhaus 1919–1933: Workshops for Modernity*, by Barry Bergdoll et al. (New York: Museum of Modern Art, 2009), 100–103. Wilk discusses the chair's likely influences within European (rather than African) craft traditions and notes that Stölzl referred to it as the "Negro" chair. For a further account of Breuer's photomontage, see Barry Bergdoll, *Marcel Breuer: Bauhaus Tradition, Brutalist Invention* (New York: Metropolitan Museum of Art, 2016), 6–7.

2. The narrative of the Bauhaus's transition from the mystical to the technorational is so ubiquitous as to elude citation. However, in reference to the "African" chair, see Wilk, "Marcel Breuer and Gunta Stölzl."

3. For art historical scholarship related to late nineteenth- and early twentieth-century mysticism and psychology, see, for example, Alexander, *Kinaesthetic Knowing*; Rosemarie Haag Bletter, "The Interpretation of the Glass Dream—Expressionist Architecture and the Crystal Metaphor," *Journal of the Society of Architectural Historians* 40, no. 1 (March 1981): 20–43; John Bramble, *Modernism and the Occult* (New York: Palgrave MacMillan, 2015), chapters 2 and 4; Juliet Koss, *Modernism after Wagner* (Minneapolis: University of Minnesota Press, 2010); and Spyros Papapetros, *The Animation of the Inorganic: Art, Architecture, and the Extension of Life* (Chicago: University of Chicago Press, 2012).

4. Regarding the intellectual property litigation over Bauhaus tubular-steel chairs, see Otakar Máčel, "Avant-Garde Design and the Law: Litigation over the Cantilever Chair," *Journal of Design History*, no. 3 (1990): 125–43.

5. In photographic reproductions, the chair's woven red, blue, and yellow threads tend to converge into secondary hues, while the paint colors on the wood have altered over time and mixed with the color of the wood. However, the chair was reported to be decorated exclusively in red, blue, and yellow.

6. Louis Althusser, "Ideology and Ideological State Apparatuses," trans. Ben Brewster, in *On the Reproduction of Capitalism: Ideology and Ideological State Apparatuses* (London: Verso, 2014), 255.

7. Karl Marx and Friedrich Engels, *The Communist Manifesto*, ed. Samuel Beer (New York: Appleton-Century-Crofts, 1955), 13.

8. Johannes Itten, "Rassenlehre und Kunstentwicklung," *Masdasnan Zeitscrhift* 6 (1923): 90.

9. On a related topic, see Papapetros, *The Animation of the Inorganic.* See also Alexander, *Kinaesthetic Knowing.*

10. Walter Gropius, "Programme of the Staatliches Bauhaus in Weimar," in *Programs and Manifestoes on 20th-Century Architecture,* ed. Ulrich Conrads (Cambridge: MIT Press, 1970), 49.

11. John Ruskin, *Seven Lamps of Architecture* (1880; repr., New York: Dover, 1989).

12. See, for example, Frederic J. Schwartz, "Utopia for Sale: The Bauhaus and Weimar Germany's Consumer Culture," in *Bauhaus Culture: From Weimar to the Cold War,* ed. Kathleen James-Chakraborty (Minneapolis: University of Minnesota Press, 2006).

13. To my knowledge, Bauhaus historiography offers only two explicit challenges to the well-rehearsed narrative concerning the two putative Bauhaus eras—the mystical expressionist era and the rational, technologically oriented era. For critiques of this narrative, see Alexander, *Kinaesthetic Knowing,* chapter 5, especially 175. See also work by Oliver Arpad Istan Botar, who examines the mysticism of Moholy-Nagy's work. Botar, "Prolegomena to the Study of Biomorphic Modernism: Biocentrism, László Moholy-Nagy's 'New Vision' and Erno Kallai's 'Bioromantik' (PhD diss., University of Toronto, 1998).

14. "The mysterious character of the commodity-form consists . . . simply in the fact that the commodity reflects the social characteristics of men's own labour as objective characteristics of the products of labour themselves, as the socio-natural properties of these things. . . . The commodity-form, and the value-relation of the products of labour within which it appears, have absolutely no connection with the physical nature of the commodity and the material [*dinglich*] relations arising out of this. It is nothing but the definite social relation between men themselves that assumes here, for them, the fantastic form of a relation between things." Marx, *Capital,* 1: 164–65.

15. Walter Benjamin, "The Work of Art in the Age of Its Technological Reproducibility, Second Version," trans. Edmund Jephcott and Harry Zohn, in *The Work of Art in the Age of Its Technological Reproducibility, and Other Writings on Media,* ed. Michael W. Jennings, Brigid Doherty, and Thomas Y. Levin (Cambridge, Mass.: Belknap Press of Harvard University Press, 2008), 19–55.

16. My reading of Benjamin's "The Work of Art" is admittedly more straightforward than Samuel Weber's imaginative reading that the withering of aura itself belongs to the structure of aura, and hence permits the persistence of aura—albeit with different forms and effects—in the age of the artwork's technological reproducibility. I believe Weber's complex analysis points to some of Benjamin's own uncertainties and revisions regarding the concept of aura. Concerning the evolution of aura in Benjamin's thinking, see Miriam Bratu Hansen, "Benjamin's Aura," *Critical Inquiry* 34, no. 2 (Winter 2008): 336–75. See also Samuel Weber, "Mass Mediauras, or Art, Aura and Media in the Work of Walter Benjamin," in *Mass Mediauras: Form, Technics, Media,* ed. Alan Cholodenko (Stanford: Stanford University Press, 1996), 84.

17. For a historic overview of modern European intellectual property, see Christopher May and Susan K. Sell, *Intellectual Property Rights: A Critical History* (Boulder, Colo.: Lynne Rienner, 2005).

18. See Lionel Bently and Brad Sherman, *The Making of Modern Intellectual Property Law: The British Experience, 1760–1911* (Cambridge: Cambridge University Press, 1999), especially part 1, "Towards a property in intangibles." See also May and Sell, *Intellectual Property Rights,* chapter 4.

19. Bently and Sherman, *The Making of Modern Intellectual Property Law,* 66.

20. Bently and Sherman, *The Making of Modern Intellectual Property Law,* 45–46. Bently and Sherman write, moreover, that reproducibility requires this claim to universality: "It has long been recognized that the property right in the intangible must extend beyond its first embodiment (the manuscript, painting, or prototype) to cover the production of replicas and

equivalents. Typically, this has been taken to mean that the intangible needs to be presented in abstract and universal terms." Bently and Sherman, *The Making of Modern Intellectual Property Law,* 51.

21. Adam Smith, *The Wealth of Nations,* ed. Edwin Cannan (New York: Random House, Modern Library Edition, 1994), chapter 5.

22. John Locke, *Second Treatise of Government,* ed. C. B. Macpherson (Indianapolis, Ind.: Hackett, 1980), 19.

23. Locke, *Second Treatise of Government,* 19.

24. Locke, *Second Treatise of Government,* 17.

25. A body of scholarship attributes modern European conceptions of authorship to either the Enlightenment or Romanticism, often with some reference to the expansion of print. I have not found scholarship claiming specifically that a Romantic construct of authorship mirrored the legal construct of intellectual property, but much of the relevant scholarship seems to tacitly suggest such a conclusion. See, for example, the following works: Tilar J. Mazzeo, *Plagiarism and Literary Property in the Romantic Period* (Philadelphia: University of Pennsylvania Press, 2007); Marilyn Randall, *Pragmatic Plagiarism: Authorship, Profit, and Power* (Toronto: University of Toronto Press, 2001); Elizabeth A. Fay, "Author," in *A Handbook of Romantic Studies,* ed. Julia M. Wright and Joel Faflak (London: John Wiley and Sons, 2016), 107–24. Also, Elizabeth Eisenstein has suggested that the notion of possessive individualism emerges with the rise of the printing press and related constructions of authorship, although she doesn't specifically link this to the legal development of intellectual property, which comes, after all, subsequent to the period she examines (primarily the fifteenth through seventeenth centuries). See Eisenstein, *The Printing Press as an Agent of Change: Communications and Cultural Transformations in Early-Modern Europe, Vol. I and II* (Cambridge: Cambridge University Press, 1980), 120–21, e-book.

26. See Máčel, "Avant-Garde Design and the Law"; T'ai Smith, "The Identity of Design as Intellectual Property," in *Bauhaus Construct,* ed. Jeffrey Saletnik and Robin Schuldenfrei (London: Routledge, 2009), 226–40; Schwartz, "Utopia for Sale."

27. Incidentally, many of the most vocal critics of technological reproduction held copyrights over technologically reproducible textile or wallpaper designs, including William Morris and A. W. N. Pugin.

28. Smith, "The Identity of Design as Intellectual Property," 233.

29. Adam Smith and Karl Marx offer somewhat different accounts of the components of a commodity's price that are not ascribable to labor time, but both authors make reference to the same agent of capital, what Smith calls "the owner of the stock which employs [the labourer]." Smith, *The Wealth of Nations,* 55–56. Marx does, however, try to account for forms of intellectual or managerial labor, describing them as "complex labor" and arguing, "More complex labour counts only as *intensified,* or rather, *multiplied* simple labour." This account hardly makes sense of how such labor could in fact come to be a multiple of itself. Marx, *Capital,* 1: 135.

30. On the Gläserne Kette, see Bletter, "The Interpretation of the Glass Dream." On Paul Scheerbart, whose writings inspired the group, see John A. Stuart, "Unweaving Narrative Fabric: Bruno Taut, Walter Benjamin, and Paul Scheerbart's *The Gray Cloth,*" *Journal of Architectural Education* 53, no. 2 (November, 1999): 61–73.

31. Bruno Taut, "A Programme for Architecture," in Conrad, *Programs and Manifestoes,* 42.

32. Emerson praises Zoroaster in "The Progress of Culture." Ralph Waldo Emerson, "The Progress of Culture," in *The Collected Works of Ralph Waldo Emerson,* vol. 8, *Letters and Social Aims* (Cambridge, Mass.: Belknap Press of Harvard University Press, 2010), 108–23. He also mentions Zoroaster in his notes and journal entries.

33. On the origins of Mazdaznan, see Peter B. Clarke, ed., *Encyclopedia of New Religious Movements* (New York: Routledge, 2006), 394.

34. Twenty-three years after Itten's departure from the school, Gropius did in fact describe Mazdaznan as an objectionable aspect of Itten's pedagogy. It is unclear, however—given that he avoided broaching Mazdaznan at the time of his argument with Itten—whether this was part of Gropius's retrospective framing of the school as technorationalist or whether it was indeed the main issue. See Fiona MacCarthy, *Gropius: The Man Who Built the Bauhaus* (Cambridge, Mass.: Harvard University Press, 2019), 137–40.

35. On Gropius's anti-Semitism, see Rose-Carol Washton Long, "Moholy's Bauhaus Photography and the Issue of the Hidden Jew," *Women's Art Journal* 35, no. 2 (Fall–Winter 2014): 35–44. Kandinsky was also known to be anti-Semitic, causing a rupture in his friendship with Arnold Schönberg. See Mark DeVoto, "Arnold Schoenberg and Judaism: The Harder Road" (lecture), accessed January 22, 2020, https://sites.tufts.edu/markdevoto/files/2015/10/Schoenberg.pdf.

36. Walter Gropius "Memorandum to the Masters of Form, 13 March 1922," in *The Bauhaus: Masters and Students by Themselves*, ed. Frank Whitford (Woodstock, N.Y.: Overlook Press, 1993).

37. Gropius, "Memorandum to the Masters of Form."

38. Marx, of course, speaks not of the alienation (*Entfremdung*) of one's "spirit" but, rather, of the alienation of one's "self" from one's labor. The Hegelian usage of "alienation," however—prevalent among Bauhäuslers—often cast it within this spiritual framework, whereby mechanistic labor was seen precisely to segregate one's spirit from one's laboring activities.

39. "Die Vorlehre von Johannes Itten, die Harmonisierungslehre von Gertrud Grunow und die Grundlagen für eine Kompositionslehre der Farbformen waren das pädagogische Rüstzeug, das wir zur Entfaltung der Bauhausidee geben konnten." Lothar Schreyer, *Erinnerungen an Sturm und Bauhaus: Was ist des Menschen Bild* (Munich: Langen Müller, 1956), 192.

40. On Grunow's laws relating colors to materials, see Gertrud Grunow, "Von der Farbe im Runden," *Kunst und Jugend* 2 (February 1938): 36–37.

41. Grunow writes: "Wie Sehweisen und Hörarten einander wirklich verwandt sind." Gertrud Grunow, "Natürliche Formentwicklung," *Kunst und Jugend*, 7 (July 1938): 139–40. See also Hildegard Heitmeyer, "Der Aufbau der lebendingen Form durch Farbe, Form, und Ton," *Die Tat, Kunst und Jugend*, March 1920, 1–4.

42. On Wolfgang Metzger's influence on her work, see Grunow, "Natürliche Formentwicklung," 139–40.

43. Gropius to Grunow, 1925. Getrud Grunow Dokumente, Mappe 1, Bauhaus-Archiv, Berlin.

44. René van der Veer, "The Making of a Developmental Psychologist," in *Heinz Werner and Developmental Science*, ed. Jaan Valsiner (New York: Kluwer Academic and Plenum, 2005), 79–81, 89–92.

45. Heinz Werner, *Comparative Psychology of Mental Development*, trans. Edward Ballard Garside (1940; repr., New York: International Universities Press, 1948), 94.

46. Werner, *Comparative Psychology of Mental Development*, 80–86.

47. Werner explains the "primitive" nature of synesthesia in a section titled "Lack of Differentiation in Primordial Perception; Synaesthesia and the Primordial Unity of the Senses," in Werner, *Comparative Psychology of Mental Development*, 86–103.

48. Werner, *Comparative Psychology of Mental Development*, chapter 11.

49. Werner, *Comparative Psychology of Mental Development*, 306–8.

50. Itten, "Rassenlehre und Kunstentwicklung."

51. "Die künstlerische Erziehung wird im wesentlichen dieselbe sein müssen wie die Eriziehung im allgemeinen, deren Ziel es ist die natürlichen Anlagen jedes einzelnen Schülers möglichst zur vollen Entfaltung und Harmonie zu bringen; das Denk-vermögen, die Sinnesvermögen und die körperlich Fähigkeiten zu entwickeln, so daβ die individuellen Kräfte sich

ungehemmt in der schöpferischen Arbeit verwirklichen können." Johannes Itten, "Kunst—Hand—Werk," manuscript in Johannes Itten, Dokumente, Mappe 23, Bauhaus-Archiv, Berlin.

52. Tadd, *New Methods in Education*, 6–7, 13–14.

53. Pennell, *Charles Godfrey Leland*.

54. Zeynep Çelik Alexander has written on Tadd's influence on Austrian and German art instruction. Alexander, *Kinaesthetic Knowing*, chapter 4. Also, for a history of the discourse on visual psychology in Vienna in the early twentieth century, see Deborah Coen, *Vienna in the Age of Uncertainty: Science, Liberalism, and Private Life* (Chicago: University of Chicago Press, 2007), chapters 6 and 9.

55. "Das hatte nichts mit dem üblichen Expressionismus zu tun, wohl aber mit dem *Grundlagen* der bildenden Kunst"; emphasis added. Itten, "Autobiographisches Fragment," in *Johannes Itten: Werke und Schriften*, by Johannes Itten, Willy Rotzler, and Anneliese Itten (Zurich: Orell Füssli, 1972), 32.

56. Itten, "Autobiographisches Fragment," 32.

57. Leah Dickerman discusses Itten's establishment of "basic units" and the importance of his emphasis on abstraction to later Bauhaus work. See Dickerman, "Bauhaus Fundaments" in Bergdoll et al., *Bauhaus 1919–1933*, 17–19.

58. Johannes Itten, "Schöpferische Automatismus," in Itten, Rotzler, and Itten, *Johannes Itten*.

59. Clare Pettit, *Patent Inventions—Intellectual Property and the Victorian Novel* (Oxford: Oxford University Press, 2004), chapter 2.

60. Johannes Itten, *Design and Form: The Basic Course at the Bauhaus*, rev. ed. (London: Thames and Hudson, 1975), 12–31.

61. One artist Itten used for this study was the fifteenth- and sixteenth-century painter Matthias Grünewald, who is considered to have preserved many features of medieval painting even though he worked during the Renaissance era.

62. "Alles, was wir sehen, hören, riechen, schmecken, tasten, fühlen, ist in Relation gesetzt zu einem Zweiten, das dem Ersten entgegengesetzt ist. " Johannes Itten, *Tagebuch von Johannes Itten* (Berlin: Verlag der Itten-schule, 1930), 54.

63. Johannes Itten, *Gestaltungs- und Formenlehre: Mein Vorkurs am Bauhaus und später* (Ravensburg, Germany: Maier, 1975), 12, 98. On the significance of breath at the Bauhaus, see Linn Burchert, "Atem- und Pulsbilder," in *Im Rhythmus: Entwürfe alternativer Arbeitsweisen von 1900 bis in die Gegenwart*, ed. Christoph Büttner and Carolin Piotrowski (Leiden: Wilhelm Fink, 2018), 59–75.

64. Itten, *Design and Form*, 34.

65. Itten, *Design and Form*, 125.

66. Itten, "Rassenlehre und Kunstentwicklung."

67. See Michael Stausberg, "Para-Zoroastrianisms," in *Parsis in India and the Diaspora*, ed. John Hinnells and Alan Williams (Oxon, UK: Routledge, 2008), 236–54.

68. Johannes Itten, "Entwicklung der Kunst," unpublished notes in Johannes Itten, Dokumente, Mappe 2, Bauhaus-Archiv, Berlin.

69. Paul Citroen, "Mazdaznan at the Bauhaus" in *Bauhaus and Bauhaus People: Personal Opinions and Recollections of Former Bauhaus Members and Their Contemporaries*, trans. Eva Richter and Alba Lorman, ed. Eckhard Neumann (New York: Van Nostrand Reinhold, 1970), 46–53. See also Whitford, *The Bauhaus*, 62–63.

70. See especially Marx, *Capital*, vol. 1, chapter 6, "The Buying and Selling of Labour Power."

71. C. B. Macpherson, *The Political Theory of Possessive Individualism: Hobbes to Locke* (1962; repr., Oxford: Oxford University Press, 2011).

72. In reference to Macpherson's text, Étienne Balibar has raised the question—as did Marx—of the transindividual nature of labor. See Balibar, "'Possessive Individualism' Reversed: From Locke to Derrida," *Constellations* 9, no. 3 (September 2002): 299–317.

73. On Moholy-Nagy's pedagogic exercises and his emphasis on "the organic," see László Moholy-Nagy, *The New Vision, 1928, 3rd Rev. Ed., 1946. And, Abstract of an Artist,* trans. Daphne M. Hoffmann (New York: Wittenborn, 1946).

74. On the connections between the Dessau Bauhaus and industrial financing, see Walter Schieffele, *Bauhaus, Junkers, Sozialdemokratie: Ein Kraftfeld der Moderne* (Berlin: Form + Zweck, 2003).

75. Walter Gropius, "Statement about the Differences of Opinion at the Bauhaus," in Whitford, *The Bauhaus,* 134; emphasis added.

76. Gropius, "Statement about the Differences of Opinion at the Bauhaus," 134.

77. Weber, "Mass Mediauras," 3.

78. Bergdoll et al., *Bauhaus 1919–1933,* 13.

3. Postwar European Modernism

1. Mark Swenarton, Tom Avermaete, and Dirk van den Heuvel, eds., *Architecture and the Welfare State* (Abingdon, UK: Routledge, 2015).

2. Alison Smithson, manuscript notes for "Team Ten Meetings 1953–1981, Team Ten Papers, box 005, folder 41, 20–22, Netherlands Architecture Institute. The archive is now with Het Nieuwe Instituut, Rotterdam. All citations of Team Ten Papers use the locater information of the Netherlands Architecture Institute.

3. On the idea of the French colonies as a laboratory for architectural experimentation, see Gwendolyn Wright, *The Politics of Design in French Colonial Urbanism* (Chicago: University of Chicago Press, 1991), chapter 2. See also Paul Rabinow, *French Modern: Norms and Forms of the Social Environment* (Chicago: University of Chicago Press, 1995).

4. On the significance of GAMMA on Team Ten, see Tom Avermaete, "From Knoxville to Bidonville: ATBAT and the Architecture of the French Welfare State," in Swenarton, Avermaete, and Van den Heuvel, *Architecture and the Welfare State,* 227–32.

5. Some noteworthy scholarship on the relations between translation and politics include Gayatri Chakravorty Spivak, "The Politics of Translation," in *Outside in the Teaching Machine* (New York: Routledge, 1993); Emily Apter, *The Translation Zone: A New Comparative Literature* (Princeton: Princeton University Press, 2006); Sandra Bermann and Michael Wood, eds., *Nation, Language, and the Ethics of Translation* (Princeton: Princeton University Press, 2005). Related scholarship on language, interpretation, and politics includes, for example, Rancière, *Dissensus.*

6. Tejaswini Niranjana, *Siting Translation: History, Poststructuralism, and the Colonial Context* (Berkeley: University of California Press, 1992), 4.

7. Alison Smithson and Peter Smithson, "Sources" document for *Parallel of Life and Art* exhibition, Smithson Family Archive, as cited in Victoria Walsh and Claire Zimmerman, "New Brutalist Image 1949–55: 'Atlas to a New World'; or, 'Trying to Look at Things Today,'" November 28, 2016, *British Art Studies,* no. 4, https://doi.org/10.17658/issn.2058-5462/issue-04/vwalsh-czimmerman.

8. On the Nid d'abeille housing project, see Monique Eleb, "An Alternative to Functionalist Universalism: Ecochard, Candilis, and ATBAT-Afrique," in *Anxious Modernisms,* ed. Sarah Williams Goldhagen and Réjean Legault (Cambridge: MIT Press, 2000), 55–73; Avermaete, "From Knoxville to Bidonville"; Ijlal M. Muzaffar, "The Periphery Within: Modern Architecture and the Making of the Third World" (PhD diss., Massachusetts Institute of Technology, 2007).

9. See Muzaffar's critique of the project as instating an intentionally compromised and partial form of modernization; Muzaffar, "The Periphery Within."

10. The most comprehensive compendium on Team Ten through 2020 is a compilation of scholarly gloss and excerpted primary-source texts: Max Risselada and Dirk van den

Heuvel, eds., *Team 10: 1953–81, in Search of a Utopia of the Present* (Rotterdam: NAi, 2005). See also Alison Smithson's compilation of writings and images in Smithson, ed., *Team 10 Primer* (1968; repr., Cambridge: MIT Press, 1974).

11. *This Is Tomorrow Catalogue* (1956), reproduced in *The Independent Group: Postwar Britain and the Aesthetics of Plenty*, ed. David Robbins (Cambridge: MIT Press, 1990), 15.

12. In a recent issue of *October* dedicated to a retrospective evaluation of new brutalism, editor Alex Kitnick perceives Banham's review as a wholly negative criticism of the *Patio and Pavilion* project. See Kitnick's preface to "This Is Tomorrow," by Reyner Banham, *October*, no. 136 (Spring 2011): 32–34.

13. Reyner Banham, "This Is Tomorrow," *Architectural Review* 120 (September 1956): 186–88; emphasis added.

14. On the savage mind's use of "signs" in lieu of "concepts," Lévi-Strauss writes, "Signs resemble images in being *concrete* entities but they resemble concepts in their powers of reference. Neither concepts nor signs relate exclusively to themselves; either may be substituted for something else. Concepts, however, have an unlimited capacity in this respect, while signs have not." Lévi-Strauss, *Savage Mind*, 16–20; emphasis added.

15. Lévi-Strauss, *Savage Mind*, 18–20.

16. Hal Foster, "Savage Minds (A Note on Brutalist Bricolage)," *October*, no. 136 (Spring 2011): 182–91.

17. On the supposedly backward-looking tendencies of *Patio and Pavilion*, see Foster, "Savage Minds," 189–90.

18. N. Katherine Hayles has argued that the human and posthuman constitute two distinct historical constructs. See Hayles, *How We Became Posthuman: Virtual Bodies in Cybernetics, Literature, and Informatics* (Chicago: University of Chicago Press, 1999).

19. Ben Highmore, instead of seeing *Patio and Pavilion* as providing a frame for sensory and semiotic order, claims that it is about a "vernacular (anti-)ordering" that mimics the quotidian. Highmore, "Rough Poetry: 'Patio and Pavilion' Revisited," *Oxford Art Journal* 29, no. 2 (2006): 282. See also Foster, "Savage Minds."

20. Siegfried Giedion, *Building in France, Building in Iron, Building in Ferroconcrete*, trans. J. Duncan Berry (Santa Monica, Calif.: Getty Center for the History of Art and the Humanities, 1995). See also László Moholy-Nagy, *The New Vision*.

21. On the Smithsons' use of Patrick Geddes's village diagram and their subsequent proposal for "scales of association," see Eric Mumford, *The CIAM Discourse on Urbanism, 1928–1954* (Cambridge: MIT Press, 2000), 253–54.

22. Marc-Antoine Laugier, *An Essay on Architecture*, Documents and Sources in Architecture, no. 1 (Los Angeles: Hennessey and Ingalls, 1977), chapter 1.

23. Vitruvius, most famously, told of the beginnings of architecture with an illustration of a "primitive hut." For a discussion of this trope, see Joseph Rykwert, *On Adam's House in Paradise*.

24. Anthony Vidler has argued that Laugier's origin myth of the primitive hut must have been influenced by an eighteenth-century preoccupation with discovering the origin of language. Moreover, he shows Laugier's hut was probably derived from the work of the missionary and ethnographer Joseph-François Lafitau, who published (largely fanciful) material on the architectures of American Indians in the French colonies of North America. See Vidler, *The Writing of the Walls*, chapter 1, "Rebuilding the Primitive Hut: The Return to Origins from Lafitau to Laugier."

25. In addition to the Team Ten examples I discuss in this chapter, architects and architectural theorists throughout the twentieth century invoked a notion of underlying essences, myths, archetypes, and far-reaching cultural roots in order to develop or justify modernist architectures. For example, proponents of Critical Regionalism were, in a sense, unwittingly

arguing for modern architecture to translate "primitive huts" (for example, to incorporate in translated form some distilled architectural idea pervasive in regional architectural heritage). See Liane Lefaivre and Alexander Tzonis, *Critical Regionalism: Architecture and Identity in a Globalized World,* Architecture in Focus (Munich: Prestel, 2003). See also Kenneth Frampton, John Cava, and Graham Foundation for Advanced Studies in the Fine Arts, *Studies in Tectonic Culture: The Poetics of Construction in Nineteenth and Twentieth Century Architecture* (Cambridge: MIT Press, 1995).

26. On architecture and pattern in relation to the technological, see Reinhold Martin, *The Organizational Complex: Architecture, Media, and Corporate Space* (Cambridge: MIT Press, 2003); Dutta, *The Bureaucracy of Beauty*; Orit Halpern, *Beautiful Data: A History of Vision and Reason since 1945* (Durham, N.C.: Duke University Press, 2014).

27. Transcripts from Team Ten meeting at Abbé de Royaumont, 1962, in Team Ten Papers, box 003, folder 22, 29.

28. Peter Smithson, "Interview Notes," in *Team Ten Papers* (Rotterdam: NAi, c. 1982); emphasis added.

29. Alison and Peter Smithson were as interested in local "indigenous" populations (for example, using Nigel Henderson's photographs of England's urban working classes) as they were in local and foreign types of indigenous architecture.

30. Christopher Alexander, *Notes on the Synthesis of Form* (Cambridge, Mass.: Harvard University Press, 1964), 32–38 and passim.

31. Alexander, *Notes on the Synthesis of Form,* 37–45 and chapter 4.

32. Alexander, *Notes on the Synthesis of Form,* chapter 4.

33. Christopher Alexander, Sara Ishikawa, and Murray Silverstein, *A Pattern Language: Towns, Buildings, Construction* (New York: Oxford University Press, 1977).

34. On cybernetic organicism as a strategy for corporate design, see Martin, *The Organizational Complex,* chapters 2 and 4.

35. On the architectural history of the Freie Universität, see Gabriel Feld, *Free University, Berlin: Candilis, Josic, Woods, Schiedelm* (London: Architectural Association, 1999).

36. Avermaete, "From Knoxville to Bidonville," 220–23.

37. Feld, *Free University, Berlin.*

38. On Van Eyck's relationship with Benedict, see Francis Strauven, "Aldo van Eyck: Modern Architecture and Dogon Culture," *Lotus International* 114 (September 2002): 120–31. See also Georges Teyssot, "Aldo van Eyck and the Rise of an Ethnographic Paradigm in the 1960s," *Joelho* 2 (2011): 50–67.

39. Alison Smithson, "How to Recognise and Read a Mat Building," *Architecture Design* 44, no. 9 (September 1974): 573–90.

40. Alison Smithson writes, "Mat-building can be said to epitomise the anonymous collective, where the functions come to enrich the fabric, and the individual gains new freedoms of action through a new and shuffled order, based on interconnection, close-knit patterns of association, and possibilities for growth, diminution and change." Smithson, "How to Recognise and Read a Mat Building," 573.

41. Smithson, "How to Recognise and Read a Mat Building," 576.

42. On orientalism as a form of representation, see Edward Said, *Orientalism* (1978; repr., New York: Vintage Books, Random House, 1994).

43. Smithson, "How to Recognise and Read a Mat Building," 580.

44. Asseel Al-Ragam offers a very different reading of the Smithsons' Kuwait City proposal, seeing its "critical nostalgia" as oppositional to European hegemony, even if not entirely successful in this endeavor. See Al-Ragam, "Critical Nostalgia: Kuwait Urban Modernity and Alison and Peter Smithson's Kuwait Urban Study and Mat-Building," *Journal of Architecture* 20, no. 1 (2015): 1–20.

45. For a transcript of Van Eyck's presentation of Blom's work and the ensuing confrontation between Van Eyck and the Smithsons, see Team Ten Papers, TTEN0003, Aanvrag 22, 218–35.

46. For an unedited transcript of Van Eyck's presentation of Blom's scheme, see Transcripts from Team Ten meeting at Abbé de Royaumont. For Van Eyck's ideas on metonymy—in relation to the Dogon and more generally—see Aldo van Eyck, *Collected Articles and Other Writings, 1947–1998* (Amsterdam: SUN, 2008). For edited versions of Team Ten discussions, see Risselada and Van den Heuvel, *Team 10*.

47. For Van Eyck's ideas on metonymy, see "A Tree Is Like a Leaf"; "Design Only Grace; Open Norm; Disturb Order Gracefully; Outmatch Need"; and "Basket—House—Village—Universe," all three in Van Eyck, *Collected Articles and Other Writings*. Van Eyck was reacting against ideas put forward in Christopher Alexander, "A City Is Not a Tree," *Architectural Forum* 122, no. 1 (April 1965): 58–62.

48. Although Kenneth Frampton's comparison between "universal civilization" and "culture" would come decades later, Frampton was drawing on an existing discursive framing according to which civilization and modernity were presumed as universal goals, while culture was equated to nonmodern traditions. Frampton, "Towards a Critical Regionalism: Six Points for an Architecture of Resistance," in *The Anti-Aesthetic: Essays on Postmodern Culture*, ed. Hal Foster (New York: New Press, 1983), 16–30.

49. Transcripts from Team Ten meeting at Abbé de Royaumont.

50. Alison Smithson and Peter Smithson, "Programme for the Architypal (UR-typal) House," presentation at *CIAM 9*, Aix-en-Provence, July 1953, transcripts in Team Ten Papers, NAi TTEN0002, folder 3.

51. Walter Benjamin, "The Task of the Translator," trans. Harry Zohn, in *Walter Benjamin: Selected Writings*, vol. 1, *1913–1926*, ed. Marcus Bullock and Michael W. Jennings (Cambridge, Mass.: Belknap Press of Harvard University Press, 1996), 253–63. See also Jacques Derrida, "Des Tours de Babel," in *Difference in Translation*, ed. Joseph F. Graham and State University of New York, Research Foundation (Ithaca, N.Y.: Cornell University Press, 1985).

52. This presentation of Benjamin's "pure language" and its relationship to architecture is distinct from Esra Akcan's reading, which proposes that Benjamin's "pure language" serves as an "aspiration for the future," interpreting the "pure language" as "the greater language . . . in which all different languages can be combined." Akcan distinguishes between this ideal form of translation and the hegemonic practices of "translatability from above." My argument is that architectural translation often operates precisely as a way to obfuscate this distinction. The structuralist aspect of "pure language"—essentially the freeing of language from its signifying function to reveal the *mode* of signification—is disturbingly akin to the hegemonic forms of translation that characterized many forms of global architectural practice. See Akcan, *Architecture in Translation: Germany, Turkey, and the Modern House* (Durham, N.C.: Duke University Press, 2012), 13–14.

53. On the one hand, translation is described as effecting a kind of tear within the fabric of language, opening onto the originary chasm separating direct, divine revelation from the inadequate mediation through which human thought renders itself into language. On the other hand, the translation also thereby struggles to overcome that chasm, thereby being suggestive of pentecostal semiotics. Samuel Weber warns that "pure language" should not be confused with a "prelapsarian language." However, given the messianic strain of Benjamin's "The Task of the Translator," it is hard to dissociate this stripped-down semiotic scaffolding from the prelapsarian. See Weber, *Benjamin's -abilities* (Cambridge, Mass.: Harvard University Press, 2008), 90.

54. Karin Jaschke discusses the spectacular media-oriented dimension of Haan's work. Jaschke, "Mythical Journeys: Ethnography, Archaeology, and the Attraction of Tribal Cultures in the Work of Aldo van Eyck and Herman Haan" (PhD diss., Princeton University, 2012), 112.

55. Herman Haan, Rogier Bedaux, Gerard Jansen, Ton Hosemans, producers, *Tellem, Verslag van een Expeditie* (Tellem, Report of an Expedition), 1975. Institut for Antropobiology, Rijksuniversiteit Utrecht. See also Van den Hout, Reinier, Mirjam Gulmans, *Andere Tijden: De Tellem Expeditie. Schedels meten in Afrika* (Other Times: The Tellem expedition. Measuring skulls in Africa). NPS VPRO, 2009.

56. On Haan's being "mistaken" for an archaeologist, see Jaschke, "Mythical Journeys," 116.

57. Van Eyck writes, "The Dogon rely on an all-pervading framework which embraces every facet of their existence, material, emotional, and transcendental. Such frameworks are so self-contained that they may tend to leave little scope for the individual whose mental structure, though moulded by them to a large extent, nonetheless never coincides fully. Not so with the Dogon, for they include within the intricate, closely knit fabric of their system a gratifying kind of scope (flexibility) which permits circumstantial and incidental modification without transgressing against the system's generative and protective potential." See Van Eyck, "Design Only Grace," in *Collected Articles and Other Writings.*

58. For the concept of binaries in Lévi-Strauss, see his *Myth and Meaning* and *The Savage Mind.* For Van Eyck's idea of the paradoxical unity of antitheses, see Van Eyck, "Design Only Grace"; Van Eyck, "Labyrinthian Clarity," in *Collected Articles and Other Writings,* 110–15.

59. Lévi-Strauss, *Myth and Meaning,* 2. See also Roman Jakobson on "inter-semiotic translation." Jakobson, "On Linguistic Aspects of Translation," in *Language in Literature,* by Roman Jakobson, ed. Krystyna Pomorska and Stephen Rudy (Cambridge, Mass.: Belknap Press, 1987).

60. Friedrich Kittler discusses the history of binary code and its relation to alphabetic representation in Kittler, "The History of Communication Media," *CTheory,* July 30, 1996, https://journals.uvic.ca/index.php/ctheory/article/view/14325/5101.

61. "Herman Haan Bracht Water in Mali," newspaper clipping, unknown source, in Herman Haan Archive / Hax0010, Netherlands Architecture Institute, archive now with Het Nieuwe Instituut, Rotterdam.

62. At Team Ten's Abbé de Royaumont meeting, Peter Smithson emphatically declared that when it came to building housing for the poor, "if you have to build for people who have no choice . . . that offer must not . . . be offered in any historically oriented way, that is, towards the reconstruction of an old way of life, but must be oriented towards the dream." That is to say, even in studying and diagramming a community's existing way of life, an architect would still offer them something else, "a dream." See Transcripts from Team Ten meeting at Abbé de Royaumont.

63. Rudofsky had used Quatremère's illustration of the way primitive or vernacular architectures had been translated into present-day forms. Van Eyck and Haan had both been asked to contribute to Rudofsky's *Architecture without Architects* exhibition. See Bernard Rudofsky, *Architecture without Architects: An Introduction to Nonpedigreed Architecture* (United Kingdom: Academy Editions, 1964); Felicity Scott, "Bernard Rudofsky: Allegories of Nomadism and Dwelling," in Goldhagen and Legault, *Anxious Modernisms.*

64. For a detailed analysis on the work of Antoine-Chrysostome Quatremère de Quincy, see Sylvia Lavin, *Quatremère De Quincy and the Invention of a Modern Language of Architecture* (Cambridge: MIT Press, 1992). See also Anthony Vidler, "The Idea of Type: The Transformation of the Academic Ideal, 1750–1830," *Oppositions,* no. 8 (1977): 95–115; Vidler, *The Writing of the Walls.*

65. According to Quatremère, architects who reject the concept of imitation "confound the idea of *type* (the original reason of the thing), which can neither command nor furnish the motif or the means of an exact likeness, with the idea of the *model* (the complete thing) which is bound to a formal resemblance." Antoine-Chrysostome Quatremère de Quincy, "Type," *Oppositions,* no. 8 (1977): 146–50.

66. Quatremère complains of East Asian architecture (typified by pagoda roofs) that "there is nothing to imitate since there is not even any change of material [from its prior

model to its architectural form].” Comparing Greek lithic architecture (derived from carpentry) to Egyptian architecture, Quatremère writes, “When stone replaced timber, by conserving all the forms of the former material the art enriched itself even more by the means suggested by the latter and thus reunited the two. . . . However, there are many people who find fault with architecture for reducing itself to imitate the first constructions of timber: they find it wrong that stone is representative of another material. . . . We have already shown that stone, in copying itself, or to put it better, by copying nothing, has offered no form to art . . . no relation to the spirit. That is proved by Egyptian architecture.” Quatremère continues, “The energetic expression of strength and all the sentiments which bind themselves to this essential virtue depends especially on the same expression of essence of architecture *or of the types that gave it its existence.* For this reason, of the three orders of architecture, the one which passes for having and which really has the most *character* is the Doric, that is to say *the primitive order where the expression of carpentry and of the constructive types of the art is stated and rendered with the greatest strength and obviousness.*” See Quatremère de Quincy, “Architecture” and “Character,” both in “Architecture, Character, Idea, Imitation: Extracts from the Encyclopédie Méthodique d'Architecture,” by Quatremère de Quincy, ed. Tanis Hinchcliffe, *9H,* no. 7 (1985): 25–34.

67. Regarding critics of the Greek temple's imitation of wood, Quatremère writes, “The tympanum and the façade have to be suppressed. All parts of the roof have to be servilely copied in detail. No convention can be admitted between wood construction and its translation into stone.” Quatremère de Quincy, “Type.”

68. Quatremère borrows from a Platonic conception of *eidos* in his concept of “type,” but he also draws from Aristotelian ideas of a telos-driven unfolding. Indeed, the kind of embryonic development of “type” resembles nineteenth-century German concepts of *Bildung,* which he may have been aware of from the work of Johann Winckelmann. Quatremère de Quincy, “Type.”

69. It should be noted that even within the discourse of “vernacular” architectures, there were opportunities to dissent from the project of universalism. Felicity Scott argues for this interpretation of Rudofsky's work. See Scott, *Disorientation: Bernard Rudofsky in the Empire of Signs* (Berlin: Sternberg Press, 2016).

70. Marcel Griaule, *Dieu d'eau: Entretiens avec Ogotemmêli* (Paris: Librairie Arthème, 1975), 34–38.

71. Griaule, *Dieu d'eau.* See also James Clifford's account of the encounter among Griaule, Michel Leiris, and the Dogon. Clifford, *The Predicament of Culture: Twentieth-Century Ethnography, Literature, and Art* (Cambridge, Mass.: Harvard University Press, 1988), chapter 2.

72. Aldo van Eyck, “Architecture of the Dogon,” *Architectural Forum* 115 (September 1961): 116–21.

73. Ogotemmêli's description is transcribed by Griaule thus: “‘Tout cela se dit en paroles. . . . Tout est symbole. . . . Tout ce qui s'exprime par symbole peut tenir sur une marche d'une coudée.’ Il employait, pour le mot symbole, une expression composée dont le sens littéral était ‘parole de ce bas monde.’” Griaule, *Dieu d'eau,* 41.

74. Foucault, *The Order of Things: An Archaeology of the Human Sciences,* translator not identified (1970; repr., New York: Routledge, 2002), xix–xx, 61–62, and passim.

75. See Rogier M. A. Bedaux, “Tellem, reconnaissance archéologique d'une culture de l'Ouest africain au Moyen Age: Recherches architectoniques,” *Journal de la Société des Africanistes* 42, no. 2 (1972): 103–85.

76. Griaule, *Dieu d'eau,* thirtieth day, “Les jumeaux et le commerce.”

77. Griaule, *Dieu d'eau,* 231.

78. Griaule, *Dieu d'eau,* 228.

79. Transcripts from Team Ten Meeting at Abbé de Royaumont.

80. See Bruno Latour on immutable mobiles in "Visualization and Cognition: Thinking with Eyes and Hands," in *Knowledge and Society: Studies in the Sociology of Culture Past and Present,* vol. 6, ed. H. Kuklick (Greenwich, Conn.: JAI Press, 1986), 1–40.

81. Muzaffar, "The Periphery Within."

82. Aldo van Eyck, *Works,* ed. Vincent Ligtelijn, trans. Gregory Ball (Basel: Birkhäuser, 1999), 127–28; emphasis added.

83. Van Eyck, *Works,* 127–28.

84. Concerning the economic and political choices leading to Robin Hood Garden's likely demolition, see Anna Minton, "London Had a Sub-prime Housing Problem. Now It Has a Super-prime Crisis," *Guardian,* April 20, 2016, https://www.theguardian.com/cities/2016/apr/20/london-housing-crisis-sub-prime-problem-super-prime. Arguing in support of public housing and discussing the case of Robin Hood Gardens, see Elain Harwood and Alan Powers, "From Downturn to Diversity, Revisiting the 1970s," *Twentieth Century Architecture,* no. 10 (2012): 8–35.

85. Paula Chakravartty and Denise Ferreira da Silva have written of a similar tendency in relation to the mortgage crisis of the early twenty-first century, noting the perpetual production of the "unsuitable economic subject." Chakravartty and Da Silva, "Accumulation, Dispossession, and Debt: The Racial Logic of Global Capitalism," in "Race, Empire, and the Crisis of the Subprime," ed. Paula Chakravartty and Denise Ferreira da Silva, special issue, *American Quarterly* 64, no. 3 (September 2012): 361–85.

86. Swenarton, Avermaete, and Van den Heuvel, *Architecture and the Welfare State.*

87. On the Smithsons' ambivalent relation to consumer culture, see, for example, Kenneth Frampton's passage on "New Brutalism and the Architecture of the Welfare State," in Frampton, *Modern Architecture: A Critical History,* 2nd ed. (London: Thames and Hudson, 1985), 265. See also Mark Crinson, "A Tree Which Grows: Stirling and Gowan, the Smithsons and Mass Culture," in *Neo-avant-garde and Postmodern: Postwar Architecture in Britain and Beyond,* ed. Mark Crinson and Claire Zimmerman (New Haven: Yale Center for British Art and Yale University Press, 2010): 177–99. See also Mark Risselada and Dirk van den Heuvel, "Introduction: 'Just a Few Houses . . . ,'" in *Alison and Peter Smithson: From the House of the Future to a House of Today,* ed. Mark Risselada and Dirk van den Heuvel (Rotterdam: 010 Publishers, 2004), 9–14.

4. Bricolage, Megastructure, Interface

1. Manuel Orazi, "The Erratic Universe of Yona Friedman," in *Arquitectura con la Gente, por la Gente, para la Gente / Architecture with the People, by the People, for the People: Yona Friedman,* ed. María Inés Rodríguez (León, Spain: MUSAC; Barcelona: Actar, 2011), 118. See Friedman's own account of his experience at Dubrovnik in Yona Friedman, *Pro Domo* (Barcelona: Actar, 2006), 11–14.

2. Dirk van den Heuvel notes that Blom in fact alluded to Friedman's megastructures as a source for his own work. See Van den Heuvel, "The Open Society and Its Experiments," in Swenarton, Avermaete, and van den Heuvel, *Architecture and the Welfare State,* 143.

3. For Friedman's own account, see "Biography," Yona Friedman (website), sponsored by the Netherlands Architecture Institute, accessed May 28, 2019, http://www.yonafriedman.nl/?page_id=1751.

4. On GEAM, see Cornelia Escher, "Nested Utopias: GEAM's Large-Scale Designs," in *Re-Scaling the Environment: New Landscapes of Design, 1960–1980,* vol. 2, *East West Central: Re-Building Europe, 1950–1990,* ed. Ákos Moravánszky and Karl R. Kegler (Basel: Birkhäuser, 2016), 81–95.

5. Yona Friedman, "Cylindrical Shelters," Yona Friedman Papers, box 60, folder 11, Getty Research Institute, Los Angeles.

6. Friedman, "Cylindrical Shelters."

7. See Giorgio Agamben, *Homo Sacer: Sovereign Power and Bare Life,* trans. Daniel Heller Roazen (Stanford: Stanford University Press, 1998), 166–80.

8. This putative neutrality of the megastructure recalls Benjamin Bratton's understanding of megastructural and electronic platforms: "Platforms are formally neutral but remain, each and every one, uniquely 'ideological' in how they realize particular strategies for organizing their publics. They are identified with neoliberalism (not without reason), but their origins lie as much within the utopian megastructures of 1960s experimental architecture, counterculture cybernetics, Soviet planning schemes, and many other systems of sociotechnical governance, both realized and imagined." Bratton, *The Stack: On Software and Sovereignty* (Cambridge: MIT Press, 2015), 46.

9. Le Corbusier's Obus plan for Algiers was almost certainly an inspiration for Friedman's early megastructural projects. In the 1960s, megastructural utopian schemes would be subsequently proposed by the Situationist structures of Constant Anton Nieuwenhuys and by the architectural group Archizoom.

10. See Bratton, *The Stack.* See also Steenson, *Architectural Intelligence.*

11. Yona Friedman, *Une architecture de survie: Une philosophie de la pauvreté* (1978; repr., Paris: Éditions de l'éclat, 2013), 33, 182–83.

12. Friedman, *Une architecture de survie,* 183.

13. Friedman, *Une architecture de survie,* 183.

14. Friedman, *Une architecture de survie,* 193.

15. Concerning Friedman's interest in cybernetics, see Yona Friedman, *Les utopies réalisables* (Paris: Union générale d'éditions, 1976).

16. Yona Friedman, "La ville totale," with Kenzo Tange, Nicholas Negroponte, and Richard Buckminster Fuller, *2000,* no. 24 (1971): 7, Yona Friedman Papers, box 5, folder 33; emphasis added.

17. Lévi-Strauss, *The Savage Mind,* 17–22.

18. Lévi-Strauss, *The Savage Mind,* 16–17.

19. James C. Scott, *Seeing Like a State: How Certain Schemes to Improve the Human Condition Have Failed* (New Haven: Yale University Press, 1998).

20. Nicholas Negroponte, "Systems of Urban Growth" (bachelor's thesis, MIT, 1966).

21. Friedman writes that Flatwriter was "conceived to enable the user to design the plan of his future home (self-planning) in the Ville Spatiale, or for a citizen to re-design his neighborhood in the Ville Spatiale." Friedman, "Flatwriter," Yona Friedman (website), sponsored by the Netherlands Architecture Institute, accessed May 27, 2019, http://www.yonafriedman.nl/?page_id=238&wppa-album=26&wppa-occur=1&wppa-photo=231.

22. The documentation for the "African Projects" credits an "S. Ketof," which presumably refers to the Italian-born Parisian engineer Serge Ketoff, although there is no clear-cut documentation identifying Ketoff's (or Ketof's) first name. Christel Frapier's research on engineers and architects working in France at this time suggests some possible discursive connections between Friedman and Ketoff. See Frapier, "Les ingénieurs-conseils dans l'architecture en France, 1945–1975: Réseaux et internationalisation du savoir technique" (PhD diss., Université Panthéon-Sorbonne—Paris I, 2009), 248.

23. Yona Friedman, "African Projects," Yona Friedman Papers, box 60, folder 7.

24. On Friedman's relationship to Israeli activities in postcolonial Africa, see Haim Yacobi, *Israel and Africa: A Genealogy of Moral Geography* (Abingdon, UK: Routledge, 2016). On Israelis in Africa more generally, see Ayala Levin, "Exporting Zionism: Architectural Modernism in Israeli–African Technical Cooperation, 1958–1973" (PhD diss., Columbia University, 2015). See also Zvi Efrat, "Proxy Colonialism: The Export of Israeli Architecture to Africa,"

in *African Modernism: The Architecture of Independence,* ed. Maneul Herz (Zurich: Park Books, 2015), 487–96.

25. On the nationalist and modernizing motivations underlying Tema's architectural design, see Iain Jackson and Rexford Assasie Oppong, "The Planning of Late Colonial Village Housing in the Tropics: Tema Manhean, Ghana," *Planning Perspectives* 29, no. 4 (2014), 475–99.

26. Friedman uses the term *ruche* (beehive) to describe the megastructures, although at one point he exchanges this term for its synonym *nid d'abeille* (bees' nest), a term used in the 1950s by the architects Candilis-Josic-Woods for their housing project in the banlieues of Casablanca, which were intended to help quell urban anticolonial unrest.

27. Yona Friedman, "Foyer Nigerien," in "African Projects." It should be noted that the archives for these "African Projects" do not clearly demarcate between the proposals for Niamey and Abidjan, thus leading to some potential confusion between the two schemes. I have endeavored to distinguish between them to the best of my abilities.

28. Friedman, "Foyer Nigerien."

29. Ginger Nolan, *The Neocolonialism of the Global Village.* See also Brian Larkin, *Signal and Noise: Media, Infrastructure, and Urban Culture in Nigeria* (Durham, N.C.: Duke University Press, 2008).

30. Yona Friedman, Yona Friedman Papers, Series II (Manuals), see especially boxes 19–25.

31. On efforts to render developmental programs more locally persuasive by adapting local media practices, see Nicole Sackley, "The Village as Cold War Site: Experts, Development, and the History of Rural Reconstruction," *Journal of Global History* 6, no. 3 (2011): 481–504. See also Subir Sinha, "Lineages of the Developmentalist State: Transnationality and Village India, 1900–1965," *Comparative Studies in Society and History* 50, no. 1 (January 2008): 68–69; Nolan, *The Neocolonialism of the Global Village.*

32. Yona Friedman, "L'UNESCO pour tous," June 1978, Yona Friedman Papers, box 8, folder 9.

33. Friedman, "L'UNESCO pour tous," 2–3.

34. Cf. Benedict Anderson, *Imagined Communities: Reflections on the Origin and Spread of Nationalism* (1983; repr., London: Verso 1991).

35. The ludic was a chief concern for Friedman. In one of his written explanations of "une architecture mobile," Friedman alludes to Johan Huizinga's *Homo Ludens.* See Friedman, "Pour une architecture mobile," *Revue Technique du Bâtiment* 2 (1960): 4.

36. Friedman, "L'UNESCO pour tous," 4.

37. On the uses, ideology, and effects of bamboo construction in India, see Ateya Khorakiwala, "Architecture's Scaffolds," *e-flux,* November 15, 2018, https://www.e-flux.com/architecture/overgrowth/221616/architecture-s-scaffolds/.

38. Friedman, "Why a Communication Centre," *Journal of Extension Systems* 1 (1985): 65.

39. Friedman, "Why a Communication Centre," 66.

40. On the logic of modernizing without financial expenditure, see Muzaffar, "The Periphery Within."

41. Friedman, "Why a Communication Centre," 63.

42. This project is described in the Yona Friedman dossier, AP FRIE, Bibliothèque Kandinsky, Centre Georges Pompidou, Paris.

43. Lévi-Strauss, *The Savage Mind,* 17; emphasis added.

5. The Earth Unfolded

1. Land artists often engaged questions of energy, entropy, ecology, and museum critique.

2. On Bayer's typography, see Jeremy Aynsley and Wolfsonian–Florida International University, *Graphic Design in Germany: 1890–1945, Weimar and Now* (Berkeley: University of California Press, 2000).

3. Bayer produced visual materials for the 1936 Olympics in Berlin.

4. For background on Paepcke and the Container Corporation of America, see James Sloan Allen, *The Romance of Commerce and Culture: Capitalism, Modernism, and the Chicago–Aspen Crusade for Cultural Reform* (Boulder: University Press of Colorado, 2002).

5. On the integration of ex-Bauhaus immigrants into U.S. social scientific endeavors, see Fred Turner, *The Democratic Surround: Multimedia and American Liberalism from World War II to the Psychedelic Sixties* (Chicago: University of Chicago Press, 2013), chapter 3.

6. The Great Books program began during World War I with War Studies and Peace Studies at Columbia University. Professors John Erskine and Mortimer Adler believed that reading the "great classics of Western Civilization" would enable students to cope with current problems of international conflict. The program was taken up by Hutchins at the University of Chicago in the 1940s and expanded into a program for local businessmen, leading to the publication of a series of books glossed by experts. For Paepcke's correspondence with Adler and Hutchins on the Great Books program, see Walter P. Paepcke Papers, box 86, Special Collections Research Center, University of Chicago Library. See also Allen, *The Romance of Commerce and Culture.* Hutchins was also associate director of the Ford Foundation at this time. See Leelah Gandhi, "The Ford Foundation and Its Arts and Culture Program in India: A Short History" (unpublished paper), accessed December 2, 2018, http://test.theatreforum.in/static/upload/docs/Ford_Fndn_A_short_history.pdf.

7. Cf. Reinhold Martin, *Utopia's Ghost: Architecture and Postmodernism, Again* (Minneapolis: University of Minnesota Press, 2010), 49. Timothy Mitchell discusses the environment redefined as an economic entity. Mitchell, *Carbon Democracy: Political Power in the Age of Oil* (London: Verso, 2011), 176.

8. For a discussion of the imbrication of scales forming conceptions of a global environment, see Anna Lowenhaupt Tsing, *Friction: An Ethnography of Global Connection* (Princeton: Princeton University Press, 2005).

9. Tim Ingold has associated the environmental construct of the "globe" with a twentieth-century form of domination, contrasting this to an older cosmographic conception of "spheres." Pursuing the same basic problematic—of how a global environment could be construed as both the perceived object and the surrounding milieu, I am, however, deviating from Ingold's nomenclature of sphere/globe. See Ingold, *The Perception of the Environment: Essays on Livelihood, Dwelling, and Skill* (London: Routledge, 2011), chapter 12.

10. Walter Paepcke, correspondence related to the Goethe Bicentennial and the theme of humanism, in Walter P. Paepcke Papers, boxes 76 and 99.

11. On the cybernetic aspects of Eero Saarinen's thinking, see Martin, *The Organizational Complex,* chapters 2 and 4.

12. Prior to their use in European churches, pendentive domes were built in mosques in the Middle East using construction techniques that were later carried into Europe, during the so-called Romanesque period of ecclesiastical architecture, as Carla Keyvanian has argued in unpublished teaching material.

13. José Ortega y Gasset, "In Search of Goethe from Within," in *The Dehumanization of Art, and Other Essays on Art, Culture, and Literature,* trans. Helene Weyl (1948; repr., Princeton: Princeton University Press, 1968).

14. Chinua Achebe, "An Image of Africa: Racism in Conrad's 'Heart of Darkness'" (lecture delivered at the University of Massachusetts at Amherst, 1975).

15. Herbert Kufferberg, "Visitor with No Message," *Boston Globe,* June 30, 1949, 20; emphasis added.

16. Albert Schweitzer, *The Forest Hospital at Lambarene,* trans. Charles Thomas Campion (New York: H. Holt, 1931), 101.

17. Albert Schweitzer, *On the Edge of the Primeval Forest and More from the Primeval Forest: Experiences and Observations of a Doctor in Equatorial Africa,* trans. Charles Thomas Campion (London: Adam and Charles Black, 1948), 93; emphasis added.

18. Michael Murray, *Albert Schweitzer, Musician* (Brookfield, Vt.: Ashgate, 1994). See also Charles Joy, *Music in the Life of Albert Schweitzer* (New York: Harper, 1951).

19. Schweitzer, *On the Edge of the Primeval Forest,* 100.

20. Murray, *Albert Schweitzer.*

21. See David Rabouin, *Mathesis universalis: L'idée de "mathématique universelle" d'Aristote à Descartes* (Paris: Presses universitaires de France, 2015).

22. Herbert Bayer, "On Typography," *Graphic Design Theory: Readings from the Field,* ed. Helen Armstrong (New York: Princeton Architectural Press, 2009), 46–47.

23. Probably influenced by the work of the typographer Walter Porstmann, who worked for the Prussian National Railway, Bayer designed a "basik alfabet" that was stripped of unnecessary swoops, dots, and serifs. Porstmann had imagined an adjusted roman-based alphabetic system through which all the languages of the world could easily be transcribed. See Aynsley and Wolfsonian, *Graphic Design in Germany.*

24. Herbert Bayer, "Gestaltung und Industrie" (manuscript for lecture, 1963), in Dokumentenssammlung Herbert Bayer, Mappe 1, Bauhaus-Archiv; emphasis added. The German text reads, "Damit will ich andeuten, dass wir weniger und weniger schreiben und lessen, und das Buch wird vielleicht vollkommen verschwinden. Mag sein, dass eine Zeit kommt, in der wir Lesen und Schreiben uberhaupt nicht mehr zu lernen brauchen; in der wir stattdessen Information absorbieren und mitteilen nicht mit Auge, Mund und Ohrh, sondern mit übernatürlich Mitteln."

25. Carothers was one of a few British experts called in from the Committee to Enquire into the Sociological Causes and Remedies for Mau Mau. David Anderson, *Histories of the Hanged: The Dirty War in Kenya and the End of Empire,* 1st American ed. (New York: W. W. Norton, 2005).

26. Perhaps responding to Franz Boas's contention that there was no innate physiological explanation for intellectual traits that appeared to inhere to different races—that differences between societies could be explained on the basis of cultural and environmental factors—Carothers presented an insidious interpretation of the relationship between race and environment. See Boas, "The Instability of Human Types," in *Papers on Interracial Problems Communicated to the First Universal Races Congress Held at the University of London, July 26–29, 1911,* ed. Gustav Spiller (Boston: Ginn, 1912). McLuhan cites at length from J. C. Carothers's article "Culture, Psychiatry, and the Written Word," *Psychiatry* 22, no. 4 (November 1959): 307–20. See also Marshall McLuhan, *Gutenberg Galaxy: The Making of Typographic Man* (1962; repr., Toronto: University of Toronto Press, 1964), 18–22, 31–39, 67; and McLuhan, *Understanding Media,* 16, and cf. 362.

27. I have written more extensively on Carothers's influence on McLuhan in *The Neocolonialism of the Global Village.*

28. McLuhan, *Understanding Media,* 92.

29. John Colin Carothers, *The African Mind in Health and Disease: A Study in Ethnopsychiatry,* World Health Organization Monograph Series (Geneva: World Health Organization, 1953), especially 120–24.

30. The Colonial Film Unit was deployed for purposes of propaganda in the British colonies—especially in African colonies—from the 1930s through the 1950s. On McLuhan's interest in the work of the Colonial Film Unit, see Nolan, *The Neocolonialism of the Global Village.* On the Colonial Film Unit in Nigeria, see Larkin, *Signal and Noise,* chapter 3.

31. Schweitzer, *On the Edge of the Primeval Forest,* 191–92.

32. Roman Jakobson, "Two Aspects of Language and Two Types of Aphasic Disturbances," in *On Language,* by Roman Jakobson, ed. Linda R. Waugh and Monique Monville-Burston (Cambridge, Mass.: Harvard University Press, 1990).

33. Claude Elwood Shannon and Warren Weaver, *The Mathematical Theory of Communication* (Urbana: University of Illinois Press, 1949).

34. Marshall McLuhan, "Introduction," *Aspen,* no. 4 (1967): 1–2.

35. McLuhan, "The Medium Is the Massage," in *Aspen,* no. 4 (1967): n.p.

36. McLuhan, *Gutenberg Galaxy.*

37. Peder Anker has written a laudatory account of the *Airways to Peace* exhibit. Anker, "Graphic Language: Herbert Bayer's Environmental Design," *Environmental History* 12, no. 2 (April 2007): 254–79. See also Peder Anker, *From Bauhaus to Ecohouse: A History of Ecological Design* (Baton Rouge: Louisiana University Press, 2010).

38. Monroe Wheeler, exhibition promotional materials, *Airways to Peace* exhibition, collection REG, folder 236, Museum of Modern Art Archives, New York.

39. In 1943, the state of New York responded by mandating that the standard Mercator maps in public schools be replaced with maps using the North Pole as the central point.

40. While Fuller has been widely credited for the development of the Dymaxion map, there were recent antecedents, most notably the maps of William Diller Matthew, the English evolutionary paleontologist. Foreshadowing the geopolitics of lebensraum, Matthew placed northern Eurasia in the center of the map and showed the "races" of the world emanating from it in southerly directions, contrary to mounting evidence of humans' shared African evolution. See David N. Livingstone, "Tropical Hermeneutics and the Climatic Imagination," *Geographische Zeitschrift* 90 (2002): 65–88.

41. "*Life* Presents R. Buckminster Fuller's Dymaxion World," *Life,* March 1, 1943, 43.

42. Wheeler, exhibition promotional materials, *Airways to Peace* exhibition.

43. Jakob von Uexküll, *A Foray into the Worlds of Animals and Humans, with a Theory of Meaning,* trans. Joseph D. O'Neil (Minneapolis: University of Minnesota Press, 2010), introduction. See also Giorgio Agamben, *The Open: Man and Animal,* trans. Kevin Attell (Stanford: Stanford University Press, 2004): especially chapters 10 through 12.

44. Uexküll writes that, owing to the environment's semiotic constitution, a bee and a cow inhabiting the same spatial area have completely different environments.

45. Beatriz Colomina, "Enclosed by Images: The Eameses' Multimedia Architecture," *Grey Room,* no. 2 (Winter 2001): 5–29.

46. Marshall McLuhan and Quentin Fiore, "The Medium Is the Massage," *Aspen,* no. 4 (1967), n.p.

47. Apart from the U.S. pavilion described by Colomina, other uses of Fuller's domed pavilions include those designed for the World Game, which simulated various global crises and resource distribution strategies. These domes instantiated a homology between architecture as a sphere of media and architecture as a sphere of global resource management. Participants would become subjects of electronic media while being simultaneously positioned as sovereigns of the global environment. Buckminster Fuller, "The World Game," *Ekistics* 28, no. 167 (October 1969): 286–92. See also Mark Wigley, "Planetary Homeboy," *ANY Magazine,* no. 17 (January 1997): 16–23; Peder Anker, "Buckminster Fuller as Captain of Spaceship Earth," *Minerva* 45 (2007): 417–34.

48. Sim van der Ryn, "Persistence of Form" (paper presented at the Twentieth International Design Conference at Aspen, 1970), International Design Conference in Aspen Papers, MSIDCA87, box 16, folder 748, folder 573, 41, Richard J. Daley Library, Special Collections and University Archives, University of Illinois at Chicago.

49. Mortimer Adler, "Some Philosophical Questions about Design" (paper presented at the Sixth International Design Conference in Aspen, 1956), International Design Conference in Aspen Papers, box 15, folder 735, 5, 1; emphasis in original.

50. Robert Maynard Hutchins, *The Great Conversation: The Substance of a Liberal Education* (Chicago: Encyclopaedia Britannica, 1952), 1.

51. Hutchins, *The Great Conversation,* 17–18.

52. Hutchins, *The Great Conversation,* 18.

53. Mitchell Duneier, *Ghetto: The Invention of a Place, the History of an Idea* (New York: Farrar, Straus and Giroux, 2016), 49, 78.

54. Nolan, *The Neocolonialism of the Global Village.*

55. Oscar Lewis, lecture on the culture of poverty (presented at the Twelfth International Design Conference in Aspen, 1962), International Design Conference in Aspen Papers, box 15, folder 741, 14–23. On Lewis's work, see Johana Londoño, *Abstract Barrios: The Crises of Latinx Visibility in Cities* (Durham, N.C.: Duke University Press, 2020), chapter 2.

56. Lewis, lecture on the culture of poverty, 18.

57. Herbert Muller, lecture on humanism (presented at the Twelfth International Design Conference in Aspen, 1962), International Design Conference in Aspen Papers, box 15, folder 741, 110–12.

58. Heinz von Foerster, lecture on environmental structure and cognition (presented at the Twelfth International Design Conference in Aspen, 1962), International Design Conference in Aspen Papers, box 15, folder 741, 29–30.

59. Uexküll, *A Foray into the Worlds of Animals and Humans,* 119–23.

60. Foerster, lecture on environmental structure and cognition, 30.

61. Foerster, lecture on environmental structure and cognition, 61.

62. Herbert Bayer, "future lecture 'on environment'" (unpublished essay), cited in Gwen Finkel Chanzit, *Herbert Bayer and Modernist Design in America* (Ann Arbor, Mich.: UMI Research, 1987), 151.

6. Harlem Speaks to Aspen

1. On the rise of environmental design and environmental psychology in the United States, see Joy Knoblauch, *The Architecture of Good Behavior: Psychology and Modern Institutional Design in Postwar America* (Pittsburgh: University of Pittsburgh Press, 2020).

2. Alice Twemlow has published several accounts of the confrontation between protesters and the IDCA's invited participants: Twemlow, *Sifting the Trash: A History of Design Criticism* (Cambridge: MIT Press, 2017), chapter 2; Twemlow, "'A Guaranteed Communications Failure': Consensus Meets Conflict at the International Design Conference in Aspen, 1970," in *The Aspen Complex,* ed. Martin Beck (Berlin: Sternberg Press, 2012); Twemlow, "I Can't Talk to You if You Say That: An Ideological Collision at the International Design Conference at Aspen, 1970," *Design and Culture* 1, no. 1 (2009): 23–49; Twemlow, "A Look Back at Aspen, 1970," August 28, 2008, *The Design Observer Group,* http://designobserver.com/feature/a-look-back-at-aspen-1970/7277. Other accounts of the event include Jean-Louis Voileau, "Jean Baudrillard, 68 et la *fonction* utopique," *Laboratoire Urbanisme Insurrectionel,* June 2012, http://laboratoireurbanismeinsurrectionnel.blogspot.fr/2012/06/baudrillard-68-et-la-fonction-utopique.html. And Felicity Scott has briefly addressed the relationships between the protesters and the IDCA in her broader discussion of Aspen. Scott, "Dataland (and Its Ghosts): Aspen Proving Grounds," in Beck, *The Aspen Complex.*

3. Reyner Banham, ed., *The Aspen Papers: Twenty Years of Design Theory from the International Design Conference in Aspen* (London: Pall Mall Press, 1974), 207.

4. Narratives covering the 1970 IDCA, the protestors, and the French group's denunciation mostly omit Cora Walker's critiques. The exception is Twemlow's passing mention of Walker, citing her remark about never having "heard of Aspen before," the same remark Houseman had cited in his summary comments. Twemlow, "I Can't Talk to You if You Say That," 37.

5. On this history, see Avigail Sachs, *Environmental Design: Architecture, Politics, and Science in Postwar America* (Charlottesville: University of Virginia Press, 2018).

6. Felicity Scott, *Outlaw Territories: Environments of Insecurity, Architectures of Insurgency* (New York: Zone, 2016), chapters 7 and 8; Halpern, *Beautiful Data,* chapter 2. See also Yates McKee, "Haunted Housing: Eco-Vanguardism, Eviction, and the Biopolitics of Sustainability in New Orleans," *Grey Room,* no. 30 (Winter 2008): 84–113.

7. Reyner Banham, "The Education of the Environmentalist" (paper presented at the Twentieth International Design Conference in Aspen, 1970), International Design Conference in Aspen Papers, box 16, folder 748, 54–60.

8. Frazier, a black American industrial designer for the Container Corporation of America, had launched the Container Corporation of America Youth Motivation Program, training young people in the poor areas of Chicago. He had sought to be included in the official conference proceedings but instead came to protest. See Frazier, "Me, Design, and Niggertown Slums," *Design Discourse Magazine* (Purdue University), 1969, 23–28.

9. Felicity Scott has written about the resonances between some constituent groups of the countercultural movement and neoliberal discourse, especially in reference to Stewart Brand and the Hog Farm commune. See Scott, *Outlaw Territories,* chapter 3.

10. Carl Koch, "Industrialized Housing: A Pure Necessity" (paper presented at the Twentieth International Design Conference in Aspen, 1970), International Design Conference in Aspen Papers, box 16, folder 748, 24–28.

11. William Houseman, *The Harlem River Yards: Bridging a South Bronx Community Need* (Bronx, N.Y.: Wave Hill, 1978), 1

12. Houseman, *The Harlem River Yards,* 4.

13. Houseman, *The Harlem River Yards,* 5.

14. The report on the Harlem River Yards does not designate particular authors for the different teams and the images they produced. It does list all the participants of the design teams: Aureo Cardona, Ruby Chin, Jeffrey Clark, Edward DeCarbo, Liviu G. Dimitriu, Esteban Figueroa, Stephen [*sic*] Holl, Robert Livesey, Millie Lopez, Michael Miler, Wilma Morten, Patrick Ping, Tse Too, Charles Smith Jr., and Della Smith. In the particular project I focus on, the representational style of Steven Holl comes across quite clearly in the images.

15. Houseman, *The Harlem River Yards,* 6. The gesture to postindustrial georgics was prescient of a legal battle that would ensue decades later between community residents and the corporation Fresh Direct, which, in 2013, won a legal battle to use the Harlem River Yards as a distribution center from which to deliver high-end groceries, mostly to neighborhoods in Manhattan and Brooklyn. One of Fresh Direct's target markets has been residents of newly gentrifying neighborhoods who do not find the local grocery stores adequate to their needs. Fresh Direct thus bridges the gap between the expectations of the wealthy and the circumstances of the poor. Just north of the Harlem River Yards, the massive wholesale food distribution center at Hunts Point has long served a similar purpose, used especially by restaurants in Manhattan.

16. Cora Walker, "Pioneering in Co-Op Programs" (paper presented at the Twentieth International Design Conference in Aspen, 1970), International Design Conference in Aspen Papers, box 16, folder 748, 77.

17. Walker, "Pioneering in Co-Op Programs," 77.

18. Walker, "Pioneering in Co-Op Programs," 79.

19. Walker, "Pioneering in Co-Op Programs," 79.

20. On the design of carceral facilities and the design of crime prevention by proponents of environmental design, see Knoblauch, *The Architecture of Good Behavior,* chapter 3.

21. Banham, "The Education of the Environmentalist," 57.

22. M. Paul Friedberg, "Energy of Communication: Tools of the Design Process" (paper presented at the Twentieth International Design Conference in Aspen, 1970), box 16, folder 748, 20.

23. Walter Orr Roberts, "Man on a Changing Earth" (paper presented at the Twentieth International Design Conference in Aspen, 1970), International Design Conference in Aspen Papers, box 16, folder 748, 74.

24. Walker, quoted in William Houseman, "A Program Chairman's Diary of Sorts" (paper presented at the Twentieth International Design Conference in Aspen, 1970), International Design Conference in Aspen Papers, box 16, folder 748, 3.

25. Walker, "Pioneering in Co-Op Programs," 77; emphasis added.

7. Pentecostal Technologies

1. Nicholas Negroponte, "Micro-electronics and Human Development" (paper presented at the Thirty-First International Design Conference in Aspen, 1982), International Design Conference in Aspen Papers, box 7, audio cassette 423.

2. Xavier Weeger, "France Seeks Cooperation in Microcomputers," *Guardian Weekly*, February 21, 1982, 11. See also Paul Lewis, "High Technology: Europe's Eureka Project Aims to Narrow U.S. Lead," *New York Times*, March 23, 1986.

3. Jean Jacques Servan-Schreiber, *The World Challenge* (New York: Simon and Schuster, 1981); originally published as *Défi mondial* (Paris: Édition Fayard, 1980).

4. Jean-Jacques Servan-Schreiber, interview in *Computerworld*, February 8, 1982, LexisNexis.

5. Servan-Schreiber, *The World Challenge*, 263–65.

6. The design was commissioned by the J. Walter Thompson advertising company.

7. This resemblance appears to have been unintentional on the part of the architect, Vittorio Mazzucconi.

8. Paul Betts, "Marseilles Pins Its Hopes on High-Tech," *Financial Times* (London), June 20, 1984.

9. "Computer Center Planned," February 5, 1982, LexisNexis.

10. Alicia Pagano, "Urban Senegal and Rural Gambia: Computer and Community Education Programs," *Childhood Education* 62, no. 3 (January 1986): 182–85, 182.

11. Jean-Jacques Servan-Schreiber, "Interview: Jean-Jacques Servan-Schreiber," interview by Rex Malik, *Computerworld*, February 8, 1982.

12. Nicholas Negroponte, "We Were Bricoleurs," interview by Molly Wright Steenson, in *A Second Modernism: MIT, Architecture, and the "Techno-Social" Moment*, ed. Arindam Dutta (Cambridge: MIT Press, 2013), 809.

13. Papert writes, "LOGO was fueled from the beginning by a Robin Hood vision of stealing programming from the technologically privileged (what I would in those early days in the 1960s have called the military-industrial complex) and giving it to children." Seymour Papert, *The Children's Machine: Rethinking School in the Age of the Computer* (New York: Basic Books, 1993), 180. See also Papert et al., "Interim Report of the LOGO Project in the Brookline Public Schools: An Assessment and Documentation of a Children's Computer Laboratory," Artificial Intelligence Memo, no. 484, Massachusetts Institute of Technology, accessed January 23, 2020, http://dailypapert.com/wp-content/uploads/2018/06/Brookline-project-1978-Logo-Memo-49.pdf; Papert, "Computers in the Classroom: Agents of Change," in *Washington Post Education Review*, October 27, 1996.

14. PLATO (Programmed Logic for Automatic Teaching Operation) was a platform engineered at the University of Illinois circa 1970. It was implemented in pilot programs around the United States and also in apartheid South Africa. On PLATO (including its implementation in South Africa), see John H. Douglas, "Learning Technology Comes of Age," *Science News* 110, no. 11 (September 11, 1976): 170–71; 174. See also Nolan, "The Pharmakon and the Machine." For a broader discussion of technological devices related to apartheid, see Edwards and Hecht, "History and the Technopolitics of Identity."

15. Some conceptual overlap between postmodernist architectural semiotics and digital research can be seen in Appleyard, Lynch, and Myer's work on roadway design, which examined signage, aesthetics, and communication while also considering new technologies of perception. Donald Appleyard, Kevin Lynch, and John R. Meyer, *The View from the Road* (Cambridge: Published for the Joint Center for Urban Studies of the Massachusetts Institute of Technology and Harvard University by MIT Press, 1964).

16. John Harwood, *The Interface: IBM and the Transformation of Corporate Design, 1954–1976* (Minneapolis: University of Minnesota Press, 2011), especially chapters 2 and 4.

17. On Friedman's computational experiments, theories of bricolage, megastructural proposals, and work for UNESCO, see Ginger Nolan, "Between Survival and Citizenship: Yona Friedman's 'Vulgar' Media," *Perspecta* 51 (2018): 61–92. See also Nolan, "Bricolage . . . or the Sudden Impossibility of Pollution."

18. Leland, "Prophesies for the Twentieth Century."

19. See Fred Turner, *From Counterculture to Cyberculture: Stewart Brand, the Whole Earth Network, and the Rise of Digital Utopianism* (Chicago: University of Chicago Press, 2006). See also Scott, *Outlaw Territories,* chapter 7; Ronald R. Kline, *The Cybernetics Moment, or Why We Call Our Age the Information Age* (Baltimore: The Johns Hopkins University Press, 2015), chapter 9.

20. See Paul Ylvisaker to Pietro Belluschi, February 11, 1958, collection AC400 6, Joint Center for Urban and Regional Studies, box 6, Department of Distinctive Collections, Massachusetts Institute of Technology Libraries. See also the Visiting Committee of the Joint Center for Urban Studies of the Massachusetts Institute of Technology and Harvard University, "Report to the President and Members of the Corporation of the Massachusetts Institute of Technology and the President and Fellows of Harvard College," July 10, 1963, Lloyd Rodwin Papers, MC 490, box 52, MIT Institute Archives. For the original report of MIT's involvement in Venezuelan urban and industrial development, see Donald Appleyard, *Planning a Pluralist City: Conflicting Realities in Ciudad Guayana,* a publication of the Joint Center for Urban Studies of the Massachusetts Institute of Technology and Harvard University (Cambridge: MIT Press, 1976). For a recent critical history of the project, see Ijlal Muzaffar, "Planning Contingency: The Joint Center of Urban Studies at Harvard and MIT and the Designing of Ciudad Guayana, 1959–1964," in Dutta, *A Second Modernism.*

21. Negroponte, "Systems of Urban Growth," 18.

22. Nicholas Negroponte, *The Architecture Machine: Towards a More Human Environment* (Cambridge: MIT Press, 1970), 2.

23. Negroponte, *The Architecture Machine,* 3; Aldous Huxley, *Brave New World* (1932; repr., New York: HarperPerennial, 1989), 2.

24. Huxley, *Brave New World,* 2.

25. Orit Halpern, "The Trauma Machine: Demos, Immersive Technologies and the Politics of Simulation," in *Alleys of Your Mind: Augmented Intelligence and Its Traumas,* ed. Matteo Pasquinelli (Luneneburg, Germany: Meson Press, 2015), 53–67.

26. The discourse on Mediterranean hill towns is linked to the interest in "anonymous" architecture discussed in chapter 2. For the Mediterranean context, Ernesto Rogers was especially instrumental in the decades following World War II in bringing the vernacular housing of Italian coasts into popular architectural culture. Negroponte borrows his imagery from Bernard Rudofsky's *Architecture without Architects* exhibition. For a discussion of the exhibition, see Scott, "Bernard Rudofsky."

27. The architect Oscar Niemeyer, a politically vocal Communist Party member, was heavily involved with Lúcio Costa's design for Brasilia.

28. Mestizoism describes twentieth-century Latin American policies of encouraging ethnoracial mixing as a way to transform indigenous societies and render them more amenable

to the state's economic agendas. On mestizoism in Bolivia, see Kevin A. Young, *Blood of the Earth: Resource Nationalism, Revolution, and Empire in Bolivia* (Austin: University of Texas Press, 2017), chapter 2. On mestizoism more generally, see Peter Gran, *Beyond Eurocentrism: A New View of Modern World History* (Syracuse, N.Y.: Syracuse University Press, 1996), 160–62; 177–78. Also, Fabiola Lopez-Duran recounts histories of eugenic policies of racial purification in relation to urban planning in Latin America. Lopez-Duran, *Eugenics in the Garden: Transatlantic Architecture and the Crafting of Modernity* (Austin: University of Texas Press, 2018).

29. Negroponte, *The Architecture Machine*, 5.

30. Negroponte, *The Architecture Machine*, 4–5.

31. Negroponte, *The Architecture Machine*, 4–5.

32. On the importance of individual agency in the Architecture Machine Group's discourse, see Aubrey Anable, "The Architecture Machine Group's *Aspen Movie Map:* Mediating the Urban Crisis in the 1970s," *Television and New Media* 13, no. 6 (2012): 498–519.

33. Adorno and Horkheimer write, "Yet the city housing projects designed to perpetuate the individual as a supposedly independent unit in a small hygienic dwelling make him all the more subservient to his adversary—the absolute power of capitalism. Because the inhabitants, as producers and as consumers, are drawn into the center in search of work and pleasure, all the living units crystallise into well-organised complexes. The striking unity of microcosm and macrocosm presents men with a model of their culture: the false identity of the general and the particular." Theodor Adorno and Max Horkheimer, *Dialectic of Enlightenment*, ed. Gunzelin Schmid Noerr, trans. Edmund Jephcott (Stanford: Stanford University Press, 2002), 94–95.

34. Negroponte, "Micro-electronics and Human Development."

35. Nicholas Negroponte, *Soft Architecture Machines*, (Cambridge: MIT Press, 1975), 103.

36. Negroponte, "2B1."

37. Servan-Schreiber, "Interview," interview by Malik.

38. Muzaffar, "The Periphery Within."

39. Negroponte, *The Architecture Machine*, 55.

40. Scott, *Outlaw Territories*, 353.

41. Negroponte, *The Architecture Machine*, 55.

42. Negroponte, *The Architecture Machine*, 55–56.

43. Negroponte, *The Architecture Machine*, 56.

44. Negroponte, *The Architecture Machine*, 57.

45. Stephen Carr and Kevin Lynch, "Where Learning Happens," *Daedalus* 97, no. 4 (1968): 1277–91.

46. Lynch credited Gyorgy Kepes at MIT with helping him develop his ideas, for they shared an interest in the cognitive aspects of detecting visual patterns. This topic was clearly also of interest to Negroponte in his work on architecture machines. See Gyorgy Kepes and Marjorie Supovitz, *Gyorgy Kepes: The MIT Years, 1945–1977* (Cambridge: MIT Press, 1978), 11–12.

47. On Lynch's mapping, see Halpern, *Beautiful Data*, chapter 2.

48. Appleyard, Lynch, and Myer, *The View from the Road.*

49. On the *Aspen Movie Map*, see Scott, *Outlaw Territories*, chapter 8. See also Steenson, *Architectural Intelligence*, chapter 6; Anable, "The Architecture Machine Group's *Aspen Movie Map*; Halpern, "The Trauma Machine."

50. See Anable, "The Architecture Machine Group's *Aspen Movie Map.*"

51. Negroponte, *The Architecture Machine*, 17; emphasis added.

52. Negroponte, *The Architecture Machine*, 15.

53. Negroponte, *Soft Architecture Machines*, 131–40.

54. Negroponte, *The Architecture Machine*, 106–7.

55. Servan-Schreiber, *The World Challenge*, 215.

56. Negroponte, "Micro-electronics and Human Development."

57. There is a large literature on the effects of structural adjustment programs on economic inequality and access to education. See, for example, Silvia Federici, Constantine George Caffentzis, Ousseina Alidou, eds., *A Thousand Flowers: Social Struggles against Structural Adjustment in African Universities* (Trenton, N.J.: Africa World Press, 2000).

8. Technological Sovereignty and the Global South

1. On the CMI pilot program in Morocco, see "Logo in Morocco," *Agora: Informatics in a Changing World* 8, no. 2 (1984): 18–19. See also Rachel Cohen and Gaston Mialaret, *Les jeunes enfants: La découverture de lécrit et l'ordinateur* (Paris: Presses Universitaires de France, 1987).

2. Pierre Drouin, "Le saut de la 'puce'" [The flea's jump], *Le Monde,* December 23, 1982, https://www.lemonde.fr/archives/article/1982/12/23/le-saut-de-la-puce_2905745_1819218.html. See also "Morocco: Informatics and Youth," *Agora: Informatics in a Changing World* 6, no. 2 (1983): 10.

3. Drouin, "Le saut de la 'puce.'"

4. Elmandjra, quoted in Drouin, "Le saut de la 'puce.'"

5. Servan-Schreiber, "Interview," interview by Malik.

6. Drouin, "Le saut de la 'puce.'"

7. U.S. House of Representatives, *Measures to Address the Impact of Computer Technology on Lesser Developed Countries: Hearings before the Subcommittee on Science Research and Technology of the Committee on Science and Technology,* 97th Congress, 2nd sess., May 19, July 15, 1982 (Washington, D.C.: U.S. GPO, 1982), 45.

8. Langaa groupe d'intiative commune en recherche et publication, *Mobile Phones: The New Talking Drums of Everyday Africa* (Cameroon: Langaa Research Common Initiative Group, 2009).

9. Ayensu in U.S. House of Representatives, *Measures to Address the Impact of Computer Technology on Lesser Developed Countries,* 45; emphasis added. The analogy between African drums and electronic media had already been drawn several decades before by Marshall McLuhan, an analogy he was led to through colonial and developmental discourse and practices. See Nolan, *The Neocolonialism of the Global Village.*

10. Pagano, "Urban Senegal and Rural Gambia."

11. Daniel Junqua, "Tiers monde: Le 'micro' aux pieds nus," *Le Monde,* September 29, 1983.

12. U.S. House of Representatives, *Measures to Address the Impact of Computer Technology on Lesser Developed Countries,* 44.

13. Seymour Papert, "Computers and People: A Concept of a Center of Excellence in the Study, Development, and Applications of Personal Computer Power" (draft, November 21, 1977), AC-0117, Secondary Technical Education Project records, box 4, Massachusetts Institute of Technology, Libraries, Department of Distinctive Collections.

14. See, for example, Sherry Turkle, *The Second Self: Computers and the Human Spirit,* 20th anniversary ed. (Cambridge: MIT Press, 2005); Seymour Papert, *Mindstorms: Children, Computers, and Powerful Ideas* (1980; repr., New York: Basic Books, 1993), passim.

15. Papert, "Computers and People."

16. Papert, *The Children's Machine,* 180.

17. Papert writes, for example, "But reading will no longer be the unique primary access road to knowledge and learning, and it should therefore no longer be the dominant consideration in the design of School." See Seymour Papert, "Obsolete Skill Set: The 3 Rs," *Wired,* no. 102 (February 1, 1993), https://www.wired.com/1993/02/1-2-papert/.

18. See Jacques Derrida, *Of Grammatology,* trans. Gayatri Chakravorty Spivak (Baltimore: The Johns Hopkins University Press, 1998).

19. Papert, "Some Poetic and Social Criteria for Education Design" (talk delivered at the HumRRO Conference, September 16–18, 1975); emphasis in the original, accessed July 2, 2016, http://www.papert.org/articles/SomePoeticAndSocialCriteriaForEducationDesign.html.

20. John Harwood points out that the Turing Test, which seeks to prove the potential indistinguishability between human and computer thought, rests on the faulty assumption (an assumption contradicted by the structure of the experiment itself) that "thought exists independently of any mediation." Harwood, *The Interface*, 61–64.

21. Negroponte, *The Architecture Machine*, 17.

22. Negroponte, *The Architecture Machine*, 17–29. See also Negroponte, *Soft Architecture Machines*, 57–67.

23. Sherry Turkle and Seymour Papert, "Epistemological Pluralism: Styles and Voices within the Computer Culture," *Signs* 16, no. 1 (1990): 129–30.

24. For Itard's writings on Victor, see Jean Marc Gaspard Itard, *The Wild Boy of Aveyron*, Century Psychology Series (New York: Century, 1932).

25. Itard, *The Wild Boy of Aveyron*.

26. Smith says, for example, that "words are Fregean, lacking the representational power of images" and that "truly productive thinking, in whatever area of cognition, takes place in the realm of images." See David Canfield Smith, "Pygmalion: A Creative Programming Environment" (PhD diss., Stanford University, 1975), 6–8.

27. Smith, "Pygmalion," 7.

28. Freud also compares the semiotics of schizophrenics and the dreamwork. See Sigmund Freud, "Metapsychological Supplement to the Theory of Dreams (1916)," in *General Psychological Theory: Papers on Metapsychology*, ed. Philip Rieff (New York: Simon and Schuster, 1991), 156–58. See also Sigmund Freud, *The Interpretation of Dreams*, trans. Joyce Clark (Oxford: Oxford University Press, 1999), passim.

29. Freud, "On Narcissism."

30. "Il s'agit de quelque chose d'assez voisin de ces messages que les linguistes appellent autonymes pour autant que c'est le signifiant même (et non ce qu'il signifie) qui fait l'objet de la communication." (This is quite similar to those messages that linguists call autonyms, in that it's the signifier itself [and not what it signifies] that is the object of communication.) Lacan, "D'une question préliminaire à tout traitement possible de la psychose," in *Écrits* (Paris: Éditions du Seuil, 1966), 537.

31. Jonathan Metzl, *The Protest Psychosis: How Schizophrenia Became a Black Disease* (Boston: Beacon Press, 2009).

32. Metzl, *The Protest Psychosis*. Metzl describes one incarcerated black man whose "gibberish" was said to be an indication of schizophrenia; see the case of Cecil Peterson in *The Protest Psychosis*, 3–4. Later, Metzl cites the coinage of the term "protest psychosis" by the psychiatrists Walter Bromberg and Franck Simon in reference to men detained for civil rights activism. The psychiatrists described the detainees' "refusal to accept the syntactical language of standard English. Often the prisoners draw pictures or write material of an Islamic nature, elaborating their ideas in the direction of African ideology with a decided 'primitive' accent." Bomberg and Simon, "The 'Protest' Psychosis: A Special Type of Reactive Psychosis," *Archives of General Psychiatry* 19 (1968): 155–60, quoted in Metzl, *The Protest Psychosis*, 100–101.

33. Gilles Deleuze and Félix Guattari, *A Thousand Plateaus: Capitalism and Schizophrenia*, trans. Brian Massumi (Minneapolis: University of Minnesota Press, 1987), especially section 10.

34. Fredric Jameson, *Postmodernism, or The Cultural Logic of Late Capitalism* (Durham, N.C.: Duke University Press, 1991), chapter 1 and passim.

35. Bernard Stiegler, *Taking Care of Youth and the Generations*, ed. Werner Hamacher, trans. Stephen Barker (Stanford: Stanford University Press; Meridian Crossing Aesthetics, 2010), 190.

36. Betsy Carpenter, "On the Trail of Nintendo's Magic," *U.S. News and World Report,* July 16, 1990.

37. Natasha Dow Schüll, *Addiction by Design: Machine Gambling in Las Vegas* (Princeton: Princeton University Press, 2012).

38. Papert et al., "Interim Report of the LOGO Project in the Brookline Public Schools."

39. Papert, *Mindstorms,* 20–23. Piaget explains these stages of development in several of his works, most notably in Piaget, *The Psychology of the Child,* ed. Bärbel Inhelder, trans. Helen Weaver (1969; repr., New York: Basic Books, 2000); Piaget and Marjorie Warden, *The Language and Thought of the Child: International Library of Psychology, Philosophy, and Scientific Method* (London: K. Paul, Trench, Trubner; New York: Harcourt Brace, 1926).

40. Piaget explains these stages of development in several works. For example, see Piaget, *The Psychology of the Child.* See also Papert, *Mindstorms,* 20–23.

41. Turkle and Papert, "Epistemological Pluralism."

42. On the CMI's pilot program in Senegal led by Papert, see Pagano, "Urban Senegal and Rural Gambia."

43. Papert, "Computers and People"; emphasis added.

44. Felicity Scott has noted a tendency among instructors at MIT's School of Architecture and Planning during the 1970s to conflate urban conditions in the global south with those in U.S. ghettoes. See Scott, *Outlaw Territories,* 341–42.

45. Papert, *Mindstorms,* 20.

46. The IBI grew out of an existing organization under UNESCO, the International Computation Center (ICI), which it replaced, and dates given for this transition vary. Fermín Bernasconi mentions 1974 as the date of the IBI's inception. The archives for the IBI describe an incremental transformation from the ICI into the IBI between 1969 and 1978. Archives of the Intergovernmental Bureau of Informatics (IBI), FR PUNES AG 15-IBI, UNESCO Archives and Documentation of Internal Organizations; Bernasconi, "Opening Address by Professor Fermín Bernasconi, Director General, IBI," in *Strategies and Policies on Informatics: IBI Background Documents Presented to the Intergovernmental Conference in Torremolinos (Spain),* August–September 1978 (New York: UNIPUB, 1979). For an outline of IBI's history in relation to UNESCO, see Abdelfettah Benchenna, "L'UNESCO," *Communication* 25, no. 1 (2006): 221–39.

47. Belisario Betancur, "The Informatics Revolution," *Agora: Informatics in a Changing World* 8, no. 2 (1984): 28.

48. Marius Franciscono, the director general of the Informatics Office of Benin, is quoted as having made this statement at a planning meeting, titled Informatics and Information, in Rome, March 12–13. "Their Banks, Our Data," *Agora: Informatics in a Changing World,* April–June 1982, 54; emphasis added.

49. Karl P. Sauvant and Beate-Katrin Graben, "Transnational Corporations and Transborder Data Flows: An Overview," cited in "The UNCTC: Strengthening the Negotiating Capacity of Developing Countries," *Agora: Informatics in a Changing World* 1 (January–March 1982): 51–53; emphasis added. See also Edward Roche, "International Computing and the International Regime," *Global Information Management* 1, no. 2 (1992): 20.

50. Joseph M. Grieco, "Between Dependency and Autonomy: India's Experience with the International Computer Industry," *International Organization* 36, no. 3 (Summer 1982): 609–32.

51. Charles and Ray Eames were commissioned by the Indian government to conduct a study on the requirements for a national design institute. Their findings were published in *The India Report* (Ahmedabad, India: National Institute of Design, 1958). The remark about cardboard computers was noted by Eames Demetrios, *An Eames Primer* (New York: Universe, 2001), 25–29.

52. Grieco, "Between Dependency and Autonomy."

53. "Economic Strategy and Informatics in India," *Agora: Informatics in a Changing World* 8, no. 2 (1984): 13–15.

54. One of the major points of contention between the Group of 77 and the United States was the issue of nonworking patents and, relatedly, nonexclusive licenses. Corporations often applied for patents in foreign nations, not with any immediate intention to manufacture a product but, rather, to block others from manufacturing it. And large corporations sometimes granted nonexclusive licenses for a patented product to small foreign manufacturing facilities to allow a market to develop for the product before then swooping in and competitively squashing the smaller manufacturers holding the nonexclusive licenses. One small way the Group of 77 wished to amend the Paris Convention and the subsequent Stockholm Conference was through provisions to curtail the abuses of nonworking licenses and patents. For a detailed discussion of these issues and, more generally, of the proceedings of the diplomatic conference, see Susan K. Sell, *Power and Ideas: North–South Politics of Intellectual Property and Antitrust,* SUNY Series in Global Politics (Albany: State University of New York Press, 1998), 107–40.

55. For histories and analyses of the Bayh–Dole Act, see Elizabeth Popp Berman, "Why Did Universities Start Patenting? Institution-Building and the Road to the Bayh–Dole Act," *Social Studies of Science* 38, no. 6 (2008): 835–71. See also Rebecca Henderson, Adam B. Jaffe, and Manuel Trajtenberg, "Universities as a Source of Commercial Technology: A Detailed Analysis of University Patenting, 1965–1988," *Review of Economics and Statistics* 80, no. 1 (1998): 119–27; David C. Mowery et al., *Ivory Tower and Industrial Innovation: University–Industry Technology Transfer before and after the Bayh–Dole Act* (Stanford: Stanford University Press, 2004). On the relationship between MIT and the Bayh–Dole Act, see Dutta, *A Second Modernism,* 65–66.

56. Nolan, *The Neocolonialism of the Global Village.*

57. Betancur, "The Informatics Revolution," 30. This article transcribes Betancur's speech given at the "Informatics and Sovereignty" conference in Cali, Colombia, which built upon what was started by the Declaration of Mexico on Informatics, Development, and Peace. Conferees included the directors general of the Andean Pact, the Latin American Integration Association (LAIA), and the UNESCO regional office; high-ranking government officials from Colombia, Venezuela, Ecuador, Argentina, Bolivia, Nicaragua, Costa Rica, Cuba, Peru, Chile, Mexico, the Dominican Republic, Brazil, Haiti, and Uruguay; and IBI director general Fermín Bernasconi. See "The Club of Cali: A New Framework," *Agora: Informatics in a Changing World* 8, no. 2 (1984): 45. On the Declaration of Mexico, see Mark B. Feldman, "Commercial Speech, Transborder Data Flows and the Right to Communicate under International Law," *International Lawyer* 17, no. 1 (Winter 1983): 87–95.

58. Bernasconi, "Opening Address."

59. "Morocco: Informatics and Youth," 10.

60. Stiegler discusses this crisis of psychic immaturity in many of his works. See, especially, Stiegler, *Taking Care of Youth and the Generations.*

61. "Morocco: Informatics and Youth," 10.

62. E. Drake Lundell, "SPIN Conference Gets Underway," *Computerworld,* September 4, 1978.

63. A "Give one, get one" campaign encouraged wealthy people to buy one laptop for themselves and donate a second one to a partner nation.

64. The price of the laptop has fluctuated between 188 and 209 U.S. dollars. Constituting a vast expenditure for most nations of the global south, purchases of OLPC have sometimes been subsidized through philanthropy, such as when Carlos Slim, Mexican billionaire and longtime friend of Negroponte, purchased fifty thousand laptops for his country. See Richard Koman, "With Peru Sale, Is OLPC on the Right Track?," *ZDNet Government,* December 3,

2007, http://www.zdnet.com/blog/government/with-peru-sale-is-olpc-on-the-right-track/3542. Stan Beer cites the Norwegian aid organization FAIR's claims that, in many of the world's poorest countries, the cost of outfitting one school with laptops and internet support for each child would be equal to ten times the school's yearly operating budget. See Beer, "War of Words between Aid Organization and OLPC Erupts," *ITWire.com*, January 24, 2007, https://www.itwire.com/home-it/war-of-words-between-aid-organization-and-olpc-erupts.html. Lee Felsenstein has made similar criticisms. Felsenstein, "Problems with the OLPC approach," Fonly Institute, November 10, 2005, http://www.fonly.typepad.com/fonlyblog/2005/11/problems_with_t.html.

65. Steve Lohr, "Buy a Laptop for a Child, Get Another Laptop Free," *New York Times*, September 24, 2007, https://www.nytimes.com/2007/09/24/business/worldbusiness/24laptop.html.

66. OPLC, "Developer's Manual," accessed January 23, 2020, http://wiki.laptop.org/go/Developers_manual.

67. In 2008 Microsoft agreed to partner with OLPC in developing its interface. Years later Bill Gates was deeply critical of the laptop's hardware. See Steve Lohr, "Microsoft Joins Effort for Laptops for Children," *New York Times*, May 16, 2008, https://www.nytimes.com/2008/05/16/technology/16laptop.html. See also Adi Robertson, "OLPC'S $100 Laptop Was Going to Change the World—Then It All Went Wrong," *Verge*, April 16, 2018, https://www.theverge.com/2018/4/16/17233946/olpcs-100-laptop-education-where-is-it-now.

68. Mark Hachman, "Negroponte: We'll Throw OLPCs out of Helicopters to Teach Kids to Read," *PC Magazine*, November 2, 2011, https://uk.pcmag.com/news/114113/negroponte-well-throw-olpcs-out-of-helicopters-to-teach-kids-to-read.

69. "New Negropontism: You Can Give Kids XO Laptops and Just Walk Away," *OLPC News*, December 10, 2010, http://www.olpcnews.com/people/negroponte/new_negropontism_you_can_give_kids_xo_laptops.html. See also "Nicholas Negroponte on Success of One Laptop per Child," *OLPC News*, September 20, 2010, http://www.olpcnews.com/people/negroponte/nicholas_negroponte_on_success.html.

70. See Greg Kennedy, "British Propaganda and the Protection of Empire in the Far East, 1933–42," in *British Propaganda and Wars of Empire: Influencing Friend and Foe, 1900–2010*, ed. Christopher Tuck and Greg Kennedy (London: Routledge, 2014). In the same volume see also James R. Vaughan, "'Two Cheers for Democracy': Empire, Cold War, and British Propaganda in Egypt, 1945–55." See also "Partners," Gearbox (website), accessed January 23, 2020, http://www.gearbox.co.ke/partners-intro.

71. Andela recently initiated major layoffs in its African branches despite windfall profits. See Jake Bright, "Africa-Focused Andela Cuts 400 Staff as It Confirms $50M in Revenue," *Tech Crunch*, September 17, 2019, https://techcrunch.com/2019/09/17/africa-focused-andela-cuts-400-staff-as-it-confirms-50m-in-revenue/.

72. See Kamau Gachigi et al., "Perspectives on Technology Transfer and Commercialization in Africa: A Focus on Kenya," in *Technology Transfer and Commercialization: Building Innovative Ecosystems*, ed. John Silbey Butler and David V. Gibson (Cheltenham, UK: Edward Elgar, 2011), chapter 2. See also Steve Daniels and Christopher Bull, *Making Do: Innovation in Kenya's Informal Economy* (self-pub., Lulu, 2010): 92–93.

Conclusion

1. Noam Chomsky's concept of generative grammar has been taken up—and transformed in its meaning—by architects interested in computation who understand a generative grammar as a set of rules guiding design operations. Peter Eisenman is the architect best known for his interest in Chomsky's ideas of grammar. See Eisenman, "Notes on a Conceptual Architecture: Towards a Definition," *Casabella* 35, nos. 359–60 (December 1971): 48–58.

On generative grammar, see Chomsky, *Topics in the Theory of Generative Grammar* (1966; repr., Berlin: De Gruyter Mouton, 2013).

2. Rancière, *Dissensus.*

3. On phatic communication (communication whose primary function lies in ritual rather than signification), see Bronislaw Malinowski, "The Problem of Meaning in Primitive Languages," in *The Meaning of Meaning,* ed. C. K. Ogden and I. A. Richards (London: K. Paul, Trench, Trubner, 1923), 296–336.

4. These observations are based on my dozen or so years affiliated with architecture schools (that is, as a PhD student and then a professor) where, like most architecture school faculty members, I serve on student design reviews and also view exhibitions of student work.

5. On the uses of data in urban planning, see Shannon Mattern, "Methodolatry and the Art of Measure," *Places,* November 2013, https://placesjournal.org/article/methodolatry-and-the-art-of-measure/. Orit Halpern and her coauthors, discussing the case of Songdo, Korea, write, "Marketed as a 'smart city,' it is presented as an entire territory whose mandate is to produce interactive data fields that will, like the natural resources of another era, be mined for wealth and, similarly, will generate subsequent infrastructure for new forms of life." Halpern et al., "Test-Bed Urbanism," *Public Culture* 25, no. 2 (2013): 272–306. Jiří Pánek offers a critique of the commercial uses of cell phone–based data mining in Kenya; see Pánek, "The Commercialisation of Public Data—How Does Participatory Data-Mining Look on a Global Scale?" *South African Journal of Geomatics* 2, no. 13 (2013): 231–45. Pánek also discusses potential means of democratizing uses of geographic information systems (GISs) in Pánek, "Participatory and Public Participation GIS: A Phenomenon of Neocartography with a High Potential in Developing Countries?" in *The Scale of Globalization: Think Globally, Act Locally, Change Individually in the 21st Century,* ed. Přemysl Mácha (Ostrava, Czech Republic: University of Ostrava, 2011), 235–43. See also John Friesen et al., "Determining Factors for Slum Growth with Predictive Data Mining Methods," *Urban Science* 2, no. 3 (2018): 81; Monika Kuffer, Karin Pfeffer, and Richard Sliuzas, "Slums from Space—15 Years of Slum Mapping Using Remote Sensing," *Remote Sensing* 8, no. 6 (2016): 455.

6. UN-Habitat, *A Practical Guide to Designing, Planning, and Executing Citywide Slum Upgrading Programmes* (Nairobi: United Nations Human Settlements Programme, 2014), 32–33.

7. UN-Habitat, *A Practical Guide to Designing, Planning, and Executing Citywide Slum Upgrading Programmes,* 32.

8. Michael Speaks, Robert Somol, and Sarah Whiting are among the recognized proponents of the postcritical position in North America. Especially noteworthy is Speaks's series of short articles on design intelligence published in various architecture magazines. See also Somol and Whiting, "Notes around the Doppler Effect and Other Moods of Modernism," *Perspecta* 33 (2002): 72–77.

9. On the rise of smartness in urban and architectural discourse, see Orit Halpern, Robert Mitchell, and Dionysius Geoghehan, "The Smartness Mandate: Notes toward a Critique," *Grey Room,* no. 68 (Summer 2017): 106–29.

10. Christina Wasson, "Design Anthropology," *General Anthropology* 23, no. 2 (2016): 1–11.

11. Artz, "Contextual Inquiry."

12. Zeynep Çelik Alexander, "Neo-Naturalism," in "New Ancients," ed. Dora Epstein Jones and Bryony Roberts, *Log,* no. 31 (Summer 2014): 23–30.

13. Alexander cites Norman Bryson's enthusiasm for art history's turn to neuroscience in his Introduction to Warren Neidich's *Blow-Up.* See Bryson, "Introduction: The Neural Interface," in *Blow-Up: Photography, Cinema, and the Brain,* by Warren Neidich (New York: Distributed Art Publishers; Riverside: UCR / California Museum of Photography, 2003). See also Zeynep Çelik Alexander, "Neurons and Signifiers," *The Aggregate* (website), 2 (March 2015), http://we-aggregate.org/piece/neurons-and-signifiers.

14. Bryson, "Introduction," 14.

Index

Page numbers in italics refer to photographs and illustrations.

GINGER NOLAN is assistant professor of architectural history and theory at the School of Architecture at the University of Southern California. She is author of *The Neocolonialism of the Global Village* (Minnesota, 2018).